365 days with Newton

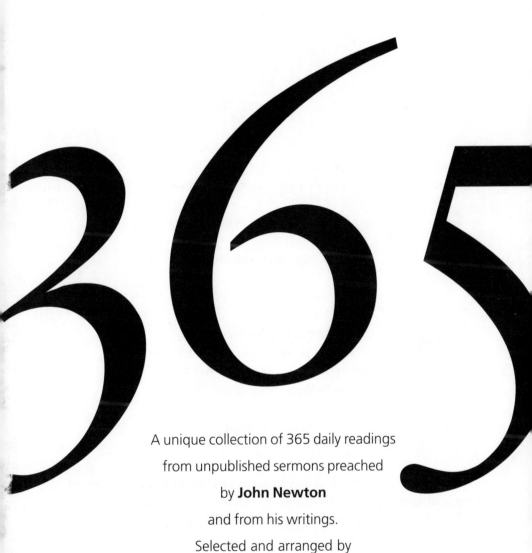

A unique collection of 365 daily readings
from unpublished sermons preached
by **John Newton**
and from his writings.
Selected and arranged by
Marylynn Rouse

DayOne

© Marylynn Rouse 2006
First printed 2006
Reprinted 2010

The right of Marylynn Rouse to be identified as the author of the work has been asserted by her in accordance with the Copyright, Designs and Patents Act 1988.

Scripture quotations are from the King James Version, unless othwise stated.

British Library Cataloguing in Publication Data available

ISBN 978–1–903087–92–3

Published by Day One Publications
P O Box 66, Leominster, HR6 0XB
☎ 01568 613 740 FAX 01568 611 473
e-mail address: sales@dayone.co.uk

Designed by Steve Devane.

This lovely book is not a version of the game, 'Who would you most like to meet from the past?' That is always a slightly meaningless matter for a Christian—for the great ones of the past whom we would most like to meet are in fact waiting to meet us in heaven!

No, the purpose of this book is not 'to meet John Newton' (lovely as that thought is) but to sit under his ministry, to enjoy today what many enjoyed yesterday, to enter into his benefit.

I have had the privilege of 'getting there first', for I have had the use of much of the material in this book ahead of publication, and have made it my daily companion. I write, therefore, not, so to speak, in a spirit of hope, but by way of testimony. Not 'Would you like to meet John Newton?' but 'Here is John Newton to meet you, to speak, teach and minister.' Come, enjoy and profit!

Newton's whole ministry bore the marks so evident in his lovely hymns: it was consistently *biblical* (to share the Word of God), *spiritual* (to promote walking with God), *simple* (to make biblical truth and principles plain), and *practical* (to inculcate personal holiness and sound relationships in church and society). In this collection every day bears these marks, so useful to every believer, so instructive for those called to minister. Newton was a rich and princely teacher, a sensitive and caring pastor, and a straight, outspoken guide.

Not only all this, but in Marylynn Rouse Newton has found a true disciple, and a skilled publicist. By enormous diligence, and self-sacrificing application, she has made herself a leading 'Newton expert', and in this sensitive compilation all that expertise is put at our disposal.

Please God, he has determined to bless this work, just as surely as he will use it to bless every individual reader!

Alec Motyer
Poynton, Cheshire
April 2006 AD

In 1758 John Newton was working as Surveyor of Tides in Liverpool docks, from an office close to the site of this World Heritage City's Albert Docks. At the prompting of friends he began to pray about entering the ministry to 'honestly and plainly declare the truths of the gospel'.

He determined to preach Christ crucified, 'the great essential points of the glories of his person and offices, his wonderful love and condescension, his power, faithfulness and readiness to save, the grandeur of his works, the perfection of his example, his life, passion, death and resurrection', which he considered, 'undoubtedly the most pleasant set of topics, so the most useful and effectual, to rouse a hatred against sin, to feed the springs of grace into the heart, to animate and to furnish every believer for his spiritual warfare'.[1]

Like Jonah, Newton had previously run away from the Lord and it had taken a tremendous storm at sea in 1748 to humble him, convict him of his defiance and stir him up to cry out to God for mercy. He would later write, 'How precious did that grace appear the hour I first believed'. For the rest of his life he set aside the anniversary of that day of his conversion, 21 March, for thanksgiving and prayer (see this date in these readings).

When Newton finally entered the ministry in 1764 through the kindness of Lord Dartmouth (later Britain's Colonial Secretary), it was as curate-in-charge of the parish church of St Peter and St Paul, Olney. For sixteen years he lived amongst the lace-making and farming cottagers, learning from their simple lifestyle, applying scriptural truths in everyday terms and gaining valuable pastoral experience.

He began preparing his sermons in a series of notebooks. Hannah Wilberforce, the aunt of William Wilberforce, MP, was one of Newton's many friends who begged to borrow his notebooks. Fortunately for us, many of these notebooks are still in existence. None of them has ever been published before,[2] so after a gap of more than 200 years, we may now join this privileged group of friends and 'borrow' his sermon notebooks.

However, we have an advantage over his contemporaries, for we can draw on his unpublished diaries and correspondence to gain a little extra insight into some of the circumstances surrounding these sermons. From his diary, for instance, we learn that *Amazing Grace* was almost certainly written for New Year's Day 1773 (see 1 January) and *Glorious things of thee are*

---

1   *Miscellaneous Thoughts on Entering the Ministry*, 1758, Lambeth Palace Library, MS 2937.
2   Except for sermons I transcribed earlier on *Amazing Grace* and *How sweet the name of Jesus sounds*.

spoken, Zion city of our God, for Easter Day 1775 (the series he was preaching from 2 Samuel 23:5 at the time certainly reflects similar thoughts—see 1 May).

Sometimes we gain more background information than mere dates. For instance, eager to learn from his Creator's handiwork, Newton loved to glean what he could of the signature of God in it. Observing an eclipse of the moon at Olney on 30 July 1776, he recorded in his diary: 'I thought my Lord, of thine eclipse. The horrible darkness which overwhelmed thy mind when thou saidst, *Why hast thou forsaken me?* Ah, sin was the cause—my sin.' He expressed these thoughts in a hymn, preached from it at the Great House (Lord Dartmouth's property) on Sunday evening, and sent a copy to his friend and sponsor John Thornton.

While many with unmeaning eye	Fain would my thankful heart and lips
Gaze on thy works in vain;	Unite in praise to thee;
Assist me, LORD, that I may try	And meditate on thy eclipse,
Instruction to obtain.	In sad Gethsemane.3

Newton's diaries, journals, hymns and correspondence are the source of meditations to accompany the sermon extracts, along with some Scripture verses. The meditations include 124 of his own hymns from *Olney Hymns*, published in 1779 during his last year at Olney. Extracts from his journal of children's meetings illustrate sermon points, together with portions of his correspondence with William Wilberforce, John Thornton (Wilberforce's uncle and a Director of the Bank of England), John Ryland (later President of Bristol Baptist College) and the Coffin family in Linkenhorne, Cornwall.

The sermon extracts in this book draw on Newton's previously unpublished notes for 105 sermons. Some of his original notes from which he later published fifty sermons based on the texts in Handel's *Messiah* are in the main sections (see for example 8 June). So too we find the sermon notes for *How sweet the name of Jesus sounds* (see 8 April), for an address to the Bible Society (now the Naval, Military and Air Force Bible Society— see 22 September) and for the funeral service of his 'right hand', Betty Abraham, an Olney watchmaker's wife, together with a hymn based on the last words she spoke, from Lamentations 3:24, *The Lord is my portion* (see 13 February).

Most of the sermons were preached in Olney between 1764 and 1780 and come from sermon notebooks owned by the Cowper & Newton Museum. Occasionally the sermons or hymns are dated (forty-one sermons and twenty-three hymns have been identified). A few of the sermons were

---

3   *Olney Hymns*, 1779, Book 2, Hymn 85, *On the eclipse of the moon*, 30 July 1776.

preached in London, for Newton went on to become the rector of St Mary Woolnoth in the heart of the city's 'square mile'. His congregations were drawn from all denominations, including Methodists, Presbyterians, Congregationalists, Baptists, Moravians and Quakers. One sermon in these daily readings was written to be preached as the annual sermon before his parishioner, the Lord Mayor of London (see 25 March).

While the events surrounding the sermons and meditations add interest, by far the greatest advantage of these readings comes from the deeply biblical approach which Newton maintained from that resolution formed in 1758 on the banks of the Mersey to 'honestly and plainly declare the truths of the gospel'.

We may consider ourselves feasting alongside Newton's breakfast party companions in London or at his Tuesday evening open-house sessions for 'Parsons, Parsonets, and Parsonettas'—the down-and-outs, like the penniless Claudius Buchanan (who became Newton's curate and subsequently Vice-Provost of Fort William in Bengal), the MPs and city bankers, such as William Wilberforce and Henry Thornton, female authors such as Hannah More (converted through reading Newton's letters, published as *Cardiphonia*), pioneer missionaries such as William Carey (en route to India), Richard Johnson (chaplain of the first fleet to Australia), and many more.

Although each page is 'self-contained', a special feature of these daily readings is the facility to follow through Newton's thinking in a series, for instance the selections from his series on the Transfiguration, where he comes at a passage from different angles with new insights at each attempt.

Finally, in the words of John Newton, which seem to apply suitably to this selection of his readings,

And with these views, I would attempt to assist your meditations on it. I may say as the woman of Samaria, *the well is deep* [John 4:11] ... Here, I think, if anywhere, we have cause to pray with the psalmist, *Open thou my eyes, that I may see the great things of thy law* [Psalm 119:18]. May this be the desire of all our hearts, and may the Lord afford a gracious answer.[4]

Marylynn Rouse
The John Newton Project
Stratford on Avon
April 2006

EDITORIAL COMMENT

All the text here is Newton's, although spellings and punctuation have been normalized for easier reading. Very occasionally a word or phrase has been adjusted, and this is shown in the footnotes. In the interests of uniform length, some minor deletions have been made from Newton's sermon notes, but these have not altered the thrust and argument of what he was saying. Round brackets indicate Newton's writings and square brackets the editor's. Although each page is complete in itself, sermons which continue further are numbered as [1/4], [2/4], etc.

ACKNOWLEDGEMENTS

My thanks to the following for permission to quote from their manuscripts: The Bodleian Library, Bristol Baptist College, Cambridge University Library, The Cowper & Newton Museum, Dr Williams's Library, Lambeth Palace Library, Princeton University Library and Mrs Hilary Aspray.

Many friends have played some part in this production through their encouragement, proof-reading and prayers along the way (and it was a long way!). Special thanks go to Alec Motyer, Bishop Timothy Dudley Smith, the trustees of The John Newton Project—John Langlois (Chairman), Tony Baker, Martin Hines, Mike Swales, Malcolm Turner and Robert Watson—and to Chris Wilson, Anna Fisher and Laurie Brokenshire. My thanks also to Brian Edwards and John Roberts for suggesting the book and to Elizabeth Knight, trustee of the Cowper & Newton Museum, Olney, historian extraordinaire, who first put Newton's sermon notebooks into my hands and so started an irreversible chain of events which is leading to the publication online of *The Complete Works of John Newton* at www.johnnewton.org.

And O that it may please thee, that this imperfect testimony of thy goodness may be bless'd to the use & advantage of any who by thy Providence shall be brought to peruse any part of it

John Newton

Amazing Grace

'*And David the king came and sat before the* LORD, *and said, Who am I, O* LORD *God, and what is mine house, that thou hast brought me hitherto? And yet this was a small thing in thine eyes, O God; for thou hast also spoken of thy servant's house for a great while to come, and hast regarded me according to the estate of a man of high degree, O* LORD *God.*'
1 *Chronicles* 17:16–17
SUGGESTED FURTHER READING: 1 Chronicles 17:1–17

The Lord bestows many blessings upon his people, but unless he likewise gives them a thankful heart, they lose much of the comfort they might have in them. And this is not only a blessing in itself but an earnest of more. When David was peacefully settled in the kingdom, he purposed to express his gratitude by building a place for the Ark. This honour the Lord had appointed for his son Solomon, but he graciously accepted David's intention, for he not only notices the poor services of his people, but even their desires to serve him when they spring from a principle of simple love, though opportunity should be wanting. He sent him a message by Nathan assuring him that his son should build the house and that he himself would build David's house and establish his kingdom. This filled his heart with praise. My text is part of his acknowledgement. Omitting David's personal concerns, I would accommodate them to our own use as a proper subject for our meditations on the entrance of a new year. They lead us to a consideration of past mercies and future hopes and intimate the frame of mind which becomes us when we contemplate what the Lord has done for us.

FOR MEDITATION: [almost certainly written for this sermon]
Faith's review and expectation
Amazing grace! (how sweet the sound)
That saved a wretch like me!
I once was lost, but now am found,
Was blind, but now I see.[1]

A wretch like me

'And David the king came and sat before the LORD, *and said, Who am I, O* LORD *God, and what is mine house, that thou hast brought me hitherto?'*
1 *Chronicles 17:16*
SUGGESTED FURTHER READING: 1 Timothy 1:12–17

Who am I? The frame of mind: humility and admiration. *Who am I ...?* This question should be always upon our minds. *Who am I?* What was I when the Lord began to manifest his purposes of love? This was often inculcated upon Israel: *Thou shalt remember*; *Look unto the pit* from which we were taken. Lord, what is man!

At that time we were miserable, shut up under the law and unbelief. What must have been the event had the Lord left us there? After a few years spent in vanity, we must have sunk to rise no more. We were rebellious, blinded by the god of this world. We had not so much a desire of deliverance. Instead of desiring the Lord's help, we breathed a spirit of defiance against him. His mercy came to us not only undeserved but undesired. Yea, few of us but resisted his calls, and when he knocked at the door of our hearts endeavoured to shut him out till he overcame us by the power of his grace. See our proper characteristics: Titus 3:3. It was the Lord against whom we sinned and who showed us mercy. He needed not. What just cause of admiration, that he should appoint such salvation, in such a way, in favour of such helpless, worthless creatures.

This calls for love, gratitude and obedience, as in Romans 12:1, *I beseech you therefore, brethren, by the mercies of God, that ye present your bodies a living sacrifice, holy, acceptable unto God, which is your reasonable service.*

FOR MEDITATION: Few living can have more cause than myself to say, What am I—that thou hast brought me hitherto? Brought me from Africa, from the house of bondage, saved me from sinking in the ocean and from a thousand deaths—raised me from a state of contempt and misery beyond the common lot of mortals—to admit me among thy children, thy servants, to know and to preach thy gospel—and this in a situation of honour and eminence. I am surrounded with mercies and comforts. Thy goodness has followed and encompassed me through another year. May my heart praise thee. May my life praise thee.[3]   *Diary*, 1 January 1780

SERMON: 1 CHRONICLES 17:16–17 [2/4]

Safe thus far

'And David the king came and sat before the LORD, and said, Who am I, O LORD God, and what is mine house, that thou hast brought me hitherto?'
1 Chronicles 17:16
SUGGESTED FURTHER READING: Exodus 18:1–12

That thou hast brought me hitherto. Here let us look back:

(i) Before conversion: his providential care preserving us from a thousand seen, millions of unseen, dangers, when we knew him not; his secret guidance, leading us by a way which we knew not, till his time of love came.

(ii) At conversion: the means by which he wrought upon us supports in the time of conviction, and the never to be forgotten hour when he enabled us to hope in his mercy.

(iii) Since we first were enabled to give up our names to him: mercy and goodness have followed us. In temporals, he has led and fed us. Many have fallen when we have been preserved, or, if afflicted, we have found him a present help in trouble. Some may say, *with my staff I passed over this Jordan* [Genesis 32:10]. In spirituals, preserving us from wasting sins, from gross errors, or restoring and healing, maintaining his hold in our hearts, notwithstanding so much opposition, so many temptations and provocations. The comforts we have had in secret and public worship, the seasonable and undoubted answers to prayer. Grace to any dear to us, peace in our families, his blessing with us a church and a people.

This calls for trust and confidence. We have good reason to cast our cares upon him, and to be satisfied with his appointments. *Hitherto he has done all things well* (Mark 7:37).

FOR MEDITATION:

'Twas grace that taught my heart to fear
And grace those fears relieved;
How precious did that grace appear,
The hour I first believed!

Through many dangers, toils and snares,
I have already come;
'Tis grace has brought me safe thus far,
And grace will lead me home.4

Homeward bound

'And yet this was a small thing in thine eyes, O God; for thou hast also spoken of thy servant's house for a great while to come, and hast regarded me according to the estate of a man of high degree, O LORD God.'
1 Chronicles 17:17
SUGGESTED FURTHER READING: 1 Chronicles 17:18–27

You have spoken about the future. Are these *small things?* Yes, compared to what follows—he has spoken *for a great while to come,* even to eternity. Present mercies are but earnests of his love, present comforts but foretastes of the joy to which we are hastening. O that crown, that kingdom, that eternal weight of glory! We are travelling home to God. We shall soon see Jesus, and never complain of sin, sorrow, temptation or desertion any more. He has dealt with us according to the estate of a man of high degree. He found us upon the dunghill and has made us companions of princes—in a wilderness and has led us to the city of God.

This calls for patience—yet a little while and we shall be at home, *for now is our salvation nearer than when we first believed* (Romans 13:11). We are spared thus far. But some, I fear, are strangers to the promises. You are entered upon a New Year. It may be your last. You are at present barren trees in the vineyard. O fear lest the sentence should go forth—*Cut it down* [Luke 13:7].

FOR MEDITATION:

The LORD has promised good to me,
His word my hope secures;
He will my shield and portion be,
As long as life endures.

Yes, when this flesh and heart shall fail,
And mortal life shall cease;
I shall possess, within the veil,
A life of joy and peace.

The earth shall soon dissolve like snow,
The sun forbear to shine;
But GOD, who called me here below,
Will be forever mine.[5]

[Note these are the original last verses to *Amazing Grace*, by Newton.[6]]

Anointed eyes

'In the beginning God created the heaven and the earth.' Genesis 1:1
SUGGESTED FURTHER READING: Psalm 19:1–14

It would make plain people more sensible of the advantage of the Word of God if they knew the uncertainty and perplexity of the wisest men, who were not favoured with this light, with respect to the most obvious truths. The world with all their wisdom knew not God. A child that has read the Bible knows more than all the philosophers of old put together. Some thought the world was eternal, others that it made itself. But the Scripture gives a clear and satisfactory, though brief, account. There is more in this first verse of the Bible than in 10,000 volumes of men's invention.

The book of creation

The book of nature open lies,
With much instruction stored;
But till the LORD anoints our eyes
We cannot read a word.

The knowledge of the saints excels
The wisdom of the schools;
To them his secrets GOD reveals,
Though men account them fools.

Philosophers have pored in vain,
And guessed, from age to age;
For reason's eye could ne'er attain
To understand a page.

To them the sun and stars on high,
The flowers that paint the field,
And all the artless birds that fly,
Divine instruction yield.

Though to each star they give a name,
Its size and motions teach;
The truths which all the stars proclaim,
Their wisdom cannot reach.

The creatures on their senses press,
As witnesses to prove
Their Saviour's power, and faithfulness,
His providence and love.

With skill to measure earth and sea,
And weigh the subtle air;
They cannot, LORD, discover thee
Though present everywhere.

Thus may we study nature's book
To make us wise indeed!
And pity those who only look
At what they cannot read.7

FOR MEDITATION: 'But God made the earth by his power; he founded the world by his wisdom and stretched out the heavens by his understanding' (Jeremiah 10:12, NIV).

SERMON SERIES: GENESIS, NO. 1 [1/4], GENESIS 1:1

In the beginning

'In the beginning God created the heaven and the earth.' Genesis 1:1
SUGGESTED FURTHER READING: Proverbs 8:22–31

In the beginning. As Adam was created on the sixth day, and the year of life assigned in which his son Seth was born, and so on in the life of each of his descendants, …it is pretty certain that the birth of Christ took place about 4,000 years after the creation—that is, to us, about 5,770 years ago[8] was the commencement of time which Moses speaks of. What then was before this beginning? I answer, the same that shall be when all these things have an end: eternity. This is too great a thought for our feeble minds to grasp. We are lost indeed when we consider eternity with respect to the future as having no end, but it is harder to conceive of it by looking back, as having had no beginning. Before anything was made that was made, God was supremely happy and glorious in himself and would have been forever if neither heaven or earth had been created, but when he pleased, he manifested his power in producing creatures to whom and in whom he might communicate and display his goodness. If a thought arises in our minds of wonder that through a whole eternity it should not please God thus to manifest himself till within a few thousand years ago, we should charge such a thought to the darkness and weakness of our minds. Supposing the beginning had been not 5,000 but 5,000 million years ago—there would have been room for the same objection, for even then there would have been an eternity before the beginning, the same as there is now. We submit then to the wisdom, will and word of God: *in the beginning he created.*

FOR MEDITATION: 'He has also set eternity in the hearts of men; yet they cannot fathom what God has done from beginning to end' (Ecclesiastes 3:10, NIV).

The Three One

'In the beginning God created the heaven and the earth.' Genesis 1:1
SUGGESTED FURTHER READING: Isaiah 42:1–7

God. Who can describe him! Guess at him by his works—but alas, we know them not. If I was qualified to speak at large of the magnitude, the motions, the regularities and order of the heavenly bodies, many of which, taken singly, are probably hundreds or thousands of times larger than the globe we live on—if I could help you to judge of their immense distances from each other and from us—if, to come lower, I could assist you to number the sand upon the seashore and the drops of water in the ocean, every one of which is as much the effect of divine power and the object of his providential care as the sun in the firmament—if I could give you a view of that great family in heaven and earth from the highest angel to the meanest worm, which all derive their being from him and could not subsist a single moment without him—this might give some assistance to help you to conceive of his greatness, his wisdom and goodness. The consideration of those things is very useful in its proper place to those who have leisure and abilities for it, but these are not the direct subjects of the gospel ministry. Such knowledge of God as is attainable from his works will neither break a hard heart nor heal a wounded conscience. I will rather speak of him as he has revealed himself in Scripture in a way more suited to sinners—the Lord Jehovah: Father, Word and Holy Spirit. The God who in the fullness of time was in Christ reconciling sinners to himself—he in the beginning created the heavens and the earth. The work of creation is ascribed to each of the glorious three: to the Word or Son (John 1:3; Colossians 1:16); to the Holy Spirit (Acts 4:24–25 compared with 1:16). Let us always keep in view the God of the Scriptures as the Three One—the Covenant God whose glory and grace is revealed to sinners in the person of Jesus Christ.

FOR MEDITATION: Although he is 'the high and lofty One' who inhabits eternity, he promises also to dwell with him who is 'of a contrite and humble spirit' (Isaiah 57:15).

His almighty power

'In the beginning God created the heaven and the earth.' Genesis 1:1
SUGGESTED FURTHER READING: Job 38:4–18

God created. God created by an immediate act of almighty power. Creatures can make, that is form one thing from another, but to give being to the first principles of things belongs to God alone. And this, in a strict and proper sense, was the work of creation. Other things were produced and disposed afterwards in the several days. When God would remind his people of his power to help them under the greatest difficulties—when he would silence the vain reasonings of their unbelief, which is so ready to say, 'How can these things be?'—he often puts them in mind of this first revelation of his Almighty Arm (Isaiah 44:24; Jeremiah 31:35; Isaiah 51:12-13; Jeremiah 5:22). And though we have a general conviction of his power, we are too apt to fail in a right application of it to our particular cases and should therefore often consider what he hath wrought.

The heaven and the earth: that is, the visible world with all their furniture and inhabitants (Genesis 2:1). Let us humbly enquire into some of the reasons for which he created all things by his good pleasure. In general they were created for the display of his glory to intelligent creatures by the order, beauty, variety and grandeur of his works, as I have already hinted, and for the effusion of his goodness in giving life and a suitable perfection to different orders of beings. In particular he formed *the earth* as a theatre to display the riches of his glorious grace in the salvation of a people chosen to himself in Christ before the foundation of the world. He formed the visible *heavens* with an immediate reference to the benefit of the earth, particularly of man for whom the earth was made. Under the term *heaven,* we may likewise understand that glorious state in which he makes himself known as the fountain of happiness and joy to his angels and redeemed people. This kingdom was prepared for them from the beginning (Matthew 25:34).

FOR MEDITATION: Believers, this God is our God. How miserable are they who have no part in him.

All in confusion

'And the earth was without form, and void; and darkness was upon the face of the deep.' Genesis 1:2
SUGGESTED FURTHER READING: Psalm 8:1–9

The matter out of which the beauty, order and variety we now observe were framed, was at first all in confusion. The earth, the water, the deep, were one mixed mass and darkness covered the whole. The earth was *without form*— without a determinate form, a crude mass—*and void*—that is, empty, unfurnished, destitute of ornaments and inhabitants and incapable of receiving any till God was pleased to put forth his mighty power and arrange everything according to his wise plan. The wisdom of man, who would fain account for everything, has endeavoured to guess by what steps the Almighty proceeded in this work; many conjectures of this sort have been started, but they are all vain and trifling, no better than waking dreams; nay, they are presumptions. The Lord pours contempt upon such proud reasoners in his sublime questions to Job (chapter 38) and intimates that his counsel is far above, out of our sight [Psalm 10:5]. It is enough for us that things were thus in the beginning, and if we endeavour [to understand] this darkness and confusion and then compare it with the creation as it now appears, so as to say with humble admiration, 'What has God wrought?' and to be affected with his greatness and goodness, then we have the true philosophy. All besides is vanity and food for pride.

FOR MEDITATION: I have been witness to a great and important revolution this morning, which took place while the greatest part of the world was asleep. A while ago, darkness reigned. Had a man dropped for the first time into our world, he might have thought himself banished into a hopeless dungeon. How could he expect light to rise out of such a state? And when he saw the first glimmering of dawn in the east, how could he promise himself that it was the forerunner of such a glorious sun as has since risen! Such strangers once were we. Darkness, gross darkness, covered us: how confined were our views! And even the things which were within our reach we could not distinguish. Little did we then think what a glorious day we were appointed to see ... We knew not that there was a Sun of righteousness, and that he would dawn and rise and shine upon our hearts.[9]

SERMON SERIES: GENESIS, NO. 2 [1/3], GENESIS 1:2–3

Ascribe all to God

'And the Spirit of God moved upon the face of the waters. And God said, Let there be light: and there was light.' Genesis 1:2–3
SUGGESTED FURTHER READING: Psalm 146:1–10

Consider the great Author of that beautiful change which took place in the course of the six days. The Spirit of God *moved*—the same word is used in Deuteronomy 32:11: 'As an eagle *fluttereth* over her young.' It signifies the powerful influence and energy which penetrated the whole mass and by a general motion prepared their separation out of that confused state in which they were blended together. And this is ascribed to the Spirit of God. It was not, as some men afterwards dreamed, by a blind and casual impulse. The Scriptures teach us to ascribe all to God. By the word of his almighty power God produced light. He said, *Let there be*—and it was. This is the most excellent and beautiful of all visible things and that by which all other things are made known. It was a direct opposition to the state just before— and there could be no tendency in darkness to produce it. Yet the word of God brought it forth immediately. From this beginning, the whole beautiful creation was gradually accomplished in the course of six days, as in the course of this chapter. For so it seemed fit to his wisdom, otherwise he could have finished all in an instant.

FOR MEDITATION:

Could all the art of man suffice
To move away the snow,
To clear the rivers from the ice,
Or make the waters flow?

No, 'tis the work of GOD alone;
An emblem of the power
By which he melts the heart of stone,
In his appointed hour.

JESUS, we in thy name entreat,
Reveal thy gracious arm;
And grant thy Spirit's kindly heat,
Our frozen hearts to warm.[10]

The wonder-working God

'And the Spirit of God moved upon the face of the waters. And God said, Let there be light: and there was light.' Genesis 1:2–3
SUGGESTED FURTHER READING: John 1:1–5

Now this account of the creation, the Scripture teaches us to use to advantage chiefly for three purposes:

(i) to help our conceptions of the wonder-working God: his wisdom (Psalm 104:24), power (Amos 4:12–13; Isaiah 40:26), goodness (Psalm 104:13–15).

(ii) to instruct us in his readiness and willingness to help his people in their greatest troubles and in the darkest times. When our hearts faint we should remember the right hand of the Most High (Isaiah 51:13; Psalm 146:5).

(iii) as a type or emblem of the new creation. The sinner has faculties and powers originally suited for the service of God—but all is in disorder. His mind is without form and void. Darkness, gross darkness, sin, ignorance and misery covers his heart, but (2 Corinthians 4:6) [*God, who commanded the light to shine out of darkness, hath shined in our hearts, to give the light of the knowledge of the glory of God in the face of Christ Jesus*], then life and fruitfulness take place and the wilderness becomes the garden of the Lord.

This God was in Christ reconciling the world to himself by the Cross—and in the Man Christ he still reigns upon a throne of grace mighty to save. Believe in his name.

FOR MEDITATION: *The old and new creation*

That was a wonder-working word	The new creation of the soul
Which could the vast creation raise!	Does now no less his power display;
Angels, attendant on their LORD,	Than when he formed the mighty whole,
Admired the plan, and sung his praise.	And kindled darkness into day.
From what a dark and shapeless mass,	Though self-destroyed, O LORD, are we,
All nature sprang at his command!	Yet let us feel what thou canst do;
Let there be light, and light there was,	Thy word the ruin can repair,
And sun and stars, and sea and land.	And all our hearts create anew.[11]

SERMON SERIES: GENESIS, NO. 2 [3/3], GENESIS 1:2–3

Mortal, transitory creatures

'For all our days are passed away in thy wrath: we spend our years as a tale that is told.' Psalm 90:9
SUGGESTED FURTHER READING: Psalm 90:1–17

In the works of creation we may observe not only a display of divine wisdom in themselves, but a particular wisdom in dispositioning them and making them subservient to the special use and occasions of mankind. Thus the sun and moon give evidence of their Maker's glory and would have done so if placed at such a distance from us that we had never seen them. But how are his wisdom and goodness confirmed to us by the benefits we receive from these heavenly bodies! Omitting other uses, I shall mention one which is expressly mentioned in Genesis 1:14. The Lord had appointed that man, after the fall, should be a mortal, transitory creature, and he knew that he would be a depraved and foolish creature, prone to bury himself in the things of this world and to forget eternity. Therefore when he fixed the sun and moon to give light to the earth he suited their various changes and revolutions to admonish man of the unceasing speed of time. Thus all things are in motion: day and night swiftly succeed each other, the moon appears, increases, declines and is again renewed and the changing seasons, in a constant succession, bring round the year. Thus *day after day uttereth speech*. The psalm before us is a prayer of Moses. The subject is the present state of human life: its uncertainty—compared to the grass which falls suddenly before the scythe (see Psalm 103:16) in verse 6—its brevity—seventy years or less for the most part, and all beyond that term pain and infirmity (verse 10)—its general vanity in itself—we spend or bring our years to end *as a tale that is told*.

FOR MEDITATION: [for New Year 1774]

While with ceaseless course the sun	Thanks for mercies past receive,
Hasted through the former year,	Pardon of our sins renew;
Many souls their race have run,	Teach us, henceforth, how to live
Never more to meet us here.	With eternity in view:
Fixed in an eternal fate,	Bless thy word to young and old,
They have done with all below;	Fill us with a Saviour's love;
We a little longer wait,	And when life's short tale is told,
But how little—none can know.	May we dwell with thee above.[12]

SERMON: PSALM 90:9 [1/3] [ALSO PREACHED 28 DECEMBER 1783]

The seeds of eternity are sown in time

'For all our days are passed away in thy wrath: we spend our years as a tale that is told.' Psalm 90:9

SUGGESTED FURTHER READING: Ecclesiastes 12:1–14

As a tale that is told. Let us consider the comparison. *As a tale:* the margin reads 'a meditation', whether silent or expressed—a thought, or a word, or a discourse. I judge our translation to be exceeding proper, suited to the scope of the passage and the nature of our life. The chief pleasure of a tale or relation lies in the hearing or telling it while it is new. When well known or often told, it ceases to please. A worn-out tale is a proverb for what is tedious. Such is our life—every year is in the main a repetition of the same poor story. Youth, when just entering upon it, are all attention—but O if old people were to speak, how insipid and tasteless is the tale of life to those who know not the pleasures of communion with God. *Few and evil*, says Jacob, *have the days of my life been* [Genesis 47:9]. Of the good, nothing remains but the remembrance—and this was mixed with so much evil that few people would have the courage to live a year over again, if they were to choose—and yet, alas, afraid to die. O the vanity of man! When the tale is told, or the word spoken, it is gone beyond recall. Many consequences often follow from one improper speech, but that which was said cannot be unsaid. In the former view, life appeared quite insignificant, but in this it appears of the greatest consequences. I have somewhere met a sentence which much struck me. I wish it may affect all who hear it: 'The seeds of eternity are sown in time.' According to our pursuits and conduct in this momentary life, such will be our condition for ever. So the Apostle reminds us in Galatians 6:7–8, *Be not deceived; God is not mocked: for whatsoever a man soweth, that shall he also reap.*

FOR MEDITATION: Time is short—and the nature of our employment while it lasts is well suited to raise our thoughts above the little concerns of such a life as this… The love of Christ, the worth of souls, the honour of being instrumental in their recovery, a glorious endless state of happiness and holiness—how light must our present sufferings appear when weighed in the scales of the sanctuary against these things. Let us not be weary in well-doing, for in due time we shall reap if we faint not.[13]

SERMON: PSALM 90:9 [2/3] [ALSO PREACHED 28 DECEMBER 1783]

Take stock

'*For all our days are passed away in thy wrath: we spend our years as a tale that is told.*' Psalm 90:9
SUGGESTED FURTHER READING: Psalm 116:1–19

It would be seasonable to take a review of our lives, especially of the past year. I would willingly assist you herein and help you to set out some of the particulars before your conscience: God's dealings with you and your returns to him. The Lord's dealings with us may be comprised under mercies, afflictions and ordinances.

(i) Mercies: as life itself—a measure of health, deliverances from danger, a supply of your returning wants; he has given to many of you the lives of your friends, comfort in your families, restored some who were dear to you from the borders of the grave. Now all temporal mercies and comforts are from his gift. They are talents and shortly you must give an account of your stewardship. How have you improved them? I trust he has taught some of you to own them as his gifts and to improve them to his glory. But alas, are there not too many who have abused his mercies to occasions of sin?

(ii) Afflictions: these indeed, when sanctified, are mercies likewise. But how many suffer in vain. Many changes have happened amongst us in a year: pain, sickness, death in our families, crosses and losses in our affairs. None of these things have happened by chance. The Lord has done it. Every rod has a voice. Have you heard it, taken it to heart? Did you humble yourself before him in affliction?

(iii) Ordinances: we have been favoured with a year more of gospel ordinances. The word of the Lord has been with you *precept upon precept, line upon line* [Isaiah 28:13]—to what effect? What have you known of Jesus? Are you convinced of sin? Are you considering your latter end?

FOR MEDITATION: If you cannot answer such an enquiry with comfort, still the Lord waits to be gracious. Now at least, cry to him for light and faith that you may receive a free pardon and be turned by the power of Jesus, for there is no other name given among men whereby we can be saved. Believers will find cause of humiliation, but you have an Advocate with the Father. Thank him for all that is past, trust him for all that's to come.[14]

SERMON: PSALM 90:9 [3/3] [ALSO PREACHED 28 DECEMBER 1783]

Finished and furnished for the praise of his glory

'And God said, Let us make man in our image, after our likeness.'
Genesis 1:26
SUGGESTED FURTHER READING: Psalm 96:1–13

When the earth was finished and furnished, a suitable inhabitant was wanting, capable of admiring the Creator's work and yielding a tribute of worship and praise. Such an inhabitant was man in his original state. Yet man was not made for the sake of the earth, but the earth for the sake of man—concerning whom the divine counsels had been engaged from eternity. And when the appointed season of his existence drew near, the earth was fitted to receive him. We may note a particular form of expression, *Let us*, which seems to intimate:

(i) that mysterious distinction in the Godhead which we call the Trinity. The word is plural, though joined with a verb in the singular (compare 3:22, *And the* LORD *God said, Behold the man is become as one of us* ...).

(ii) the excellency and importance of the design. This is pointed out to our weak capacity by the idea of an act of council and agreement. And indeed the great events and the manifestation of the divine glory which depended upon the creation of man, give us cause to consider this as the chief of all the works of God.

FOR MEDITATION: 'Father, I will that they also, whom thou hast given me, be with me where I am; that they may behold my glory, which thou hast given me: for thou lovedst me before the foundation of the world. O righteous Father, the world hath not known thee: but I have known thee, and these have known that thou hast sent me. And I have declared unto them thy name, and will declare it: that the love wherewith thou hast loved me may be in them, and I in them' (John 17:24–26).

Designed for eternity

'And the LORD *God formed man of the dust of the ground, and breathed into his nostrils the breath of life; and man became a living soul.'*
Genesis 2:7
SUGGESTED FURTHER READING: Ezekiel 37:1–14

The LORD *God formed man.* The formation of man's body:

(i) The materials: *the dust of the ground,* and yet by nature capable of immortality; for that man was afterwards liable to death was the consequence of sin. Here we may observe that everything is what it is in consequence of the divine appointment. Dust, by the will of God, may be immortal, and stones become bread.

(ii) The expression *formed*: the word is properly used of the skill and power of the potter over the clay which he moulds according to his own will, and makes it very different from what it was in the mass. Much of the wisdom of God is manifest to an attentive eye in the admirable structure of our bodies. We are fearfully and wonderfully made.

The LORD *God breathed.* The communication of life: he *breathed*, which seems to import the union of an immortal soul—for the animals were living creatures likewise, yet no such expression is used of them. The life of the soul was distinct from the life of the body and did not, like that, depend upon his obedience, for the wicked are immortal. Only sin perverts this primitive blessing and honour into the greatest curse. *Consider this, ye that forget God* [Psalm 50:22]—you are not creatures of a day, but designed for eternity.

FOR MEDITATION: O for a new heart, a new sight, that my mind may be active. Leave me not to my own foolishness but lead me and guide me and restore unto me the joy of thy countenance for thy name's sake. Amen.[15]

Diary, 8 and 17 November, 1755

SERMON SERIES: GENESIS, NO. 3 [2/4], GENESIS 2:7

Made in his image

'And God said, Let us make man in our image, after our likeness.' 'In the day that God created man, in the likeness of God made he him.' Genesis 1:26, Genesis 5:1
SUGGESTED FURTHER READING: Colossians 1:15–20

In his own image, or *likeness*. I will not be scrupulous about distinguishing these expressions. Taken together, I apprehend they signify:

(i) Man was formed in the image of God as his representative here below, honoured with the subordinate dominion of the earth and all its creatures (1:27).

(ii) Perhaps the expression may intimate 'in the image and likeness of that body which the Word of God would in time take into union with himself.' For this was in his purpose before either man or the earth was made. Man was therefore formed according to the resemblance of him who now sits upon the throne—the Head of the whole creation.

(iii) The capacities of man bore some faint image of the divine perfections—understanding, consciousness, will, and vast affections— which the possession of all the creatures could not satisfy (verse 20). And this natural dignity and vastness of the soul, which makes it incapable of being satisfied with anything short of an infinite good, still remains under the ruin of the fall—though this likewise becomes a curse and punishment, sin having rendered a union between the soul and its chief good impracticable without the interposition of free grace.

(iv) Man was created in the moral image of God, indeed with a portion of his goodness, holiness and truth, by which he was qualified for communion with his Maker and fully enabled for obedience to his righteous law (Ephesians 4:24; Colossians 3:10). This image was totally lost and defaced by sin and therefore the work of grace which restores it is called a new creation.

This account agrees likewise to the woman, though she was made afterwards and immediately from the substance of the man.

FOR MEDITATION:

On man in his own image made,   The whole creation homage paid,
How much did GOD bestow?   And owned him, LORD, below![16]

Ruins restored

'And God said, Let us make man in our image, after our likeness.'
Genesis 1:26
SUGGESTED FURTHER READING: Genesis 1:26–2:3

The subject we are upon is so mysterious and so briefly related that it would be easy to start curious speculations—but it is our wisdom to avoid an attempt of being wise above what is written. Let us fix to what is profitable.

(i) Cause for lamentation: How is the gold become dim! how is the most fine gold changed! ... The precious sons of Zion, comparable to fine gold, how are they esteemed as earthen pitchers... (Lamentations 4:1–2). What an awful difference—instead of dominion, misery and confusion. Instead of the moral image of God, the image of Satan full drawn upon the soul. Nothing remains but immortality and capacity—and these constitute our wretchedness, so that if men have no more than sin has left them, they will one day wish they had been dogs or toads to crawl upon the earth awhile and then be for ever forgot.

(ii) Cause of praise: to say, 'Blessed be God for Jesus Christ—this ruin is under his hand.' He is come that we may have life and that we may have it more abundantly [John 10:10]. Believe in him and your souls shall live.

FOR MEDITATION:
Oh! When flesh and heart shall fail,
Let thy love our spirits cheer;
Strengthened thus, we shall prevail
Over Satan, sin and fear:
Trusting in thy precious name,
May we thus our journey end;
Then our foes shall lose their aim,
And the Judge will be our Friend.[17]

Paradise gained

'And the LORD *God took the man, and put him into the garden of Eden to dress it and to keep it. And the* LORD *God commanded the man, saying, Of every tree of the garden thou mayest freely eat: but of the tree of the knowledge of good and evil, thou shalt not eat of it: for in the day that thou eatest thereof thou shalt surely die.' Genesis 2:15–17*
SUGGESTED FURTHER READING: Luke 4:1–13

We have reason to believe that before sin brought a curse upon the creation, the whole earth was a *Garden of Eden* in comparison of[with] what it is now. Yet when all was good, it pleased God to make a further display of his goodness in favour of man, and to enrich and beautify a peculiar spot for his residence. In this paradise man was placed with a general permission of the right and use of all that he could desire—with only the one exception mentioned in my text where we may note the name: *the tree of knowledge of good and evil.*

On the conduct of our first parents (for they were both included, see 3:2) with respect to this tree, depended their knowledge of that good for which they were created, or the evil which was yet unknown that would be the consequence of disobedience. Note that Adam's whole duty to God consisted in abstinence from the forbidden fruit—for we have shown that his being made in the divine image signified that he had the law of love, holiness and righteousness written in his heart. But his ability to maintain communion with his Maker was suspended upon his observation of this positive precept.

FOR MEDITATION: 'I go to prepare a place for you' (John 14:2).
'To him that overcometh will I give to eat of the tree of life, which is in the midst of the paradise of God' (Revelation 2:7).

'In the midst of the street of it, and on either side of the river, was there the tree of life, which bare twelve manner of fruits, and yielded her fruit every month: and the leaves of the tree were for the healing of the nations. And there shall be no more curse: but the throne of God and of the Lamb shall be in it; and his servants shall serve him' (Revelation 22:2–3).

SERMON SERIES: GENESIS, NO. 4 [1/2], GENESIS 2:15–17

Paradise lost

'And the LORD *God commanded the man, saying, Of every tree of the garden thou mayest freely eat: but of the tree of the knowledge of good and evil, thou shalt not eat of it: for in the day that thou eatest thereof thou shalt surely die.' Genesis 2:16–17*
SUGGESTED FURTHER READING: Romans 7:5–13

The great God had a just right to make such an exception: when he of his mere bounty had given everything else to his creature, man was furnished with sufficient strength to obey and warned of the danger if he rebelled.

The prohibition: *Thou shalt not eat*—to remind him:

(i) of his state of dependence on God, and that he was not absolute Lord of himself.

(ii) that God was his chief good, and nothing truly desirable but in subordination to him.

(iii) to intimate that he was not as yet established in happiness, but in a state of probation.

The sanction or condition with which this prohibition was attended:

(i) The penalty of disobedience—death:

(a) *spiritual*, which immediately took place when he had transgressed.

(b) *temporal*, to which he became immediately subject though the execution was deferred. And,

(c) *eternal*, which is necessarily opposed to that life which is by the gospel (Romans 6:23) and which is inflicted upon impenitent sinners and was therefore included in the first penalty, for we cannot suppose the righteous Judge would inflict a greater punishment than he had threatened.

(ii) Since he was not to die unless he sinned, a promise of continuance in life and happiness was necessarily implied (Romans 10:5).

This is what is frequently called the 'Covenant of Works'.

FOR MEDITATION:

LORD, what is man! extremes how wide,	Divine at first, a holy flame
In this mysterious nature join!	Kindled by the Almighty's breath;
The flesh, to worms and dust allied,	Till, stained by sin, it soon became
The soul, immortal and divine!	The seat of darkness, strife and death.[18]

SERMON SERIES: GENESIS, NO. 4 [2/2], GENESIS 2:15–17

Bridging the generation gap

'And thou, Solomon my son, know thou the God of thy father, and serve him with a perfect heart and with a willing mind...' 1 Chronicles 28:9
SUGGESTED FURTHER READING: Deuteronomy 11:1–25

David was a man of great experience, and though upon some occasions he showed himself to be a poor, sinful man like others, yet the prevalence of his zeal and spirituality gave him the honourable title of the man after God's own heart. He was warmly devoted to the Lord, preferred the light of his countenance to all earthly joys, and felt a concern for the honour of his name, worship and people, to the close of his life. The Lord greatly prospered him in many respects, and yet exercised him with many sharp trials. The sharpest of these were perhaps those he met with in his own family. One of his sons, Amnon, wickedly defiled his own sister, which afterwards cost him his life at a drunken feast. Absalom, another of his sons, rose up in rebellion against his own father. A third, Adonijah, attempted by fraud to possess the kingdom. The history of David's family affords a caution to parents, not to connive at sin in their children, and a caution to youth, not to give way to their headstrong and ungoverned passions.

We have only the names of several of his children, but his principal hope and comfort was Solomon. The words I have read are his dying charge to this dear child. He was soon to take upon him the care and government of a great people, in the discharge of which he would need much wisdom, and a peculiar blessing. The death of his father would soon leave him at full liberty, and at the same time deprive him of an affectionate and experienced guide. But in my text David points out to him a resource for every difficulty, a supply for every want: *Know thou the God of thy father and serve him* and it shall be well with thee.

FOR MEDITATION: [written to be sung after this sermon]

O David's Son, and David's LORD!	Like David, when this life shall end,
From age to age thou art the same;	We trust in thee sure peace to find;
Thy gracious presence now afford,	Like him, to thee we now commend
And teach our youth to know thy name!	The children we must leave behind.[20]

SERMON: 1 CHRONICLES 28:9 [1/5] [FOR THE YOUNG PEOPLE]

Knowing God

'And thou, Solomon my son, know thou the God of thy father, and serve him with a perfect heart and with a willing mind: for the LORD searcheth all hearts, and understandeth all the imaginations of the thoughts: if thou seek him, he will be found of thee; but if thou forsake him, he will cast thee off for ever.' 1 Chronicles 28:9
SUGGESTED FURTHER READING: Jeremiah 23:23–24

You must *know* the Lord before you can serve him, and you will serve him if you know him. You are as Solomon: the means by which God is known are afforded you. To these you must attend. In the knowledge of God is eternal life—and you must know Christ as the way, for none knoweth the Father but the Son, and he to whom the Son will reveal him. You are not called to attempt this by your own power. O that you could be sensible of your inability, then a great point would be gained. He has revealed himself in his word, yet still you need the Spirit of his Son.

What is it to *know* God?

(i) To be duly impressed with a sense of his awesome majesty and greatness—such a sense as may abase us before him, and teach us to fear him.

(ii) To know the way in which he holds communion with sinners. If you think of him as One who can suffer you to approach in any way but by faith in Christ, or who will afford you any pardon or spiritual good but through the atoning blood, you know him not aright.

(iii) To conceive of him as the only desirable portion of your souls, who alone is capable of making you happy.

(iv) To know him as reconciled—as your God and Father, who has accepted you in the beloved. This is the knowledge which brings peace into the soul and gives strength for his service.

FOR MEDITATION: 'And this is life eternal, that they might know thee the only true God, and Jesus Christ, whom thou hast sent' (John 17:3).

SERMON: 1 CHRONICLES 28:9 [2/5] [FOR THE YOUNG PEOPLE]

Serving God

'...Serve him with a perfect heart and with a willing mind: for the LORD *searcheth all hearts, and understandeth all the imaginations of the thoughts...' 1 Chronicles 28:9*
SUGGESTED FURTHER READING: Deuteronomy 10:12–22

Serve with a perfect heart and a willing mind, otherwise you cannot serve him at all. You cannot serve two masters. He says, *My son, give me thy heart* [Proverbs 23:26]. If you will serve God you must renounce the service of sin and glorify him in your body and spirit which are his. And this service must be free, not by force or any constraint but by the constraint of love. A formal service, urged by slavish fears and performed for merely selfish ends, is not accepted. Without faith you cannot please him [Hebrews 11:6]. To draw near him with your lips is not enough. Therefore if you think of serving God, consider the argument—to pray for *a perfect heart* and *willing mind*. He *searcheth* and *understandeth*. He has a perfect knowledge of you, from your birth to this hour—your hearts and ways are all open to him. I am persuaded the best and the worst of you would blush and tremble to have some things of which your conscience reminds you, exposed to the view of this congregation—and yet what are we? Worms like yourselves! But thus you are exposed to the view of the heart-searching God. Do you not then see a necessity of his grace? And will not such a conviction engage you to give yourselves wholly to him? You may deceive men, and even yourselves, but not him. There is comfort as well as caution in this thought—he knows your fears, your wants, your disappointments, how long and how often you have been seeking happiness where it is not to be found. Therefore he invites, calls you, to know and serve him, which is life and peace. Unworthy and sinful as he sees you are, yet he opens a door of mercy and says, *Seek ye my face and live.*

FOR MEDITATION: May my heart be divested of all prepossession and self-seeking; may I be enabled to see and follow my duty; and may I maintain the comfortable testimony of a sincere, teachable and obedient conscience in thy sight. O may thy Spirit witness in my heart, and my conversation witness in the world, that I am indeed thy disciple, thine without reserve, thine and not another's, thine and not my own—Amen.[21]

Miscellaneous Thoughts, Friday 23 June 1758

SERMON: 1 CHRONICLES 28:9 [3/5] [FOR THE YOUNG PEOPLE]

Seeking God

'...If thou seek him, he will be found of thee; but if thou forsake him, he will cast thee off for ever.' 1 *Chronicles* 28:9
SUGGESTED FURTHER READING: Psalm 34:1–22

This leads to the encouragement: *if you seek him he will be found.* It is his own promise—Seek and him ye shall find. Come and he will receive you. But do you ask, What is it to come or to seek? To come to Christ is to venture yourselves as poor, perishing creatures upon his blood and promise; and to seek him is to wait upon him according to his word for grace and power to do so. Though you are not sufficient in yourselves to come to Christ, yet you cannot, without stifling and rebelling against the light he has given you, put off seeking him a day longer. Seek him by prayer. Entreat him to make you truly sensible of these things, to soften your hearts, to give you the knowledge of himself. Search the Scriptures. Attend upon the ministry of the gospel. Be found in the way. If you are sincere in your desires, you will break off from sinful and ensnaring company and the things which you yourselves know are contrary and displeasing to him. Thus he will be found of you. And he says, *He that findeth me findeth life* [Proverbs 8:35]. O blessed shall ye be of the Lord, if you thus seek him. When you receive faith you will receive pardon, peace; you will find access to a communion with the great God. Heaven will begin in your soul while upon earth. He will guide you by his counsel and afterwards receive you to his glory. O that I could tell you the sweetness of the hidden manna, but it can only be known by tasting—some of you I trust have tasted that he is gracious.

FOR MEDITATION:

Our LORD, who knows full well
The heart of every saint;
Invites us, by a parable,
To pray and never faint.

Though unbelief suggest,
Why should we longer wait?
He bids us never give him rest,
But be importunate.

'Twas thus a widow poor,
Without support or friend,
Beset the unjust judge's door,
And gained, at last, her end.

Then let us earnest be,
And never faint in prayer;
He loves our importunity,
And makes our cause his care.[22]

SERMON: 1 CHRONICLES 28:9 [4/5], [FOR THE YOUNG PEOPLE]

Do not forsake him

'...If thou seek him, he will be found of thee; but if thou forsake him, he will cast thee off for ever.' 1 Chronicles 28:9
SUGGESTED FURTHER READING: Hebrews 3:7–4:6

The close of my text is awful. If you will not hear, my eye shall weep for you in secret. Attend to the caution—*If you forsake him* ... This is not contrary to what we preach of his unchangeable love to his own people. If you seek him, you shall so find him that nothing shall separate you from him. But if you neglect his call, if you reject him in your hearts, he will cast you off for ever—in life, at death, at the great day. In life you shall be a poor, miserable creature without God in this world, given up to unruly lusts and follies, strangers to peace, without hope or relief. At death—when your soul is plunging into eternity, torn from your idols. At the great day—do you not tremble at the thought? My heart trembles for you. But I would hope better things and things which accompany salvation. I would hope this is a season of grace, that prayer is heard, that the Lord is now about to exert the power of grace and that he will show himself mighty to save. I hope none will think that because I am especially to speak to young persons tonight, that therefore they only are concerned in the subject. If you have lived many years a stranger to God, surely it is high time that you should seek him, for if you do not know him, you must assuredly perish. What though you have lived forty, fifty, sixty, seventy years and are a slave to sin this hour—why, you are, for ought you know, upon the very brink of ruin. Yet it is not too late. *Seek him* now while he may be found. If your hearts are not utterly hardened against his voice, there is yet hope. But O beware of delays. It is the eleventh hour with some of you. May the God of all grace snatch you as brands out of the burning.

FOR MEDITATION: Some of you he has called out of darkness into his marvellous light. Be thankful unto him and bless his name. Follow hard after him. Be of good courage. Fightings and fears you must expect, but he is faithful who has called, who also will do it.

SERMON: 1 CHRONICLES 28:9 [5/5] [FOR THE YOUNG PEOPLE]

God's law—his prescribed course

'But we know that the law is good, if a man use it lawfully.' 1 Timothy 1:8
SUGGESTED FURTHER READING: 1 Timothy 1:1–11

Ignorance of the nature and design of *the law* is at the bottom of all our mistakes in religious concerns. This is the root of self-righteousness and the grand reason why the gospel of Christ is no more regarded. Without a due knowledge of the law, the gospel cannot be rightly preached or understood. And there are and have been too many like those mentioned in the preceding verse, *desiring to be teachers of the law; yet not knowing what they say and affirm.* Notice what we are to understand by the law. The law in many passages of the Old Testament signifies the whole revelation of the will of God, as in Psalm 1:2 and 19:7; but the law, strictly speaking, is distinguished from the gospel, as shown at large in the Epistles to the Romans and Galatians. In the chapter before us the Apostle plainly intends the law of Moses, but in order to understand the nature and design of the law of Moses, it is necessary to go a little higher. The law of God then in the largest sense is that rule, or prescribed course, which he has appointed for his creatures, according to their several natures and capacities, so as to answer the end for which he has created them. Thus it extends to things without life. So it is said, the wind and storm fulfil his word or law. So he hath appointed the moon for its seasons and the sun knoweth his going down, or going forth, and performs all its revolutions according to its Maker's pleasure. If we could suppose the sun was an intelligent being and was to refuse to shine, or was to wander from the path in which God has appointed it to move, it would be a transgressor of the law. But there is no such disorder in the natural world. The law of God in this sense, or what is frequently called the law of nature, is no other than the impression of God's power whereby all things continue to his original purpose. For he spake and it was done, he commanded and it stood fast.

FOR MEDITATION: 'For we are his workmanship, created in Christ Jesus unto good works, which God hath before ordained that we should walk in them' (Ephesians 2:10).

SERMON SERIES: 1 TIMOTHY 1:8, NO. 1 [1/2]

Under the law or under grace?

'But we know that the law is good, if a man use it lawfully.' 1 Timothy 1:8
SUGGESTED FURTHER READING: Galatians 4:21–5:1

Jesus having finished the law, all other sacrifices are unnecessary and vain. The blessed gospel supplies the place of the ceremonial law, to the same advantage as the sun makes the twinkling of the stars and the feeble glimmering of moonlight no longer necessary. May the Lord help you to understand whether you are under the law or under grace. Do you love God? Have you always done so? Do you love your neighbour as yourself, perfectly and constantly doing to others as you would they should do unto you? Can you hear the Ten Commandments read and say deliberately, 'I am free from the breach of every one, either in thought, word or deed?' Will you say, why do I ask such vain questions? Why, nothing less than this can save you from hell, if you seek salvation by the law. The Lord help you to understand it, that you may embrace the gospel. By Jesus we are justified from those things for which the law of Moses would condemn us.

But if you are under grace, if you have put your trust in Jesus, then be of good cheer, he is able to save to the uttermost. You need not be afraid of the law; it is magnified and made honourable by your surety. Study it therefore as your rule and pray to him for grace that you may have a growing conformity to it in your temper and conversation, that he may be glorified in you and by you.

FOR MEDITATION: Thy grace is sufficient for me, but not the notion in my head—it must be the efficacy in my heart. Forgive the past, heal my wounds and anoint me with fresh oil. Let my soul live and it shall praise thee. O my Lord, thine eye beholds many hearts and hands and eyes waiting upon thee this morning for a blessing. Behold me among them. And shine upon me this day, that I may feel the importance of the truths and their sweetness in my soul, and may with an enlarged heart declare them to the people.[23]

Diary, 15 and 16 June 1776

The law is good

'But we know that the law is good, if a man use it lawfully.' 1 Timothy 1:8
SUGGESTED FURTHER READING: Psalm 1:1–6

When the mind is enlightened and instructed by the Word and Spirit of God, then the law is known to be *good*.

(i) It is holy. It manifests the holiness of God and, when obeyed, communicates an impression of his holiness to man. A conformity to this divine law is the perfection of human nature. There can be no excellence in man but so far as he is influenced by this law. Without it, the greater his natural powers and abilities are, so he is but so much the more detestable and mischievous.

(ii) It is just. God had a just right and authority to appoint this rule; it was suited to the relation and ability of his creatures. And though we, by sin, have lost our power, his just right remains and therefore he can justly punish transgressors.

(iii) It is *good*—good for man, his obedience to the law and the favour of God therein being but another word for his proper happiness. And it is impossible for him to be happy in any other way. Only to sinners these things must be applied according to the gospel as fulfilled in Christ, who has obeyed the law and made atonement for sin in behalf of all who believe in him. So that through him they are delivered from condemnation and entitled to all the benefits of his obedience. Thus God is just in justifying the believers. From him likewise they receive the law as a rule enforced by his example and their peculiar obligations to his redeeming love. This makes obedience pleasing and the strength they receive from him makes it easy.

FOR MEDITATION: Till the law is thus approved, there can be no hatred of sin as sin, though it may be avoided in particular instances. If you say the law is good and the gospel is good and see how they illustrate each other, and yet are walking in a spirit of bondage, it is owing to the weakness of your faith. Your judgement may be clearer than your experience, but wait on the Lord and both in due time shall be established. You would as soon as eat poison, as allow yourself in sin, if you knew the *good*ness of the law.

Learning to walk worthy

'But we know that the law is good, if a man use it lawfully.' 1 Timothy 1:8
SUGGESTED FURTHER READING: Matthew 5:17–30

The law is *lawfully* used as a rule of life. The grace of God, received by faith, disposes us to obedience in general, but, through remaining darkness and ignorance, we are much at a loss as to particulars. We are therefore sent to the law to learn how to walk worthy of God and every precept has its place and use. It is *lawfully* used as a test whereby to judge of the exercise of grace. Believers differ so much from what they once were and from what others yet are, that without this right use of the law, comparing themselves with themselves, or with others, they would be prone to think much more highly of their attainments than they ought. But when they try themselves by the standard, they sink into the dust and cry with Job, *I cannot answer thee one of a thousand* [Job 9:3]. From hence you may see how the law is good to him who uses it *lawfully*. It furnishes them with a comprehensive view of the will of God and the path of duty. By the study of it they acquire an habitual spiritual taste of what is right or wrong. The exercised believer, like a skilful workman, has a rule in his hand whereby he can measure and determine with certainty, whereas others judge, as it were, by the eye—can only make a random guess, in which they are generally mistaken. The law makes or keeps them humble. It endears Christ the law-filler [Matthew 5:17] to their hearts and puts them in mind of their obligations to him and dependence upon him every moment.

FOR MEDITATION: 'This book of the law shall not depart out of thy mouth; but thou shalt meditate therein day and night, that thou mayest observe to do according to all that is written therein: for then thou shalt make thy way prosperous, and then thou shalt have good success' (Joshua 1:8).

Satan as himself

'And no marvel; for Satan himself is transformed into an angel of light.'
2 Corinthians 11:14
SUGGESTED FURTHER READING: Revelation 12:7–12

False teachers are Satan's instruments: he works in and by them, and can work without them. We may observe from this text that Satan has two general methods: open and like himself, or under a borrowed garb as *an angel of light.* Consider the first: he uses no disguise upon some occasions to multitudes of sinners, who are so bent upon sinning that they do not put him to the trouble of transforming himself. They are as ready to sin as he to tempt. Shall we say he uses any art or pains with swearers, drunkards, Sabbath-breakers? These are his willing servants that commit uncleanness with greediness. Alas, how many will not have the poor excuse to plead that they were deceived. They know in their consciences that those who do such things are worthy of death. He often acts like himself to poor convinced sinners, inflaming their wounds with his poisoned darts and labouring to persuade them that their sin is too great to be forgiven. He likewise often visits believers with temptations of a dark and black nature, horrid blasphemies, etc., which leave no room to doubt who is their proper author.

FOR MEDITATION:

Forest beasts, that live by prey,
Seldom show themselves by day;
But when daylight is withdrawn,
Then they rove and roar till dawn.

Then, my soul with terror hears
Worse than lions, wolves, or bears,
Roaring loud in every part,
Through the forest of my heart.

Thus when JESUS is in view,
Cheerful I my way pursue;
Walking by my Saviour's light,
Nothing can my soul affright.

Wrath, impatience, envy, pride,
Satan and his host beside,
Press around me to devour;
How can I escape their power?

But when He forbears to shine,
Soon the traveller's case is mine;
Lost, benighted, struck with dread,
What a painful path I tread!

Gracious LORD afford me light,
Put these beasts of prey to flight;
Let thy power and love be shown,
Save me, for I am *thine* own.[24]

SERMON: 2 CORINTHIANS 11:14 [1/2]

An angel of light

'*...Satan himself is transformed into an angel of light.*' 2 Corinthians 11:14
SUGGESTED FURTHER READING: 2 Kings 10:15–31

Sometimes Satan transforms himself into *an angel of light*:

(i) by abuse of gospel principles. He will, upon some occasions, bear a testimony to the truth—but always to serve a wicked end. He will allow and plead for the atonement and righteousness of Jesus Christ—does he not look like *an angel of light*? But his end is to depreciate holiness. He will at other times preach up duties and good works, sanctification; this looks well, but O he is only transformed. His design is to set forwards such things in opposition to the blood of Christ, and the work of the Spirit. He will cry up free grace and prove from God's word that we can do nothing. This is a truth even in Satan's mouth, but his conclusions from it show who he is. He means to make sinners [feel] secure and careless and negligent of the means.

(ii) by a false humility. He is very troublesome to sincere souls this way, persuading them that such great sinners as they ought not to believe.

(iii) by a false zeal—that makes a show and sets up self, under a pretence of God's glory, as in the case of Jehu [2 Kings 10:31].

(iv) by false comforts—working upon their passions and imaginations, while their own hearts are yet buried in the love of sin and the world.

What need to pray to be kept! What good news that Jesus is revealed to destroy the works of the devil!

FOR MEDITATION: I now see more clearly than ever the reason of my former small proficiency, and of my frequent relapses into folly: I see that I had not that perfect dependence on Jesus my Saviour and him only for justification and acceptance, as I thought I had. I see that I was inclined insensibly to exalt my own wretched self, to the prejudice of his honour and grace, and was in some things under the influence of a legal spirit; and that was sufficient cause for my Lord to keep back his influence, and to leave me to weave my spider's webs to my own shame and confusion. Yet he was determined not to forsake me wholly, for his love is everlasting and unchangeable, and blessed be his name, I trust he has shown me my error, and will by his grace prevent me falling grossly into it again.[25]

Diary, 5 July 1754 [after meeting Capt. Alexander Clunie in St Kitts]

SERMON: 2 CORINTHIANS 11:14 [2/2]

For an anniversary

'Praise the LORD, O Jerusalem; praise thy God, O Zion. For he hath strengthened the bars of thy gates; he hath blessed thy children within thee. He maketh peace in thy borders, and filleth thee with the finest of the wheat.' Psalm 147:12–14
SUGGESTED FURTHER READING: Psalm 147:1–20

Zion signifies the church: recovered by Jesus, the true David, out of the hand of his enemies; the seat of royal residence and of spiritual worship. The name is applicable to each of the hills of Zion: the congregations of believers. Happy the people that are in such a case as my text describes. The Lord grant it may in some measure be our case and that we may be thankful. I have chosen the subject as not unsuitable to what I believe is upon many of our hearts on the return of this day. Here we have protection, provision, blessing and peace.

Protection: *he strengtheneth the bars of thy gates*. Zion is a besieged city, but kept by the power of God. Satan is always endeavouring to break in, attempting to hurt them by erroneous doctrines or licentious practices. Therefore we are called upon to watch and stand fast in the faith, to quit ourselves like men and be strong.

He blesseth thy children. An increase in graces, making them thriving, giving them appetite as well as food and enabling them to show forth his praise in a holy conversation. An increase in numbers, calling them into the state of children who were by nature strangers and aliens.

FOR MEDITATION:
Blest inhabitants of Zion,
Washed in the Redeemer's blood!
JESUS, whom their souls rely on,
Makes them kings and priests to GOD:
'Tis his love his people raises
Over self to reign as kings
And as priests, his solemn praises
Each for a thank-offering brings.[26]

Peace and provision

'Praise the LORD, *O Jerusalem; praise thy God, O Zion. For he hath strengthened the bars of thy gates; he hath blessed thy children within thee. He maketh peace in thy borders, and filleth thee with the finest of the wheat.' Psalm 147:12–14*
SUGGESTED FURTHER READING: Leviticus 26:3–13

Provision. The quality: *the finest wheat*, the doctrines and truths of the gospel in their power and purity. This is the bread of life—Jesus Christ dispensed in the word and received by faith. The quantity: *filleth*, when ordinances are attended not only now and then, but frequently, and when by the Spirit's application they are made lively and savoury.

Peace. Peace is threefold:

(i) peace in their own souls, when they grow into an established peace with God by Jesus Christ (Romans 5:1).

(ii) peace amongst themselves, when the power of his grace prevents all those jealousies, envyings, discords, which wherever they prevail are dishonourable, uncomfortable and hurtful to the works.

(iii) outward peace. A full peace with the world cannot be expected, but I mean liberty to enjoy our privileges without interruption or ill-treatment— a mercy with which we are singularly favoured.

Now the most of the blessings and benefits I have mentioned depend under God upon the continuance of a gospel minister. This some of you will know, and therefore when the Lord seemed to threaten a removal you were pained. Woeful are the consequences when the Lord removes his candlestick—then profession languishes, errors creep in, dispensations and discords take place—the spirit of the world takes place, and the most established feel a want and a loss. Let us remember we are still dependent upon him. As the time of distress is his time of help, so the hour of security is the hour of danger.

FOR MEDITATION:

Round each habitation hovering	Thus deriving from their banner
See the cloud and fire appear!	Light by night and shade by day;
For a glory and a covering,	Safe they feed upon the Manna
Showing that the LORD is near:	Which he gives them when they pray.[28]

SERMON: PSALM 147:12–14 [2/2] [ON THE COTTINGHAM ANNIVERSARY]

Nurture the rising generation

'And Pharaoh's daughter said unto her, Take this child away, and nurse it for me, and I will give thee thy wages. And the woman took the child, and nursed it.' Exodus 2:9
SUGGESTED FURTHER READING: 2 John 1–13

Though these words were first spoken on a particular occasion by Pharaoh's daughter to the mother of Moses, yet they express the sense of God's revealed will and command to all parents. And the subject is one of those which his ministers ought at times to press upon their hearers. And it is a point of much importance. The hopes of the church and nation depend upon the rising generation. The people of God are fewer, and dropping away daily. How little success the preaching of the gospel has upon those who are grown old and hardened in sin, experience shows. Surely except the Lord of hosts has a remnant among those who are growing up, we shall soon be as Sodom and be made like unto Gomorrah. And yet perhaps there is nothing in which believers are so generally negligent as in this. And though some of the chief arguments I would use can only be fully understood by believers, yet I will speak as much at large as I can, for it is a common concern, which all ought to lay to heart.

Children are the gift of God—when his hand is seen, and his glory regarded in them, they are blessings. You that have children, there was a voice with the providence; the voice said to you, *take this child and nurse it for me*. Bring it up in the nurture and admonition of the Lord.

FOR MEDITATION: Lord, do thou strengthen my hands, and water my poor endeavours, and grant that some of these little ones may look back with thankfulness to thee for these opportunities, when I am laid low in the dust.[29]
Journal of children's meetings at Olney, 28 March 1765

We, when companions together in youth, enjoyed the same scenes of childhood under the kind instruction of Good Mr Newton and have united in singing those sweet hymns in Dr Watts's little book[30] in the Great House Meeting as we used to call it. Those reflections were a source of comfort to her—your dear mother.[31]
[by a former member of the children's meetings, c.1842]

SERMON: EXODUS 2:9 [1/3]

Watch over your children

'And Pharaoh's daughter said unto her, Take this child away, and nurse it for me, and I will give thee thy wages. And the woman took the child, and nursed it.' Exodus 2:9
SUGGESTED FURTHER READING: Hebrews 12:5–13

Parents, being evil, know how to give good gifts to their children—the good things of this life—to feed, clothe them, and so on,—but to *nurse* and bring them up for the Lord signifies more:

(i) to endeavour to instil into them religious principles. I mean more by this than to teach them a catechism by rote as you would teach a parrot. They should be conversed with and every occasion laid hold of to explain and make them know that God sees and hears them, and that this God is only to be known and worshipped in Jesus.

(ii) to watch over and govern their temper—this is vastly needful, to take them while they are young—yet how sadly are they hurt by a fond and blind indulgence to their faults and humours. And if any correction or restraint is attempted, it is often in anger and heat, so that the end is not answered. It is but like Satan casting out Satan. If you do not bring in the authority of God and act in a spirit of meekness and steadiness, you may make them fear you, but you will do but little good.

(iii) to take care in particular that they attend on the worship of God on the Lord's Day, and are not suffered to break the Sabbath. I am afraid many parents have much to answer for in this point. But almost all the evils and abominations to which youth are in time addicted enter at this door.

(iv) to set them a good example. Without this indeed the rest will ordinarily do little. But alas, for many poor children are forced to blush every day for the behaviour of their parents. If you love them, be careful of laying stumbling blocks in their way.

FOR MEDITATION: My dear child [Betsy], ... When you read our Saviour's discourses, recorded by the evangelists, attend as if you saw him with your own eyes, standing before you; and when you try to pray, assure yourself before you begin, that he is actually in the room with you, and that his ear is open to every word you say. ... You are not speaking into the air, or to One who is a great way off; but to One who is very near you—to your best Friend.[32]

SERMON: EXODUS 2:9 [2/3]

Just wages

'And Pharaoh's daughter said unto her, Take this child away, and nurse it for me, and I will give thee thy wages. And the woman took the child, and nursed it.' Exodus 2:9
SUGGESTED FURTHER READING: 2 Samuel 18:24–33

If you conscientiously endeavour to bring up your children for the Lord he will pay you your wages—you shall not lose your reward. Let us begin with the lowest first. Your children will love and reverence you. Even though you should not be so successful as you could wish, yet if you thus honour the Lord, he will honour you in your children's eyes. You will generally see them preserved from those excesses which so often wound the hearts of parents. For though it is a true and common observation that grace does not run in the blood and good people have often wicked children, yet it will generally appear that when they break out very bad and profligate in youth, they have been spoiled and neglected in childhood. Who knows but you may be made instruments of the Lord to save your children's soul—then with what joy will you meet at the great day. But if you will not bring them up for the Lord, you will bring them up for Satan—and what wages do you think you will receive (by God's righteous judgement) from that hard master? You must expect they will despise your authority, fly in your face and wound your hearts by their disobedience. O what a heartbreaking hour will that be. Think what David felt for Absalom [2 Samuel 18:33].

FOR MEDITATION: 'Train up a child in the way he should go: and when he is old, he will not depart from it' (Proverbs 22:6).

My dear Eliza is still spared to me, and in her attention and affection I find the best substitute (in the removal of my dear wife) that the nature of the case can possibly admit. But it is to thy mercy and blessing that I owe her attention and kindness. Accept my praise. Above all I thank thee for the causes and tokens I have to believe that thou hast called her by thy grace. Lord, keep her as the pupil of thine eye, hide her under the shadow of thy wings, reward her for her attention to me in my old age, and after a short separation, at thine appointed time, may we meet in thy presence above to part no more.[33]   *Diary*, 2 February 1801 [re his adopted daughter]

SERMON: EXODUS 2:9 [3/3]

He knows our hearts

'What prayer and supplication soever be made by any man, or by all thy people Israel, which shall know every man the plague of his own heart, and spread forth his hands toward this house: then hear thou in heaven thy dwelling place, and forgive, and do, and give to every man according to his ways, whose heart thou knowest; (for thou, even thou only, knowest the hearts of all the children of men).' 1 Kings 8:38–39
SUGGESTED FURTHER READING: Jeremiah 17:5–10

The Lord gave Israel to understand from first to last, and especially when he was affording them signal mercies, that he knew them and knew what returns they would make to him. He knew them, and long experience taught them to know themselves. Therefore it was often sounded in their ears, *Not for your own sakes* [Ezekiel 36:32]. The song of Moses was published with this view before they entered Canaan, that the grant might be known to be wholly of grace. The most glorious day perhaps ever seen by Israel was at the dedication of the first temple. The Lord had wrought wonderfully for them, subdued their enemies, given them rest, plenty riches, a king who was the wisest of men. The temple, built by divine direction, was finished in all its beauty and glory; the people, to appearance, all of one heart and mind; the sacrifices immense, the congregation innumerable, the glory of the Lord in view filling the house in token of his favour and acceptance. Yet the Lord then saw a day coming, which they were little aware of, when Israel would be delivered up into the hands of their enemies and their temple destroyed— not one stone left upon another. The prayer of Solomon upon this occasion was doubtless pronounced under the immediate influence of the Holy Spirit, and gives throughout a prophetic intimation of the changes that would take place.

FOR MEDITATION: *Take heed to thyself*, for there the principal danger lies. The world and the devil will undoubtedly spread all their snares, and join all their force against thee, but thy principal danger lies at home. As nothing from without entering into a man defileth him, so it may be said that nothing from without that befalleth a man can either hurt or hinder him in his spiritual progress unless he himself become one of the party. Thou that art devoted to God, take heed of thyself.[34]

SERMON: 1 KINGS 8:38–39 [1/6]

Direct your hearts and eyes to the Great Temple

'What prayer and supplication soever be made by any man, or by all thy people Israel, which shall know every man the plague of his own heart, and spread forth his hands toward this house ...' 1 Kings 8:38
SUGGESTED FURTHER READING: John 2:13–22

The people were directed to pray toward the temple, which we find was observed by Daniel when captive in a far distant country. Those of the Jews who went no farther than the literal sense, and trusted in their outward privileges, have been long in a hopeless state; their temple and priesthood have been destroyed more than 1700 years, since which they have been incapable upon their own principles of offering one acceptable prayer, for they have no temple whither to direct their supplications. But the design of the prayer is made good to the spiritual Israel. Before the temple made with hands was finally destroyed, God was pleased to raise up another made without hands, of which the other was but a type, as our Lord himself teaches us in John 2 [19–22]. In these happy, gospel times wherein God is made known in Christ, we have the full blessings of which the worship in Solomon's temple conveyed but the emblem and foretaste. The Lord give us faith to direct our hearts and eyes to the Great Temple in which the fullness of the Godhead unchangeably dwell, and may the glory of the Lord be revealed to our souls.

FOR MEDITATION: 'But I say unto you, That in this place is one greater than the temple... Destroy this temple, and in three days I will raise it up. Then said the Jews, Forty and six years was this temple in building, and wilt thou rear it up in three days? But he spake of the temple of his body. When therefore he was risen from the dead, his disciples remembered that he had said this unto them; and they believed the scripture, and the word which Jesus had said' (Matthew 12:6; John 2:19–22).

'And he carried me away in the spirit to a great and high mountain, and showed me that great city, the holy Jerusalem, descending out of heaven from God... And I saw no temple therein: for the Lord God Almighty and the Lamb are the temple of it' (Revelation 21:10,22).

SERMON: 1 KINGS 8:38–39 [2/6]

The true Temple

'*What prayer and supplication soever be made by any man, or by all thy people Israel, which shall know every man the plague of his own heart, and spread forth his hands toward this house: then hear thou in heaven thy dwelling place, and forgive, and do, and give to every man according to his ways, whose heart thou knowest; (for thou, even thou only, knowest the hearts of all the children of men).*' 1 Kings 8:38–39
SUGGESTED FURTHER READING: 2 Corinthians 3:7–18

I shall speak of the true Temple. The type points out to us several things. Though the whole earth was filled with the providence and goodness of the Lord, he was only known in the temple worship. No other place or people had tokens of God's presence amongst them. Thus God is only known in Christ. The book of nature and even the book of Scriptures give us no comfortable apprehensions of him, any farther than Jesus the true Temple is acknowledged. If men have not eyes to see what is taught of the person, offices and saving work of Christ, even the Scripture is a sealed book to them, and with the Word of God in their hands and in their mouth, they stumble like the blind at noonday. Many who acknowledge the Scripture in words know no more of God in a way of comfortable dependence and influence than the heathens. All acceptable service was confined to the temple, or immediately referred to it. No sacrifices could be offered anywhere else, and prayers by those at a distance must be directed towards it. Thus, as there can be no knowledge of God, so no communion with God, but by Christ. He is the door and the way, and no one cometh to the Father but by him. In the temple there was a veil separating the things within it from the people's view, intimating the state of distance of the church under the law. But this veil was removed, and every partition broken down at his death. The hidden glories are revealed. All the Lord's people are priests and have right of access, and the temple, no more confined to one space, is open to people of all languages and nations.

FOR MEDITATION: 'Behold the tabernacle of God is with men, and he will dwell with them, and they shall be his people, and God himself shall be with them, and be their God' (Revelation 21:3).

SERMON: 1 KINGS 8:38–39 [3/6]

All persons and all cases

'What prayer and supplication soever be made by any man, or by all thy people Israel, which shall know every man the plague of his own heart, and spread forth his hands toward this house: then hear thou in heaven thy dwelling place, and forgive ...' 1 Kings 8:38–39
SUGGESTED FURTHER READING: Revelation 7:9–17

When we meet in the name of Christ in his ordinances, we are at the gate of the temple. The Lord is near, his eye upon us, his ear open to us, and his arm stretched forth to bestow upon us the blessings of his goodness—therefore the promise and encouragement. What Solomon asked, the Lord put in his heart because it was his pleasure to perform. Here is leave given for all persons and all cases.

(i) All persons—that is, all who account it a privilege, *every man who knows the plague of his own heart*. How strongly does unbelief work when those who do have[35] a right, make the ground of that right an objection against themselves! Do you say, 'Ah, I am such a sinner, such a backslider, I dare not come?' Is not this rather a proof that you *know the plagues of your own heart* and are therefore invited by name?

(ii) All cases—*what prayer and supplication soever*. This is a large word. Let no one say, 'I am shut out.' They who *know the plague of their own hearts* will have matter for various supplications. A sense of our wants and wills will teach us to pray. What is this plague? Let the Lord know and direct your prayers to the Temple and you shall be heard.

FOR MEDITATION:

Behold the throne of grace!
The promise calls me near;
There Jesus shows a smiling face,
And waits to answer prayer.

That rich atoning blood,
Which sprinkled round I see;
Provides for those who come to GOD,
An all-prevailing plea.

My soul ask what thou wilt,
Thou canst not be too bold;
Since his own blood for thee he spilt,
What else can he withhold.

Beyond thy utmost wants
His love and power can bless;
To praying souls he always grants,
More than they can express.[36]

SERMON: 1 KINGS 8:38–39 [4/6]

The plague in our hearts

'What prayer and supplication soever be made by any man, or by all thy people Israel, which shall know every man the plague of his own heart, and spread forth his hands toward this house: then hear thou in heaven thy dwelling place, and forgive ...' 1 Kings 8:38–39
SUGGESTED FURTHER READING: Mark 2:1–12

I can tell some of you what *the plague of your heart* is. It includes such things as these:

(i) guilt. *I have sinned against the LORD* [2 Samuel 12:13]. Well, there is forgiveness with him—for those who are beginning to come to him and for those who have backslidden from him.

(ii) unbelief. This is always with us. I see the gospel is good and true. I know and in my judgement approve the way of salvation, and yet I cannot make it my own. Look to the temple and say, 'Lord, increase my faith.'

(iii) indwelling sin. Some may say, O I am ready to be swept away by the stream of corrupt nature, and especially in one instance: I have an enemy who knows where I am weak and threatens to overpower me. But in this temple there is a treasury of grace.

[contd in 6/6]

FOR MEDITATION:

Physician of my sin-sick soul,
To thee I bring my case;
My raging malady control,
And heal me by thy grace.

I would disclose my whole complaint,
But where shall I begin?
No words of mine can fully paint
That worst distemper, sin.

It lies not in a single part,
But through my frame is spread;
A burning fever in my heart,
A palsy in my head.

It makes me deaf, and dumb, and blind,
And impotent and lame;
And overclouds, and fills my mind,
With folly, fear, and shame.

A thousand evil thoughts intrude
Tumultuous in my breast;
Which indispose me for my food,
And rob me of my rest.

LORD I am sick, regard my cry,
And set my spirit free;
Say, canst thou let a sinner die,
Who longs to live to thee?[37]

SERMON: 1 KINGS 8:38–39 [5/6]

He hears the feeblest cry for mercy

'What prayer and supplication soever be made by any man, or by all thy people Israel, which shall know every man the plague of his own heart, and spread forth his hands toward this house: then hear thou in heaven thy dwelling place, and forgive, and do, and give to every man according to his ways, whose heart thou knowest; (for thou, even thou only, knowest the hearts of all the children of men).' 1 Kings 8:38–39

SUGGESTED FURTHER READING: Psalm 35:1–28

[contd from 5/6]
The plague of your heart includes:

(i) temptation. This takes in all the foregoing. Satan strengthens unbelief, stirs up corruption, and fixes guilt upon the conscience. 'He has near access to my heart and I feel that within which agrees with all his proposals. My mind is filled with hard thoughts of God, blasphemies and evil imaginations.' A part of Solomon's prayer was for Israel when smitten before their enemies.

(ii) deadness of spirit. 'I know and believe the truth, but it seems not to touch me. I pray without life, I hear without pleasure, my mind is wandering to the ends of the earth and I cannot fix it.' There is relief in this place also. A coal of fire from the golden altar of this temple will warm your heart, and quicken your affections to divine things.

(iii) impatience. 'I am in trouble and my heart rebels against the Lord. I do not find affliction sanctified.' Look to the temple, to him who drank the cup of wrath for us. I cannot mention every case; whatever it be, here is provision.

FOR MEDITATION: But what is it to direct the prayer to the temple? It is to pray in the name of Jesus, as King, and expecting—for his sake only. See what is asked: *hear, forgive* and *do*. He will *hear* the feeblest cry, *forgive* the greatest sins, and *do* the hardest things. *For thou only knowest.* He knows before you ask; he that searcheth the heart knoweth what is the mind of the Spirit. We are going to the Lord's table. May he enable us to carry with us a sense of *the plague of our own hearts* and of his abundant love, compassion and power. May he show careless sinners *the plague of their hearts*, that they may cry for mercy.

SERMON: 1 KINGS 8:38–39 [6/6]

Certain deliverance

'How is Babylon become a desolation among the nations!' Jeremiah 50:23
SUGGESTED FURTHER READING: Jeremiah 50:1–10

Babylon was the great enemy of Israel, and by God's permission triumphed over it for a season, laid Jerusalem in heaps and led the people into captivity. But the prophet in this chapter foretells the destruction of Babylon, and that in consequence of it, Israel should return to their own land in the manner described in my text [50:5]. But the Scriptures principally testify of Christ. The prophecies concerning Israel are not to be confined to the literal and immediate sense; they are typical, and receive their full accomplishment and signification when referred to gospel times. Mystical Babylon is the kingdom of Satan—Jesus, the true Cyrus, triumphed over him and destroyed his power by his death. Then he spoiled principalities and powers, broke the gates of brass asunder, and effected the deliverance and redemption of his people, which now is not suspended upon any conditions on their parts, but wholly depends upon the efficacy of his grace and promise. He has made their deliverance not only possible but certain. He has said, *They shall ask the way,* and he has likewise said, 'They that seek shall find' [Luke 11:9].

FOR MEDITATION: I began to pray. I could not utter the prayer of faith: I could not draw near to a reconciled God, and call him Father. My prayer was like the cry of the ravens, which yet the Lord does not disdain to hear ... One of the first helps I received (in consequence of a determination to examine the New Testament more carefully) was from Luke 11:13 ... Here I found a Spirit spoken of, which was to be communicated to those who ask it. Upon this I reasoned thus: if this book is true, the promise in this passage is true likewise: I have need of that very Spirit by which the whole was written, in order to understand it aright. He has engaged here to give that Spirit to those who ask. I must therefore pray for it; and if it is of God, he will make good his own word. ...About this time I began to know that there is a God that hears and answers prayer. How many times has he appeared for me since this great deliverance![38]

Narrative, 1764, Letter 8

SERMON: JEREMIAH 50:5 [2/7] [TO THE YOUNG PEOPLE]

When every creature comfort fails

'The LORD is my portion, saith my soul; therefore will I hope in him.'
Lamentations 3:24
SUGGESTED FURTHER READING: Acts 27:13–44

The prophet Jeremiah and the spiritual worshippers of God in his time lived in a cloudy and dark day. Though the Lord set a mark upon them for good and gave them their lives for a prey, yet were they deeply affected with the common calamity of their people. It is no small trial to the people of God to live where wickedness prevails, suppose they suffer no more than from what they see and hear around them, but when the Lord arises to take vengeance, when he sends his desolatory judgements, when he breaks the staff of bread and water, or says to the sword, *Sword, go through the land* [Ezekiel 14:17], his people, as well as others, have a share in the trouble—and that justly, for they have not been so faithful as they ought in bearing a testimony against sin, neither have they been so deeply humbled before God on this account as became them. However, at the worst they have two consolations: firstly that his providence is with them to support and bring them safe through all they meet, and secondly that he himself is their friend, their God, their portion—a portion which no change of circumstance can deprive them of. And here we see the triumph of faith that can rejoice in the Lord when every creature comfort fails and can claim an interest in him when all things seem against them. The believers at this time saw their country laid waste, their cities destroyed, their temples burnt by fire, their neighbours and friends cut off by sword and pestilence, they themselves rooted out from their pleasant dwellings and sent captives into a strange land. Yet in the midst of all this desolation they could say, *The LORD is my portion,* therefore though cast down, we are not destroyed—*I will hope in him.*

FOR MEDITATION: We have had a great blow at Olney. Betty Abraham is gone. We prayed for her continuance, but the time when Jesus had prayed she might be with him to see his glory being come, we could not keep her, nor is it fitting we should. My soul desires to say, *Thy will be done.* Yet I feel as if I had lost a right hand[39] ... I preached her funeral last night from Lamentations 3:24, which were some of the last words she spoke.[40]
John Newton to John Ryland jnr, 14 February 1774

SERMON: LAMENTATIONS 3:24 [1/4] [FOR BETTY ABRAHAM'S FUNERAL]

It's all of grace

'The LORD is my portion, saith my soul; therefore will I hope in him.'
Lamentations 3:24
SUGGESTED FURTHER READING: Psalm 119:57–72

Happy indeed are the people who have the Lord for their God. Let us consider how the Lord becomes a *portion*. If the holy angels should use these words they would not seem strange, but when sinful worms are not ashamed or afraid to say so, it seems wonderful indeed. How different our portion by nature: sin our choice, misery our state, wrath our inheritance. Such were once all those who have now the Lord for their portion. They did not obtain their portion as that which Jacob speaks of: by his sword and his bow [Genesis 48:22]. It was all of grace. It pleased the Lord to make them his people, to choose them for his portion, and then he gave himself to be a portion for them.

(i) He spared and waited for them (Ezekiel 16:6).

(ii) He opens their understandings, to look upon themselves and desire him.

(iii) He gives them faith—then they claim him as their own.

FOR MEDITATION:

Once perishing in blood I lay,
Creatures no help could give,
But Jesus passed me in the way,
He saw, and bid me live.

At length the time of love arrived
When I my Lord should know,
Then Satan, of his power deprived,
Was forced to let me go.

Though Satan still his rule maintained,
And all his arts employed;
That mighty Word his rage restrained,
I could not be destroyed.

O can I e'er that day forget
When Jesus kindly spoke!
'Poor soul, my blood has paid thy debt,
And now I break thy yoke.

Henceforth I take thee for my own,
And give myself to thee;
Forsake the idols thou hast known,
And yield thyself to me.'[41]

SERMON: LAMENTATIONS 3:24 [2/4] [FOR BETTY ABRAHAM'S FUNERAL]

What a portion!

'The LORD is my portion, saith my soul; therefore will I hope in him.'
Lamentations 3:24
SUGGESTED FURTHER READING: Lamentations 3:19–24

What a portion! The word implies two things:
   (i) excellence. None account anything a portion but what is (in their esteem at least) valuable.
   (ii) propriety. However excellent a thing may be, if it is not ours, or if we have no hope of attaining it, we cannot look on it as our portion.
   Now the Lord is deservedly a portion to believing souls, for he is most excellent in himself, and he gives them a right to call him their own. Compare this with the portions and desirable things of this life. They are:
   (i) hard to get.
   (ii) unsatisfactory when obtained. The want of one thing will spoil the sweetness of many, as Haman [in Esther].
   (iii) hard, nay impossible, to keep.
   But the Lord is:
   (i) a free portion. None that sincerely desire him shall be rejected. Grace reigns, and sinners, though vilest and most unworthy, are welcome.
   (ii) an all-sufficient portion, exceeding all their capacities, wants and desires.
   (iii) an everlasting portion: in life, in death and for ever.

FOR MEDITATION: We had a full house and I hope a good time in the evening. The subject, death—it being the first time of our meeting there since Betty Abraham was removed; I had made a hymn upon the occasion.[42]
Diary, Sunday evening 20 February 1774

From pole to pole let others roam,	JESUS, who on his glorious throne
And search in vain for bliss;	Rules heaven and earth and sea;
My soul is satisfied at home,	Is pleased to claim me for his own,
The LORD my portion is.	And give himself to me.[43]

[hymn prompted by Betty Abraham's death; first used 20 February 1774]

SERMON: LAMENTATIONS 3:24 [3/4] [FOR BETTY ABRAHAM'S FUNERAL]

Hope in him

'The LORD *is my portion, saith my soul; therefore will I hope in him.'*
Lamentations 3:24
SUGGESTED FURTHER READING: Psalm 130:1–8

Consider to whom he is a *portion*. Those who have the Lord for their portion are:

(i) humble. They have abasing thoughts of themselves, admiring thoughts of his grace and condescension. They say as Mephibosheth in 2 Samuel 19:28.

(ii) spiritual. A carnal principle indeed still cleaves to them, but their prevailing desire is towards their portion.

(iii) obedient. A sense of his love constrains them; they acknowledge that they are not their own.

If so, does not the Word of God assure some of you that as yet you have no part or lot in this portion? What can the self-righteous, the worldly and the self-willed claim here? Which of us may not take up a lamentation and say, *my leanness* [Isaiah 24:16]? If we have the beginnings of these gracious principles, yet how weak and faint. However, there is a comfortable and safe conclusion. If the Lord is your portion, your desire, you may hope in him:

(i) for that renewed pardon you want.

(ii) for a clearer manifestation of your interest.

(ii) for increase of grace.

(iv) that he will not cast you off for ever.

FOR MEDITATION: [prompted by Betty Abraham's death]

His person fixes all my love,
His blood removes my fear;
And while he pleads for me above,
His arm preserves me here.

For him I count as gain each loss,
Disgrace, for him, renown;
Well may I glory in his cross,
While he prepares my crown!

His word of promise is my food,
His Spirit is my guide;
Thus daily is my strength renewed
And all my wants supplied.

Let worldlings then indulge their boast,
How much they gain or spend!
Their joys must soon give up the ghost,
But mine shall know no end.[44]

SERMON: LAMENTATIONS 3:24 [4/4] [FOR BETTY ABRAHAM'S FUNERAL]

Beware your adversary

'*Now the serpent was more subtle than any beast of the field which the* LORD *God had made.*' Genesis 3:1
SUGGESTED FURTHER READING: James 4:1–10

To the Word of God we are indebted for the knowledge we have of the first state of things. We have here the mournful account concerning the entrance of evil, which is given not to indulge our curiosity, but because it most highly concerns us to know it and to be suitably affected with it.

The serpent. Yet he was not a mere serpent, but that evil spirit who is called in Scripture (I suppose upon this account) the old serpent the devil (John 8:44; Revelation 12:9). The Scripture is very brief in the account it gives us of the invisible world. But this much is clear: that there is in the scale of God's creatures an order of beings, superior to man in powers and knowledge, called angels, formed for the service and vision of God; that many of these angels kept not their first estate, but rebelled against God, were cut off from his light and holiness, and became fallen, apostate and hopeless spirits, or in other words, devils; that the word 'devil', singularly in Scripture, seems used sometimes collectively for the whole body and interest of these powers of darkness, and sometimes to denote one chief spirit or head amongst them who is called the prince of the bottomless pit and (from the advantages he gained over our first parents) the god of this world; that Satan and all his associates in misery are filled with malice, enmity and rage against God and his creatures. Their study is to defile and to destroy, and though they are chained by the power of God and cannot do all they would, yet they have a permissive liberty, which God by his holy wisdom makes subservient to his own glory. In brief we may collect from Scripture that Satan, or the head of these apostate angels, was suffered to tempt Adam to break God's commands—force him he could not.

FOR MEDITATION: Be sober—be vigilant. You have an adversary. Did he attempt thus against Adam in Paradise and shall you escape? If you do not find him assaulting and endeavouring to deceive you, it is because you are asleep in his hands. He thinks he has you sure—he has blinded your eyes and stopped your ears and is leading you captive at his will.

Arts and crafts

'Now the serpent was more subtle than any beast of the field which the Lord God had made.' Genesis 3:1

SUGGESTED FURTHER READING: 1 Corinthians 10:1–13

The design of Satan was doubtless to dishonour and affront God and to destroy man, whose happiness he envied. But see how he was taken in his own craftiness: hereby occasion was opened for the revelation of God's glory in justice and in grace, and man was raised from the misery into which Satan plunged him, to a nobler and more established happiness than that in which he was at first created. We may admire and say as Romans 11:33 [*O the depth of the riches both of the wisdom and knowledge of God! how unsearchable are his judgements, and his ways past finding out!*]

Observe his wiles. I doubt not but in this first temptation might be noticed the chief traces of all the arts he practises to this day upon Adam's posterity and that the steps by which he prevailed show much of the workings of the hearts of all men under his influence. But I do not believe that the line of my experience is sufficient to sound the depths of this mystery of iniquity. It is a mercy if we can say, *We are not altogether ignorant of his devices* [2 Corinthians 2:11].

You that are seeking the Lord, wonder not that Satan is against you. Be humble and continue in prayer. But remember who has conquered him. Make the name of Jesus your high tower and take to you the armour of God.

FOR MEDITATION:

The castle of the human heart
Strong in its native sin;
Is guarded well, in every part,
By him who dwells within.

For Satan there, in arms, resides,
And calls the place his own;
With care against assaults provides,
And rules, as on a throne.

But JESUS, stronger far than he,
In his appointed hour
Appears, to set his people free
From the usurper's power.

'This heart I bought with blood,' he says,
'And now it shall be mine';
His voice the strong one armed dismays,
He knows he must resign.45

Satan's subtlety

'*Now the serpent was more subtle than any beast of the field which the Lord God had made.' Genesis 3:1*
SUGGESTED FURTHER READING: Matthew 16:13–28

What I can observe to you may be gathered from Satan's appearance, his address and his arguments. He appeared as a serpent, either in the likeness of a serpent or rather, as I suppose, he actually possessed a real serpent. If I was to tell you the conjectures of the learned upon this subject, it might be more for your amusement than edification. I would say as little as possible that is not founded upon the sure word. It is plain the serpent was degraded by the sentence and therefore was a more excellent creature before the Fall than since. It did not go upon its belly or feed upon dust; what other properties it might possess we know not. Satan's principal reason for choosing this creature is assigned—he was the most *subtle*, and therefore Eve was the less liable to be surprised at the subtlety of Satan under such a form. From hence we may note in general that Satan knows how to avail himself of the fittest instruments. In all succeeding times, Satan's work is carried on by subtle instruments. When he would oppose the commands of God, when he would deprave the doctrines of the gospel, when he would darken the glories of Christ and deny the operations and influences of the Holy Spirit, he does not ordinarily employ fools in these services, but men of parts and abilities, of genius and learning. We shall hardly find one dangerous or damnable error that had considerable prevalence in the church but what has been started and maintained by persons of this sort. Had they been ignorants and blockheads, as we say, their dreams might have been quickly despised and forgot.

FOR MEDITATION: Hence none should be proud of natural abilities, or a turn for reasoning, or the furniture of learning. The more of these things a man has, if they are not sanctified by grace, they make him but so much a fitter instrument for Satan, and qualify him for the greater mischief. Many wise men and great scholars who have admired themselves and been admired by the world for their ingenuity will one day wish they had been born idiots.

Be sober—be vigilant

'Now the serpent was more subtle than any beast of the field which the Lord God had made.' Genesis 3:1
SUGGESTED FURTHER READING: 1 Corinthians 1:18–31

A lesson of caution: let none be carried away by great names, so as to take things upon trust because the person who teaches them is called a scholar, a divine, a doctor or a pope. For ought I know, if Satan had appeared to Eve as an ass she might have disdained to confer with him. But the serpent was so subtle and engaging that he caught her attention. Now perhaps some of you would not be so willing to venture your souls upon your own righteousness to think so meanly as you do of the person and gospel of Christ, if you did not know that the same sentiments are maintained by persons whom you suppose wiser than yourselves. But if you are blindly led by those who are wrong themselves (and the wisdom of man is foolishness with God) what must the issue be?

We have as yet but entered upon this important subject and our time draws to a close. I must therefore only add a word of exhortation: Be sober—be vigilant. You have an adversary.

FOR MEDITATION: An advance in years and the changing dispensations of thy providence have put an end to many of my conflicts; but my heart is still the same... O make me wise and watchful, diffident of myself and wholly dependent upon thee! As my ground changes, my enemy can change his mode of attack. My wisdom is not a match for his subtlety, nor my utmost efforts equal to his strength. I am still liable to many snares, and there are many ways in which I might still grieve thy Spirit, wound my own conscience, and even openly dishonour my profession. But if thou art pleased to hold me up, I shall be safe, and nothing short of that power which sustains the stars in their orbits can suffice to keep me from falling.[46]

Diary, 15 December 1796 (aged 71)

SERMON SERIES: GENESIS, NO. 5 [4/4], GENESIS 3:1

He does not quench the smoking flax

'Nicodemus saith unto him, How can a man be born when he is old? Can he enter the second time into his mother's womb, and be born?' John 3:4
SUGGESTED FURTHER READING: John 3:1–21

When we read our Lord's discourse with Nicodemus, we may well say what some said who heard him speak themselves, *Never man spake like this man* [John 7:46]. Here we see a depth of doctrine explained and illustrated by the most familiar and condescending comparisons. We see something of that tenderness and freedom with which he received all that came unto him. He did not despise the day of small things; he did not quench the smoking flax, but cherished it into a flame. We see likewise the power and efficacy of his words, how they cause light to spring out of darkness, instruct the most ignorant and confirm the most fearful. Nicodemus, who at first came to Jesus by night, attained at length so much boldness in his cause, that when he hung upon the cross, wounded and dead, when his apostles had all forsaken him, he durst appear in the midst of his enemies as an open disciple and assist in taking down his body and preparing it for the funeral. Let this encourage those who are now seeking him in much darkness and many fears. His arm is not shortened, nor his ear heavy, nor his compassions abated to this hour.

FOR MEDITATION: The religion I then possessed my Lord, thou knowest, scarcely deserved the name. For I knew little of thee as a Saviour, and while I trusted thee in temporals, I was not aware of my greatest wants and dangers. In my spiritual concerns, I chiefly depended upon myself. I knew I had been very bad, I had a desire to be better, and thought I should in time make myself so. Surely if I had any light, it was but as the first and faintest streak of dawn. Yet if this glimmering had not been from thee, it could not have advanced. Thou who wilt not forsake the work of thine own hands, nor break the bruised reed, nor quench the smoking flax, wast pleased to pardon, accept and bring me forward. May the remembrance of thy patience and gentleness towards me, teach me forbearance and candour to others, in whom I observe the smallest indications of a desire to seek and serve thee![47]

Annotated *Letters to a Wife*, 21 February 1795

SERMON SERIES: JOHN 3:1–2, NO. 1 [1/7]

Hear as if your last opportunity

'For God so loved the world, that he gave his only begotten Son, that whosoever believeth in him should not perish, but have everlasting life.' John 3:16
SUGGESTED FURTHER READING: Luke 23:32–43

As I conceive that this discourse will afford a large scope for doctrine, for instruction in righteousness, I propose, if opportunity is afforded, to go through it all. To enlarge upon all that the verses before us contain in reference to these subjects will be a work of time. Perhaps many who are present at my entrance upon this passage may not live to see the close of it, even if I should be spared to complete it. May the Lord therefore enable me to speak and you to hear every discourse as if it were the last opportunity we should enjoy on this side of eternity. It may be summarized by four principal points:

(i) the nature and necessity of the new birth (from John 3:3–8).

(ii) concerning the certainty and evidence of divine truth and the insufficiency of man to receive the clearest and most necessary doctrines, unless he is taught from above (verses 9–13).

(iii) our Lord declares the great design of his coming into the world, to give life to those who were at the point of death (verses 14–17).

(iv) the happiness of those who should believe, and the aggravated condemnation of those who reject his gospel (verses 18–21).

FOR MEDITATION: I am willing to hope that you will be made a messenger of light and peace to his soul. The Lord's hand is not shortened that he cannot save. He can do great things in a small time, as you know from your own experience. In a moment, in the twinkling of an eye, he can command light to shine out of darkness. If he speaks, it is done… One glimpse of the worth of the soul, the evil of sin, and the importance of eternity, will effect that which hath been in vain attempted by repeated arguments.[48]

John Newton to William Cowper, 22 February 1770
[re Cowper's brother, John, converted on his deathbed a few days later]

SERMON SERIES: JOHN 3:1–2, NO. 1 [2/7]

The most unlikely persons

'*There was a man of the Pharisees, named Nicodemus, a ruler of the Jews: the same came to Jesus by night, and said unto him, Rabbi, we know that thou art a teacher come from God: for no man can do these miracles that thou doest, except God be with him.*' John 3:1–2
SUGGESTED FURTHER READING: Joshua 2:1–24

Who Nicodemus was: by profession *a Pharisee*, in rank *a ruler*, and, it was probable from John 7:50, a member of their chief council—that council which afterwards condemned him to death. The Pharisees were our Lord's professed and implacable enemies upon all occasions, and the rulers and rich men, if they did not directly join with them in seeking his destruction (which many did), yet in general thought him beneath their notice. The publicans and sinners, the poor and the miserable, flocked about him, but as to the rest, they were either so careless or so obstinate, that his enemies could boldly say, *Have any of the Pharisees and rulers believed on him?* [John 7:48]. This was therefore a singular case. We may observe from it that the grace of God can, and often does, triumph over the greatest difficulties and show itself sovereign in calling the most unlikely persons. Who would have thought of an Obadiah in the court of the wicked? A Rahab? Or an enquirer after Jesus among the Pharisees and rulers? The Lord draws some in every situation and character of life. He can break through the greatest prejudices and the strongest temptations, can soften the heart of a proud Pharisee, and make a rich man poor in spirit. It is true not many of these are called, but some there are, and we know not who will be the next. It should therefore give us encouragement and teach us patience concerning those who as yet sit in darkness. We are apt to condemn by the lump, and give up whole bodies of men as desperate, but those we have little hopes of may ere long outstrip us in the Christian profession.

FOR MEDITATION: Though he does not see things clearly I have reason to hope the Lord has begun a good work in his heart [9 May 1776]. O my Lord, I thank thee for thy goodness to him; I think he goes forward into the light of thy truth [2 September 1777]. I think I can see he has got before me already. Lord, if I have been useful to him, do thou, I beseech thee, make him now useful to me [11 December 1778].[49]

Diary, Newton's prayers for the Rev. Thomas Scott

The Lord's secret friends

'And after this Joseph of Arimathea, being a disciple of Jesus, but secretly for fear of the Jews, besought Pilate that he might take away the body of Jesus ... And there came also Nicodemus, which at the first came to Jesus by night ... Then took they the body of Jesus ... to bury.' John 19:38–40
SUGGESTED FURTHER READING: Acts 9:1–22

When Nicodemus came to Jesus he was not reproached with what he had been. Our Lord was of no party; even one that came from among his professed enemies, he received with freedom and kindness. He is the same still. No matter what you have been, whether Pharisee or publican, if you seek him you shall be welcome.

Observe that the truth has some secret friends amongst those who seem engaged for its overthrow. Jesus had a Nicodemus and a Joseph in the council of his enemies, who perhaps moderated and kept back their wicked designs till the appointed time, and then openly appeared in his behalf. The Lord has often preserved his church and professed people in this manner. And perhaps it is to answer the designs of his providence that some whose hearts are touched with this love, are kept for a season from that increase of light and knowledge which, if they could immediately obtain, would break them off from those connections where he has at present occasion for their service.

FOR MEDITATION: If my testimony should not be necessary or serviceable, yet, perhaps, I am bound in conscience to take shame to myself by a public confession, which, however sincere, comes too late to prevent or repair the misery and mischief to which I have formerly been accessory. I hope it will always be a subject of humiliating reflection to me, that I was once an active instrument in a business at which my heart now shudders. I have ... written ... simply from ... a conviction that the share I have formerly had in the trade, binds me in conscience to throw what light I am able upon the subject, now it is likely to become a point of parliamentary investigation. I ought not to be afraid of offending many, by declaring the truth. ... [against] a commerce so iniquitous, so cruel, so oppressive, so destructive, as the African Slave Trade![50]

Thoughts upon the African Slave Trade, 1788 (copies given to every MP)

SERMON SERIES: JOHN 3:1–2, NO. 1 [4/7]

Come and hear for yourself!

'There was a man of the Pharisees, named Nicodemus, a ruler of the Jews: the same came to Jesus by night, and said unto him, Rabbi, we know that thou art a teacher come from God: for no man can do these miracles that thou doest, except God be with him.' John 3:1–2
SUGGESTED FURTHER READING: 1 Kings 5:1–15

What Nicodemus did: he *came to Jesus*. And thus his weak, infant faith expressed in his words, was justified by his works. He had heard much against Jesus, but then the power of his miracles struck him—he thought there must be something extraordinary. Though he was a ruler and Jesus, to outward appearance, a despised and poor man, he thought it worthwhile to go and see him. He did not send others to judge, but went to hear for himself. In this his example is a reproof to many. As there were disputes about Jesus in person—some saying he was a good man and others, *Nay, he deceiveth the people* [John 7:12]—so it is now wherever his gospel is preached. When it comes first into a place, it occasions a talk all around the country. Many are hasty to charge it with folly and madness—a strange doctrine that frightens some people out of their wits. The men that have turned the world upside down are come in our neighbourhood likewise. And O, what numbers of poor ignorant souls are kept back by such foolish reports and take up with lies and falsehoods at second hand, when if they could but be persuaded to come and hear for themselves they might perhaps receive conviction. I can only pity and pray for those that will not come; the absent cannot hear me.

FOR MEDITATION:

LORD, I am come! thy promise is my plea,	Bowed down beneath a heavy load of sin,
Without thy word I durst not venture nigh;	By Satan's fierce temptations sorely pressed,
But thou hast called the burdened soul to thee,	Beset without, and full of fears within,
A weary burdened soul, O LORD, am I!	Trembling and faint I come to thee for rest.

Be thou my refuge, LORD, my hiding-place,
I know no force can tear me from thy side;
Unmoved I then may all accusers face,
And answer every charge, with, 'JESUS died.'[51]

What think you of Christ?

'There was a man of the Pharisees, named Nicodemus, a ruler of the Jews: the same came to Jesus by night, and said unto him, Rabbi, we know that thou art a teacher come from God: for no man can do these miracles that thou doest, except God be with him.' John 3:1-2
SUGGESTED FURTHER READING: Acts 8:26-40

Nicodemus's example is an encouragement to such as are like him. Perhaps some of you are much in his case. You have heard strange stories about the gospel preaching, much evil and some good. You have been considering, 'If the doctrine is false, how comes it that so many flock to hear it? Surely they cannot be all fools. If, as I hear, it breaks people off from their sins, teaches liars to speak truth, drunkards to live sober, and those who were bad neighbours to become good ones, how can this be a delusion? Well, if it please God, I'll go soon and know, if I can, what it is that causes all the stir.' And now you are come. Well then, take encouragement. It's a good thing to be enquiring after Jesus, as Nicodemus found it. He came very ignorant, as you may be now—he seemed to come, as it were, only to satisfy his curiosity, but he heard what he did not expect and by degrees became a faithful friend and follower of Christ. I hope the Lord who brought you now will incline you to come again, for I have many things to say to you. Perhaps you are not aware that the comfort of your life and the salvation of your soul is closely concerned in the judgement you make of what you hear amongst us.

Do not think I take upon me too much in saying this. I have reason to doubt of myself, but I am sure of my doctrine. Do you ask what is preached here? I answer, We preach Christ crucified—Christ the wisdom of God and the power of God; Christ the sinner's friend, Christ the sure foundation, Christ the only hope and refuge for lost man. Surely then you will attend.

FOR MEDITATION: Should I ask this question: What think you of Christ?—perhaps some of you could give me no answer. But perhaps you have never considered that according to your thoughts of Christ, so will your eternal state prove. If you go out of the world with low, dishonourable thoughts of Jesus, you are lost for ever. But observe, Nicodemus was ignorant too till the Lord taught him, and he will teach you likewise if you seek him with your whole heart.

Afraid of the daylight

'There was a man of the Pharisees, named Nicodemus, a ruler of the Jews: the same came to Jesus by night, and said unto him, Rabbi, we know that thou art a teacher come from God: for no man can do these miracles that thou doest, except God be with him.' John 3:1–2
SUGGESTED FURTHER READING: Isaiah 51:1–8

Nicodemus came *by night*. Some ascribe this to prudence and modesty; he would not interrupt Jesus in the day but waited for his leisure. For my own part I made no doubt he came by night because he was afraid to come by daylight. He was under the sinful fear of man lest he should be persecuted or laughed at. He was not willing to run the risk of being thought a follower of Christ, at least till he was sure that he was right. We have many such spirits that would hear if they durst, would be glad of the opportunity of a strange place or a dark night, but so afraid of being called mad or a Methodist [an evangelical]. I doubt not but you are acquainted with some who are afraid of coming to us for that reason, and perhaps some of you are thinking how you shall face your acquaintance when you go back. However, it's well you are come at all. Our Lord did not reprove Nicodemus on this account, though it was quite wrong, but he is very gracious and gentle to young beginners. I shall only advise to pray to him for strength, and the oftener you come and the more diligently you hear, the bolder you will grow.

FOR MEDITATION: [re the conversion of William Wilberforce] To the Rev. John Newton: Sir, I wish to have some serious conversation with you ... PS Remember that I must be secret, and that the gallery of the House [of Commons] is now so universally attended, that the face of a Member of Parliament is pretty well known.[52]
William Wilberforce to John Newton, 2 December 1785

I saw Mrs [Aunt Hannah] Wilberforce today, and left her in tears of joy. She says you may depend on her strictly observing your requisitions. The reason I mentioned at first that Saturday was not convenient was only from the possibility of your being known and noticed by somebody—which reason now seems not so mighty as it was then.[53]
John Newton to William Wilberforce, 22 December 1785

SERMON SERIES: JOHN 3:1–2, NO. 1 [7/7]

He gives quietness

'When he giveth quietness, who then can make trouble? and when he hideth his face, who then can behold him?' Job 34:29
SUGGESTED FURTHER READING: Job 34:21–30

True quietness and peace is not our portion by nature (Isaiah 57:21). It is the gift of God and, as the first communication, so the continuance depends upon him—*if he hideth*. The way in which he gives (for it is a free gift) we are taught in Isaiah 32:17. See also Psalm 29:11 and 85:8. When the righteousness of God by Jesus is made known, approved and received by faith, the effect is quietness. All can witness it is not to be found in the ways of sin, or in attempts to establish our own righteousness—or, if a seeming peace, it is not solid such as will bear examining. Therefore such are angry. But God's peace—the more lived by his word, the more confirmed. As this quietness depends upon God, so upon him only—no matter who frowns, if he smiles (so Romans 8:31). It will stand the brunt against all charges: the law cannot disturb—an answer is prepared and the soul can admit every charge and yet plead Jesus; indwelling sin cannot remove it—this causes mourning, but the blood and grace of Jesus are effectual; changes of frames—these for a season occasion great searchings of heart and are always cause of humiliation, but, as faith grows, it can rejoice in an unchangeable God; temptations—these indeed are war, but the Lord can give peace in the midst of war; much less, outward afflictions—hear the Apostle who drank deep of this cup: *Therefore I take pleasure in infirmities, in reproaches, in necessities, in persecutions, in distresses for Christ's sake: for when I am weak, then am I strong* (2 Corinthians 12:10).

FOR MEDITATION:

The tempter, who but lately said,
I soon shall be his prey;
Has heard my Saviour's voice and fled
With shame and grief away.

But JESUS pitied my distress,
He heard my feeble cry;
Revealed his blood and righteousness,
And brought salvation nigh.

O wondrous change! but just before
Despair beset me round;
I heard the lion's horrid roar,
And trembled at the sound.

Beneath the banner of his love,
I now secure remain;
The tempter frets, but dares not move
To break my peace again.⁵⁵

SERMON: JOB 34:29 [1/2] [ON THE FAST DAY]

When he hides his face

'When he giveth quietness, who then can make trouble? and when he hideth his face, who then can behold him?' Job 34:29
SUGGESTED FURTHER READING: Psalm 13:1–6

When he hideth. Here it is supposed that the Lord may hide his face from those to whom he has once given quietness. This for wise reasons:

(i) to show them what is in their hearts. When the sun sets, beasts come forth.[56]

(ii) to keep them from spiritual pride.

(iii) to make them value peace the more.

(iv) to teach them how to walk with others.

(v) to chastise them for unfaithfulness in their walking.

When he does hide his face, who can behold him? We can then gain little help from:

(i) knowledge. We may speak, read, hear of divine truths, but there is little life and comfort in them till the Lord returns.

(ii) experience. We think in our happy times, 'Sure I shall never forget this.' But we may be left to doubt of all.

(iii) helps from men. All are then found miserable comforters.

For a close: this is scriptural, agreeable to the experience of the most—in this path you may see the footsteps of the flock. Be not surprised if some talk otherwise, but keep close to your Bibles. I would press believers to assurance, but not to be strong in themselves as if they had a stock of grace and comfort within. Our strength is in the Lord.

FOR MEDITATION: See the necessity of walking humbly and closely with the Lord in his ways. Not as the condition of salvation—this is in Christ alone—but as the means of keeping the evidence clear. If thus with the Lord's people, what must the sinner and ungodly expect? To believers, though the streams fail, the fountain is sure. But O if the Lord should hide his face in death, or frown upon from his judgement seat.

Satan's wily methods

*'Now the serpent was more subtle than any beast of the field which the
LORD God had made. And he said unto the woman, Yea, hath God said,
Ye shall not eat of every tree of the garden?' Genesis 3:1*
SUGGESTED FURTHER READING: 2 Samuel 11:1–26

The serpent said to the woman, who was created to be a helpmeet for the
man. Adam was the immediate head of the creation and God gave him the
woman to be his companion. We may believe they were each furnished
suitably for the different parts assigned them in life—equal with respect to
their great end, the knowledge and love of God, but the woman in some
respects subordinate to the man even in Paradise. It seems probable that
Satan expected more easily to prevail over her, that he was afraid of being
discovered and repulsed if he applied directly to man, but if he could deceive
the woman first, he hoped by her means to draw the man into transgression
likewise, as the event proved (see 1 Corinthians 11:3,9; 1 Timothy 2:13–14).
In this first temptation we may see something of his general methods to this
day.

It seems that Satan was well acquainted with Adam's ability, therefore he
proceeded cautiously; he knew his situation and suited himself accordingly.
The Scripture, as I have observed, intimates that even in the state where both
were perfect, the woman was in a sense the weaker vessel, therefore he began
with her, watching an opportunity, as it should seem, when Adam was
absent. And thus he besets and watches us all, especially awakened souls. He
will not ordinarily come upon you in your strength, at a season when you are
best prepared and most upon your guard, but will wait his advantage. He
did not tempt Peter to deny his master when upon the Mount, but when he
found him in the high priest's hall. He will not tempt you by directly
thwarting your knowledge and judgement, but will tempt you when you are
weaker, by your imaginations, passions or prejudices.

FOR MEDITATION: 'Be self-controlled and alert. Your enemy the devil prowls
around like a roaring lion looking for someone to devour' (1 Peter 5:8, NIV).

Our greatest snares

'Now the serpent was more subtle than any beast of the field which the LORD *God had made. And he said unto the woman, Yea, hath God said, Ye shall not eat of every tree of the garden?' Genesis 3:1*
SUGGESTED FURTHER READING: Job 2:1–10

Satan tempted Eve by a serpent, Adam by Eve herself. She was bone of his bone, his dearest friend, his other self. By sin she was brought under Satan's power and became his instrument, so that then he had access to Adam in the least suspected and the most ensnaring way. If he did not prevail thus, he could have little hope of success in any other method. And alas, he took his measures surely. Adam hearkened to the voice of his wife. By the subtlety of Satan, our best earthly comforts and the choicest gifts of God may become our greatest snares. If it was so in Paradise, how much more are we exposed to this danger now. Do you rejoice in the possession of many blessings and comforts? Rejoice with trembling. The enemy is watching to make that which is good an occasion of your falling. There is not one of them but may draw you into sin. We know not how often our nearest friends may (perhaps unawares to themselves) be influenced by the enemy to tempt us to sin. He will not so frequently solicit us by those we hate, as by those we love. And when they mean us well, they may be acting the part, to our hurt, which a professed enemy could not attempt. Thus Satan employed Peter to discourage our Lord from his purpose of love to us; but he saw that though the words were Peter's, the suggestion was from Satan and treated it accordingly (Matthew 16:23).

FOR MEDITATION: This consolation he himself gives, *Be of good cheer, I have overcome the world* [John 16:33]. Jesus likewise overcame in himself and overcame in his people all that is in the world suited to poison and alienate their hearts, so that by faith in him they are enabled to withstand not only its frowns but its smiles, which are perhaps the more dangerous weapons with which the world can assault them.[57]

Sermon: Revelation 19:13, 7 September 1777

Don't doubt the sure word of God

*'Now the serpent was more subtle than any beast of the field which the
LORD God had made. And he said unto the woman, Yea, hath God said,
Ye shall not eat of every tree of the garden?' Genesis 3:1*
SUGGESTED FURTHER READING: Psalm 119:9–24

Satan's arguments. We shall find a train of Satan's subtleties in his discourse
with the woman, and in her answers we shall see how he prevails by degrees,
when he can get us to listen to his reasonings. He does not show all his
design, but begins with starting a doubt... 'Is it possible?—I can hardly
believe it' ... and this he expresses ambiguously—*of every tree?*—as if he
asked for information. Such questioning, where the command of God was
concerned, the woman ought not to have indulged. Here seems to have been
the beginning of sin and we are often endangered the same way. Satan's
doubt respected:

(i) the reality of the command. And so still he prevails, persuading many
that the precepts and threatenings in the Bible are not the sure word of God.
Yea, he would sometimes force such doubts even upon believers.

(ii) the reasonableness of it. Why should God say so? Thus he teaches
sinners to reason: 'If God has threatened, he will not make his threatenings
good; sure he will not punish me with everlasting misery for taking my
pleasures here a few years.'

So there are many points of doctrine as plainly expressed as words can
express them, yet Satan teaches men to reason about them till they deny and
disbelieve them totally. Even some of God's dear children are kept in
suspense to their hurt.

FOR MEDITATION: But I must stop for the present, adding a word concerning
Jesus, who was revealed to destroy the works of the devil. In him there is
pardon for all transgressions and wisdom to enable us to withstand Satan.
Without him sinners must perish—but those who believe in him shall be
made more than conquerors and placed out of Satan's reach for ever. Seek
his face therefore and your souls shall live.

SERMON SERIES: GENESIS, NO. 6 [3/3], GENESIS 3:1

Sinning with our eyes open

'And the woman said unto the serpent, We may eat of the fruit of the trees of the garden: but of the fruit of the tree which is in the midst of the garden, God hath said, Ye shall not eat of it, neither shall ye touch it, lest ye die.' Genesis 3:2–3
SUGGESTED FURTHER READING: Proverbs 2:1–22

If the enemy of our souls can seduce us so far as to parley with him, we seldom come off unhurt. Something there was, in his appearance and in the manner of his speaking, that drew the attention of Eve. She might have been upon her guard, for had he meant well, he would rather have commended the goodness of God to her than have started a doubt concerning his command.

Her answer includes an acknowledgment of the bounty and blessings she enjoyed. This heightens the ingratitude and folly of her compliance afterwards and left her without excuse. How unreasonable, as well as rebellious, to disobey a good God who had given all things richly to enjoy. The devil tempts poor sinners to think God a hard master, but if you will be his servants you will find nothing is forbidden you but what hurts you and what it would be your interest to avoid, even if you were not to give an account of yourself to God.

She owns the prohibition, and therefore sinned *with her eyes open*. Why was not Satan discouraged when he found she had the precept in mind? Probably he saw, or judged, she was beginning to yield—that though she remembered the precept she wished it was otherwise.

FOR MEDITATION:

Sin, when viewed by Scripture light,
Is a horrid, hateful sight;
But when seen in Satan's glass,
Then it wears a pleasing face.

When the gospel trumpet sounds,
When I think how grace abounds,
When I feel sweet peace within,
Then I'd rather die than sin.[58]

God's commands are perfect

'And the woman said unto the serpent, We may eat of the fruit of the trees of the garden: but of the fruit of the tree which is in the midst of the garden, God hath said, Ye shall not eat of it, neither shall ye touch it, lest ye die.' Genesis 3:2–3
SUGGESTED FURTHER READING: Psalm 119:89–104

Observe Satan will not be afraid of those who have much light in their heads, if their hearts are insincere before God. It is not talking about Christ and grace and holiness that will preserve you from the power of temptation, if your hearts desire the forbidden thing. But it is a high aggravation to sin against such light. It is the case of many amongst us. You do it not ignorant—you know the judgements of God. Satan can hardly be said to cheat you, for you obey him with your eyes open. Eve seems to add to God's word. He said *not eat*—she puts in *not touch*. Perhaps Satan used this to advantage against her, and when she found she did not die for touching it, she might venture more boldly to eat it. However, men are very prone to add their own inventions to the Word of God, which in many ways becomes a snare to them. The commands of God are perfect and cannot be amended. And they are so broad as to call for all our strength and time to observe them. If we do more than we are commanded we shall infallibly leave something unattended to that he has made our duty.

FOR MEDITATION:

When the cross I view by faith,
Sin is madness, poison, death;
Tempt me not, 'tis all in vain,
Sure I ne'er can yield again.

What before excited fears,
Rather pleasing now appears;
If a sin, it seems so small,
Or, perhaps, no sin at all.

Satan, for a while debarred,
When he finds me off my guard,
Puts his glass before my eyes,
Quickly other thoughts arise.

Often thus, through sin's deceit,
Grief and shame, and loss I meet;
Like a fish, my soul mistook,
Saw the bait, but not the hook.

Made, by past experience, wise, Let me learn thy word to prize;
Taught by what I've felt before, Let me Satan's glass abhor.[59]

SERMON SERIES: GENESIS, NO. 7 [2/4], GENESIS 3:2–5

An endangered species

'And the serpent said unto the woman, Ye shall not surely die: for God doth know that in the day ye eat thereof, then your eyes shall be opened, and ye shall be as gods, knowing good and evil.' Genesis 3:4-5
SUGGESTED FURTHER READING: Psalm 119:105-120

In Satan's reply we may note:

(i) From starting a doubt concerning the threatening, he proceeds to a bold denial. This, Eve could hardly have borne at first—but by listening to the first, she was prepared for the second. And now we may pronounce her fallen. She had sinned in her heart, though she had not actually eaten the fruit, for the law is spiritual and reaches to the thoughts (as Matthew 5:28).

(ii) He instils hard thoughts of God, as though he withheld something which he knew would increase their happiness. *God doth know* and therefore he forbid. This, said of the old serpent, abounds in our fallen nature. Why are sinful pleasures pursued, but upon a secret surmise that we shall be more happy by following our own will than the will of our Creator?

(iii) He opens his temptation to suit that spirit of pride and curiosity with which he had already infected her. And flattered her with:

(a) an advance in state: not only impunity but advantage. *You shall be as gods.* Thus Self sits in the throne of God and the creature is drawn off from subjection to a desire of independence.

(b) an increase of knowledge: what this was to be she could only learn by making the experiment. Then she found a knowledge of guilt and shame was all she gained. Ever since, vain man would be wise, but acquires nothing but vanity and vexation of spirit.

FOR MEDITATION:

Alas! by nature how depraved,
How prone to every ill!
Our lives, to Satan, how enslaved,
How obstinate our will!

The holy Spirit must reveal
The Saviour's work and worth;
Then the hard heart begins to feel
A new and heavenly birth.[60]

Repairing the ruins

'And the serpent said unto the woman, Ye shall not surely die: for God doth know that in the day ye eat thereof, then your eyes shall be opened, and ye shall be as gods, knowing good and evil.' Genesis 3:4–5
SUGGESTED FURTHER READING: James 1:13–15

When Satan has drawn us from the belief of the truth, there is nothing so false, absurd and dangerous but he can persuade us to receive. How vain was the thought, that she could be better than she was without the Lord's leave and in defiance to his will. Learn the deceitfulness and hardening nature of sin, how it prevails by degrees, till at length the soul ventures the loss of all for present gratification—and is equally unmindful of past obligations and future consequences of disobedience.

As pride and self-seeking were the first sins, so the first work of God's Spirit when he comes to renew the sinner is to lay the axe to these roots of the evil tree, which he does by a conviction of sin upon the conscience and giving affecting views of the humiliation of Jesus—man would be as God, therefore God became man. O admire this grace and look to this Saviour who alone is able to repair the ruin we have brought upon ourselves.

FOR MEDITATION: [for New Year's Evening 1773]

Ensnared, too long, my heart has been	LORD, I have hated thee too long,
In folly's hurtful ways;	And dared thee to thy face;
O, may I now, at length, begin	I've done my soul exceeding wrong
To hear what Wisdom says!	In slighting all thy grace.
Approach my soul to Wisdom's gates	Now I would break my league with death,
While it is called today;	And live to thee alone;
No one who watches there and waits	O let thy Spirit's seal of faith,
Shall e'er be turned away.	Secure me for thine own.[61]

Open my eyes

'And after six days Jesus taketh Peter, James, and John his brother, and bringeth them up into an high mountain apart.' Matthew 17:1
SUGGESTED FURTHER READING: Nehemiah 8:1–8

Though our Lord Jesus, in his humbled state, was despised and rejected by the unbelieving Jews, who judged only by his outward appearance, yet his true disciples beheld and acknowledged his glory. There was such wisdom in his words, such power in his works, such grace and goodness in his whole conduct, such a virtue went from him, drawing, teaching and comforting their hearts, that they could say, We *believe and are sure thou art the Christ* [John 11:27]. On some occasions he made a more perceptible and open display of his glory, and in an extraordinary sense manifested himself to them as he did not to the world. This was eminently the case at the solemn and memorable season of his transfiguration, recorded by three Evangelists. It seems a subject well suited to strengthen the faith and promote the edification of his people. And with these views, I would attempt to assist your meditations on it. I may say as the woman of Samaria, *the well is deep* [John 4:11]. In going through the passage, we shall perhaps be led to speak of some of the most important and difficult points both of doctrine and experience. Here, I think, if anywhere, we have cause to pray with the psalmist, *Open thou my eyes, that I may see the great things of thy law* [Psalm 119:18]. May this be the desire of all our hearts, and may the Lord afford a gracious answer.

FOR MEDITATION:

The woman who for water came,   Taught from her birth to hate the Jews,
(What great events on small depend)   And filled with party-pride; at first
Then learnt the glory of his name,   Her zeal induced her to refuse
The Well of life, the sinner's Friend!   Water, to quench the Saviour's thirst.

But soon she knew the gift of GOD,
And JESUS, whom she scorned before,
Unasked, that drink on her bestowed,
Which whoso tastes shall thirst no more.[62]

Strengthened for trials

'And after six days Jesus taketh Peter, James, and John his brother, and bringeth them up into an high mountain apart.' Matthew 17:1
SUGGESTED FURTHER READING: Luke 22:39–53

If the reasons are enquired why our Lord was transfigured upon the mount, though we must not expect by searching to find out his work to perfection, we may humbly suppose some of the reasons to be: to confirm the disciples' faith and that they might afterwards declare themselves eyewitnesses of his glory (2 Peter 1:16–17); to exhibit a proof to them of the realities of the unseen world, against the cavils of Sadducees and infidels; to give them a pattern of that glory in which his people shall be raised at the last day (Philippians 3:21). We may observe the time:

(i) It was soon after Peter's noble confession (Matthew 16:16). Thus the Lord rewards his people's faith with farther discoveries, as he promised to Nathaniel (John 1:50). Surely if we could give him more of the honour due to his name, by steadfast believing, he would show us more of his glory. Let us pray for more faith, that we may have more comfort.

(ii) It was soon after he had so expressly spoken of his sufferings, which Peter could not bear only to hear of, and which, when they came on him, put all his disciples to a stand. This was therefore a seasonable and gracious revelation to prepare and strengthen them for their approaching trial. And thus he is often pleased to confirm and strengthen his people for an hour of trouble. And when he is pleased to favour them with particular nearness and sweetness and to shine remarkably upon their souls, they may ordinarily expect a trial is at hand.

(iii) It was soon after he had been enforcing the necessity of self-denial (Matthew 16:24). This may teach us that the knowledge of Christ in his power, glory and love, is the great means to make self-denial necessary and pleasant.

FOR MEDITATION: 'And he … kneeled down, and prayed, saying, Father, if thou be willing, remove this cup from me: nevertheless not my will, but thine, be done. And there appeared an angel unto him from heaven, strengthening him. And being in an agony he prayed more earnestly: and his sweat was as it were great drops of blood falling down to the ground' (Luke 22:41–44).

SERMON SERIES: ON THE TRANSFIGURATION, NO. 1 [2/4]

All of grace

'And after six days Jesus taketh Peter, James, and John his brother, and bringeth them up into an high mountain apart.' Matthew 17:1
SUGGESTED FURTHER READING: Romans 12:1–8

The persons: *Peter, James and John.* It does not become us to enquire too curiously why he admitted only three of his disciples to be witnesses of his glory, or why these three rather than any of the rest. Yet since we are told it was his pleasure so to do, it may be proper to draw an observation or two from this circumstance.

I do not lay any stress upon the number three. It is plain that on several occasions these three were distinguished from the others. Some think because they were more eminent for grace—if they were so, I should judge this was the effect rather than the cause of the preference the Lord gave them. They who are most with him, will be most like him. It is true that humble, diligent waiting is the way to enjoy peculiar nearness, but we can render nothing to him, but what we first receive from him. It is sufficient to say he has a right to do what he will with his own. He admitted these three to a nearer intimacy and John was favoured beyond them all (John 13:23). He is called, by way of eminence, the disciple whom Jesus loved, though he loved them all. So he loves all his people, yet makes a difference between some and others in providence, in grace, in comforts. Some have two talents, some five, some of the good ground bears thirtyfold, other sixty, other one hundred—all according to his wise appointment, and yet so as that there is encouragement for everyone in the use of means to open their mouths wide and desire the best things: an abundance of grace and peace, and the fruits of holiness. They who seek shall surely find. However, these apostles were not without their faults. Peter was often wrong, and afterwards denied him. James and John would have called fire from heaven. His favours are all of grace.

FOR MEDITATION: [to precede the New Year's Day sermon]

Now, gracious LORD, thine arm reveal,　　Help us to venture near thy throne,
And make thy glory known;　　　　　　　And plead a Saviour's name;
Now let us all thy presence feel,　　　　　For all that we can call our own,
And soften hearts of stone!　　　　　　　Is vanity and shame.[65]

Keeping a balance

'And it came to pass about an eight days after these sayings, he took Peter and John and James, and went up into a mountain to pray.' Luke 9:28
SUGGESTED FURTHER READING: 2 Corinthians 12:1–10

These three disciples were appointed witnesses of his passion. They saw him in his agony, and therefore he first gave them a view of his glory. If their joy was now great, their sorrow after was proportionable. It seems the Lord generally keeps a balance in the experiences of his people. They who have the strongest comforts have the sharpest conflicts; they who have the strongest trials have the most powerful supports. Thus, as in the gathering of the manna, they that have much have nothing over, they that have little have no lack. If he gives great enlargement and consolation, he will send something to keep us humble and low; if he calls to great temptations, he will give cordials that we be not swallowed up and overmuch sorrow.

Perhaps he distinguished these three that by his example he might sanctify and authorize our Christian friendships. If we love the Lord Jesus, we are bound to love all his people and to love them with a pure heart fervently. But with respect to relationships we are not bound to treat them all alike, nor is it possible in the present state of things to do so. A suitableness in temperament, in way of life, and many occasions of connection in the course of his providence, lead us into greater nearness of affection with some than with others. And our practice herein, while we keep within Scripture bounds and do not set up our friends as idols, is unanswerably justified by the conduct our Lord observed himself. Thus he graciously suited himself to our circumstances in all respects.

Let me close with entreating each of you to consider whether you are yet in the number of Christ's disciples—if not as one of the three, or one of the twelve, yet a sincere follower.

FOR MEDITATION: 'Blessed be God, even the Father of our Lord Jesus Christ, the Father of mercies, and the God of all comfort; Who comforteth us in all our tribulation, that we may be able to comfort them which are in any trouble, by the comfort wherewith we ourselves are comforted of God. For as the sufferings of Christ abound in us, so our consolation also aboundeth by Christ' (2 Corinthians 1:3–5).

SERMON SERIES: ON THE TRANSFIGURATION, NO. 1 [4/4]

Far from the madding crowd

'And after six days Jesus taketh Peter, James, and John his brother, and bringeth them up into an high mountain apart.' Matthew 17:1
SUGGESTED FURTHER READING: Exodus 33:12–34:7

The place to which he led his disciples: this was *a high mountain*. What mountain, or where situated, is a point of more curiosity than use. The reason of his choosing such a place seems obvious—it was doubtless for the opportunity of retirement. When he would show them his glory, he took them aside from the crowd. He taught frequently in public, in the temple and in the streets, but he revealed himself more intimately to his disciples when he had them apart from the world. Hence we observe the Lord withdraws his people from the hurries of the world to show them his goodness and his glory. To this he calls them by his Word and Spirit and oftentimes by his providence. Not that they are to forsake their stations and services in life—he will give them grace and wisdom for their public callings also—but they must not be engrossed with these. They must have seasons of waiting upon him in the mountain apart, or they will deprive themselves of their best privileges. The ordinances, though public in one sense (as with regard to their outward administration they are open to all), are, in another, private. Many can tell what a retreat they find in them from the noise and cares of the world. Therefore they are glad to go up to the house of the Lord, which is called the mountain of his holiness. In their own houses they are in the midst of hurry and confusion, and they expect when they return to meet new trials at the very threshold of the door. But while they are in the mountain they are at peace—there for a little season they forget their distractions, they get balm for their wounds and are renewed in strength for the warfare. How sweet are Sabbaths and ordinances in this view! They say with Peter, *It is good to be here* [Luke 9:33], and here, if it might be, they would stay—and return to an ensnaring, troublesome world no more.

FOR MEDITATION:

How welcome to the saints, when pressed
With six days' noise, and care, and toil,
Is the returning day of rest,
Which hides them from the world awhile?

Now, from the throng withdrawn away,
They seem to breathe a different air;
Composed and softened by the day,
All things another aspect wear.[66]

SERMON SERIES: ON THE TRANSFIGURATION, NO. 2 [1/5], LUKE 9:28

Get above the world

'And it came to pass about an eight days after these sayings, he took Peter and John and James, and went up into a mountain to pray.' Luke 9:28
SUGGESTED FURTHER READING: 1 Kings 19:1–18

The exercise of secret prayer is as a retired mountain where the Lord promises to meet and shine upon his people. Satan knows that he cannot greatly prevail against those who are frequent and fervent in prayer, and therefore he bends his chief strength and subtlety to divert or discourage them from it. And indeed, so to speak, this hill of prayer is steep. It is pleasant when we can reach the top, but the ascent is wearisome to the flesh. But there are happy seasons when the Lord, as it were, leads them by the hand; then they mount up as with eagles' wings [Isaiah 40:31]—they get above the world and he causes his goodness to pass before them [Exodus 33:19].

Sometimes afflictions answer the purpose of this mountain. Perhaps a believer has imperceptibly given way to a worldly spirit, is hurried about many things, multiplying cares and burdens without necessity; another is seduced into wrong compliances, to mix with unprofitable company and waste the time—that time that might be better employed. When either of these is the case, the soul cannot thrive. And as there is no medium, not to go forward is to go back. There are some who need not be asked by those who know them, *Why art thou lean from day to day?* [2 Samuel 13:4]. They are ensnared by easy, besetting temptations, and mix their food with ashes. Many have suffered this way and have reason to bless the Lord that he sent some affliction—perhaps a fit of sickness—which put a stop to their worldly pursuits, gave them leisure to consider their ways, and proved as a mountain to them, where they sought and obtained a new blessing.

FOR MEDITATION:

With joy they hasten to the place,
Where they their Saviour oft have met;
And while they feast upon his grace,
Their burdens and their griefs forget.

This favoured lot, my friends, is ours,
May we the privilege improve;
And find these consecrated hours,
Sweet earnests of the joys above![67]

Seasons of refreshment

'*And it came to pass about an eight days after these sayings, he took Peter and John and James, and went up into a mountain to pray.*' Luke 9:28
SUGGESTED FURTHER READING: Psalm 84:1–12

The Lord affords his people seasons of refreshment which the world knows nothing of. The scribes and Pharisees who despised Jesus could not but despise his followers. They little thought of what passed upon this mountain. Had they seen him transfigured they would not so much have wondered at the disciples' attachment to him. It is thus still. The world see that the Lord's people have their trials, dejections and infirmities, but they know nothing of their consolations. Therefore they either pity or despise them, and suppose they lead a poor, melancholy life. They would not think so if they knew all. His people have indeed their heart bitternesses, but *a stranger intermeddleth not with their joys* [Proverbs 14:10]. One gracious visit from his presence makes them amends for many sufferings. A day, or an hour, of communion with him, is better than a thousand.

The experiences of different believers are very different at the same time. While some are rejoicing, others are sorrowing. These three were happy upon the mount—the rest had a sharp exercise of their faith in their master's absence (Luke 9:40).

FOR MEDITATION: I had long *believed* and often told others, that our God is *all-sufficient*, but in the year '90, I could say, I not only believe him to be all-sufficient, but I have found him so. He enabled me to trust in him, and I am helped. Yes, I am persuaded that no power, short of that which sustains the stars in their orbits, could have supported me. To this day, she is seldom an hour out of my waking thoughts, but the recollection gives me no pain. I can say from my heart, *he has done all things well.* He gave, and he took away. I praise his goodness and wisdom for both. I compare creature comforts to candles. While they burn they waste, and if we live long we may see them all go out in succession. But if we are interested in the Sun of Righteousness, the Fountain of Light, Life and Power and Comfort, he can well supply their place, and he has promised that he will. Habakkuk 3:17–18.[68]
John Newton to William Wilberforce, 30 September 1800
[Newton preached his wife's funeral sermon from Habakkuk 3:17–18.]

SERMON SERIES: ON THE TRANSFIGURATION, NO. 2 [3/5], LUKE 9:28

Persevere in prayer

'And it came to pass about an eight days after these sayings, he took Peter and John and James, and went up into a mountain to pray.' Luke 9:28
SUGGESTED FURTHER READING: Luke 18:1–8

The last circumstance mentioned in this verse is the design: he went up into the mountain *to pray*. His purpose indeed was to be transfigured before them, but he does not appear to have told them this. But while they were attending him in the way of duty, he afforded them this favour beyond what they could have expected. We may note the sweetest tokens believers obtain of the Lord's presence and goodness are usually in a time of prayer. No doubt the disciples would have gone with great eagerness, had they expected to have seen their Lord transfigured. But this was kept from them, that their going might rather be an act of obedience to his will, than to gratify a selfish motive of their own. We are often greatly blameable in this matter. No complaints more frequent than of an unwillingness to pray— but why? Chiefly because we look too much to our own pleasure. If we were assured beforehand that we should see Jesus in his glory, that we should enjoy a very lively state of mind and feel our hearts burn like fire, we should want little persuasion to pray. But we are but half-inclined to duty farther than we find it connected with comfort. Hence we have sometimes said, 'To what purpose shall I pray, when I find myself not at all the better?' This is too much like the spirit of those who followed the Lord for the loaves and the fishes. The difficulties and conflicts, the deadness and temptations we meet with in our attempts to pray, are not pleasant, yet to persevere in prayer in the midst of such discouragements is one of the best proofs of our sincerity and that we serve the Lord upon a right principle and for his own sake. These things are the trials of faith, and we cannot be well assured that our faith is right until it has stood trials. Every hypocrite may continue to pray, so long as he finds it pleasant.

FOR MEDITATION: 'Likewise the Spirit also helpeth our infirmities: for we know not what we should pray for as we ought: but the Spirit itself maketh intercession for us with groanings which cannot be uttered. And he that searcheth the hearts knoweth what is the mind of the Spirit, because he maketh intercession for the saints according to the will of God' (Romans 8:26–27).

SERMON SERIES: ON THE TRANSFIGURATION, NO. 2 [4/5], LUKE 9:28

Wait simply on Him

'And it came to pass about an eight days after these sayings, he took Peter and John and James, and went up into a mountain to pray.' Luke 9:28
SUGGESTED FURTHER READING: Luke 2:25–38

The Lord always accepts his people that wait simply upon him, though visits resembling what is here recorded are vouchsafed but now and then. The disciples were constantly with Jesus and often attended him when praying, but they only saw him transfigured once. He has many ways of doing us good besides that of giving sensible comfort. A season of special consolation is often near at hand when least expected, and therefore while we are waiting in the use of means, we have cause to be expecting good from the Lord—for he has not said to any, *Seek ye me in vain* [Isaiah 45:19].

They that live without prayer are out of the way of peace and comfort. You must not charge the Lord foolishly; if you seek him you shall find him— if you neglect him, the fault is your own. It is a dismal state to be prayerless. Why, are you not afraid to close your eyes at night, or to go out of your houses in the morning?

FOR MEDITATION:

When my prayers are a burden and task,   I have heard of thy wonderful name,
No wonder I little receive;   How great and exalted thou art;
O LORD, make me willing to ask,   But ah! I confess to my shame,
Since thou art so ready to give   It faintly impresses my heart:
Although I am bought with thy blood,   The beams of thy glory display,
And all thy salvation is mine;   As PETER once saw thee appear;
At a distance from thee my chief good,   That transported like him I may say,
I wander, and languish, and pine.   'It is good for my soul to be here.'

But if thou hast appointed me still, To wrestle, and suffer, and fight;
Oh make me resigned to thy will, For all thine appointments are right:
This mercy, at least, I entreat, That knowing how vile I have been,
I with MARY may wait at thy feet, And weep o'er the pardon of sin.[69]

SERMON SERIES: ON THE TRANSFIGURATION, NO. 2 [5/5], LUKE 9:28

The dignity and privilege of prayer

'And as he prayed, the fashion of his countenance was altered, and his raiment was white and glistering.' Luke 9:29
SUGGESTED FURTHER READING: Romans 11:33–36

This change of our Lord's appearance, when the beams of his glory shone through the veil of flesh which he assumed for our sakes, is called his transfiguration. Matthew and Mark say, *He was transfigured before them* [Matthew 17:2; Mark 9:2]. Luke adds a farther circumstance which is worthy of our attention, that it took place *while he was praying*. If, as it is probable, this was the subject of his prayer, that his glory might be manifested to his disciples, he obtained an immediate and signal answer, and no wonder, for he is always heard. He never asked in vain. Here lies the safety and comfort of his people, that he has engaged to intercede for all that come unto God by him, and therefore, because he pleads their cause, they cannot be overpowered. But our Lord, when in the action of prayer while he was upon earth, may be considered not only as their Advocate, but their Exemplar and Pattern. He commanded them to pray, he taught them to pray, and he added force to his precept by his own example. And he gave them here a great encouragement to persevere in prayer and that they might hope that when they drew near to God in duty, he would draw near to them, for *as he prayed, he was transfigured*. In this view I shall propose one observation for our improvement at present, before I come to consider the transfiguration itself. Prayer is the great instituted means of impressing the soul with such a sense of the glory of God as transforms it into his resemblance and raises it to a kind of transfiguration. Or, the sweetest and most transforming impressions of divine things are usually afforded in a season of prayer. As it was with the Head, so it is with the members: while they are praying they are transfigured.

FOR MEDITATION: Many arguments may be offered to enforce this practice of prayer—from duty, as we are the Lord's creatures; from necessity, as we depend upon him for our continual support—but this argument arising from the dignity and privilege should have an especial weight with all who have tasted that the Lord is gracious.

Waiting on God in secret

'But thou, when thou prayest, enter into thy closet, and when thou hast shut thy door, pray to thy Father which is in secret; and thy Father which seeth in secret shall reward thee openly.' Matthew 6:6
SUGGESTED FURTHER READING: Matthew 6:5–18

Prayer is the ordinance in which we have most immediate access to God. It is the most spiritual part of worship, which is the reason why our carnal hearts are most averse to it. In conversing and hearing, it is more easy to keep up some attention without the actual exercise of grace. And therefore we find many ready enough to talk with Christians, or to hear sermons, who know but little of waiting upon God in secret. To keep up this communion, the soul must be habitually disposed to seek the Lord for his own sake. In prayer, if spiritually performed, we turn our backs upon creatures, and call home our thoughts to fix them immediate upon God in Christ, as seated on his throne of glory. It seems plain therefore that this exercise is especially suited to engage our hearts. Hence they that live much in prayer may be said to live much with God, and as frequency of visits gives acquaintance and freedom, they are most in the way of receiving special manifestations from him. On this account, I would remark that though it is very desirable to maintain a praying frame at all times and in all places, so as to be able to lift up our hearts to him in spontaneous and secret prayer—in our common occasions, and as we are walking in the streets—yet it is our wisdom to be punctual in observing set times of approaching him. There are some great ends in prayer, particularly the contemplation of his glory, which seem to require a retired and solemn attendance upon him.

FOR MEDITATION: Think of him as often as you can; make a point of praying to him in secret, remembering that when you are most alone, he is still with you. When you pray, endeavour simply to express your wants and feelings just as if you were speaking to me. Fine words and phrases, some people abound in; but true prayer is the genuine language of the heart, which the Lord understands and accepts, however brokenly expressed. The woman of Canaan only said, 'Lord, help me!' The publican's prayer was almost as short, 'God be merciful to me a sinner'; and both were heard.[70]

John Newton to his niece, 23 October 1783

SERMON SERIES: ON THE TRANSFIGURATION, NO. 3 [2/4], LUKE 9:29

Characteristics of prayer

'And as he prayed, the fashion of his countenance was altered, and his raiment was white and glistering.' Luke 9:29
SUGGESTED FURTHER READING: Psalm 62:1–12

The graces which are most immediately exercised in prayer are those having a special tendency to raise the soul above itself and above the world such as:

(i) faith. The enlightened mind, when addressing itself to wait on God, will often feel a question rising, 'Why dost thou this? How dare you, a poor sinner, approach the Holy God?' Faith answers this question and pleads the Redeemer's name, his life, death and mediation. These thoughts lead the soul to take a view of the mystery of redemption, to see the strong foundation which God has laid in Zion. Hence arise admiration and praise. Now the Apostle says that so far as we by faith behold the glory of the Lord, we shall be changed into the same image from glory to glory.

(ii) love. When we find ourselves brought into the presence of the great King, and that unworthy and as unfaithful as we are, we have a right to call him Father, we are led to reflect, 'To what do I owe this privilege?' Thus the love of God and the love of Jesus are brought to mind. 'O I was afar off once—I little thought he would do this for me.' A sense of this love kindles love in our heart. And the more we love the more we are transfigured—for he that dwelleth in love, dwelleth in God and God in him.

(iii) trust. While we are conversing with creatures, we are prone to rest too much upon them, but in prayer we leave them all, and charge our souls as David, *wait thou only upon God* [Psalm 62:5]. By faith we apprehend his power engaged on behalf of his people; by love we give ourselves to him and appropriate his all-sufficiency to ourselves, and thus are enabled to trust in God, which is a grace that refines and enables the soul and frees it from all vain and selfish pursuits, which, in whatever degree they prevail, are chiefly owing to a want of confidence in God.

(iv) humiliation. A sight of God gives us a sense of our imperfection, and abases us into the dust before him. So Job, Isaiah, Daniel and John found it. Now this is the frame of mind to which the Lord has promised to look; when we are thus abased, he will honour.

FOR MEDITATION: 'Lord, teach us to pray' (Luke 11:1).

SERMON SERIES: ON THE TRANSFIGURATION, NO. 3 [3/4], LUKE 9:29

That we may see God

'And as he prayed, the fashion of his countenance was altered, and his raiment was white and glistering.' Luke 9:29
SUGGESTED FURTHER READING: John 15:1–27

Here and there we may see the ground of what has been frequently observed, that declensions of religion begin at the closet door. To omit prayer, is to omit the best means in which the principal graces of the divine life are exercised, strengthened and fed. For the discharge of this duty we are promised the assistance of God's Holy Spirit, to show us the things of Jesus, to remind us of our wants, to put arguments in our mouths. Our prayers, so far as they are spiritual, are not our own. They are not to be judged of by the outward expressions; perhaps we cry and chatter like a swallow, but he powerfully helpeth, even when his people can only bring forth groanings which cannot be uttered. What wonder then, considering the Spirit pleads in them below, while Jesus pleads for them above, that they sometimes find the light of heaven and glory opening upon their hearts. If these things are so, may we not take up a lamentation that we are so unskilful, or so remiss, in this great mystery of holding communion with God in prayer? Let me speak to your hearts and mine. If we would be successful and comfortable in prayer, we must be frequent. Even friends lose intimacy and freedom if they are not often together. We may stay from a person we love till we hardly care about them. We must guard against formality. There is too much of this ready to steal even upon believers. We dare not omit prayer, but are careless in the performance. Formality is the bane of every duty, but especially of this. We should have this especially in view when we pray: that we may see God. Watchfulness must be joined with prayer. Indeed, one is not practicable without the other.

FOR MEDITATION: The Lord Jesus, like the sun, is in all places at once. Go where we will, we are not far from him, if we have but eyes to perceive him. … he is complete and all-sufficient, the Sun of righteousness, the Fountain of life and comfort; his beams, wherever they reach, bring healing, strength, peace and joy to the soul. Pray to him, my dear, to shine forth and reveal himself to you.[71]

John Newton to his niece, 22 October 1779

SERMON SERIES: ON THE TRANSFIGURATION, NO. 3 [4/4], LUKE 9:29

Much to be observed

'Howbeit for this cause I obtained mercy, that in me first Jesus Christ might show forth all longsuffering, for a pattern to them which should hereafter believe on him to life everlasting.' 1 Timothy 1:16
SUGGESTED FURTHER READING: Ezra 6:19–22

When Moses has related the deliverance of Israel from Egypt, he adds, *It is a night much to be observed*, and they were accordingly directed to keep it in solemn remembrance. Much to be observed and remembered likewise is the time where it can be clearly known, of the Lord's appearance to deliver his people from Satan's bondage. I say when it can be known, for many are brought in so gradual a way, that they cannot distinctly mark the beginning. Others can certainly tell when he signally appeared in their behalf. The return of this day has I believe never been wholly forgotten by me, for twenty-five years past, though I have never thought of it with a thousandth part of thankfulness and sensibility which it demands. It is the day when the Lord sent from high and saved me from sinking in the deep water. It is the first time since I came to Olney that it happened on a Sunday, and as the Lord has been pleased (which is rather more than I could have hoped for two or three days since) to enable me to stand before you this afternoon, I would hope he will graciously fulfil my text amongst us at this time. And that I shall not speak of such an amazing instance of his mercy, and stand up as a pattern of his longsuffering before you in vain.

My manner of life till that period and the dreadful extremity to which I was then brought is pretty well known. Surely there never was one to whom a part of the Apostle's words were more applicable than myself. I was indeed a persecutor, a blasphemer and injurious, but I obtained mercy because I did it ignorantly in unbelief. O to say from my heart, I thank Christ Jesus my Lord.

FOR MEDITATION: My subjects today were suggested from my own circumstances. This being the anniversary of ye day in the year 1748 when the Lord delivered me from sinking at sea, and made the first impression upon my heart after my dreadful apostasy, I preached upon the occasion in the afternoon, and was favoured with liberty. O that I could preach effectually to my own heart. Lord do thou make it soft and sensible.[72]

Diary, 21 March 1773

SERMON: 1 TIMOTHY 1:16 [1/4]

The chief sinner

'Howbeit for this cause I obtained mercy, that in me first Jesus Christ might show forth all longsuffering, for a pattern to them which should hereafter believe on him to life everlasting.' 1 Timothy 1:16
SUGGESTED FURTHER READING: 3 John 1–14

The Lord in showing mercy to Paul had a farther view than to himself. He designed him to stand as a pattern how he would deal with others. Had all the apostles and ministers been like Nathaniel, they might have preached the gospel, but could not have been such striking instances of its power, as Paul and those who, like him, have been stopped and changed in the height of open rebellion.

The words *in me first* should rather be *in me the chief*—the expression is the same as in the former verse—a pattern of patience to sinners should be taken from a chief sinner. But how is it he says, *I obtained mercy because I did it ignorantly*? It should seem then that he was not the chief—his ignorance and unbelief were some excuse. But surely the Apostle could not mean to lessen his faults—this ignorance was wilful, his unbelief obstinacy, he had means of being informed. It can only mean that he did not act against the conviction of his conscience that Jesus was the Christ. This makes a great difference between common sinners and apostates; those who have felt the power of the Word of God, and afterwards absolutely renounce the gospel are in a deplorable condition indeed. This Paul who is a pattern of longsuffering to others, tells us that it is impossible to renew them to repentance. Ignorance and unbelief when the means of grace are afforded is an aggravation of sin rather [than] an excuse. However, the case of Paul is left to assure us that the state of such is not yet desperate. I likewise sinned with a high hand and against great advantages and warnings, yet I stand here this day to tell other sinners there is forgiveness with him.

FOR MEDITATION: How wonderful the mercy I then received, how wonderful the mercies that led to it. What rich various accumulated mercies have followed it. And yet, alas, what a poor unprofitable servant I am still. O Lord, poor as I am, I am thine; thou hast chosen, called, accepted me and made me willing and desirous to devote myself to thee. Confirm thine own good work and keep me near to thyself.[73]   *Diary*, 21 March 1773

SERMON : 1 TIMOTHY 1:16 [2/4]

Longsuffering and grace

'Howbeit for this cause I obtained mercy, that in me first Jesus Christ might show forth all longsuffering, for a pattern to them which should hereafter believe on him to life everlasting.' 1 Timothy 1:16
SUGGESTED FURTHER READING: Zephaniah 3:14–20

The whole power and authority is here ascribed to Jesus Christ. Though as Mediator he was the Father's servant, he has life in himself and gives it to whom he pleases. It is he with whom we have to do. Too many in their views of attaining mercy, think little or nothing of Jesus Christ. But may we all take note that he is upon the throne and keeps the keys of life and death, of heaven and hell. If we enquire what is the will and pleasure of this great and only Potentate, we are told it is to show forth all longsuffering and grace. Having wrought our salvation by himself he bestows it freely. So his promises run: *Whosoever will—him that cometh I will in no wise cast out.* Because we are slow of heart to believe, he confirms his words by examples. You that think yourself not good enough to believe, or that your sins have shut you out from hope of mercy, think of Paul. Had you seen him when he was approaching Damascus, could you have thought him likely to be a vessel of mercy? Yet how suddenly changed, how freely accepted and pardoned. Lest we should think such cases peculiar to the first preaching of the gospel he still affords such instances. Permit me to speak of myself. I had cast off all fear of God and man, and being left to my own evil heart and the power of Satan, was seated in the chair of the scorner before I was twenty years of age. Not only slighted the gospel, but treated it as a fable—was hardened beyond the sense of conviction, and like Ahab sold myself to work wickedness. In this state of mind and practice, I was overtaken by that terrible storm, all hope of being saved quite gone, and I had not the least probability of surviving one quarter of an hour, but I obtained mercy, and it was not to me only but to some of you. The Lord thought of you then and preserved me alive that I might be a witness for him at Olney.

FOR MEDITATION: I could stand forth and propose myself instead of a thousand arguments … as a pattern of thy longsuffering to all that should repent and believe.[74]

Miscellaneous Thoughts, Saturday 24 June 1758

Speaking from experience

'Howbeit for this cause I obtained mercy, that in me first Jesus Christ might show forth all longsuffering, for a pattern to them which should hereafter believe on him to life everlasting.' 1 Timothy 1:16
SUGGESTED FURTHER READING: Acts 26:4–18

I speak not from books but experience:
(i) of the folly of self-righteousness. Before I became so exceedingly wicked, I laboured long to obtain salvation by the works of the law. I read the Scripture much, got much of it by heart, spent many hours in a day in what I called meditation and prayer, abstained from many sins which had hurt my conscience, but all the while sin and self reigned in my heart, and though I named the name of Christ I knew no more of him than a heathen [did]. Satan seeing me thus building upon the sand, suffered me to go on a good while for he knew he could presently shake it all down. And so it proved—so it will always be with self-righteousness.

(ii) of the evil of sin. I cannot doubt but when I speak of the little satisfaction that sinners find in their evil ways, I describe what passes in some of your hearts because I speak from my own. I boasted of liberty, I pretended to pity the poor precise creatures that minded religion, I forced my face to wear a smile, and stifled arguments with a jest, when at the same time my heart was full of madness, rage and misery and I would gladly have changed conditions with a dog or a toad. My life was often insupportable, and nothing but the Lord's secret overruling power could have kept me from destroying myself. I cannot doubt but it is thus with many who would fain be thought happy by others.

(iii) of the vanity of all excuses. Some may perhaps charge their ruin, possibly their sins, upon the decrees of God. But when you have eternity as full in your view as I then had, your mouth will be stopped as mine then was. I saw I had destroyed myself, and thought it next to impossible that I could escape damnation, if the Lord was wise and just and able to punish.

FOR MEDITATION: But he enabled me to hope against hope. He saved me from the sea by a miracle of providence, and from hell by a miracle of grace, that he might show in me a pattern of his longsuffering. Once a rebel, now a messenger, I come in Christ's name, as though he did beseech you by me—*be ye reconciled to God.*

SERMON: 1 TIMOTHY 1:16 [4/4]

True righteousness

'Righteousness exalteth a nation: but sin is a reproach to any people.'
Proverbs 14:34
SUGGESTED FURTHER READING: Proverbs 14:12–35

The usual judgement of mankind on almost every important point is so very different from the decision of Scripture, that both cannot possibly be true. National prosperity is more commonly estimated by the extent of dominion, by the success of arms in war, and the increase of riches and commerce in peace; whether righteousness flourisheth or not, is seldom taken into account. And the prevalence of sin, of infidelity, dissipation and profligacy, is deemed a small reproach compared with a diminution of power and wealth. When our fleets and armies triumphed over all resistance and spread terror and desolation to the remotest parts of the globe, and the treasures of the East began to pour in upon us with an almost boundless profusion, this nation was supposed to be highly exalted. But nothing less than the progress of righteousness and the suppression of sin can render us truly honourable or take away our reproach if the Word of God, the great Governor of the earth, be truth. And this happy change would do it, though we should lose one province and one empire after another, and we should be deprived of our boasted consequence among the nations of the earth. The sentences in the book of Proverbs are for the most part contrasted and we may therefore fix the sense of righteousness in this passage by considering it as the opposite to sin. Sin, which is the reproach of our nature, of every person, family, village, city and kingdom in which it is found, is that inward principle of the heart and that outward course of conduct which is contrary to our relation to God as his creatures and to the tenor of his revealed will. A right disposition of heart towards God and a conduct in all points regulated by the authority and rule of his Holy Word, is this *righteousness which exalteth a nation*, and so far is this wanting, the most powerful, opulent, civilized and enlightened empire, with all its supposed attainments, advantages and distinctions, is clearly[76] the subject of reproach and contempt.

FOR MEDITATION: 'I have not hid thy righteousness within my heart; I have declared thy faithfulness and thy salvation: I have not concealed thy lovingkindness and thy truth from the great congregation' (Psalm 40:10).

SERMON: PROVERBS 14:34 [1/7] [FOR THE ANNUAL CHARITY SERMON]

The character of the righteous man

'Righteousness exalteth a nation: but sin is a reproach to any people.'
Proverbs 14:34
SUGGESTED FURTHER READING: 1 John 2:28–3:10

I shall delineate the character of a righteous man. That mankind is very far from original righteousness is the doctrine of our Church (Article 9). But the authority of our church, or of any church, would be of small weight unless supported and proved by the testimony of Scripture. They are *so very far* gone, that when God looked down upon the children of men, to see if there were any good among them, the result of his enquiry is declared (Psalm 14, Romans 3), *There is none righteous, no, not one, there is none that understandeth, there is none that seeketh after God*. That sobriety, benevolence and equity which entitle men to respect as members of society, is very far short of righteousness unless connected with the knowledge, love and fear of the great God in whom we live and move and have our being. He is our Creator, Supreme Lawgiver and Benefactor, and therefore our first and highest regards are due to him. Unless we love, serve, trust, believe and obey him, we are not righteous, we are not honest. Morality, so much praised, so little practised, implies the right discharge of all our relative duties and our first and highest relation being that in which we stand to our Maker; if he is left out, our pretence to morality is vain. The righteous man has been convinced of loving, serving or trusting the creature more than the Creator—of preferring his own will to the will of God, of seeking happiness in something short of the favour and glory of God, and, in the prophetic language, of forsaking the fountain of living waters and hewing out to himself broken cisterns that can hold no water. The righteous man has therefore seen himself to be a sinner and he has taken his measures of sin from the majesty and goodness of God against whom he has sinned. He believes the record God has given of his Son, obeys the command and accepts the invitation to trust in this Saviour, renouncing very other hope.

FOR MEDITATION: The righteous man, therefore, is he who has peace with God through Jesus Christ, who, as redeemed by blood from the desire and dominion of sin, is no longer his own. He is now the willing servant of God, devoted to his will and glory.

SERMON: PROVERBS 14:34 [2/7] [FOR THE ANNUAL CHARITY SERMON]

Good citizens

'Righteousness exalteth a nation: but sin is a reproach to any people.'
Proverbs 14:34
SUGGESTED FURTHER READING: Romans 13:1–4

Consider how a nation (which is composed of a multitude of individuals) would be exalted if this character was universally or even generally prevalent. Whatever be the situation of the righteous man, he is an ornament and a blessing to the community. If he be in authority, he ruleth over men in the fear of God. Whether seated upon a throne, or in a subordinate station in public life, his power, influence and example, so far as they extend, are employed in promoting the public good, to encourage the love of righteousness in others, to vindicate the oppressed, maintain order and suppress wickedness. The God whom he serves teaches him for his station and supports him. His principles render him superior to the selfish craft which often passes for wisdom in the world, and the fear of God secures him from that fear of man which bringeth a snare. The righteous man is the true patriot, who wrestles for his country by prayer in secret and devotes his talents to promote the good of all around him. The righteous man in private life is a good citizen. He respects and obeys the government and laws under which he lives. He is willingly subject to lawful authority (and obeys), not from constraint, or for the sake of filthy lucre, but for conscience' sake. If he be rich, the grace of God teaches him to be humble, moderate and benevolent. If he be poor, it teaches him patience and contentment, to be quiet in the land, diligent in his calling. As a relative, the righteous man is a kind and compassionate master, a good husband, a punctual trader, a faithful, upright servant, in every relation endeavouring to approve himself to God and to do unto others as he would wish others in a like situation should do unto him. He is sober and temperate in all things, gentle, forbearing and forgiving, because in every situation he endeavours to adore the doctrine of God his Saviour in all things, and is no farther directly concerned in the affairs of this life, than to let his light so shine in his allotted department, that others may glorify God on his behalf.

FOR MEDITATION: 'Lead me, O LORD, in thy righteousness' (Psalm 5:8).

SERMON: PROVERBS 14:34 [3/7] [FOR THE ANNUAL CHARITY SERMON]

Left to ourselves, ruin is certain

'Righteousness exalteth a nation: but sin is a reproach to any people.'
Proverbs 14:34
SUGGESTED FURTHER READING: Daniel 9:1–19

I think it undeniable that if this righteousness were diffused among all ranks and orders of men, there would be reason to say, happy are the people that are in such a state. Discord, envy, hatred, prodigality, covetousness, sensuality and a long train of evils which fill the world with woe, would be banished from among them. Each one in his sphere would contribute to the good of the whole, and God thus served, and thus honoured, would be their bulwark and shield, a wall of fire round about them and a glory in the midst of them. But where sin, the neglect of God and of his laws, prevail—it is a present reproach—it will prove them a foolish and unwise, an ungrateful and base spirited people. A want of public spirit in superiors, a readiness to sacrifice every valuable consideration to the selfish calls of ambition or interest—and, in the inferior [socially lower] classes, impatience of subordination, licentiousness under the pretence of liberty, the indulgence of hurtful passions—in general: dissensions, riots, weak counsels, rash enterprises, ruined fortunes and constitutions, distracted families, tyrannical masters, treacherous servants, bankruptcies, robberies, rapes and murders, crowded jails and places of worship almost empty, would mark the character of the nation and of the times. And these things would in their own nature, not only be a reproach, but tend to the ruin of the people.

FOR MEDITATION: God has sometimes shown his displeasure against sin by public and severe judgements—thus he brought a flood upon the old world and destroyed Sodom and Gomorrah with fire. But if he only leaves a people to themselves, their ruin will be equally certain, and perhaps equally terrible. He inflicted no heavier punishment than this upon the Jews after they had filled up the measure of their iniquities by crucifying the Son of God. He did not visit them with earthquakes or hurricanes, but he gave them up to the way of their own hearts. Their ruin quickly followed; they brought it upon themselves, with such a complicated concurrence of calamities as were never suffered by any other people upon earth.

SERMON: PROVERBS 14:34 [4/7] [FOR THE ANNUAL CHARITY SERMON]

Contribute to our national honour

'*Righteousness exalteth a nation: but sin is a reproach to any people.*'
Proverbs 14:34
SUGGESTED FURTHER READING: Acts 17:16–34

Whether we are a people exalted by the love and practice of righteousness, or whether sin, enormous sin, be our reproach, and a just cause for fear lest it involve us in ruin, I leave to your observation and to your consciences. I hope there are amongst you many righteous persons, and many more who feel some concern for the wickedness and misery around you. May God enable you, according to your several opportunities, to contribute to our national honour and to the removal of our reproach by joining heartily in the cause of righteousness, and by discountenancing sin.

This will lead you to countenance the preaching of the gospel, which is the appointment and power of God to salvation through faith in this name. The people are destroyed for lack of knowledge. The glorious gospel of Christ is like the sun: when this light shines and is perceived, the darkness of iniquity and misery flee before it.

FOR MEDITATION: Let those lament the speed of time whose hearts and hopes are confined to the present world! I trust we may rejoice that our complete, full salvation is much nearer than when we first believed, and is still advancing apace. Months that are gone, are gone for ever, and have borne away each its own load. *Our* chief concern with the flight of time is to endeavour to make the most of it as it passes and to work while it is day, for the night cometh. Considered as an opportunity, which, if let slip, can never be recalled, life is precious. It is *here* only, that we can bear testimony to the grace of God in the midst of sinners and improve our talents and influence, be they more or less, to alleviate the miseries or to promote the welfare of our fellow creatures.[77]

John Newton to William Wilberforce, 22 December 1795

Stretch out a friendly hand

'Righteousness exalteth a nation: but sin is a reproach to any people.'
Proverbs 14:34
SUGGESTED FURTHER READING: Amos 5:4–15

Much may be done by the united efforts of persons of character and influence to enforce the laws of the land. The gross and shameful profanation of the Lord's Day, the multitudes of unhappy prostitutes who throng our streets to ensnare the unwary, the many vile prints and pamphlets exposed to sale which are calculated to excite and disseminate lewdness, are no less contrary to law and sound policy than to religion. They are a disgrace to our *police*, and though tolerated with impunity in a land called Christian, would not, I am persuaded, have been permitted under the ancient heathen governments of Greece and Rome. How many are the snares spread for unexperienced youth, which too frequently counteract the advantages of education and good example. But the children of the poor, destitute of these advantages, many of them without advice and without restraint if no friendly hand is stretched out for their relief, are peculiarly exposed. It is a subject of lamentation, rather than wonder, that numbers grow up in the habits of idleness, drunkenness and dishonesty, that they are bold in the way of evil and neither fear God nor regard man, that from smaller they proceed to greater wickedness, that beggars and thieves abound everywhere, that neither our persons nor our property, nor dwellings, are safe, and that so many are brought to an untimely end at every sessions and assize. Who can say how many of these evils are prevented by the charitable institutions and support of schools for poor and otherwise friendless children?

FOR MEDITATION: I spoke to them of the love of Jesus in submitting to all these indignities for our sakes, of the wickedness of man in treating him who did nothing but good in this manner. I made them observe progress in wickedness. These ungodly men who crucified Christ were once children— began with little things, and so grew hardened as they grew old—from hence I showed them the necessity of praying to God to keep us, for if he should leave us to ourselves, we know not what we may come to.[78]
Journal of children's meetings at Olney, 24 January 1765

Especially to the young people

'Righteousness exalteth a nation: but sin is a reproach to any people.'
Proverbs 14:34
SUGGESTED FURTHER READING: Exodus 1:22–2:10; Hebrews 11:23–29

If some, if but a few, if even but one of the children [of the Charity School] before you, besides being put in the path of honest industry, should be partakers of that righteousness which I have described, it will compensate for the expense. Who that had seen Moses cast out upon the water, would have expected that he would one day become the deliverer and leader of Israel?[79] I would animate you with the hope that amongst these children there may be some who in future life will appear in a very different situation, and by the providence and grace of God be qualified for great usefulness in society—patterns and promoters of that righteousness that exalteth a nation. May God so enthuse the hearts of this assembly, and so direct you to improve the talents he has entrusted you with, that in the great day of his appearance you may be found in the number of those who have been instrumental in turning many to righteousness, and who shall shine as the brightness of the firmament and like the stars for ever and ever. Amen.

FOR MEDITATION: Now I look to thee for strength and for a blessing this evening. I am going to speak in thy name, and especially to the young people. May I carry thy message. May thy power apply it. May thy voice be heard, thy presence felt, thy glory seen amongst us. May the grace of our Lord Jesus Christ be abundantly known tonight, and may some good work be wrought which may be recorded to thy praise in the annuls of eternity.[80]

Diary, 1 January 1783

Of one mind?

'And the whole earth was of one language, and of one speech. And it came to pass, as they journeyed from the east, that they found a plain in the land of Shinar; and they dwelt there. And they said one to another, Go to, let us make brick, and burn them throughly. And they had brick for stone, and slime had they for morter.' Genesis 11:1–3
SUGGESTED FURTHER READING: Genesis 11:1–9

The tenth chapter [of Genesis] is a map of the origin of all nations as branching from the sons of Noah. It seems probable that Noah fixed his residence not far from where the Ark rested, and that as his posterity increased, they extended themselves and formed new settlements on every side. We have here an account of the spirit and enterprise of one branch of the people, which travelled eastward, and the confusion of tongues with which they were furnished (for till then, there was but one language spoken upon the earth). Note the occasion. This was twofold:

(i) *they found a plain,* a convenient place for building, and that afforded fit materials—brick and mortar. Thus God has been pleased to fill the earth with his goodness and furnished it in great variety for the accommodation of its inhabitants. And he has given a wisdom to men to avail themselves of what they find and to maximize all materials to their own use. They did not find bricks, but having clay, they were instructed to make them. That spirit of invention and improvement which is the spring of so many arts and callings in life, and applies the productions of the earth to many different uses, is the gift of God, though seldom acknowledged and thought of—and for the most part, as in this instance, the skill and ingenuity of men are employed in purposes of wickedness and in defiance of God who gave them.

(ii) they were unanimous—of one mind and one tongue. This encouraged and enabled them to undertake great things. Union where there is not the fear of God is but a conspiracy against him. But seldom anything considerable, either of good or evil, is done without it.

FOR MEDITATION: 'Unless the Lord builds the house, its builders labour in vain. Unless the Lord watches over the city, the watchmen stand guard in vain' (Psalm 127:1, NIV).

Hold on to the truth

'*And they said, Go to, let us build us a city and a tower, whose top "may reach" unto heaven; and let us make us a name, lest we be scattered abroad upon the face of the whole earth.*' Genesis 11:4
SUGGESTED FURTHER READING: Joshua 24:1–24

Note their attempt to build a city and a tower: a city for residence and a tower for worship—this seems the meaning of the expression '*whose top— to the heavens*' [verse 4]. The words 'may reach' are in italics [in the AV], as not belonging to the Hebrew, and therefore only express the private judgement of the translator. It is not probable they thought to reach heaven. And if they had intended it as a refuge in case of another flood, they would have rather built upon a mountain than in a plain. At most the expression is hyperbolical, to signify a very high tower. But some supply the words, 'whose top shall be sacred to the heavens'. This seems to have been the first open establishment of idolatry and the tower designed for a temple, dedicated to the worship of the host of heaven—that is the sun, moon and stars. Man, considered as a member of society, is naturally disposed for religious worship and there has no nation so distant or barbarous been found, but pays some acknowledgement to superior powers—excepting only in places where the light of the gospel has been resisted (in that case, a few have been so hardened and given up to a reprobate mind, as to renounce all thoughts of religion). Man—as a fallen creature—though he will have a religion, will always incline to and take up with a false one, if not prevented by grace. And mankind are disposed to relinquish the truth when they have known it. These were the descendants of Noah who worshipped the true God, and yet soon became idolaters. And human nature is the same still— prone to leave the truth and to follow after vanity.

FOR MEDITATION: Parents: endeavour to inculcate the truths of the gospel upon your children and pray to the Lord to open their hearts. Or else, like the family of Noah, they will surely forsake their parents' God.

Children: think not to say, *We have Abraham for our father* [John 8:39]. Trust not to notions and the restraints of a religious education. If you do not attain to an experimental hold of the truth, you will not hold it long.

Self on the throne

'And they said, Go to, let us build us a city and a tower, whose top "may reach" unto heaven; and let us make us a name, lest we be scattered abroad upon the face of the whole earth.' Genesis 11:4
SUGGESTED FURTHER READING: Deuteronomy 8:1–20

Note their aim and design. This was to keep together in a large body and to get themselves *a name*, that they might have their own wills, their own ways, and be admired or feared by others. The spirit of self-seeking and applause which set the builders of Babel to work, is natural of every man since the Fall. This is the essence of our departure from God. His throne in the heart is usurped by self. Every one of us has attempted to build some Babel to our own praise and advantage. Forgetfulness of God puts sinners upon such attempts as lead to their own confusion. What they design for their *name*, shall prove to their shame, and what they propose comfort from, will lead to torment. Upon this ground, I would preach Jesus, as the deliverer from self and sin.

[Newton subsequently added a note in the margin: 'Almost silenced in the delivery of this discourse and did not finish the subject.']⁸¹

FOR MEDITATION:

Can they whom pride and passion sway,
Who Mammon and the world obey,
In envy or contention live,
Presume that they indeed believe?

True faith unites to CHRIST the root,
By him producing holy fruit;
And they who no such fruit can show,
Still on the stock of nature grow.

LORD, let thy word effectual prove,
To work in us obedient love!
And may each one who hears it dread
A name to live; and yet be dead.⁸²

Don't be deceived

'Be not deceived; God is not mocked: for whatsoever a man soweth, that shall he also reap.' Galatians 6:7
SUGGESTED FURTHER READING: Obadiah 1–17

There is a lamentable proneness in mankind to *deceive* themselves in matters of the highest importance. Indeed in worldly affairs they are quite unwilling to be imposed upon. If they have a purchase to make, how cautious are they lest there should be a flaw or mistake in the title. But with regard to the salvation of their souls, any poor pretence or show of a hope will content them. Their hearts are deceitful, and Satan the great deceiver is dextrous in putting cheats upon them. Against this, we are now warned. May the Lord impress the warning upon every heart. Let us consider some of the ways in which men are deceived:

(i) by the love of the world. The Scripture pronounces it all vanity, but it appears something to a carnal eye. Satan tempted our Lord this way. To avoid this deceit, consider Matthew 16:26.

(ii) by the love of sin. Sin is called deceitful; it blinds the eyes and hardens the heart. How many are convinced in their cooler hours, but when the temptation presents itself powerfully again, they forget what they knew.

(iii) by trusting to their own strength. When they have made a few hasty resolutions, or perhaps only purposed to resolve, they think they shall stand. How often have some of you been deceived thus!

(iv) by vain hopes, founded on the general mercy of God, their own righteousness and a formal profession of the gospel.

FOR MEDITATION:

How David, when by sin deceived,
From bad to worse went on!
For when the Holy Spirit's grieved,
Our strength and guard are gone.

When sin deceives it hardens too,
For though he vainly sought
To hide his crimes from public view,
Of GOD he little thought.

His eye on Bathsheba once fixed,
With poison filled his soul;
He ventured on adultery next,
And murder crowned the whole.

Let those who think they stand beware,
For David stood before;
Nor let the fallen soul despair,
For mercy can restore.[83]

SERMON: GALATIANS 6:7 [1/1]

A great shaking

'For thus saith the LORD *of hosts; Yet once, it is a little while, and I will shake the heavens, and the earth, and the sea, and the dry land; and I will shake all nations, and the desire of all nations shall come: and I will fill this house with glory, saith the* LORD *of hosts.' Haggai 2:6–7*
SUGGESTED FURTHER READING: Exodus 19:16–25

God shook the earth when he proclaimed his law to Israel from Sinai. The description, though very simple, presents to our thoughts a scene unspeakably majestic and grand, but unspeakably awful likewise (Exodus 19:16–19). The mountain was in flames at the top and trembled to its basis. Dark clouds, thunderings and lightnings filled the air. Not only the mountain, but the hearts of the people, of the whole people, trembled, and Moses himself said, I exceedingly fear and quake. Then, as the apostle referring to this passage observes in Hebrews 12:26, *The voice of the Lord shook the earth.* But the prophet speaks of another, a greater, a more important and extensive concussion. *Yet once more I shake not the earth only but the heaven.* If we really believe that the Scriptures are true, that the prophecies were delivered by holy men who spake as they were moved by the Holy Ghost, and that not one jot or tittle shall fail, how studious should we be to attain a right understanding of passages and events in which we are nearly [closely] interested, so as to be duly and properly affected by them.

FOR MEDITATION: *On the earthquake,* 8 September, 1775

But if these warnings prove in vain,	Should the deep–rooted hills be hurled,
Say, sinner, canst thou tell,	And plunged beneath the seas;
How soon the earth may quake again,	And strong convulsions shake the world,
And open wide to hell?	Your hearts may rest in peace.
But happy they who love the LORD	JESUS, your Shepherd, LORD, and Chief,
And his salvation know;	Shall shelter you from ill;
The hope that's founded on his word,	And not a worm or shaking leaf
No change can overthrow.	Can move, but at his will.[84]

Is the King in you?

'*Now why dost thou cry out aloud? Is there no king in thee? Is thy counsellor perished? For pangs have taken thee as a woman in travail.*'
Micah 4:9
SUGGESTED FURTHER READING: Micah 4:6–13

He checks the excess of their grief and reproves their unbelief. Observe reproof and consolation joined. *Is there no king ...?* Two comfortable views of the Lord Jesus are here presented: our *King*, our *Counsellor*. The soul over whom he reigns as King must be safe and happy. The soul for whom he pleads as Advocate will surely gain its cause.

Is there no king in thee? If there is, you have no reason to sorrow without hope, for he is mighty to save. A king has great power—but none like the King and saints (Matthew 28:18). He has power over the *heart*, the *world* and the *devil*. A king is sovereign. If he will pardon, who will condemn? It is spoken of as Nebuchadnezzar's prerogative (Daniel 5:19). Much more, is it true of Jesus. Though you owe ten thousand talents, this King can clear you by an act of grace. A king is rich and can easily make his friends so. What a change did Pharaoh's favour make for Joseph. But you will say, 'It is good news for some, but if I am asked, I fear I must say, No, he is not in me—at least, I know it not. How shall I be sure?' There is no end of reasoning with unbelief. What would satisfy you?

The King has described those in whom he is: *but to this man will I look, even to him that is poor and of a contrite spirit, and trembleth at my word* (Isaiah 66:2). What can you oppose to this, but those things which the Scripture declares is common to all the people of God? What can you say, more than St Paul has said of himself (Romans 7)?

FOR MEDITATION: I long to hear that you are entered into the peace and liberty of the gospel. Why will you rather listen to an enemy who grudges you peace, and who you know beforehand was a liar from the beginning? He aims to distress you. The chief point of the gospel is very simple and plain—it is only to believe that Jesus died and rose again, and is now preparing a place in his kingdom and that all he did and suffered, with all the blessed effects of his atonement and mediation, is for your sake, if you put your trust in him.[85]

John Newton to Mrs Jean Coffin, 27 June 1793

SERMON: MICAH 4:9 [1/2]

Have you a Counsellor in heaven?

'Now why dost thou cry out aloud? Is there no king in thee? Is thy counsellor perished? For pangs have taken thee as a woman in travail.'
Micah 4:9
SUGGESTED FURTHER READING: Psalm 16:1–11

But is thy counsellor perished? thy advocate? thy friend? Have poor sinners a manager in heaven or have they not? If Satan would object to purpose, he should prove either that Christ did not die, or that death had full dominion so that he could not rise again. But see Romans 8:34, *Who is he that condemneth? It is Christ that died, yea rather, that is risen again, who is even at the right hand of God, who also maketh intercession for us.* Well, if he is not perished but still lives, see what follows:

(i) He pleads for us. How? In general see John 17, in particular see Luke 22:30–31 [31–32].

(ii) He answers for us (Zechariah 3:2).

(iii) He makes our prayers (poor as they are) acceptable (Revelation 8:3).

(iv) He obtains and bestows every needful blessing (Psalm 68:18).

In consequence of all this, he is able to save to the uttermost (Hebrews 7:25), and as willing as able. Why is not his Word worthy your credit? See John 6:37. Why then dost thou cry and refuse to be comforted? It is because your heart still cleaves to the old covenant—because you do not look simply to Christ, but are labouring for something in yourself, which you will not be able to find.

To some I might change the question—Why do not you cry? Your lives, your language proclaim there is no King in you—unless I should say, the prince of darkness. But Jesus is not your King, or Counsellor. He lives and pleads, but you have no good hope that he pleads for you. On the contrary, you crucify him afresh and put him to open shame. Is it not time to stop? If you have him not for your Saviour, he will be your Judge. If you do not cry now, you will cry for ever. Yet despair not—there is still hope. There is forgiveness with him.

FOR MEDITATION: We have indeed no sufficiency in ourselves, but our sufficiency is of God. Jesus is *able to save to the uttermost*. May this good and great Shepherd ever be your guide, your guard, your counsellor, and your consolation.[86]

John Newton to William Wilberforce (the MP's uncle), 19 October 1767

SERMON: MICAH 4:9 [2/2]

The name of Jesus

'Thy name is as ointment poured forth.' Song of Solomon 1:3
SUGGESTED FURTHER READING: 1 Peter 2:4–10

I knew nothing about the fear of God. I never had a hearty desire to keep his commandments, till I began to know a little of Christ. I was starving and he fed me; I was sick and he visited me; I was naked, destitute of all good, and he clothed me with his own righteousness; I was shut up in the prison of sin and he came and burst open the doors and set me at liberty. How great is his goodness; how great is his beauty. In comparison of this tree of life, all the tallest of the sons of men are empty and barren. He is the chief among ten thousands and altogether lovely. The soul ranges, as it were, through the whole creation to find some worthy similitudes of her Lord, but all are scanty and insufficient. Let us consider this in my text. It may lead our thoughts not only to the excellency that is in Christ, but to his suitableness to us, and afford a glass in which you may see yourselves and be able to judge by the light of the Holy Spirit whether you are indeed worthy the name of Christians.

Thy name. This in general means his person (as in Revelation 3:4), or rather the manifestation of his person, that by which he is known. The name of Christ includes the whole revelation concerning him, who he is, what he has done—all that we read of his love, his power and his offices, make a part of his great and glorious name. The soul that is taught by the Word and Spirit of God to understand a little of these things, receives such a sense of love and joy, that the very sound of his name is sweeter than music to the ears, sweeter than honey to the taste. He is named a Saviour, to save from guilt, sin and hell. This implies a Mediator. There is an important concern between us and God—but how shall we approach?—who shall interpose? This name affords a comfortable answer. He is named a Husband. Our wants, debts and fears are many. But he is made known by this name (Isaiah 54) and he is rich enough to supply all.

FOR MEDITATION:

Dear name! the rock on which I build,
My shield and hiding place;
My never-failing treasury filled
With boundless stores of grace.

JESUS! my Shepherd, Husband, Friend,
My Prophet, Priest and King;
My LORD, my Life, my Way, my End,
Accept the praise I bring.[87]

SERMON: SONG OF SOLOMON 1:3 [1/5]

His name like ointment

'Thy name is as ointment poured forth.' Song of Solomon 1:3
SUGGESTED FURTHER READING: Luke 10:29–37

This name is compared to *ointment*. These were more frequent in use, and many of more costly composition, than common amongst us.

Some were healing, applied to wounds and bruises and putrefying sores. Now the sinner, when he is awakened and comes to himself, finds himself like the man (Luke 10) stripped and wounded and half dead. Jesus, like the good Samaritan, comes with an eye of pity to pour in the ointment of his name. This is a certain and the only cure for the wounds of sin. Many can witness to this. How, when they began to feel their misery and see their danger, they made use of many means, but found them all physicians of no value. Like the woman in the Gospel, when they had spent all their time and strength in this way, they were no better but rather grew worse. But this ointment made them whole.

Some were cordial and reviving. The believing soul is subject to fainting—it has but little strength and meets many discouragements—but is relieved from time to time by the good savour of this ointment. The name of Christ refreshes it with new strength under the remains of sin, assaults of Satan and troubles of life.

FOR MEDITATION: O the name of Jesus—indeed it is as ointment poured forth.[88]

[John Newton to Thomas Haweis, Liverpool, May 1763]

How sweet the name of JESUS sounds
In a believer's ear!
It soothes his sorrows, heals his wounds,
And drives away his fear.

It makes the wounded spirit whole,
And calms the troubled breast;
'Tis manna to the hungry soul,
And to the weary rest.[89]

A distinguishing savour

'Thy name is as ointment poured forth.' Song of Solomon 1:3
SUGGESTED FURTHER READING: Isaiah 61:1–3

Ointments were used in feasts (Luke 7:46; hence Psalm 23:5), and the name of Jesus is a precious banquet to the believing soul. This fills him as with marrow and fatness; this puts an honour and a beauty upon him; therefore (verse 4) *more than wine*.

Precious ointments have a savour, a perfumed smell, which distinguishes the person that bears them. So this ointment of the name of Jesus, when poured into a believer's heart, it makes him smell as a field which the Lord has blessed. It is this communication of grace and holiness which they have received from their beloved which makes them known to each other and distinguishes them from the world.

Who have a right to the bread and wine? Even all those who see the value and long to know more of the virtue of this ointment. Fear not, ye who seek Jesus, but come. Are you wounded? Are you fainting? Let not this keep you away, but rather constrain you. You cannot do without it.

FOR MEDITATION:
By Thee my prayers acceptance gain
Although with sin defiled;
Satan accuses me in vain
And I am owned a child.[90]

Yes, dear Mrs Barham[91] is gone home. She lived honourably and died peaceably. Were I to preach a funeral sermon, I should say but little about her; but I would make the people stare, if I could, by telling them what a wonderful Friend she had; one who paid all her debts, and was so attentive to her that his eye was never off her by night or day for a long number of years; one who, by looking at her, could sweeten her pains, renew her strength, and fill her with wisdom, grace and peace. She is gone to see her best Friend; and I hope, one day to see her with him.[92]

John Newton to William Bull, 13 October 1781

Filled with his fragrance

'Thy name is as ointment poured forth.' Song of Solomon 1:3
SUGGESTED FURTHER READING: Psalm 22:1–31

How *poured forth?* We read in Mark 14 that the woman brought precious ointment in a box—and when she broke the box, then and not before, the whole house was filled with its fragrance. Thus the grace and virtue of this name was confined and known but to few while our Lord conversed upon earth—but afterwards it was *poured forth* when he suffered. The precious vessel that contained this precious ointment was broken upon the cross— the savour of his name, his love, his blood, poured out from every wound in his sacred body. *See from his head, his hands, his feet, sorrow and love flow mingling down.*93 From that hour, it was quickly spread and diffused far and near. And here we are still to look for it. When we desire a new savour of this ointment, let us turn our eyes, our thoughts, to Golgotha. To behold him by faith as he hung bleeding and dying, with outstretched arms inviting our regards and saying, See if any sorrow was like to my sorrow. This is a sovereign balm for every wound and a cordial for our care.

FOR MEDITATION:

When on the cross, my Lord I see
Bleeding to death, for wretched me;
Satan and sin no more can move,
For I am all transformed to love.

Here I forget my cares and pains;
I drink, yet still my thirst remains;
Only the fountain-head above,
Can satisfy the thirst of love.

His thorns, and nails, pierce through my heart,
In every groan I bear a part;
I view his wounds with streaming eyes,
But see! he bows his head and dies!

O, that I thus could always feel!
LORD, more and more thy love reveal!
Then my glad tongue shall loud proclaim
The grace and glory of thy name.

Come, sinners, view the Lamb of GOD,
Wounded and dead, and bathed in blood!
Behold his side, and venture near,
The well of endless life is here.

Thy name dispels my guilt and fear,
Revives my heart, and charms my ear;
Affords a balm for every wound,
And Satan trembles at the sound.94

SERMON: SONG OF SOLOMON 1:3 [4/5]

Refreshing ointment

'Thy name is as ointment poured forth.' Song of Solomon 1:3
SUGGESTED FURTHER READING: Acts 13:32–52

This ointment was *poured forth* in the preached gospel. It was appointed for this end. And everything that bears the name of preaching, if it does not diffuse the knowledge of this good ointment, is dry and tedious, unsavoury and unprofitable. But by this foolishness of preaching it is spread abroad. The scene of our Lord's life was confined to a few places and it was a long while ago—but the ointment thus poured out has reached to distant lands and ages. Countless thousands have experienced its efficacy, and blessed be God, it is still fresh and still flowing. It is poured out amongst us at this day.

Farther, the expression *poured forth* may signify abundance (there is enough to spare) and freeness (it is not enclosed but open and common to all who know its value, as the light or water).

The Lord has likewise special seasons of pouring it into the hearts of his people. These are called times of refreshment (Acts 3:19): usually at the time of their first conversion; often in an hour of distress and trouble. They may expect it likewise at the hour of death. He often meets them with it in the ordinances—particularly when they approach his table. At this feast he revives them with the savour of his ointment and pours it upon their heads. He anoints them with this oil of joy and gladness above their fellows.

FOR MEDITATION:
Weak is the effort of my heart
And cold my warmest thought;
But when I see thee as thou art,
I'll praise Thee as I ought.

Till then I would thy love proclaim
With every fleeting breath;
And may the music of thy name
Refresh my soul in death.95

Kingdoms shaken

'For thus saith the LORD of hosts; Yet once, it is a little while, and I will shake the heavens, and the earth, and the sea, and the dry land.' Haggai 2:6
SUGGESTED FURTHER READING: Jeremiah 9:7–16

The effects of Messiah's appearance: *shaking the heavens and the earth.* The prophecy was, in a measure, fulfilled literally: at his birth—a new star; at his death—the sun withdrew its shining, the earth quaked, the rocks rent, and the dead arose. In his life, he often suspended and overruled the usual laws of nature and exercised supreme power over the visible and invisible world. He shook the kingdom of darkness, spoiled principalities and powers. He shook the kingdoms of the earth—the idols trembled and disappeared before his gospel, till at length the Roman Empire renounced heathenism and embraced the Christian name. But the language of prophecy is highly figurative. Mountains and trees, land and water, sun and moon, heaven and earth, often signify nations, peoples and states. And particularly heaven and earth are used to denote the religious and political establishment of Israel—or, as we say, their constitution of Church and State. This, without doubt, is the primary sense here. The appearance of the Messiah shall be accompanied with the total dissolution of the Jewish economy. The whole of their Levitical institution was fulfilled, superseded and abrogated by the Messiah. Before he died he said, *It is finished* [John 19:30]; the veil of the temple was rent in twain from the top to the bottom. And in a few years the temple itself was destroyed and therefore their former worship rendered utterly impracticable. Their civil state likewise was dissolved, they were extirpated from the promised land and sifted as with a sieve among all nations. Though in one view they are preserved a distinct people, in another view they are not a people—having neither settlement nor government, but living dispersed as strangers and foreigners among the nations (Hosea 3:4).

FOR MEDITATION: Nothing like this ever happened to any people. It is a striking, obvious and perpetual proof of the truth of the Scriptures. What was foretold by Moses and the succeeding prophets, is fulfilled to a demonstration in our eyes. How unlikely that it should be so, yet it must be so because the mouth of the Lord had spoken it.

SERMON SERIES: MESSIAH, NO. 3 [4/5], HAGGAI 2:6–7

The King of Glory

'For thus saith the LORD *of hosts; Yet once, it is a little while, and I will shake the heavens, and the earth, and the sea, and the dry land; and I will shake all nations, and the desire of all nations shall come: and I will fill this house with glory, saith the* LORD *of hosts.' Haggai 2:6–7*
SUGGESTED FURTHER READING: Psalm 24:1–10

He shall *fill this house with* his glory. When he visited it he displayed his glory. The blind and the lame came thither to him and he healed them. Children felt this power and sang, Hosanna to the Son of David, and when the Pharisees rebuked them he said, If these held their peace, the stones would cry out [Luke 19:40]. As the Lord in his own house, he purged the temple and drove out those who profaned it. And when he left it the last time, with sovereign authority he denounced that awful sentence which was soon after executed both upon the temple and the nation. His glory filled the temple when he was an infant, so that Simeon and Anna then acknowledged his character and spoke of him to those who were waiting for the consolation of Israel. Especially, his glory was manifested when he proclaimed himself the fountain of life and invited every thirsty, weary sinner to come to him to drink and live [John 7:37–38].

The temple has long been destroyed. But he has still a house—a house not made with hands. This house is his church, his people. He dwells in each individually. He dwells among them collectively in their societies and solemn assemblies. But before he takes possession of a heart, there is usually a shaking. He shakes the heavens and the earth; their former views of God and themselves are changed. All that they have been building in religion is shaken to the ground—their vain hopes are shaken to the foundation. This makes way for the perception of his glory as a Saviour. In this day of his power, the heart is willing to throw open its gates that the King of Glory may come in [Psalm 24:7–10].

FOR MEDITATION: 'Hallelujah! Salvation and glory and power belong to our God' (Revelation 19:1, NIV).

The capital point

'Blessed be the God and Father of our Lord Jesus Christ, which according to his abundant mercy hath begotten us again unto a lively hope by the resurrection of Jesus Christ from the dead.' 1 Peter 1:3
SUGGESTED FURTHER READING: 1 Corinthians 15:1–11

Great is the difference between the notion and experience of divine truths. When they are truly known, they warm the heart and put life into our words. The Apostle was a poor and afflicted man. He wrote to a scattered and afflicted people. Yet see how he begins. They who can make these words their own may be joyful in tribulation.

The way in which believers have a right to the inheritance:

(i) They are *begotten again*. They have it as children, not by nature—Ephesians 2:3 ... *and were by nature the children of wrath, even as others*—but by grace and adoption, born of the incorruptible seed of the word, quickened by the Spirit—an adoption accompanied with a real change: by the former a right, by the latter a suitability.

(ii) The ground or cause: *abundant mercy*, considering the objects (sinners), the greatness of the blessings, the procuring cause (John 3:16 *For God so loved the world, that he gave his only begotten Son, that whosoever believeth in him should not perish, but have everlasting life*).

(iii) The great means—*the resurrection of Jesus Christ*. This is the capital point in which all gospel truths centre. *And if Christ be not risen, then is our preaching vain, and your faith is also vain. And if Christ be not raised, your faith is vain; ye are yet in your sins'* (1 Corinthians 15:14,17).

FOR MEDITATION:

'I Am,' saith CHRIST our glorious head,
(May we attention give)
'The resurrection of the dead,
The life of all that live.

By faith in me, the soul receives
New life, though dead before;
And he that in my name believes,
Shall live, to die no more.'

Thy power and mercy first prevailed
From death to set us free;
And often since our life had failed,
If not renewed by thee.

To thee we look, to thee we bow;
To thee, for help, we call;
Our life and resurrection thou,
Our hope, our joy, our all.[96]

SERMON: 1 PETER 1:3 [1/2]

A living hope

'Blessed be the God and Father of our Lord Jesus Christ, which according to his abundant mercy hath begotten us again unto a lively hope by the resurrection of Jesus Christ from the dead.' 1 Peter 1:3
SUGGESTED FURTHER READING: John 14:15–31

The knowledge and appearance: *a lively* or *a living hope*, or enlivening. They are heirs, but at present under age and therefore under restraint, but they know what they are born to. A king's son while very young has but faint thoughts of his state and rank, but as he grows up, and the nearer he comes to possession, his views enlarge. So believers grow in hope. From the first there is a pleasure to know what they are born into. This hope is *lively*, the object great, the ground sure, being the promise of God and the resurrection of Christ, who has said, *Because I live, ye shall live also* [John 14:19]. It is *living hope* because it springs from a living faith—and it is *enlivening*, comforting and supporting them under all the griefs and troubles of life (1 Corinthians 15:19). What could we do without it?

The inheritance:

(i) incorruptible, cannot waste or come to nothing. The soul is immortal and must be miserable except its portion was enduring.

(ii) undefiled, uncrossed with trouble, disappointment, temptation and sin.

(iii) unfading. A flower is the emblem of all worldly good—if it looks fair it is but for a season, and soon withers. Such are our pleasures. They always end in weariness and if not plucked from us fade of themselves. But not so hereafter. O for a manifestation of the Spirit, that we may receive an impression of this glory that shall be revealed.

FOR MEDITATION: The frame of mind to which these thoughts should raise us:

(i) Praise to *the God and Father of our Lord Jesus Christ*—in the Old Testament, the God of Abraham, Isaac and Jacob; to us, *the God and Father of our Lord Jesus Christ*, and thus he is *our* God and Father. This is the language of faith, love, trust and joy.

(ii) Praise to Jesus by whom we have access to God. We had continued strangers if he had not brought us nigh.

SERMON: 1 PETER 1:3 [2/2]

Legal fears and gospel hopes

'And the Spirit and the bride say, Come. And let him that heareth say, Come. And let him that is athirst come. And whosoever will, let him take the water of life freely.' Revelation 22:17
SUGGESTED FURTHER READING: Romans 15:1–13

The manner in which the Word of God addresses our consciences affords a proof that it is indeed from him who knows our frame. Hope and fear are the main principles of our conduct. And what so worthy of our fear as the terrors of the Lord? His justice, power, holiness, his hatred of sin, and the wrath that hangs over sinners, is therefore set forth in lively colours that we may be stirred up to flee for refuge to Jesus. But alas in vain, unless he is pleased to accompany the letter of the word with the operation of the Spirit—then the sinner hears and trembles and can no longer put the thoughts away, but cries out with earnestness, 'Alas! *What must I do to be saved?'* [Acts 16:30]. As the law is designed to awaken our fears, so the gospel is sweetly suited to engage our hopes. How glorious are the revelations there made of the Lord Jesus Christ—the riches of his grace, and the happiness of the eternal world—to a believing soul. In comparison with these, everything else appears but loss and dung. This prospect enlivens the soul to tread upon every difficulty and to press on to the prize. When faith obtains a view of that which is within the veil, hard things become easy and bitter things sweet. With respect to all that stands in the way it says, 'None of these things move me.' But it is seldom thus at the first setting out. Faith in the beginning is small as a grain of mustard, weak as a bruised reed. A sight of sin, the workings of unbelief, the temptations of Satan, unite to discourage the sensitive sinner. Thus it is, thus the Lord knew it would be. And therefore he has provided the most tender, endearing and repeated invitations. He says: Matthew 11:28; John 6:37; Isaiah 1:18; and in many other places to the same effect.

FOR MEDITATION:

A Word from JESUS calms the sea,	'Upon my promise rest thy hope,
The stormy wind controls;	And keep my love in view;
And gives repose and liberty	I stand engaged to hold thee up,
To tempest-tossed souls.	And guide thee safely through.'97

SERMON: REVELATION 22:17 [1/6] [EASTER MONDAY EVENING]

The Spirit says, Come

'And the Spirit and the bride say, Come. And let him that heareth say, Come. And let him that is athirst come. And whosoever will, let him take the water of life freely.' Revelation 22:17

SUGGESTED FURTHER READING: Romans 8:5–27

I shall take the words in the order they lie. Here is a joint invitation: *the Spirit and the bride say, Come.*

The Spirit: the Holy Spirit that searcheth the deep things of God and reveals his mind to men—the Spirit whose office it is to glorify Jesus. Here then is a sufficient warrant for poor sinners. Why are you poring upon yourselves, doubting whether such as you have any ground of hope, when the Spirit himself says, *Come?* Do you think he speaks to mock you? Indeed if you know nothing of God but by the law, you might expect and fear he would rather say, Depart, but now it is *Come.* For:

(i) Christ has died. Justice is satisfied.

(ii) Christ is pleading—he presents his own blood and is accepted. Therefore the Spirit assures us that God is reconciled and bids us, *Come.*

FOR MEDITATION: The Spirit is our prompter, that stirs up our hearts to lay hold of the golden opportunity. Our hearts are dull and backward to pray but when the Spirit shows us a glimpse of the things of Christ, of the glories of heaven, of the peace, honour and happiness of the Lord's people, this quickens us. How forgetful are we, but the promise is fulfilled. We often approach the throne of grace, dumb, and are unwilling to go because we think we have nothing to say—rather dragged by conscience than drawn by love. Yet when at length we try to begin, how sweetly is one want, promise, blessing, after another, brought to our minds so that at last we are as loath to leave off as we were at first to begin.[98]

Sermon on Romans 8:26, *The Searcher of Hearts*

The bride says, Come

'And the Spirit and the bride say, Come. And let him that heareth say, Come. And let him that is athirst come. And whosoever will, let him take the water of life freely.' Revelation 22:17
SUGGESTED FURTHER READING: Revelation 14:1–7

The bride, that is, the church (Ephesians 5:25): the 'church triumphant' and the 'church militant'—a double family. Both echo to the Spirit's call and say, *Come*.

The church triumphant are nearer us perhaps than we are aware. Those who have escaped from this tempestuous world and are safe before the throne, have a regard for their brethren below, and most probably a knowledge of what passes here. We are told there is joy in heaven over a sinner that repenteth. They say, '*Come*, do not cleave to that poor earth, but raise your thoughts and prepare to follow us upwards. O could you see and know where we are and how we live, surely you would come. *Come*, be not afraid of the King, we have found him merciful. Distrust not his promises, we have found them all fulfilled. We were once as you are, sinful, distressed and almost despairing, but we overcame by the blood of the Lamb, and so shall you. Therefore, *Come*.'

John Newton to William Wilberforce, 30 March 1797:
Yes Sir! I trust you and I shall soon join in their songs, and share in their joys without abatement, interruption or end! And may we not believe that it will be some addition to our happiness, to meet with those whom we loved, with whom we took sweet counsel, and went to the house of God in company? Surely I shall not see my late, dear and honoured friend Mr Thornton without peculiar emotions of gratitude and joy! Shall I not be glad to thank your kind aunt, for all the kindness she showed me when she was below? There too I hope to meet my dear Mary and Eliza, and many more. Perhaps this paper could not contain the names of all who were once dear to me upon earth, and are now happy in heaven![99]

FOR MEDITATION: Oh, for more faith, to break through the veil, and obtain a clearer and more affecting realizing view of the glories of the unseen world! To behold the Lamb upon the throne, to hearken to the songs of the harpers, to contemplate the immense multitude who are already made more than conquerors through him who loved them![100]

SERMON: REVELATION 22:17 [3/6] [EASTER MONDAY EVENING]

Those who hear say, Come

'And the Spirit and the bride say, Come. And let him that heareth say, Come. And let him that is athirst come. And whosoever will, let him take the water of life freely.' Revelation 22:17
SUGGESTED FURTHER READING: 1 Chronicles 29:10–20

The church militant: the church on earth. Though they have not yet fully attained, yet they have known enough of the Lord to invite others to taste and see. And this is the desire of every gracious heart, that many may partake of the same grace. The world unjustly calls them uncharitable. None are or can be truly charitable but they. Their eyes are spared to see sin and its consequences and when they get a little hope for themselves, they soon look round and think, O that my parents, children, friends and neighbours might know it too. How do they pity sinners. And when the Lord comforts them they long to tell. Nay, they cannot wholly keep silence, though they often get little thanks for their pains. And indeed this is their duty, for so it is said.

Let him that heareth say, *Come*. This, however, means the understanding ear—so the word signifies, as in John 6:60 [*This is an hard saying; who can hear it?*]. Those who know not for themselves, *cannot* recommend it to others. We are sure, however, they will not. Perhaps there are some now hearing, who, instead of joining with the Spirit and bride, fight against them and say, 'Keep away.' You come perhaps to listen if you can find something amiss, or to misrepresent, that you may confirm others in their prejudices against the truth.[101] You may jest at what you hear now, but you will not jest in the day when God shall require your soul.

FOR MEDITATION: But you that hear and understand, remember you are bid to repeat the invitation and say, *Come*. Has the Lord opened eyes and cast out the evil spirits? Go then, and upon every fair occasion be ready to commend him to others—and especially seek out and comfort afflicted souls.

SERMON: REVELATION 22:17 [4/6] [EASTER MONDAY EVENING]

The thirsty come

'*And the Spirit and the bride say, Come. And let him that heareth say, Come. And let him that is athirst come. And whosoever will, let him take the water of life freely.*' *Revelation 22:17*
SUGGESTED FURTHER READING: Isaiah 55:1–5

The persons called: *him that is athirst.* In a sense, this includes *all*, and I think the Word of God warrants such a general call (Isaiah 55:1–2). You that are thirsting after happiness and seeking it where it is not to be found, in creature comforts and sinful pleasures, spending your money for that which is not bread, this Spirit calls on you to come for the Bread of Life. The pearl of great price is set before you. The water of life is pointed out to you. *Come*, there is room enough and water enough. If you never thought of it before, begin now. What? No desire after the water of life? Alas, if you put it from you, you will perish. If you despise this invitation it will lie heavily upon your conscience hereafter. What will you say to the Lord of the feast? That you never heard of it? That you were not warned? I take that poor excuse from you now. I call upon everyone now in the Lord's presence—I adjure you by his cross and passion that you seek him for the water of life. But alas, I cannot persuade you or turn your hearts. Lord, put forth thy power.

The words, I hope, will be welcome to awakened souls. Do you not thirst, and for these very things which the Lord has promised? You know the nature of thirst is that nothing can assuage it but drink. Are your desires thus? Then you are called, as it were, by name. As sure as there is a water of life, so sure you have a right to it.

FOR MEDITATION: See the Lord says whosoever *will.* Are you *willing?* Then here is no exception of persons. Whatever you have been in time past, no matter, if you are now willing. Surely you would not have been so, had not the Lord made you. He says *freely.* You are spiritually poor, and if it was to be bought you must go without, for you have nothing to pay. But did you ever pay for the rain? Or sunshine? No, these blessings are bestowed freely, bountifully. All the wealth in the world could not purchase them, but they come without money and without price. Just so free is gospel grace to every seeking soul.

Go with a pail

'And the Spirit and the bride say, Come. And let him that heareth say, Come. And let him that is athirst come. And whosoever will, let him take the water of life freely.' Revelation 22:17
SUGGESTED FURTHER READING: Ezekiel 47:1–12

What they are called to: *water* of life. This, no doubt, stands for the communication of every grace from Jesus Christ. He is the fountain, John 7:37–39. It is compared to water, for it is plenty. There is abundance of grace—a fountain, a river, an ocean (Isaiah 44:3). Water is used for cleansing, refreshing, as in Ezekiel 36:25 and Isaiah 41:17. Freeness—water is open to all. If people beg wine they take a small vessel, but if they ask for water they go with a pail. So you need not straiten yourself, but open your mouth wide.

It is water *of life*. It makes alive (Ezekiel 47:9), it keeps alive, it is a pledge of life everlasting (John 4:14).

Are these things so? Then once more, sinners, take heed how you refuse—it is at the peril of your souls. If you will stand out, a time will come when you will want a drop of water to cool your tongues. You are athirst—what more can you want? The fountain is pointed out and you are invited. Do you say as the woman in John 4:11? The ordinances are buckets with which you shall draw water out of the wells of salvation (Isaiah 12:3). The Lord shall give you refreshing draughts in prayer.

FOR MEDITATION: But remember, when you have drunk you must drink again. Do not live upon present tastes, but rejoice that the fountain is made over to you. Believers, let us keep close to this fountain. O let it not be said of us as in Jeremiah 2:13 [*For my people have committed two evils; they have forsaken me the fountain of living waters, and hewed them out cisterns, broken cisterns, that can hold no water*]. As you have received Christ Jesus, so walk in him—your first beginnings and your increase must be in the same way. Thus you shall go on from strength to strength and at last be brought to the fountainhead, where you shall thirst no more.

Although ...

'Although my house be not so with God; yet he hath made with me an everlasting covenant, ordered in all things, and sure: for this is all my salvation, and all my desire, although he make it not to grow.'
2 *Samuel 23:5*
SUGGESTED FURTHER READING: 2 Samuel 23:1–5

The beginning of this chapter is commended to our notice as the last words of David—the last words of a man of eminent spirituality, so as to receive the title of 'the man after God's own heart' [Acts 13:22], and of one who had been long and variously exercised. He had been in troubles from his youth—sometimes so pressed that he almost despaired—yet always seasonably supported. In this verse he is speaking of the two points which, respecting his personal concern, lay nearest his heart—his family and his soul. The truths he here contemplates and the manner of his expression afford room for more discourses than one. At present, and by way of introduction to what I may offer hereafter from the passage, I shall endeavour to give you a brief exposition upon the word and to raise a few observations for general use. May the Lord command his blessing.

Although. From this word and the case referred, compared with the general case of Scripture, I would observe that the people of God, however situated[102] or circumstanced, have each their trials. David was a child, a prophet, of God. He was a warrior and a king. He had great riches and great honours. But still he had an '*although*'.

Let this encourage some. Why do you complain as though none were exercised like yourself (1 Peter 5:9)? Let it teach others what to expect. You may possibly for a little while think yourselves well in all points—but whether believers or not, you will find a cross. Pray that trials may be sanctified. Escape them you cannot.

FOR MEDITATION: 'Although he was a son, he learned obedience from what he suffered, and, once made perfect, he became the source of eternal salvation for all who obey him' (Hebrews 5:8–9, NIV).

Spiritual concern for our family

'Although my house be not so with God; yet he hath made with me an everlasting covenant, ordered in all things, and sure: for this is all my salvation, and all my desire, although he make it not to grow.'
2 Samuel 23:5
SUGGESTED FURTHER READING: 1 John 3:1–14

My house. David was prosperous in many respects, but afflicted in his family. One son slain by another, and he that murdered his brother proved a rebel and traitor to his father. He had many children, but few that he could hope were the Lord's children. His sorrow on this account found a place even in his last words. Observe hence: a good man longs for the spiritual welfare of his children and family. Indeed those who have tasted that the Lord is gracious, wish that all around them were partakers of the same mercy, but charity will, in this sense at least, begin at home. I think those of you who have dear relatives may try yourselves by this test. Do you travail, as it were, in birth for those who are dear to you? It is a good sign, and if your desires prompt you to the use of every probable and appointed means, and if a failing of success with them gives you a deep, perceptive concern, and excites your prayers to God for them yet more earnestly, be not discouraged, you may yet have the desire of your hearts. But remember, grace does not run in the blood. David had Amnon and Absalom. Manasseh, who was brought up under good Hezekiah, was wicked beyond all that were before him. Nothing but the power of God can change the heart. Therefore:
    (i) Beware of trusting to outward privileges (Matthew 3:9).
    (ii) Be not discouraged if you have not had them in early life. They could not have saved you of themselves, and if you seek the Lord Jesus he can save you without them.

FOR MEDITATION: A letter from Brother Harry yesterday ... May it be given me to pray earnestly for him. If his disappointments are sanctified to lead him to the one thing needful, they will be blessings, and the greatest success upon other terms would be a curse.[103]

Diary, 9 September 1773

'Just so' with God

'Although my house be not so with God; yet he hath made with me an everlasting covenant, ordered in all things, and sure: for this is all my salvation, and all my desire, although he make it not to grow.'
2 *Samuel* 23:5
SUGGESTED FURTHER READING: Philippians 3:1–11

Not so with God. David's children were something in the sight of men: king's sons and honourable. But alas, says he, what will this avail, unless they are precious in the Lord's sight? We are all 'just so' and no otherwise than as we are with God. His judgement is right. Those whom he favours are happy in a cottage. All others are and will be miserable though they may be rich and honourable in the sight of the world. Examine, my dear friends, do you truly think so? Do you regard his loving kindness as better than life, and account all things but loss and dung in comparison with Christ? [Philippians 3:8]. If not, unless the Lord change your mind, how miserably will you be disappointed when the things you love must leave you and you be constrained to appear before God? Here is a rule for parents: do you wish your children well? Then remember to seek for them the kingdom of God and his righteousness in the first place. Endeavour to impress them with a sense of the importance of eternal things. Pray for their souls. If you neglect this and only put them in a way and set them an example of heaping up wealth, you are not their friends but their enemies.

FOR MEDITATION: *And give unto Solomon my son a perfect heart.*
1 Chronicles 29:19.
[When Newton was just a toddler, his mother's pastor, David Jennings, challenged the parents in his church from the above prayer of David's: 'Did you ever pray this prayer for your children in good earnest? Lord give them a perfect heart. What pains have you taken to instruct and teach them the good ways of holiness? ... O! be earnest and importunate with God, be daily intercessors with him for the souls of your dear children. Beg it of him, who is the God of grace, that he would give your children a perfect heart.' Newton recalled his mother praying for him with tears.[104]]

Yet …

'Although my house be not so with God; yet he hath made with me an everlasting covenant, ordered in all things, and sure: for this is all my salvation, and all my desire, although he make it not to grow.'
2 *Samuel* 23:5
SUGGESTED FURTHER READING: Jeremiah 31:31–34

Yet he hath made. As every believer has an *although*, so likewise a *yet* to balance it. Many are the comforts provided for the children of God, but none like the consideration of this covenant. Observe the parts:

(i) *a covenant*: an engagement in which the great God condescends to bind himself to performance.

(ii) *everlasting*: from everlasting in its glorious contrivance, to everlasting in its blessed effects.

(iii) *ordered*: prepared, disposed. The Lord foresaw whatever would be wanted and has provided accordingly. A fullness of grace, a supply for every want, is treasured up in this blessed covenant, and in a way wonderfully suited for the encouragement and consolation of unworthy sinners.

(iv) *sure*: not suspended upon uncertain conditions, but established with and in Christ, confirmed by promises, by oath and by blood.

FOR MEDITATION:

Encouraged by thy word
Of promise to the poor;
Behold, a beggar, LORD,
Waits at thy mercy's door!
No hand, no heart, O LORD, but thine,
Can help or pity wants like mine.

Thy thoughts, thou only wise!
Our thoughts and ways transcend,
Far as the arched skies
Above the earth extend:
Such pleas as mine men would not bear,
But God receives a beggar's prayer.[105]

A hardened heart

'And when the woman saw that the tree was good for food, and that it was pleasant to the eyes, and a tree to be desired to make one wise, she took of the fruit thereof, and did eat, and gave also unto her husband with her; and he did eat.' Genesis 3:6
SUGGESTED FURTHER READING: 1 John 2:3–17

So true is that word in James 1:15: *Then when lust hath conceived, it bringeth forth sin: and sin, when it is finished, bringeth forth death.* The serpent had so entirely perverted the woman's judgement and hardened her heart that nothing now appeared so desirable as what God had expressly forbid. We have her motives. In the view we had of this fruit, we may see the leading principles by which sin has always deceived, which the Apostle enumerates as the chief branches of the spirit of this world (1 John 2:16).

(i) *It was pleasant to the eye.* Great reason we have to make David's prayer (Psalm 119:17) and with Job to make a covenant with our eyes [Job 31:1], for they are the inlet of many temptations. In many countries there are still pleasant trees that bear poisonous fruit. Had not the eye of her mind been blinded, she had not made this judgement.

(ii) And *good for food.* If she had been starving, this might have seemed the more plausible, but she had abundance and variety of what was really good and liberty to use it. Because it looked pleasant she thought it good, for she had not tried; the serpent told her so, or perhaps she saw him eat it.

(iii) *Desirable to make one wise.* Besides the gratification of her sensual appetites, she was drawn away by the pride of her heart and this perhaps was the chief snare. The fruit of other trees was probably as pleasant, and she knew was good for food, but none but this flattered her ambition to be raised higher in rank and knowledge.

FOR MEDITATION: Observe: when the heart is resolved upon sin, every pretence and presumption becomes a strong argument for compliance. When Satan has gained the will and made us careless of God's command and authority, his work is done. The grossest temptations will then be welcome. How else could sinners think there was something good and desirable in drunkenness, uncleanness, blasphemy and other vile abominations which he urges them to do?

SERMON SERIES: GENESIS, NO. 8 [1/3], GENESIS 3:6–7

Guilty!

'And when the woman saw that the tree was good for food, and that it was pleasant to the eyes, and a tree to be desired to make one wise, she took of the fruit thereof, and did eat, and gave also unto her husband with her; and he did eat.' Genesis 3:6
SUGGESTED FURTHER READING: 2 Timothy 2:15–3:9

The facts. Eve completed the transgression by actually eating the fruit, in a daring spirit, despising the threatening of the God who made her. *She gave to her husband and he did eat.* It should seem Adam was absent at first, but now sin had hardened her heart, she sought him out to make him partner in her iniquity. I suppose she used some arguments, because the Lord charges Adam not only with taking the fruit from her hand, but with hearkening to her voice. As she had eaten and was yet alive, she might, from that circumstance, tempt him to doubt and disbelieve the threatening as she had done before him. Observe:

(i) When Satan has prevailed upon any to sin, he will not suffer them to sin alone, but employs them as instruments to tempt others. Many of you know this but too well. It is a small thing for you to break God's commands yourself, unless you can seduce others. When Adam came to consider what he had done, his answer to the Lord intimates that he wished he had never seen the face of Eve. O what a miserable greeting will those have in the other world who have helped to ruin each other in this. How will they revile and charge and curse each other!

(ii) The patience of God which ought to lead sinners to repentance, is a means of hardening them (Ecclesiastes 8:11). If Adam had found Eve struck dead upon the spot for eating the fruit, it would have terrified him from a compliance. But now her impunity made him bold.

FOR MEDITATION: I met with a young man who had formerly been a midshipman on board the *Harwich* ... I gave him a plain account of the manner and reason of my change, and used every argument to persuade him to relinquish his infidel schemes. He would remind me that I was the first person who had given him an idea of his liberty. He was exceedingly profane, and grew worse and worse. I saw in him a most lively picture of what I had once been. He died convinced but not changed.[106] *Narrative*, 1764, Letter 13.

Full of shame

'And the eyes of them both were opened, and they knew that they were naked; and they sewed fig leaves together, and made themselves aprons.'
Genesis 3:7
SUGGESTED FURTHER READING: Psalm 25:1–22

The immediate consequences for Adam and Eve were:

(i) *Their eyes were opened.* Satan had blinded them but, when the Lord pleased, they came to themselves; they knew now the difference between good and evil. The full meaning of these expressions I am not able to explain. They were naked before, but now they were sensible of such a change in their state, that they were ashamed of themselves.

(ii) They made a covering of *fig leaves.* An emblem of the poor expedients of sinners, to supply their own wants, to hide their own shame and to satisfy their consciences by their own performances.

Here was the first sin—which indeed contained all other sins in one—idolatry, rebellion, robbery and murder—yet they found mercy. Here is encouragement to convinced souls—the Lord Christ who was revealed to them as the Seed who should break the serpent's head is preached amongst you. Say not your sin is great and therefore no hope—so was Adam's, but where sin abounded, grace has much more abounded.

FOR MEDITATION:

O, speak that gracious word again,
And cheer my drooping heart!
No voice but thine can soothe my pain,
Or bid my fears depart.

Oh then let saints and angels join,
And help me to proclaim,
The grace that healed a breach like mine,
And put my foes to shame!

And canst thou still vouchsafe to own
A wretch so vile as I?
And may I still approach thy throne,
And Abba, Father, cry?

Dear LORD I wonder and adore,
Thy grace is all divine;
Oh keep me, that I sin no more
Against such love as thine![107]

SERMON SERIES: GENESIS, NO. 8 [3/3], GENESIS 3:6–7

Jesus, our gracious Mediator

'… Yet *he hath made with me an everlasting covenant* …' *2 Samuel 23:5*
SUGGESTED FURTHER READING: 1 Timothy 2:5–6

This *covenant* of grace was established with and in our Lord Jesus Christ for the recovery and salvation of all that should believe in his name. The Scripture speaks of transactions between the Father and the Son before the foundation of the world. If we understand it of the divine persons in the Trinity, it intends a mutual consent that the work of our redemption should be brought about in such a way. But if we understand it of the God–man Christ Jesus, the Word made flesh, appearing in our nature and cause, we may say that the covenant of grace to us was to him a covenant of works, strictly speaking. He was the Mediator between God and sinners. He engaged for men to God and for God to men. He engaged to God on the behalf of men, to vindicate the honour of his broken law by his voluntary obedience unto death, fulfilling all the commands of God in his own person and making atonement for transgression with his own blood. He received authority on the behalf of God, to bring many sons to glory, even all who should embrace the message of his love and put their trust under the shadow of his wings (John 12:30; Isaiah 53:11). He is our surety, on whom our debt was charged, and, having paid it, he proclaims a free discharge to every weary, wounded soul. When their hearts are pricked with a sense of those sins which caused his death, he, like another, Joseph, says by his gospel, 'Let it not grieve you that your sins brought sorrow and death upon me—for so God appointed, and so I readily engaged to save your lives and to preserve your souls from death.' Jesus is the sum and substance of the *everlasting covenant*.

FOR MEDITATION:

Thus dragged by my conscience , I came,
And laden with guilt, to the Lord;
Surrounded with terror and shame,
Unable to answer a word.

But oh! what surprise when he spoke,
While tenderness beamed in his face;
My heart then to pieces was broke,
O'erwhelmed and confounded by grace:

'Poor sinner, I know thee full well, By thee I was sold and was slain;
But I died to redeem thee from hell, And raise thee to glory to reign.'[108]

Fixed on an immovable rock

'Although my house be not so with God; yet he hath made with me an everlasting covenant, ordered in all things, and sure: for this is all my salvation, and all my desire, although he make it not to grow.'
2 Samuel 23:5
SUGGESTED FURTHER READING: Psalm 71:1–24

Some, I doubt not, have their desires to this covenant, but guilt and fear keep them. Satan says as Jehu [2 Kings 9:18], '*What hast thou to do with peace?* If the covenant blessings were for you, the Lord would not let you wait so long without comfort.' O resist that enemy. Put yourself into the hands of Jesus; his compassions are infinite, and he shall exalt you in due time. Did you ever hear of any who trusted in him and perished? How could you ever have had a desire towards him unless he had put it into your hearts?

Believers—rejoice in this covenant. Walk about this Sion,[109] consider her foundations and all the towers thereof and mark well the bulwark. See how it is fixed upon an immovable rock, guarded by almighty power, encompassed with infinite love, and enriched with all desirable blessings, and then with a holy indifference to all the trials of the present hour, rejoice and say: *Although my house be not so with God, yet he has made with me an everlasting covenant, ordered and sure....*

FOR MEDITATION: [for Easter Sunday 16 April 1775]
Glorious things of thee are spoken,
Zion, city of our GOD!
He, whose word cannot be broken,
Formed thee for his own abode:
On the rock of ages founded,
What can shake thy sure repose?
With salvation's walls surrounded
Thou may'st smile at all thy foes.[110]

His surpassing glory

'*For thus saith the* LORD *of hosts; Yet once, it is a little while, and I will shake the heavens, and the earth, and the sea, and the dry land; And I will shake all nations, and the desire of all nations shall come: and I will fill this house with glory, saith the* LORD *of hosts.' Haggai 2:6–7*
SUGGESTED FURTHER READING: Ezra 3:10–13

The Jews, on their return from the captivity, met with many discouragements in their attempts to rebuild the temple—not only from the opposition and arts of their enemies, who prevailed for a time to compel them to desist from their work, but from the comparison which some of the old men were led to make between the magnificence of the first temple and the expectation they formed of the utmost they should be able to perform in the building of the second (verse 3 compared with Ezra 3:12–13). In these circumstances the prophets Haggai and Zechariah were sent to animate the people by a promise that, mean and poor as the second temple might appear compared with the first, the glory of the latter house should be greater than that of the former. Had this depended upon a profusion of silver and gold, the Lord could have provided it. But the glory spoken of was of a different kind and would be abundantly verified by the personal appearance of the Messiah. His presence in the second temple would confer honour and glory upon it far surpassing the external pomp of the temple of Solomon, and would be attended with greater consequences than when he appeared on Mount Sinai. Then he only shook the earth, but under the latter temple he would shake the heavens and the earth, the sea and the dry land, to introduce the Messiah who should thus fill the house with his glory.

FOR MEDITATION: 'I did not see a temple in the city, because the Lord God Almighty and the Lamb are its temple. The city does not need the sun or the moon to shine on it, for the glory of God gives it light, and the Lamb is its lamp' (Revelation 21:22–23, NIV).

On the very brink of eternal ruin!

'And they heard the voice of the LORD *God walking in the garden in the cool of the day: and Adam and his wife hid themselves from the presence of the* LORD *God amongst the trees of the garden. And the* LORD *God called unto Adam, and said unto him, Where art thou?' Genesis 3:8–9*
SUGGESTED FURTHER READING: Joel 2:12–17

Though sin through its deceitfulness may appear pleasing in the commission, in the end it bites like a serpent. Guilt, shame and fear had seized our first parents, but what was past could not be recalled or undone.

(i) The Lord's appearance. The expression is remarkable—*the voice of the* LORD *God walking.* Some think the word *walking* agrees with *voice.* They heard the *voice* or the *word* of the Lord, that is, he whose glorious and essential name is the Word of God. He who in the fullness of time was to put away their sin by the sacrifice of himself, was now coming to deal with them, not in judgement but in mercy.

(ii) The effect on them. They *hid themselves.* How great a change! Before, no doubt, his visits were welcome, but now they trembled, because they had sinned. They no longer deserved the knowledge of God. Thus it is with all their posterity. Instead of gaining an increase of knowledge, sin had made them so stupid that they thought to hide themselves from an all-seeing eye—at least it intimates the greatness of their terror. Thus when the Lord visits a sinner's conscience, how fain would he hide, and seek a refuge in lies: 'I am not so bad as others' or, 'I will be better' and so on.

But the Lord calls, Adam *where art thou?* Why not joyful at my approach as formerly? Thus he speaks, not for information, but to bring them forth and to bring them to a confession. *Where art thou?* Alas, how fallen! *Where art thou,* sinner? Alas, under the curse of the law, in a state of enmity with God and, of course (if mercy prevent not) upon the very brink of eternal ruin.

FOR MEDITATION: I hardly feel any stronger proof of remaining depravity than in my having so faint a sense of the Amazing Grace that snatched me from ruin, that pardoned such enormous sins, preserved my life when I stood upon the brink of eternity and could only be preserved by miracle, and changed a disposition which seemed so incurably obstinate and given up to horrid wickedness. Well may I say, 'O to grace how great a debtor'![111]

Trembling under God's righteous law

'And the LORD God called unto Adam, and said unto him, Where art thou? And he said, I heard thy voice in the garden, and I was afraid, because I was naked; and I hid myself. And he said, Who told thee that thou wast naked? Hast thou eaten of the tree, whereof I commanded thee that thou shouldest not eat? And the man said, The woman whom thou gavest to be with me, she gave me of the tree, and I did eat. ...And the woman said, The serpent beguiled me, and I did eat.' Genesis 3:9–13
SUGGESTED FURTHER READING: Psalm 51:1–8

At length they are constrained to appear. Adam confesses his fear, but not his sin. He was stubborn, but the Lord followed him closer. Hast thou—is it possible?—hast thou made light of my command? He is forced to own it, but still would find excuse. He lays the fault upon the woman and in effect upon the Lord himself for giving him such an ensnaring companion. The woman in her turn tries to remove the blame to the serpent. Hitherto the Lord had not revealed his gracious purpose of forgiveness—but they stood trembling under the convictions of having broken his righteous law. From hence we may observe that legal convictions will never humble the sinner's heart to a true and gracious repentance for sin. Nothing that passed as yet reveals the frame of Adam's mind to have been better than that of the serpent himself. I mention this for the sake of some who are ready to question whether they are right because they have not been in such great terrors as some others. If you felt the terrors of Judas, they could not effect one gracious desire. Again, whatever uneasiness people may sometimes feel on account of sin, if their hearts are not humbled under a sense of its vileness, we cannot be sure that it is the effect of a good work upon their hearts.

FOR MEDITATION: The calling is wrought by the Spirit of God and it lays hold of the spirit of the sinner. It is something more than that alarm and uneasiness which is often felt while the sound of the preacher's voice is in the ear and from which people quickly recover as soon as they get into the open air. It is more than a half reformation from a few gross sins. It is the voice of God that brings the law to the conscience and the conscience to the bar, that cuts off every plea for hope and brings the soul into the state of a trembling prisoner, till a way of escape is opened by the knowledge of Christ.[112]

SERMON SERIES: GENESIS, NO. 9 [2/3], GENESIS 3:8–13

Black despair turned to hope

'I was afraid, because I was naked; and I hid myself.' Genesis 3:10
SUGGESTED FURTHER READING: Psalm 51:9–19

Observe that a sinner that feels the condemning power of the law would never expect or even ask for mercy, if the Lord did not first reveal that there is forgiveness with him. A true law work without any gospel light would shut the soul up in black despair.
Narrative, 10 March 1748:
… almost every passing wave breaking over my head … Indeed I expected that every time the vessel descended in the sea, she would rise no more; and though I dreaded death now, and my heart foreboded the worst, if the Scriptures, which I had long since opposed, were indeed true; yet still I was but half-convinced, and remained for a space of time in a sullen frame, a mixture of despair and impatience. I thought if the Christian religion were true, I could not be forgiven; and was therefore expecting, and almost at times wishing, to know the worst of it… Thus, as I have said, I waited with fear and impatience to receive my inevitable doom.[113]

Therefore, we may be sure that those who venture upon general and unscriptural notions of mercy, never truly knew what the word *sin* means, considered as an offence against the majesty and holiness of God. When a soul has had such a conviction and yet, in the midst of many fears and faintings, continues waiting and hoping for salvation by Jesus, cannot seek it in any other, cannot give over seeking it in him, there is certainly a degree of faith.
Narrative, 10 March 1748:
I now began to think of that Jesus whom I had so often derided: I recollected the particulars of his life, and of his death—a death for sins not his own, but, as I remembered, for the sake of those who in their distress should put their trust in him. … He was pleased to show me at that time, the absolute necessity of some expedient to interpose between a righteous God and a sinful soul. Upon the gospel-scheme I saw at least a peradventure of hope, but on every other side I was surrounded with black unfathomable despair.

FOR MEDITATION: O bless him for Christ—that ever that precious name sounded in your ears.

SERMON SERIES: GENESIS, NO. 9 [3/3], GENESIS 3:8–13

An everlasting covenant

'*Although my house be not so with God; yet he hath made with me an everlasting covenant, ordered in all things, and sure: for this is all my salvation, and all my desire, although he make it not to grow.*'
2 *Samuel* 23:5
SUGGESTED FURTHER READING: Revelation 1:12–18

Having spoken of the covenant in general, I now come to speak particularly of its properties. It is *everlasting*, *ordered* and *sure*. Each of these would bear a whole discourse but I shall endeavour to comprise them all in one.

Everlasting. This in two senses:

(i) *From* everlasting. It is not a new and hasty contrivance, but was established in the counsels of God from before the foundation of the world (Titus 1:2). Christ as the head of the covenant was set up from everlasting (Proverbs 8:23). And from hence we may prove that there never was but one true religion since the fall of Adam, though under various dispensations (see Hebrews 11), and that salvation is all of grace.

(ii) *To* everlasting. It is unchangeable. It is inexhaustible. It has been the refuge of the people of God in all ages. It is so to us, and thousands yet unborn shall rejoice in it when we are gone off the stage of this life. It is not the weaker for all the assaults that have been made against it, it is not the poorer for all the supplies that have been derived from it, but, like its great Author, is *the same yesterday, today and for ever* [Hebrews 13:8]. It will be still the same to eternity.

FOR MEDITATION:

The promised land of peace
Faith keeps in constant view;
How different from the wilderness
We now are passing through!

Here griefs, and cares, and pains,
And fears, distress us sore;
But there eternal pleasure reigns,
And we shall weep no more.

Here often from our eyes
Clouds hide the light divine;
There we shall have unclouded skies,
Our Sun will always shine.

LORD pardon our complaints,
We follow at thy call;
The joy, prepared for suffering saints,
Will make amends for all.[114]

Ordered and sure

'Although my house be not so with God; yet he hath made with me an everlasting covenant, ordered in all things, and sure: for this is all my salvation, and all my desire, although he make it not to grow.'
2 Samuel 23:5
SUGGESTED FURTHER READING: Psalm 111:1–10

Ordered in all things. The word signifies disposed, suited, provided, in such a manner as to answer every case and necessity that should arise. O this is a comfortable thought when the soul is enabled to look round. See how everything in this covenant is exactly fitted to its state (1 Corinthians 1:30). The Lord knew what would be wanted and has provided accordingly (1 Timothy 4:8). The poor awakened soul is distressed and terrified by the guilt of sin, but here is pardon—free pardon—a pardon bought with blood. It is distressed by fears and unbelief which make it shrink back and say, 'For others it may be, but not for me.' But here are many, great, exceeding, precious promises. It sees itself all over wants, but the ordered covenant contains an infinite fullness. It is alarmed with numerous enemies, but when we look to the covenant, we see there are more with us than against us. There is a dreadful heart of unbelief tempting to depart from God, and when it is felt, the believer thinks, 'This enemy will be too hard for me at last.' 'Nay,' says the covenant, 'that cannot be. I will put my fear into thy heart.' Thus every objection and complaint being provided for and answered, the covenant is *sure*, or as the word is, *secured*—freed from any possibility of miscarrying. It is *sure* by the word of God (Psalm 111:5,9; Isaiah 54:10), by the oath of God (Psalm 110 [verse 4]; Hebrews 6:17), by the power of God (Deuteronomy 33:27), by the blood of Christ (Zechariah 9:11), by the intercession of Christ (Hebrews 12:24) and by the government of Christ (Matthew 28:18).

FOR MEDITATION: O what comfort does the consideration of this covenant afford! Hence you that desire to be established in faith and peace, meditate much on this subject. You will never get strength by poring only upon your own hearts. Let all examine (concerning your faith in Christ, if you are united to him) this covenant which is made in and with him. You may say of it, as David, 'He has made it *with me.*'

SERMON SERIES: 2 SAMUEL 23:5, NO. 3 [2/3]

All my salvation, all my desire

'Although my house be not so with God; yet he hath made with me an everlasting covenant, ordered in all things, and sure: for this is all my salvation, and all my desire, although he make it not to grow.'
2 Samuel 23:5.
SUGGESTED FURTHER READING: Revelation 21:1–7

Can you adopt David's words, *this is all my salvation, and all my desire?*

Is it *all your salvation?* Do you understand this way? Do you approve it? The whole of it? Is Christ precious to you? In all his offices? If so, the covenant is yours. If not, you are yet in covenant with death, under the covenant of the law, bound down with a curse.

Is it *all your desire?* Then you are waiting upon the Lord, you are weary of sin, you love his ordinances, you account all things loss and dung compared with the blessings of the covenant. Such shall not be disappointed. Although your house be not as you could wish, although you are not made to grow so fast as you are taught to pray for, yet here is comfort: the Lord has made *an everlasting covenant.* He has made it known to you, drawn your heart to approve and desire it. This is a sign you are surely interested in it. Can you, with respect to disappointment, see sufficient compensation if you could be able to say upon good grounds, *he hath made with me an everlasting covenant...?* Without his grace you could not have made this choice.

Fear not. You are in a good care. You have committed yourself to the Lord and none can snatch you out of his hands. Press on, read, pray, attend diligently on his means, and you shall know more and more of this covenant while you live, and ere long shall be put in possession of all its blessings in a better world. Amen.

FOR MEDITATION: Most gracious Lord, my all is in thy hands, my heart open to thee, my desires before thee. There is a liberty, a freedom, to which thou invitest thy people! O admit me to it and let me apply to thee as my best friend, counsellor and benefactor, and pour into thy gracious ear the incidents of the day and the reflections of my heart.[115]

Diary, 16 October, 1775

SERMON SERIES: 2 SAMUEL 23:5, NO. 3 [3/3]

A way of escape

'And I will put enmity between thee and the woman, and between thy seed and her seed; it shall bruise thy head, and thou shalt bruise his heel.'
Genesis 3:15
SUGGESTED FURTHER READING: Psalm 68:1–20

If I was to dwell upon every circumstance and expression in this chapter, it would confine me too long. I shall therefore chiefly insist upon this memorable verse in which the first and great promise of mercy and salvation to fallen man is contained. The curse of God fell heavily and absolutely upon Satan whose doom is couched in figurative expressions suitable to the figure of the serpent he assumed. Our first parents likewise received a sentence implying much misery, pain and labour in the present life, to terminate only with death. But in this verse, a way of escape is provided from the eternal death which their sin had justly deserved. In the words [we have] a promise of the Redeemer, a brief intimation of his sufferings and success, and these so expressed as to be applicable to all his people.

We have a promise—*the seed of the woman*. The Redeemer [is] thus spoken of to intimate that he should be truly a man made of a woman and partaker of our very nature (Galatians 4:4; Hebrews 2:14), and that his incarnation should be miraculous and extraordinary—made of a woman, but without a human father, by the agency of the Holy Spirit (Luke 1:35).

FOR MEDITATION:

Prepare a thankful song
To the Redeemer's name!
His praises should employ each tongue
And every heart inflame!

Upon the cross he died,
Our debt of sin to pay;
The blood and water from his side
Wash guilt and filth away.

He laid his glory by,
And dreadful pains endured;
That rebels, such as you and I,
From wrath might be secured.

And now he pleading stands
For us, before the throne;
And answers all the Law's demands,
With what himself hath done.

Though pressed, we will not yield, But shall prevail at length,
For JESUS is our sun and shield, Our righteousness and strength.[116]

SERMON SERIES: GENESIS, NO. 10 [1/4], GENESIS 3:15

Sin's guilt removed

'*And I will put enmity between thee and the woman, and between thy seed and her seed; it shall bruise thy head, and thou shalt bruise his heel.*'
Genesis 3:15
SUGGESTED FURTHER READING: Romans 6:1–14

The nature of the Redeemer's work is set forth by a conflict with the serpent and his seed, in which:

(i) Christ should be completely victorious, removing the guilt of sin, the curse of the law from his people; that he should destroy death and him that had the power of death (that is the devil). These great things he has already done. Sin is expiated—God is reconciled, death is disarmed of its sting and Satan is a vanquished enemy who can do nothing but by permission. And there is a day appointed which will openly solemnize this triumph and *bruise* this enemy finally under his feet.

(ii) He should conquer by suffering. Yet great as these were in the garden and upon the cross, his bloody agony and bloody death, only his *heel* was affected—his human nature and that life which he took on purpose that he might lay it down. His *head* was invulnerable; his divine nature and his life that he had in himself were out of the enemy's reach (Romans 6:9; Revelation 1:18).

FOR MEDITATION:

I saw one hanging on a tree,
In agonies and blood;
Who fixed his languid eyes on me,
As near his cross I stood.

Alas! I knew not what I did,
But now my tears are vain;
Where shall my trembling soul be hid?
For I the LORD have slain.

Sure, never till my latest breath,
Can I forget that look;
It seemed to charge me with his death,
Though not a word he spoke.

A second look he gave, which said,
'I freely all forgive;
This blood is for thy ransom paid,
I die, that thou may'st live.'

My conscience felt, and owned the guilt,
And plunged me in despair;
I saw my sins his blood had spilt,
And helped to nail him there.

Thus, while his death my sin displays,
In all its blackest hue;
(Such is the mystery of grace)
It seals my pardon too. [117]

Seeds of perpetual warfare

'And I will put enmity between thee and the woman, and between thy seed and her seed; it shall bruise thy head, and thou shalt bruise his heel.'
Genesis 3:15
SUGGESTED FURTHER READING: 1 Peter 1:3–12

The name of Christ includes both head and members in one mystical body (1 Corinthians 12:12). As all who believed in Christ are in him denominated as the *seed* of the woman and the *seed* of the promise, so the *seed* of the serpent includes all the wicked, according to John 8:44 and 1 John 3:8. There is an opposition, a war between these respective *seeds*—an irreconcilable war in which each party is supported and strengthened by its proper head. The carnal mind is enmity against God, his Christ, his truth and his people. And though the Lord's *seed* do not hate the persons of wicked men, yet his grace enables them to set their ways, practices and spirit at defiance, so that they will by no means make peace and league with them. In the course of this warfare they are made conformable to their Head. The serpent and his *seed* occasion them much trouble, sorrow and suffering and thus *bruise their heel*—but can do no more than wound them in their present concerns in this mortal state. And they, by his strength, finally *bruise his head*, overcome all assaults by his blood and the word of his testimony, and are made more than conquerors through him who has loved them.

FOR MEDITATION: And I greatly need a blessing for myself, for though the Lord mercifully supports me in public, I am far from having attained those privileges in my retired walk, which he has given me an idea of as belonging to my profession. I still find a warfare. The foundation of my peace and hope stands firm, but I mourn under a languor and distance of spirit, which I am sometimes ready to think peculiar to myself. I trust he will continue to support me, and that when he has tried me I shall come forth like gold. Though my conscious feelings are faint, I trust Jesus is precious to my soul. I account his favour better than life, and see nothing truly worth living for, but to seek his face and to be employed in his service.[118]

John Newton to John Thornton, 18 May 1775

SERMON SERIES: GENESIS, NO. 10 [3/4], GENESIS 3:15

Stand fast in the battle

'And I will put enmity between thee and the woman, and between thy seed and her seed; it shall bruise thy head, and thou shalt bruise his heel. ... And Adam called his wife's name Eve; because she was the mother of all living. Unto Adam also and to his wife did the LORD *God make coats of skins, and clothed them.' Genesis 3:15, 20–21*
SUGGESTED FURTHER READING: Exodus 14:10–31

Notice two things that follow in the chapter:

(i) an intimation of Adam's faith in this promise, in the name he gave his wife (verse 20). He called her *Eve*, which is derived from a word signifying life. The reason is given: because, in her seed, the true life, the dead in sin should live to God and thus she was to be *the mother of all living*.

(ii) the seal of this promise on the Lord's part—clothing them with *skins*—the skins, without doubt, of beasts slain for sacrifice and thus I doubt not the imputation of the righteousness of the great sacrifice was typically set forth to their faith.

We may preach the gospel to poor sinners. Jesus is here revealed as set apart of God from the beginning to destroy the works of the devil. Believe in him and you shall be saved. We may remind believers of the nature of their calling—think not of stable peace and rest here—the serpent and his seed are in close conspiracy against you; pray therefore for the whole armour of God that you may stand fast in the evil day.

FOR MEDITATION:

Begone unbelief,	Why should I complain
My Saviour is near,	Of want or distress,
And for my relief	Temptation or pain?
Will surely appear:	He told me no less:
By prayer let me wrestle,	The heirs of salvation,
And he will perform,	I know from his Word,
With CHRIST in the vessel,	Through much tribulation
I smile at the storm.	Must follow their LORD.[119]

The true meaning of Scripture

'And, behold, there talked with him two men, which were Moses and Elijah: who appeared in glory, and spake of his decease which he should accomplish at Jerusalem.' Luke 9:30–31
SUGGESTED FURTHER READING: 1 Corinthians 1:17–31

Why were there any witnesses summoned from the heavenly world? Why saints rather than angels? Why only two? And why these two, preferable to the cloud of witnesses who had lived upon earth? Some of these questions are perhaps best referred to the divine will. God does not see fit to acquaint us with all the reasons of his proceedings. We may safely rest in a persuasion that all his appointments are wise and expedient, and hereafter, perhaps, we shall clearly know what at present is not revealed. To give the disciples and to give us, from their testimony, a confirmation that there is a blessed state beyond the present life, two persons who had once been partakers of our afflictions and infirmities, now appeared with Jesus in glory. I know not that there is any stress to be laid upon the number two. These two were selected, and we may observe concerning *Moses and Elijah*, their resemblance. There had been a resemblance in several parts of their history, in which they had been particularly differenced from all other servants of God. Both had seen the glory of God in the Mount, both had been supernaturally sustained without food, forty days and nights. Both had been eminent instruments in their day. By Moses the law had been given—by Elijah the knowledge and practice of it had been restored in a very degenerate time. The Scriptures which were then known, were generally summarized by two sections—the law and the prophets. Moses the lawgiver and Elijah as a representative of the prophets appeared, to signify that all that was written in the law and the prophets terminated in Jesus. The Jews professed a great regard to the writings of Moses and the prophets, yet they rejected their testimony in favour of Christ. The disciples, by this interview, were convinced how little their professed teachers knew of the true meaning of the Scriptures.

FOR MEDITATION: 'And he said unto them ... all things must be fulfilled, which were written in the law of Moses, and in the prophets, and in the psalms, concerning me. Then opened he their understanding, that they might understand the Scriptures' (Luke 24:44–45).

SERMON SERIES: ON THE TRANSFIGURATION, NO. 5 [1/3], LUKE 9:30–31

Partakers of the resurrection

'*And, behold, there talked with him two men, which were Moses and Elijah: who appeared in glory, and spake of his decease which he should accomplish at Jerusalem.*' Luke 9:30–31
SUGGESTED FURTHER READING: Deuteronomy 34:1–12; 2 Kings 2:1–12

In one thing *Moses and Elijah* differed: Elijah was translated without tasting death. The circumstances of Moses' death were uncommon and honourable, yet he did die. Now he appeared in glory upon equal advantage with Elijah. I see no reason to suppose that he assumed a body upon this occasion, or the appearance of a body only. I rather think that he was partaker of the resurrection of Jesus, before the great day of the general resurrection, as it is certain several were soon afterwards (Matthew 27:53). Though they left this world in different ways, they now appeared in the same glory. Various are the dispensations through which the Lord's people pass in the present life, and by which they pass out of it, but they shall all appear at last in the same glory. And thus their redemption draweth nigh. How the disciples knew Moses and Elijah, we are not told. Perhaps our Lord informed them, either when they appeared or after they departed. Or, for ought we know, an impression attended their appearance that satisfied the disciples who they were. It seems not at all improbable that when we mingle with the world of spirits, we shall know as we are known—without needing information. How sweet will the communion be which believers shall have with each other, not only with those whom they walked with here below, but with all who have died in the Lord. O to sit down with Abraham, Isaac and Jacob in our Father's kingdom. But these things, as yet, are hid. We cannot order our speech concerning them by reason of darkness.

FOR MEDITATION:

In vain my fancy strives to paint	Thus much (and this is all) we know,
The moment after death;	They are completely blest;
The glories that surround the saints,	Have done with sin, and care, and woe,
When yielding up their breath.	And with their Saviour rest.[120]

The grand topics of heaven

'And, behold, there talked with him two men, which were Moses and Elijah: who appeared in glory, and spake of his decease which he should accomplish at Jerusalem.' Luke 9:30,31
SUGGESTED FURTHER READING: Luke 9:28–36

If we had only heard that Moses and Elijah came down to converse with Jesus, we should have felt some desire or wish to know the subject of their conference. Here we are told, and it is worthy our notice. They spake not of such trifling incidents as the world accounts great, not of the rise and fall of kingdoms. Their conversation turned entirely upon him, his sufferings and the glorious event of his undertaking. These are the grand topics of heaven and heaven-born souls. Alas for poor mortals, to many of whom the Redeemer's sufferings and glories, which is the delightful theme and song of angels, is tasteless, tedious and offensive. They *spake of his decease* or his departure—his Exodus—it is the word by which we call the book that relates the departure of Israel from Egypt and may be understood of:

(i) his departure out of life, in agonies and sufferings. This was foretold by Moses and the prophets; this was now confirmed by Moses and Elijah. It was an interesting subject to them. They were redeemed by that price which he was soon to pay. They saw more clearly the dignity of his person and the value of his redemption than we can do in this imprisoned state. We may believe they did not speak of it in that cold and careless manner which we often do.

(ii) his departure out of the world. When having completed his purpose, he would return victorious to heaven. As he had his sufferings in view, so likewise his glory.

FOR MEDITATION: Let us learn to imitate the glorified saints and talk more of Jesus, what he has done and what he is doing where he is. Let us aspire to be with them that we may know more and praise better. We are too much tied to the things of sense, too willing and well satisfied to live at a distance from our home. Our willingness to wait the Lord's time for our dismission should be an act of submission and resignation to his will—and not because we are pleased with the world. Salvation—a good hope that you shall join the heavenly host.

SERMON SERIES: ON THE TRANSFIGURATION, NO. 5 [3/3], LUKE 9:30–31

Fly to Jesus, the stronghold

'*And the dove came in to him in the evening; and, lo, in her mouth was an olive leaf plucked off: so Noah knew that the waters were abated from off the earth.*' Genesis 8:11

SUGGESTED FURTHER READING: Genesis 7:24–8:12

Awful have been the effects of sin in every age and country. But never had death such a general triumph over sinners as in the days of Noah. When he and his family were safely shut up, in that very day, the sentence long before denounced was executed, and all mankind, having corrupted their ways before God, were swept away with a flood. What heart can conceive the horror and dismay when destruction presented itself in every quarter, and the ark, which before they had slighted, and which was the only possible way of escape, was shut against them. This is an emblem of a still severer day of vengeance when the wicked shall be destroyed, not by water, but by a deluge of wrath and fire. O think of it in time and fly to Jesus, the stronghold, as *prisoners of hope* [Zechariah 9:12].

FOR MEDITATION:

Saved by blood, I live to tell
What the love of CHRIST hath done;
He redeemed my soul from hell,
Of a rebel made a son:
Oh, I tremble still, to think
How secure I lived in sin;
Sporting on destruction's brink,
Yet preserved from falling in.

Shame and wonder, joy and love,
All at once possessed my heart;
Can I hope thy grace to prove,
After acting such a part?
'Thou hast greatly sinned,' he said,
'But I freely all forgive;
I myself thy debt have paid,
Now I bid thee rise and live.'

In his own appointed hour,
To my heart the Saviour spoke,
Touched me by his Spirit's power,
And my dangerous slumber broke.
Then I saw and owned my guilt,
Soon my gracious LORD replied;
'Fear not, I my blood have spilt,
'Twas for such as thee I died.'

Come, my fellow-sinners, try,
JESUS' heart is full of love;
Oh that you, as well as I,
May his wondrous mercy prove!
He has sent me to declare,
All is ready, all is free;
Why should any soul despair,
When he saved a wretch like me?[121]

SERMON SERIES: GENESIS, NO. 18 [1/3], GENESIS 8:11

Guidance: divine & DIY

'And the dove came in to him in the evening; and, lo, in her mouth was an olive leaf plucked off: so Noah knew that the waters were abated from off the earth.' Genesis 8:11
SUGGESTED FURTHER READING: Nehemiah 2:11–18

We have the resting of the ark upon a mountain, guided thither by God and not steered by Noah's prudence. The Lord has times of rest for his people. A convinced sinner is like the ark tossed upon the waves, but in due time guided to *the Rock that is higher than* he [Psalm 61:2]. When the ark had rested some time, Noah was desirous of intelligence. He saw the tops of the hills from the window of the ark, but was solicitous to know when the earth should be dry and fit to receive him. God had told him the day when the flood should come, but not when it should subside. The knowledge of the one was necessary, the other not so. The one he could not have known but by revelation, but he might in due time discover the other in the use of ordinary means. The knowledge the Lord affords his people is not to indulge their curiosity or to make them indolent, but so graciously managed, that, while nothing truly profitable is held from them, their own diligence and application is still needful.

FOR MEDITATION: I wish I could advise you about your sons, but here likewise I am at a loss. Dispose of your children in any way, you cannot keep them out of the infectious air of the world's evil atmosphere. When you have made the most prudent use in your power of the means that the providence of the Lord affords, you can do nothing further than to commend them to him by frequent, fervent prayer, and then in faith, patience and hope, wait for the issue: and if you give them up to him (when you have done your part), you must leave him (if you can) to answer your prayers in his own time and way; for he often brings the blind by a way they know not.[122]

John Newton to James Coffin, 19 February 1799

Sweet messenger of rest

'And the dove came in to him in the evening; and, lo, in her mouth was an olive leaf plucked off: so Noah knew that the waters were abated from off the earth.' Genesis 8:11
SUGGESTED FURTHER READING: Isaiah 51:12–16; Matthew 11:28–30

Noah sent forth first the raven, which returned no more, then a dove, which, not finding rest, returned to the ark—but the second time brought an olive leaf. It was probably from an imperfect tradition of this circumstance that an olive branch has been considered an emblem of peace among all nations. The raven is an unclean bird. A bird of prey, it was confined in the ark and glad of its liberty, for it could find subsistence abroad. But the dove could not live upon ravens' food and therefore returned till the earth was fully dried. Thus the carnal heart can find satisfaction in the world, but the believer can find no rest but in the ark. As Noah put forth his hand to receive her, so Jesus graciously receives the weary soul into his rest.

The dove, though it came back unsuccessful, is sent forth again and at last brings the token. The peace of God is revealed to persevering prayer, and when the heart has been humbled by the Word and brought into a meek and gentle spirit. The peace of God is made known not to ravens but to doves. At last the dove likewise took its flight and returned no more. The earth was dried and the fruits ready for its food. Believers go forth upon the wing of faith and prayer; they receive tokens of good and are witnesses and messengers of the Lord's mercy. But in time their hope is exchanged for possession and they take their flight from the church below to the land of eternal rest, from whence they shall come back no more.

FOR MEDITATION:

Does the gospel-word proclaim
Rest, for those who weary be?
Then, my soul, put in thy claim,
Sure that promise speaks to thee:
Marks of grace I cannot show,
All polluted is my best;
Yet I weary am I know,
And the weary long for rest.

Safely lodged within thy breast,
What a wondrous change I find!
Now I know thy promised rest
Can compose a troubled mind
You that weary are like me,
Hearken to the gospel call;
To the ark for refuge flee,
JESUS will receive you all![123]

SERMON SERIES: GENESIS, NO. 18 [3/3], GENESIS 8:11

The sweet savour of Jesus

'And the LORD smelled a sweet savour; and the LORD said in his heart, I will not again curse the ground any more for man's sake; for the imagination of man's heart is evil from his youth; neither will I again smite any more every thing living, as I have done.' Genesis 8:21
SUGGESTED FURTHER READING: Genesis 8:13–22

The Lord's answer of peace to Noah: here is a gracious promise, *I will not again curse the ground*. The reason is assigned: *for the imagination of man's heart is evil from his youth up*. This seems a reason of the same kind as that before assigned for the destruction of the earth—the *for* may be rendered *though*.

(i) Sin is so deeply rooted that judgements cannot remove it. If the aboundings of sin were to be always followed with a deluge, there must be a new flood at least in every generation. God, having once shown his displeasure this way, will wait to be gracious. But this we owe to the sweet savour of Jesus. The Lord saw and knew that the new race of mankind would be no better than the old.

(ii) The evil of man cannot frustrate the grace of the Lord. Vile as they are, he will have a people out of them that shall show forth his praise.

(iii) The continuance of the seasons is an earnest and pledge of the Lord's faithfulness to every part of his Word. We expect harvests and obtain them because he thus was pleased to engage himself to Noah. So all that his people hope for, from his Word, shall be surely fulfilled, and so likewise the weight of all his threatenings shall fall heavy upon the heads of the wicked, for he is *not a man that he should lie or the son of man that he should repent* [Numbers 23:19].

FOR MEDITATION: The gospel gives a blessed freedom from the power of outward sin, but the root of sin in the heart still remains and will yield bitter fruit: unbelief, self-will, self-righteousness and pride, a wandering heart, a vain, ungoverned imagination, a numbness of spirit amounting to an almost total indisposition to divine things. ... But though sorrowful, we may be always rejoicing, for we have a mighty and a merciful Saviour, and in him we have righteousness and strength. In him we are complete and he is full of compassion. He knows our frame and remembers that we are but dust.[124]

SERMON SERIES: GENESIS, NO. 19 [1/1], GENESIS 8:21

The call of God

'Now the LORD had said unto Abram, Get thee out of thy country, and from thy kindred, and from thy father's house, unto a land that I will show thee.' Genesis 12:1
SUGGESTED FURTHER READING: Hebrews 11:8–16

The command was to leave his family and country and to go to an unknown land which God would show him. The calling of Abraham is supposed to have been less than 400 years after the flood. In this space of time it seems the knowledge of God was again almost lost upon the earth, and Abraham's family, as well as others, was sinking into idolatry. The Lord was now about to fulfil his purpose of selecting a particular people to himself, by whom he would be known and worshipped, and amongst whom the types and prophecies concerning the Messiah should be revealed and perpetuated till, in the fullness of time, the Messiah should come of that nation, to be a light and salvation to the ends of the earth. He who has a right to do what he will with his own, as the potter over the clay, chose Abraham to be the head and origin of this nation, and marked out, long before they were a people, the land in which they should be fixed. And in the meanwhile he permitted, by his providence, that the land allotted to his own people should be settled by that branch of Noah's family who, at his appointed season, should be cut off for their wickedness, and thereby make room for Abraham's posterity. Thus Abraham is to be considered in a twofold light: as a public person—the head of the Israel of God—and likewise personally as a believer, and a pattern of the life of faith.

FOR MEDITATION:

If he his will reveal,
Let us obey his call;
And think whate'er the flesh may feel,
His love deserves our all.

We should maintain in view
His glory, as our end;
Too much we cannot bear, or do,
For such a matchless friend.

His saints should stand prepared
In duty's path to run;
Nor count their greatest trials hard,
So that his will be done.

With JESUS for our guide,
The path is safe though rough
The promise says, 'I will provide',
And faith replies, 'Enough!'[125]

SERMON SERIES: GENESIS, NO. 22 [1/3], GENESIS 12:1FF.

The God of glory

'The God of glory appeared unto our father Abraham, when he was in Mesopotamia.' Acts 7:2
SUGGESTED FURTHER READING: Acts 7:1–8

When Abraham was in a state of ignorance, and probably an idolater, God revealed himself unto him (Acts 7:2) as *the God of glory*. Thus the work begins in all his people. If not idolaters in the gross sense, yet in a spiritual sense we are all idolaters—self-worshippers, lovers of the world, lovers of pleasure more than of God, and this is idolatry. The Lord finds his people when they seek him not—indeed they seek him, and sometimes for a long space and under many discouragements before they know him to their comfort, but he begins with them before they can seek him at all. This is universally true whatever advantages they may have of outward means, yet till he speaks to their hearts they know him not, nor have any true desire after him. The Lord begins by revealing himself to the soul as *the God of glory*. When the Lord appeared, then Abraham saw the vanity of idols. Even the notions we have of God by nature, are so unsuitable to the representation he has made of himself by his Word and Spirit, that while we pretend to worship him, we may be said to worship an idol. If we do not apprehend him as *the God of glory*, glorious in holiness, justice and truth, we worship not the true God but an imagination of our own hearts. Many, if they would examine their own hearts, might be convinced they have in a manner thought him such a one as themselves; they deny his most essential attributes, or they could not presume on his favour while they live in their sins.

FOR MEDITATION: In those early days there was no written word. But now we have the Scriptures complete we are not to expect to hear a voice or see a glory with our bodily eyes. He makes himself known by his Word and Spirit. And this, though a silent way and unperceived by others, is accompanied with no less certain evidences of his presence and power than if he was to speak in thunder and appear to us in the awful manner he did to Israel at Mount Sinai. Such an outward display of majesty might indeed overawe the carnal heart for a season, but would not change it. The glory of God can only be seen to good purpose by the eyes of the mind (2 Corinthians 4).

SERMON SERIES: GENESIS, NO. 22 [2/3], GENESIS 12:1FF.

Called to leave

'Now the LORD had said unto Abram, Get thee out of thy country, and from thy kindred, and from thy father's house, unto a land that I will show thee.' Genesis 12:1
SUGGESTED FURTHER READING: Matthew 10:32–39

The Lord called Abraham to leave his father's house. By this is signified the effect of a gracious call: it will suffer a person no longer to remain in the love and practices of a wicked world, but to separate in these things from their nearest and dearest friends if they walk not in the Lord's ways—not literally to forsake their houses, but to hold no more communion with them in sin. This is the first visible effect of his call. A change appears in their conversation and conduct. He gives them a sight of the evil and danger of sin, and of his own glory, and thus he makes them willing in the day of his power [Psalm 110:3]. It was doubtless a trial to Abraham's natural affections to forsake his family, and many of his people have no less trial while they live with them. When a person's foes begin to be of their own household, when parents or children, the wife of the bosom, or a friend who is as one's own soul, shall employ all their influence, persuasions, promises, threats, kindness, unkindness, pity and surly turns, to persuade the soul whom the Lord has called, to disobey his call, this is very hard to flesh and blood.

Abraham knew not particulars, but he might be well assured that as the Lord called him he should gain by the exchange. He knew not wither he went, but he knew whom he followed, and therefore he consulted not with flesh and blood. Do you likewise. The Lord whom you serve is able to make you amends ... Go you forth at his command, live upon him for today, trust in him for tomorrow ...

FOR MEDITATION:

His call we obey
Like Abram of old,
Not knowing our way,
But faith makes us bold;
For though we are strangers
We have a good Guide,
And trust in all dangers,
The LORD will provide.

No strength of our own,
Or goodness we claim,
Yet since we have known
The Saviour's great name;
In this our strong tower
For safety we hide,
The LORD is our power,
The LORD will provide.[126]

SERMON SERIES: GENESIS, NO. 22 [3/3], GENESIS 12:1FF.

The promise

'And I will make of thee a great nation, and I will bless thee, and make thy name great; and thou shalt be a blessing: and I will bless them that bless thee, and curse him that curseth thee: and in thee shall all families of the earth be blessed.' Genesis 12:2–3
SUGGESTED FURTHER READING: Galatians 3:1–18

From the consideration of God's command [in verse 1] we are led to the promise. For when the Lord calls his people out of the world, he does not bid them forsake all for nothing. A mistake in this point is the reason why they are pitied because they no longer run in the same excess of riot. So children might affect to pity grown people because they are no longer pleased with their childish sports. A part of this promise was personally to Abraham, that he should be the father of a great nation, and that in him—that is to say, as it is elsewhere expressed, in his seed—*all the families of the earth* should be blessed. This St Paul applies to Christ (Galatians 3). Here the promise first given in general terms, of a seed of the woman, is restrained to One of Abraham's posterity and it was his especial honour and privilege to be the head of God's chosen people and the root from whence, according to the flesh, the Saviour of men should spring. Here Abraham began to see the day of Christ, and it was by faith in him, who in the fullness of time was to descend from him, that the covenant was established to Abraham himself.

FOR MEDITATION: 'A record of the genealogy of Jesus Christ the son of David, the son of Abraham: Abraham was the father of Isaac, Isaac the father of Jacob, Jacob the father of Judah, … Jesse was the father of David the king,… the father of Joseph, the husband of Mary, of whom was born Jesus, who is called Christ' (Matthew 1:1–2,16, NIV).

'Therefore it is of faith, that it might be by grace; to the end the promise might be sure to all the seed; not to that only which is of the law, but to that also which is of the faith of Abraham; who is the father of us all' (Romans 4:16 NIV).

The inheritance

'And I will make of thee a great nation, and I will bless thee, and make thy name great; and thou shalt be a blessing.' Genesis 12:2
SUGGESTED FURTHER READING: Colossians 2:1–15

I will bless thee. Here we say, *Whoso the Lord blesses shall be blessed*. To this purpose the touching petition of Jabez—O that thou wouldst bless me *indeed* [1 Chronicles 4:10], for thou only art able. For the sum of this blessing see Genesis 15:1—*I will preserve thee from all evil and satisfy thee with all good*. How safe are they who have the Almighty for their defence; how rich who have the all-sufficient God for their portion. Thus it is with all his people. Then why fear, or why complain? Sure they may be willing to leave the world to those who have no God.

And make thy name great. Abraham's name has been recorded with honour—and there is an honour to all his people. What is it that gives people a great name in the world?

(i) A noble descent. But the lowliest believer is of more honourable birth than the greatest king, if not partaker of grace. He is born from above, born of God—sons and daughters of the Lord Almighty.

(ii) Great possessions. Here likewise they have the advantage. They are joint heirs of Christ and all things are theirs.

(iii) Great actions. Thus captains and warriors who are skilful and successful in destroying mankind, are renowned. But the believer is engaged in a more important and difficult warfare and by the power of grace he overcomes the devil, the world and himself. He that ruleth his spirit is greater than he who taketh a city (Proverbs 16:32). We have in Hebrews 11 a specimen of the mighty acts of faith, and each believer's *exploits* shall at last be made known before angels and men. Then their name shall be great indeed, though now by an unbelieving world cast out as evil (Daniel 11:32).

FOR MEDITATION: 'Praise be to the God and Father of our Lord Jesus Christ! In his great mercy he has given us new birth into a living hope through the resurrection of Jesus Christ from the dead, and into an inheritance that can never perish, spoil or fade—kept in heaven for you, who through faith are shielded by God's power until the coming of the salvation that is ready to be revealed in the last time' (1 Peter 1:3–5, NIV).

SERMON SERIES: GENESIS, NO. 23 [2/3], GENESIS 12:2

Gracious living

'And I will make of thee a great nation, and I will bless thee, and make thy name great; and thou shalt be a blessing.' Genesis 12:2
SUGGESTED FURTHER READING: Ephesians 4:17–5:21

And thou shalt be a blessing: blessed in thyself and a blessing to others. Believers indeed are by the world accounted a burden, as Lot was in Sodom, yet each one is a public blessing. Thus they are compared to light, to salt, and so forth. Consider:

(i) their usefulness. The grace of God teaches them benevolence and usefulness. If any professor [of the faith] lives to himself it is a bad sign. I hope we have not so learnt Christ.

(ii) their example. They cannot do all they would, yet their example has some good effect, to restrain the boldness of sin and to draw others to seek after the Lord likewise (1 Peter 3:1).

(iii) their prayer. If Sodom had not been dreadfully abandoned, the prayer of Abraham would have saved it; and had there been ten of these blessings found in it, it would have escaped destruction.

(iv) [their protection]—by their interests and concerns being interwoven at present in the world. They are the wheat, for whose sake the tares are so long spared. If the world could have its wish and the people whom they hate were quite removed, they would not be suffered to go on long with impunity.

FOR MEDITATION: *Tempus fugit* very fast indeed. I am already more than three months in my seventy-second year. So the almanac tells me, otherwise I should scarcely perceive it. I preach Jesus Christ and him crucified, and tell my hearers that if they love him for his great love to them, they ought to love one another. I have nothing to do with controversies. Church folks, dissenters, methodists of all sorts come to hear me, and they are all welcome, and all sit very quietly. I am waiting for my dismission, which I trust I shall receive at the best time. I have some longing (though I am not impatient) to be at home—there to see my dear Mary and Eliza—and above all to see him, whom having not yet seen, I trust is the Lord and beloved of my heart. To see him as he is, and to be like him. This is worth dying for, and worth living for, till he shall say, Come up hither.[127]

John Newton to John Ryland, 26 November 1796

SERMON SERIES: GENESIS, NO. 23 [3/3], GENESIS 12:2

Room for the exercise of faith

'And the LORD *appeared unto Abram, and said, Unto thy seed will I give this land...' Genesis 12:7*
SUGGESTED FURTHER READING: Romans 4:13–25

God's promises still leave room for the exercise of faith. So Abraham found it. The land which he saw was for his *seed*, which was cause of rejoicing, but attended with two abatements.

(i) Though it was given to his seed, he himself had no possession, but was a sojourner in tents all his days. Yet he was not disappointed as to his own best interests; he was taught to consider this earthly inheritance as a type of a better [one], that is, an heavenly (Hebrews 11:10,13–14). So the promises run to believers: all things are theirs; they shall inherit the earth. In the meanwhile many of them are destitute and in want of all things. Here sense is ready to complain, but faith takes up the best meaning. All things are mine so far as the Lord sees good, and I shall have his blessing with them, but my great inheritance is on high, therefore none of these things move me.

(ii) His chief [abatement] was that the promise was made to his *seed*, when as yet he had no child and little prospect of any, for his wife was barren and he himself advancing in years. This difficulty grew harder every day as he and his wife grew older, and though his faith surmounted it, yet it was not without conflicts, as we may gather from 15:2. In this instance the faith of Abraham is especially commended to our imitation (Romans 4:18–22). Great things believers expect in their walk with God: peace, joy, strength and sweet communion. Nor shall they be disappointed if they believe. But when they are acquainted with the evil of their own hearts and the temptations belonging to their warfare, they are in much the same situation as Abraham, who could never have had a comfortable hope of a child, if he had given way to the reasonings of flesh and blood. He waited twenty-five years and when at last it seemed impossible, then his desire was fulfilled.

FOR MEDITATION: Two considerations supported the Word and the power of God: he had promised, and he was able to perform. Apply this to yourself, poor soul. Are you saying, *Can these dry bones live?* [Ezekiel 37:3] Can grace and comfort ever dwell in this heart? Yes. The Lord has spoken, and therefore you may rejoice, for he who has promised is able also to perform.

SERMON SERIES: GENESIS, NO. 24 [1/4], GENESIS 12:7

Sunshine through the clouds

'And the LORD *appeared unto Abram, and said, Unto thy seed will I give this land: and there builded he an altar unto the* LORD, *who appeared unto him.' Genesis 12:7*
SUGGESTED FURTHER READING: Revelation 21:22–22:6

Though the Lord was always with Abraham to protect and bless him, he manifested himself or *appeared* to him but now and then. Thus with respect to all necessary supplies of grace and strength, and a liberty to seek his direction and blessing, he is ever with his people—but there is a gracious presence, the light of his countenance, which they do not always enjoy. In this sense he visits them but does not abide, as the sun gives us every day for necessary uses, but does not always shine upon us. When it does, it casts an inimitable glory and gilds every object. Be thankful for the light and for eyes to behold it, but pray likewise for the breaking forth of the Sun of righteousness. If you have it, rejoice in it, yet expect a change. There are reasons both on the Lord's part and on ours why he does not always shine. But in yonder happy world we shall have unclouded skies.

FOR MEDITATION:

As when the weary traveller gains
The height of some o'er-looking hill;
His heart revives, if cross the plains
He eyes his home, though distant still.

The thought of home his spirit cheers,
No more he grieves for troubles past;
Nor any future trial fears,
So he may safe arrive at last.

While he surveys the much-loved spot,
He slights the space that lies between;
His past fatigues are now forgot,
Because his journey's end is seen.

'Tis there, he says, I am to dwell
With JESUS, in the realms of day;
Then I shall bid my cares farewell,
And he will wipe my tears away.

Thus, when the Christian pilgrim views
By faith, his mansion in the skies;
The sight his fainting strength renews,
And wings his speed to reach the prize.

JESUS, on thee our hope depends,
To lead us on to thine abode;
Assured our home will make amends
For all our toil while on the road.[128]

SERMON SERIES: GENESIS, NO. 24 [2/4], GENESIS 12:7

An altar

'And the LORD *appeared unto Abram, and said, Unto thy seed will I give this land: and there builded he an altar unto the* LORD*, who appeared unto him.'* Genesis 12:7
SUGGESTED FURTHER READING: Hebrews 13:9–16

Abraham erected *an altar*. This shows:

(i) his faith—in the great sacrifice, the virtue of which was set forth by all the sacrifices before under the law.

(ii) his gratitude. When God had appeared to him and given him such promises, immediately he raises an altar. Who is there amongst you, upon whom the Lord has lately shone? Has he answered your prayers, prevented your fears, taken off your sackcloth and girded you with gladness? O say, *the vows of God are upon me* [Psalm 56:12]. O may your heart be as an altar upon which *the sacrifice of praise* is continually offered [Hebrews 13:15].

(iii) his profession. He was among a people that knew not God, but he was not so affected by the custom of the country as to be ashamed or afraid to have it publicly known that he worshipped the Lord. Everything that looks like ostentation should be avoided, but if the Lord has called us out of darkness into light, we should not be unwilling to be marked and known by our neighbours and friends as those who have given themselves to him.

FOR MEDITATION: The points of his public profession of religion from which I think he cannot warrantably recede, are such as these: he will say with Joshua, or his example and conduct will say it for him, *As for me and my house, we will serve the Lord.* He will neither be afraid nor ashamed to have it publicly supposed or known that he worships God, in his closet, and (allowing for unavoidable interruptions) in his family; and that so far as his example, persuasion and authority can influence, he will endeavour that all who live under his roof shall be restrained from evil, and taught and encouraged to serve the Lord with him.[129]

John Newton to William Wilberforce, 1 November 1787
[responding with advice on embarking on the abolition of the slave trade]

Family prayers

'And the LORD *appeared unto Abram, and said, Unto thy seed will I give this land: and there builded he an altar unto the* LORD, *who appeared unto him.'* Genesis 12:7
SUGGESTED FURTHER READING: Ruth 1:1–18

Abraham had a family and therefore he had *an altar*. He was not content to pray in his closet, but worshipped God with his household. I remember my fault today. I have spoken too seldom and too faintly upon this topic—it is a very important point. Let me entreat you, as many as fear the Lord, to see to it that you set up an altar in your houses. Your children, your servants, if you have any, are entrusted to you for this end. How is Abraham commended on this account! *I know him*, says the Lord, *that he will command his children and his household after him* [Genesis 18:19]. Family mercies require family acknowledgement. If you would have obedient children and faithful servants and peace, the peace of God in your dwellings, live not without family prayer. The flesh will plead excuses, the devil will help to furnish them, but it is your duty and will be your honour and your blessing, and the neglect of it will prove like a thorn in your foot to make your progress in other things slow and painful. If you think yourself unable to lead prayer in a family, make use of a good [published] form rather than omit. Beginnings are always difficult, but if you simply look up to the Lord, he will strengthen and guide you.

FOR MEDITATION: [Newton's three-year-old nephew holidayed with him in Olney. His mother later wrote:]
    Soon after he came home to us, he asked why we had not prayer as often as at his uncle's, and expressing his liking their way best. I think this early impression upon his mind of a holy life was, with God's blessing, owing to their good example and instructions.[130]

Elizabeth Cunningham (Mary Newton's sister)

Trifling with God's majesty

'Thou shalt not take the name of the LORD *thy God in vain; for the* LORD *will not hold him guiltless that taketh his name in vain.' Exodus 20:7*
SUGGESTED FURTHER READING: Revelation 11:15–19; 19:11–16

The foundation of true religion is laid in a right knowledge of God and ourselves. How deficient we are in each of these, how far fallen from original righteousness, is strongly implied in this prohibition, which would be altogether unnecessary were we not altogether sunk in stupidity and wickedness. That such worms should be liable to trifle with the majesty whose presence fills heaven and earth, before whom the angels hide their faces—that such frail, dependent creatures have need to be cautioned that we do not profane the name of the God in whom we live, move and have our being—is as striking an instance of our depravity as our daring to break through this caution, and slighting the awful threatenings with which it is closed, is a dreadful aggravation of our guilt.

These words were first delivered in flames and thunder. Such a scene, or rather infinitely more dreadful, shall hereafter take place when the Lord shall again descend and be revealed in flaming fire to take vengeance. Then shall sinners be convinced not only of their ungodly deeds, but their hard speeches—and shall know the meaning of that terrible exception I have read: He will not hold *them* guiltless.

FOR MEDITATION: … foolish and perverse again. What can I say? but that I am vile beyond expression—weak as water and wilful as an ass's colt. Silly creature to trifle with thee and to wound myself, and that for a mere nothing. Lord, humble and strengthen me. Let me plead thy blood, thy promise. Let me again see I have an Advocate with the Father, and enable me to come to thee in faith, that I may obtain and find grace to help in time of need.[131]

Diary, 7 July 1776

Trivial escapes

'Thou shalt not take the name of the LORD *thy God in vain: for the* LORD *will not hold him guiltless that taketh his name in vain.' Exodus 20:7*
SUGGESTED FURTHER READING: Colossians 3:1–17

What shall we say of the throng of profane swearers, who wound our ears and pollute our language by a horrid mixture of execrations and blasphemies in their common conversation? *Their throats are an open sepulchre—their mouths are full of cursing and bitterness, the poison of asps is under their lips* [Romans 3:13–14]. The Lord will not hold them guiltless. In vain their thoughtless plea, 'they mean no harm'. In vain their presumptuous comparison of themselves with others—as though those were trivial escapes that did not affect the peace of society. If these were small sins singly, their frequency would make a vast amount. But is it a small sin, to rush against the bosses of God's buckler [a small shield: Job 15:26], to despise so terrible a threatening as this! A habit of swearing is a sure sign not only of an unsanctified heart, but of a conscience hardened and, as it were, seared with a hot iron, callous and insensible [1 Timothy 4:2]. May the Lord awaken such.

Will any that live in a Christian land and have the Bible at hand plead ignorance of this in the great day? Surely no! Let your future lives be devoted to him who loved you.

FOR MEDITATION: I stood in need of an almighty Saviour, and such a one I found described in the New Testament. I heartily renounced my former profaneness … I was quite freed from the habit of swearing, which seemed to have been deeply rooted in me as a second nature.[132]

Narrative, 1764, Letter 9

'With the tongue we praise our Lord and Father, and with it we curse men, who have been made in God's likeness. Out of the same mouth come praise and cursing. My brothers, this should not be' (James 3:9–10, NIV).

'… revere this glorious and awesome name …' (Deuteronomy 28:58, NIV).

Only lip service

'Thou shalt not take the name of the LORD thy God in vain: for the LORD will not hold him guiltless that taketh his name in vain.' Exodus 20:7
SUGGESTED FURTHER READING: Isaiah 58:1–14

Some would applaud themselves and think themselves clear thus far, but are there no other ways of taking God's name in vain? Yes, many do it as often as they pray. See Matthew 15:8. Do you ask what you do not desire and confess what you do not feel? Is not this to take the name of God in vain? Does it not prove that you think him altogether such a one as yourselves, nay, more easily imposed on, more safely to be trifled with, than a poor fallible mortal? Strange it is to think that many not only content themselves with this lip service, but make it the meritorious ground of their hope, and fancy themselves religious because they come so often to church to mock the power that made them. But hardly can any wickedness be imagined more daring and provoking to the Most High than such a religion as this. Farther, as many of you as choose to be called Christians and live in the allowed practice of known sin, your whole lives may be considered as one continual breach of this command. In all you say and do, you blaspheme that holy name by which you are called—and still more so, if you are professed friends and favourers of the gospel. By your means the ways of truth are evil spoken of. You give occasion to those offences of which it is said, *Woe to that man by whom the offence cometh* [Matthew 18:7]. You injure the cause, stumble the weak, grieve the Lord's people and make his enemies rejoice. Better it would be never to have known the way of righteousness, than thus to abuse your knowledge. Your case is awfully dangerous indeed.

FOR MEDITATION: 'And when you pray, do not be like the hypocrites, for they love to pray standing in the synagogues and on the street corners to be seen by men. I tell you the truth, they have received their reward in full. But when you pray, go into your room, close the door and pray to your Father, who is unseen. Then your Father, who sees what is done in secret, will reward you' (Matthew 6:5–6, NIV).

The price of riches

'And Abram went up out of Egypt, he, and his wife, and all that he had, and Lot with him, into the south. And Abram was very rich in cattle, in silver, and in gold. And Lot also, which went with Abram, had flocks, and herds, and tents. And the land was not able to bear them, that they might dwell together: for their substance was great, so that they could not dwell together. And there was a strife between the herdmen of Abram's cattle and the herdmen of Lot's cattle: and the Canaanite and the Perizzite dwelled then in the land.' Genesis 13:1–2, 5–7
SUGGESTED FURTHER READING: Genesis 13:1–18

Notice the *riches* of Abraham and Lot. They forsook their own country and went into a strange land at the Lord's command, and he provided well for them. It is true the promises of the gospel chiefly respect better and spiritual blessings, yet they include the things of this life likewise. I would observe from it that the best way to prosper as to worldly concerns is to observe the Lord's commandments. I am afraid some of you, yea some believers, think otherwise. To this is owing the profanation of the Lord's Day, which so sadly prevails amongst us. I know some allow themselves in what their consciences condemn, because they cannot trust the Lord with their substance or character. They seem desirous to serve him if they could do it without offending the world. This is for a lamentation.

Note the inconvenience attending their riches: *strife*—not immediately between themselves, but their herdsmen strove, and Abraham and Lot were in danger of taking part with their respective servants as to have some difference. We may see from hence that though the Lord will give his people every needful good, yet for the most part he withholds riches from them. It is in mercy. Great possessions are usually accompanied with great cares, troubles and snares. Our life and comfort does not depend upon them; rather, they endanger peace and safety. Abraham and Lot wished to live in peace, but their servants had strife, and strife is like the kindling of a fire, which spreads far and wide from small beginnings.

FOR MEDITATION: 'They that will be rich fall into temptation and a snare, and into many foolish and hurtful lusts, which drown men in destruction and perdition' (1 Timothy 6:9).

A lover of peace

*'And Abram said unto Lot, Let there be no strife, I pray thee, between me
and thee, and between my herdmen and thy herdmen; for we be brethren.
Is not the whole land before thee? separate thyself, I pray thee, from me: if
thou wilt take the left hand, then I will go to the right; or if thou depart to
the right hand, then I will go to the left.'* Genesis 13:8–9
SUGGESTED FURTHER READING: Ephesians 2:13–22

Abraham's conduct:

(i) his desire: *Let there be no strife.* He was a blessed man, a lover of peace,
and to the utmost of his power a peacemaker. Happy are they to whom the
Lord gives such a spirit, for peace is that to the mind which health is to the
body—there is nothing can be enjoyed without it.

(ii) his argument: twofold, taken from their relation, *We are brethren*, and
their situation, *the Canaanite were in the land* [verse 7]. They knew that Lot
and Abraham were the servants of God, and what would they think of their
religion if they observed them living in strife? Besides, it might give their
enemies encouragement to fall upon them.

(iii) his proposal: he showed himself a true lover of peace. Though he was
probably the person aggrieved, he makes the first offers, and though he was
the elder, and superior, he gives up his right of choice to Lot and is
determined to be pleased if Lot can but please himself. Too often when
people talk of peace and reconciliation they are too selfish to let anything be
affected. If you allow everything they have said and done to be right, and give
up everything they ask, they will try to be peaceable.

FOR MEDITATION: 'I urge, then, first of all, that requests, prayers, intercession
and thanksgiving be made for everyone—for kings and all those in
authority, that we may live peaceful and quiet lives in all godliness and
holiness. This is good, and pleases God our Saviour' (1 Timothy 2:1–3, NIV).

'If it be possible, as much as lieth in you, live peaceably with all men'
(Romans 12:18).

A sad choice

'And Lot lifted up his eyes, and beheld all the plain of Jordan, that it was well watered everywhere, before the LORD *destroyed Sodom and Gomorrah, even as the garden of the* LORD, *like the land of Egypt, as thou comest unto Zoar. Then Lot chose him all the plain of Jordan; and Lot journeyed east: and they separated themselves the one from the other.'*
Genesis 13:10–11
SUGGESTED FURTHER READING: Luke 18:18–30

Lot's choice: though he feared the Lord, his great possessions blinded his judgement. He made too light of the privilege of dwelling with Abraham and was more intent upon providing well for his cattle than for himself. Because the land of Sodom was *well watered* and fruitful, he went to reside there, though they were notoriously wicked. See what was the consequence—he was soon involved in the effects of war. He had not been long in Sodom before he was taken prisoner and lost all his flocks and herds which had occasioned the strife and had tempted him to take up his dwelling in a place where there was no fear of God. He recovered them afterwards, but this was owing to Abraham's kindness, who forgot the slight put upon him and undertook his rescue. While he dwelt in Sodom his soul was daily grieved with the wickedness of the inhabitants [2 Peter 2:8], and while Abraham was honoured, he was despised, opposed and persecuted for his profession's sake. At last he saw the place he had chosen destroyed with fire from heaven [Genesis 19:24] and he was glad to escape for his life, leaving all his substance behind him.

FOR MEDITATION:

How hurtful was the choice of Lot,
Who took up his abode
(Because it was a fruitful spot)
With them who feared not GOD!

Yet still he seemed resolved to stay
As if it were his rest;
Although their sins from day to day
His righteous soul distressed.

A prisoner he was quickly made,
Bereaved of all his store;
And, but for Abraham's timely aid,
He had returned no more.

Awhile he stayed with anxious mind,
Exposed to scorn and strife;
At last he left his all behind,
And fled to save his life.[135]

SERMON SERIES: GENESIS, NO. 25 [3/4], GENESIS 13:12–13

Guidelines for choosing

'Abram dwelled in the land of Canaan, and Lot dwelled in the cities of the plain, and pitched his tent toward Sodom. But the men of Sodom were wicked and sinners before the LORD *exceedingly.' Genesis 13:12–13*
SUGGESTED FURTHER READING: Proverbs 24:1–27

This affords a lesson to us, especially to people that are newly setting out in the world. Look not at outward advantages only. Prize the people and ordinances of God, and pray that your lot may not be cast at a distance from them. If you know the Lord, you will meet many trials by living in a dark place where there are no means of grace to help you forward, but, on the contrary, continual hindrances to strive against. You will hardly meet anything can make you amends for the loss it will prove to your souls. If your lot is already fixed like Lot in Sodom, yet may you at least imitate him in being a witness for his truth and in grieving for the abounding of sin around you. Then you shall find the Lord whom you serve is able to deliver and protect you [Daniel 3:17]. The land of Sodom was well watered for a season, but sin brought upon it a storm of fire. So sinners may be favoured a while with outward prosperity, but judgement is at the door. Remember what our Lord said of Sodom: it was a wicked place, but it had not the gospel. *It shall be more tolerable for Sodom and Gomorrah* than for many called Christians in the great day [Luke 10:12].

FOR MEDITATION:

In vain his sons-in-law he warned,
They thought he told his dreams;
His daughters too, of them had learned,
And perished in the flames.

His wife escaped a little way,
But died for looking back:
Does not her case to pilgrims say,
'Beware of growing slack'?

Yea; Lot himself could lingering stand,
Though vengeance was in view;
'Twas mercy plucked him by the hand,
Or he had perished too.

The doom of Sodom will be ours
If to the earth we cleave;
LORD quicken all our drowsy powers,
To flee to thee and live.[136]

No loser

'And the LORD *said unto Abram, after that Lot was separated from him, Lift up now thine eyes, and look from the place where thou art northward, and southward, and eastward, and westward: for all the land which thou seest, to thee will I give it, and to thy seed for ever.' Genesis 13:14–15*
SUGGESTED FURTHER READING: Romans 8:28–39.

Happy is he who has the God of Israel for his help ... [Psalm 146:5]. Whatever changes or trials he may meet, he has a sure resource. From these verses we may take note of the time: *after Lot had separated.*

Observe:

(i) Abraham had given up something for the sake of peace—now he is made amends. It is good to be willing to suffer for the Lord's sake and to commit our cause to him. Such shall be no losers.

(ii) Abraham had lost the company of a dear friend and associate. But the Lord visited him. We are liable to be separated from those we love, by many things, but who shall separate from the Lord? Communion with him can make up the want of creature converse and creature assistance.

(iii) The land was designed for Abraham's family, not Lot's—it was necessary that Lot should settle elsewhere, yet his own fault was the immediate occasion. Thus the Lord overrules the mistakes as well as the good intentions of his people, and in general the actions of mankind, to his own glory (Genesis 45:8; Luke 2:1). When Lot was gone, the promise was confirmed.

FOR MEDITATION:
Since all that I meet
Shall work for my good,
The bitter is sweet,
The medicine is food;
Though painful at present,
'Twill cease before long,
And then, oh! how pleasant,
The conqueror's song![137]

SERMON SERIES: GENESIS, NO. 26 [1/2], GENESIS 13:14–18

God's promise for believers

'...For all the land which thou seest, to thee will I give it, and to thy seed for ever. And I will make thy seed as the dust of the earth: so that if a man can number the dust of the earth, then shall thy seed also be numbered. Arise, walk through the land in the length of it and in the breadth of it; for I will give it unto thee.' Genesis 13:15–17
SUGGESTED FURTHER READING: Colossians 1:9–14

The promise: *to thee and to thy seed*. This was Israel's security. How often did they forfeit it by disobedience, but it was promised before to Abraham. Herein we have a type of a better covenant with Jesus, which is sure to all his seed. What Lot had was by choice, but Abraham's by promise—therefore his right was preferred when the other's was lost. There is no security like the promise of God.

The command: *arise and walk*. The promise was not completely fulfilled to Abraham, for it terminated in his seed. In the meantime he was to take a survey, and by faith call it all his own. Thus believers should contemplate the full meaning of gospel promises respecting time and eternity and say, *The lines are fallen to me in a pleasant place* [Psalm 16:6]. Whatever the Lord has said shall be fulfilled. What an inheritance then is the believer's? The Lord is his *Sun and Shield* [Psalm 84:11]. *Thy Maker is thy Husband* [Isaiah 54:5]. *The Lord is thy portion* [Lamentations 3:24] and heaven is thy home.

FOR MEDITATION:

'Thou hast my promise, hold it fast,
The trying hour will soon be past;
Rejoice, for lo! I quickly come,
To take thee to my heavenly home.

'A pillar there, no more to move,
Inscribed with all my names of love;
A monument of mighty grace,
Thou shalt for ever have a place.'

Such is the conqueror's reward,
Prepared and promised by the LORD!
Let him that has the ear of faith,
Attend to what the Spirit saith.[138]

Comfort in Zion

'Comfort ye, comfort ye my people, saith your God. Speak ye comfortably to Jerusalem, and cry unto her, that her warfare is accomplished, that her iniquity is pardoned: for she hath received of the LORD's hand double for all her sins.' Isaiah 40:1–2

SUGGESTED FURTHER READING: Jeremiah 31:10–14

If, as some eminent commentators suppose, the prophet in this passage had any reference to the restoration of Babylon, it is certain his principal object was much more important. Indeed the history of their return from captivity and their state afterwards seems not to correspond with the magnificent images here used. Though they rebuilt their city and temple, they met with many insults, and much opposition, and continued a tributary and dependent people. I shall therefore waive the consideration of this sense. The prophet's thoughts seem fixed upon one august personage who was approaching to enlighten and bless a miserable world, and before he describes the circumstances of his appearances, he is directed to comfort the mourners in Zion with an assurance that this great event was sufficient to compensate them for all their sorrows. The state of Jerusalem, the representative name of the people or church of God, was very low in Isaiah's time. How different from the time of Solomon! Iniquity abounded, security prevailed, and judgements were impending. The words of many were stout against the Lord, but there were a few who feared him, whose eyes affected their hearts, and who mourned the evils they could not prevent. These and these only were strictly the Lord's people, and to these the message of comfort was addressed: *Speak to Jerusalem comfortably*, speak to her heart, to her case—there is an answer to all her desires, a balm for all her griefs, in this one consideration: the Messiah is at hand.

FOR MEDITATION: It is needful that we sometimes meet with sharp and painful changes to teach us, by our own experience, what we cannot so sensibly learn from books or sermons, that this is not our rest—that we are and must be dependent upon him, to whom we belong …But the light of his countenance, which is better than life itself, and which may more especially be hoped for when the streams of creature comfort run low or fail, is a sovereign balm to every wound, a cordial for every care.[139]

SERMON SERIES: MESSIAH,[140] NO. 1 [1/4], ISAIAH 40:1–2

For you, the war is over!

'Speak ye comfortably to Jerusalem, and cry unto her, that her warfare is accomplished ...' Isaiah 40:2
SUGGESTED FURTHER READING: Romans 7:14–8:4

Through and by the Messiah, *her warfare will be accomplished*. Two ideas are included in the original term: a state of service connected with hardship, like that of the military life, and an appointed time, as it is rendered in Job 14:14.

These ideas equally apply to the Mosaic dispensation. It was a state of comparative servitude, distance, fear and labour. The ceremonial law was a yoke, a burden, which Peter says neither we nor our fathers were able to bear. But the gospel was to supersede it, and to bring in a state of life, liberty and confidence. Such likewise is the time of conviction. The awakened sinner feels terror, distress and bondage—but it is for an appointed time. To such we are commanded to preach *comfort*, by leading their thoughts to the Messiah. The Lord God, who knows the human heart—its wants, feelings and desires—when he would comfort and speak to the heart, proposes one object, and only one, as the necessary and all-sufficient source of comfort. This is the Messiah. Jesus in his person and offices, known and received by faith, affords a balm for every wound, a cordial for every care.

FOR MEDITATION:

Approach, my soul, the mercy-seat
Where JESUS answers prayer;
There humbly fall beneath his feet,
For none can perish there.

Thy promise is my only plea,
With this I venture nigh;
Thou callest burdened souls to thee,
And such, O LORD, am I.

Bowed down beneath a load of sin,
By Satan sorely pressed;
By war without, and fears within,
I come to thee for rest.

Be thou my shield and hiding-place!
That, sheltered near thy side,
I may my fierce accuser face,
And tell him, thou hast died.

Oh, wondrous love! to bleed and die,
To bear the cross and shame;
That guilty sinners, such as I,
Might plead thy gracious name.

'Poor tempest-tossed soul, be still,
My promised grace receive';
'Tis JESUS speaks—I must, I will,
I can, I do believe.[141]

SERMON SERIES: MESSIAH, NO. 1 [2/4], ISAIAH 40:1–2

An offer of pardon

'Speak ye comfortably to Jerusalem, and cry unto her, that her warfare is accomplished, that her iniquity is pardoned: for she hath received of the LORD'S *hand double for all her sins.' Isaiah 40:2*
SUGGESTED FURTHER READING: Hebrews 10:11–18

Her iniquity is pardoned. The Messiah is coming to put away all sin by the one full, sufficient sacrifice of himself. We know that he is come, the atonement made, the ransom paid and accepted, and a throne of grace established to which whoever comes shall in no wise be cast out. To be capable of this comfort, the heart must be in a state suited to it. A free pardon is a comfort to a malefactor, but it implies guilt, and therefore they who have not broken the laws would be rather offended than comforted by an offer of pardon. Could we suppose that a company of people, who were all trembling under an apprehension of the wrath of God, constrained to confess the justice of the sentence, but not as yet informed of any way to escape, were to hear this message for the first time and to be fully assured of its truth and authority, they would receive it as life from the dead. But, for want of knowing themselves, it is to be feared that many who have received pleasure from the music of the *Messiah*, neither found nor expected nor desired to find any comfort from the words.

FOR MEDITATION:

My soul is beset
With grief and dismay,
I owe a vast debt
And nothing can pay:
I must go to prison,
Unless that dear Lord,
Who died and is risen,
His pity afford.

The death that he died,
The blood that he spilt,
To sinners applied,
Discharge from all guilt:
This great Intercessor
Can give, if he please,
The vilest transgressor
Immediate release.

When nailed to the tree,
He answered the prayer
Of one, who like me,
Was nigh to despair;
He did not upbraid him
With all he had done,
But instantly made him,
A saint and a son.[142]

Abundant grace

'Speak ye comfortably to Jerusalem, and cry unto her, that her warfare is accomplished, that her iniquity is pardoned: for she hath received of the LORD's *hand double for all her sins.'* Isaiah 40:2
SUGGESTED FURTHER READING: Ephesians 1:1–10

She has received double. Not, as some suppose, that her afflictions had already been over-proportioned to their procuring cause—sin. We shall always have reason to say, He has not dealt with us according to our iniquities. Others, who are rather too eager to strain texts beyond their proper import in order to support a favourite doctrine, suppose that the suffering of the Messiah would be greater than the exigency of the case— more than necessary. But the truth is best proved and supported by texts which expressly teach it. The efficacy of the atonement is indeed greater than the actual application and sufficient to save the whole race of mankind, if they believed in the Son of God. But he groaned and bled upon the cross till he could say, It is finished [John 19:30]—but no longer. It becomes us to refer to infinite wisdom the reasons why his sufferings were for such a precise time, but we may be sure they were not beyond what the cause required. I think the true sense of the words is that Jerusalem should receive blessings double, much greater, than all her former afflictions. And in general to us, to every believing sinner, that the blessings of the gospel would be an unspeakably great over-balance and compensation for all afflictions of every kind by which we have been or can be exercised. Afflictions are the fruit of sin, and because our sins have been many, our afflictions may be many. But where sin has abounded, grace has much more abounded.

FOR MEDITATION: Behold the goodness of God. Infinitely happy and glorious in himself. He has provided for the comfort of those who were rebels against his government and transgressors of his law.

Of sinners the chief, And viler than all,
The jailer or thief, Manasseh or Saul:
Since they were forgiven, Why should I despair,
While Christ is in heaven, And still answers prayer?[143]

SERMON SERIES: MESSIAH, NO. 1 [4/4], ISAIAH 40:1–2

Hope and quietly wait

'It is good that a man should both hope and quietly wait for the salvation of the LORD.*' Lamentations 3:26*
SUGGESTED FURTHER READING: Lamentations 3:25–33

This observation is recorded for the use of the church and has been confirmed by the experience of the Lord's people. I shall endeavour to show the meaning of the need. I would not have any go away with a mistake and say, 'If so, I am right enough; to be sure I hope to be saved, and I am *quietly waiting* for it.' But enquire whether you have any ground for your hope, whether you know what the salvation is, and what it is *quietly* to *wait*. *Salvation* is a deliverance from sin and a renewal of heart, and the having or obtaining this salvation is to arrive at well grounded persuasion that it is thus with us, that our sins are forgiven, that we have the spirit of adoption which is the earnest of the full inheritance. The *hope* here spoken of implies a sense of the worth of this salvation and a regard to the promise of God. It is suited to the case of a convinced soul. If you see you have deserved to perish and believe there is forgiveness with God, it is good and right for you to hope that though at present you cannot feel an interest in this salvation so as to call it your own, yet in the Lord's due time it shall be yours. *Quietly* to *wait* for it is not to sit down easy and careless about it. This is not good, but dangerous, and, if persisted, destructive. Neither is it possible when once the evil and bitterness of sin is known. To *wait* signifies a careful and diligent attendance on the means of grace, as it is expressed in Proverbs 8:34, *watching daily at my gates, waiting at the posts of my doors.* And the word *quietly* expresses the temper in which it becomes a sinner to wait—without complaining or repining—to be content to wait on, whatever delays or seeming disappointments we may meet with.

FOR MEDITATION: Surely, O Lord, the word that thou hast spoken concerning thy creature and upon which thou hast enabled me beyond hope to believe in hope shall not be spoken in vain. I trust that thou who hast said it art also fully able to perform all thy good promises in me and that as thou never yet didst finally cast out any poor wretch that came to thee for mercy, thou wilt not suffer me to be the first.[144]

Diary, 1 July 1752

SERMON: LAMENTATIONS 3:26 [1/3]

But I want it *Now*!

'It is good that a man should both hope and quietly wait for the salvation of the LORD.*' Lamentations* 3:26
SUGGESTED FURTHER READING: Nehemiah 4:1–23

Observe the need of such a word as this. It is much like the design of the parable which our Lord delivered to encourage us to pray earnestly and not to faint. The reasons arise:

(i) partly from the manner of his dispensation—he has promised to hear and answer—but it is likewise his pleasure to exercise our faith and patience. He seldom carries on his work any other way. When he promised Israel deliverance, he permitted Pharaoh to double his opposition. When he set them upon rebuilding the temple, he permitted their enemies to interrupt them. So when he stirs up a soul to seek his salvation, he seems at times to hide his face; their fears prevail, and their ease seems to grow worse. Yet his purpose stands good, and he tells them it is good for them both to *hope and quietly wait*.

(ii) partly from the tendency of our spirits to impatience and unbelief. A convinced sinner seeks mercy, but he must have it immediately; he can brook no delay, and is often brought to say or think, Wherefore should I wait any longer?

FOR MEDITATION:

The lion that on Sampson roared,
And thirsted for his blood;
With honey afterwards was stored,
And furnished him with food.

The world and Satan join their strength,
To fill their souls with fears;
But crops of joy they reap at length,
From what they sow in tears.

Believers, as they pass along,
With many lions meet;
But gather sweetness from the strong,
And from the eater, meat.

Afflictions make them love the Word,
Stir up their hearts to prayer;
And many precious proofs afford,
Of their Redeemer's care.

The lions rage and roar in vain,
For JESUS is their shield;
Their losses prove a certain gain,
Their troubles comfort yield.

The lions roar but cannot kill,
Then fear them not, my friends,
They bring us, though against their will,
The honey JESUS sends.[145]

SERMON: LAMENTATIONS 3:26 [2/3]

Wait *patiently?*

'It is good that a man should both hope and quietly wait for the salvation of the Lord.*' Lamentations 3:26*
SUGGESTED FURTHER READING: Isaiah 54:1–7

The truth of it is *good*. The word *good* may be understood in several senses.

First, it is reasonable, considering:

(i) the greatness of this salvation, which is such that you must allow, if the Lord was to suffer you to go on beset with tears and temptations to the last hour of life, if he showed you mercy at last you would have the utmost reason to praise him. You will say, 'Oh, if I knew this'; but it is reasonable to wait, though you know it not at present, that you may know it hereafter.

(ii) that as a sinner you have no right to make terms. What an inconsistence is it, at one time to confess the Lord might justly send you to hell, and yet perhaps the next hour repine because he makes you wait a while for the blessing.

(iii) that this is, as I have observed, the Lord's usual way. Search the Scripture: you will find it so. Ask his people who set about before you: they will tell you the same. Why should you expect he will change his methods for you? You want to be sure you are right and yet you are discouraged because you are led in that very path in which you see the footsteps of the flock before.

Secondly, it is profitable.

(i) It makes our waiting more pleasant to wait quietly and to maintain a hope upon the general promise, whereas to give way to another spirit lets in a storm upon the soul and opens a door to the worst temptations.

(ii) It is profitable to others, for they have the same exercises—if by your complaints you bring up an evil report of the good land, you lay a snare in the way of seekers and tempt the world to speak evil of your profession.

Thirdly, it is safe. It is good because those who thus hope and wait shall never be disappointed or ashamed. See such promises as Isaiah 54:7–8.

FOR MEDITATION: 'I waited patiently for the Lord; and he inclined unto me, and heard my cry' (Psalm 40:1).

A voice in the wilderness

'The voice of him that crieth in the wilderness, Prepare ye the way of the Lord, *make straight in the desert a highway for our God.' Isaiah 40:3*
SUGGESTED FURTHER READING: Luke 1:57–80

The general style of the prophets is poetical. Simplicity is the grand, inimitable characteristic of the whole Bible. But the magnificence and variety of imagery, which constitute the life and spirit of poetry, evidently distinguishes the style of the Psalms, Isaiah, and the other poetical books, from that of the historical parts in our common version. The various rules and properties of Hebrew poetry are not, at this distance of time, certainly known. But the present Bishop of London,[146] in his lectures on this subject, and in the discourse prefixed to his translation of Isaiah, has fully demonstrated one property. It usually consists of parallel expressions in which the same thought for substance is repeated in a different manner. I may open the book anywhere, almost, to explain my meaning—as chapters 59, 55 and Psalm 114. The knowledge of this peculiarity may often save us the trouble of enquiring minutely into the meaning of every single word, when one plain and comprehensive sense arises if the whole passage be taken together. Thus in this place, though it be true that John the Baptist was long retired in the wilderness and began to preach in the wilderness of Judea, yet the word does not entirely foretell that circumstance. The expressions are parallel. The prophet, rapt into future times, hears a voice proclaiming the Messiah's approach. And this is the majestic language: *In the wilderness prepare ye the way of the Lord. Make straight in the desert a highway for our God.* The wilderness and the desert are the same, as likewise in chapter 35, where the happy, the sudden, the unexpected, effects of his appearance, are described.

FOR MEDITATION: Now to see with the eye of faith the glory of the Redeemer in his appearance, to see power divine preparing the way before him, to enter into the gracious and wonderful design of his salvation, to acknowledge, admire and adore him as the Lord, humbly to claim him as *our* God, affords a pleasure very different from that which the finest music, however well adapted to the words, can possibly give.

The wilderness becomes a garden of the Lord

'The voice of him that crieth in the wilderness, Prepare ye the way of the LORD, *make straight in the desert a highway for our God. Every valley shall be exalted, and every mountain and hill shall be made low: and the crooked shall be made straight, and the rough places plain.'* Isaiah 40:3–4
SUGGESTED FURTHER READING: Psalm 105:1–45

When the eastern monarchs travelled, harbingers [forerunners] went before to give notice that the king was upon the road, and proper persons likewise to prepare the way and to remove obstacles. Some of them, if we may depend upon history, in the affectation of displaying their pomp and power, effected extraordinary things upon such occasions. For man, though vain, would appear wise; though a mere worm he would fain be great. We read of their having actually filled up valleys, and levelled hills to make a commodious way for themselves or their armies through places otherwise impassable. The prophet thus illustrates great things by small, and accommodates the language and usages of men to divine truth. The Messiah is about to visit a wilderness world, and those parts of it which he blesses with his presence shall become the garden of the Lord. Till then it is all desolate—rocky, wild and barren. But his way shall be prepared, mountainous difficulties shall sink before him into plains, in defiance of hindrances and difficulties; his glory shall be revealed in the wilderness and all flesh shall see it, for the mouth of the Lord hath spoken.

FOR MEDITATION: They say the times are very dark: they seem so to us; clouds and darkness are about his throne, but light will in due time shine out. He is carrying on his work by a straight line. If you or I were engaged in a plan which we had much at heart, we would not suffer anything to hinder our purpose, if we could prevent it: much less he, who has all power in heaven and earth...The times are dark; but perhaps they were darker in England sixty years ago. Some of those places were as a wilderness in my remembrance, and now they are gardens of the Lord. I am not sure that in the year 1740 there was a single parochial minister, who was publicly known as a gospel preacher, in the whole kingdom: now we have, I know not how many, but I think no fewer than four hundred.[147]

John Newton to John Campbell, 18 July 1795

SERMON SERIES: MESSIAH, NO. 2 [2/4], ISAIAH 40:3–5

Withstanding Messiah's progress

'The voice of him that crieth in the wilderness, Prepare ye the way of the Lord, *make straight in the desert a highway for our God. Every valley shall be exalted, and every mountain and hill shall be made low: and the crooked shall be made straight, and the rough places plain.' Isaiah 40:3–4*
SUGGESTED FURTHER READING: Isaiah 5:1–7

The state of the Jewish church and nation and the heathen when our Lord came: *a wilderness.* Israel, once the beloved people, was now, with a few exceptions, totally degenerated. The Lord's vineyard brought only wild grapes. They had the temple, the Scripture, the name of Abraham's seed. The prophet's lamentation (in 1:21) was still more applicable afterwards: *How is the faithful city become an harlot!*

The heathen world is described as sitting in darkness and in the region of the shadow of death. Philosophers had talked of wisdom and morality from age to age. But their speculations were mere swelling words of vanity, and did no real good. There were philosophers, poets, painters, musicians, eminent in their way, but the world was buried in idolatry and abominable wickedness (Romans 1:23 to the end). Everything was diametrically opposite to the design and spirit of that kingdom the Messiah was about to set up, and therefore disposed, as the event proved, to withstand his progress.

FOR MEDITATION:

Happy are they, to whom the Lord
His gracious name makes known!
And by his Spirit, and his word,
Adopts them for his own!

Then mountains sink at once to plains,
And light from darkness springs;
Each seeming loss improves their gains,
Each trouble comfort brings.

Though men despise them, or revile,
They count the trial small;
Whoever frowns, if Jesus smile,
It makes amends for all.

Though meanly clad, and coarsely fed,
And, like their Saviour, poor;
They would not change their gospel bread
For all the worldling's store.[148]

Providential preparation

'The voice of him that crieth in the wilderness, Prepare ye the way of the LORD, *make straight in the desert a highway for our God. Every valley shall be exalted, and every mountain and hill shall be made low: and the crooked shall be made straight, and the rough places plain.'* Isaiah 40:3–4
SUGGESTED FURTHER READING: Luke 2:1–20

A way was prepared for the Messiah in providence:

(i) by Alexander's conquests, which spread the knowledge of the Greek language among many nations—and the Scriptures being afterwards translated into Greek became more common. An expectation of some Great Deliverer was raised far and wide, and the Messiah became in this sense the desire of many nations.

(ii) by the establishment and growth of the Roman power, which was in its height at our Lord's birth; the principal part of the then known world was united in one empire—and as all the provinces were connected with Rome, an intercourse was opened on every side for the reception of the truth.

(iii) by John's ministry and its effects. These were so great that John himself seems to have been astonished at the numbers and character of those who came to his baptism.

It was to Judea our Lord came, and there especially were the great obstructions to be removed. For he came:

(i) to exalt the valleys—to preach the gospel to the poor, to fill the hungry with good things, to save the chief of sinners, to open the kingdom to publicans and harlots; likewise to correct the low thoughts the Jews had indulged of the law of God, the office and kingdom of the Messiah.

(ii) to bring low every mountain and hill—to detect the wickedness and confound the pride of the Pharisees and rulers, to pour contempt on all human glory, and to show that the το ὑψηλον[149] of man is abomination in the sight of God (see chapter 2[verses 11,17], or 10:4–6).

(iii) to rectify the perverse disposition of the hearts of men—to soften and subdue their spirits and to make them willing in the day of his power.

FOR MEDITATION: 'And the glory of the LORD shall be revealed, and all flesh shall see it together: for the mouth of the LORD hath spoken it' (Isaiah 40:5).

Finding true happiness

'Blessed are the poor in spirit: for theirs is the kingdom of heaven.'
Matthew 5:3
SUGGESTED FURTHER READING: Matthew 5:1–12

The desire of happiness is natural to man, but all are bewildered and disappointed in the present, except those who are enriched and taught by the Spirit of God to seek it by Christ Jesus. He came down from heaven that by his doctrine, life and death he might correct our mistakes concerning happiness and show us wherein it consists, how it is to be attained, and remove every obstacle that would deprive us of the possession. Full happiness is not upon earth, it is only to be expected in the kingdom of heaven, and true happiness in any degree is restrained to them who by his grace are brought into his appointed way to that kingdom. His people are happy here in comparison with others and shall be happy for ever. They derive their title from his blood, their temper and characters from his Spirit. These heavenly and gracious tempers are enumerated here, but they are never found singly or separate. Whoever has truly one, has received the seeds of them all, though they are not equally called out to lively exercise at all times and in all persons. Whoever is entirely destitute of any one, is destitute of the rest. May the Spirit of God help us to examine ourselves by this test for our consolation, conviction, and instruction in righteousness.

FOR MEDITATION: But I find among these illiterate and uninformed people, some who are truly wise, wise unto salvation. They know themselves, they know the Lord. The know the *summum bonum*,[150] the true happiness of man, wherein it consists and how it is to be obtained. They have learnt to taste the goodness of God in their brown bread, to be content and satisfied with a low estate—to cast all their cares upon God, and to be assured that he careth for them. They know how to obtain an audience of the King of kings. They have more in hand than the world can either give or take away.[151]

John Newton to William Wilberforce, 19 June 1794
[writing from a village inn in Cambridgeshire]

Be poor in spirit

'Blessed are the poor in spirit: for theirs is the kingdom of heaven.'
Matthew 5:3
SUGGESTED FURTHER READING: Luke 5:1–11

To be *poor in spirit* is to be humble, to know ourselves, and to judge ourselves to be what we are. There would be no excellency in this poverty of spirit if it was not founded in truth and suited to our circumstances. It is such a temper of mind as becomes a sinner under a dispensation of mercy and grace. When we hear a rich man talk of his wealth, furniture and servants, we are not surprised or offended, but if a beggar who has neither food, raiment or dwelling, should affect an air of importance and talk at the same rate, we should think him mad. No less an impropriety is it for one of fallen Adam's race to fancy that he has any wisdom, strength or goodness of his own. Yet thus we all dream by nature. Vain man would be wise. Sinful man labours to establish his own righteousness. He knows not that he is poor and miserable and blind and naked, but is trusting and boasting in a power which he has not. When we are awakened from this dream by the Spirit of God, we become *poor in spirit*, or humble—truly so in a measure, but imperfectly at the best. Now there are three discoveries made to the soul, which strip us of our fancied riches and attainments and make us poor. Those who know the most of these are the most advanced in poverty of the spirit:

(i) a humbling sense of the sinfulness of our hearts. When this is known it causes as sudden a change of thought as it would if a man should unexpectedly find he had the plague upon him. How little then would he think of all his possessions! So the convicted sinner.

(ii) a humbling sight of the majesty of God. How greatly did this affect Job and Isaiah (chapter 6). But especially,

(iii) a humbler taste of his love. A manifestation of God reconciled in Christ humbles the soul to purpose. Without a hope of this sort, the former would lead to despair. But when this hope arises to a strong, well-grounded persuasion, when the Lord shines upon the soul, then there is true poverty of spirit.

FOR MEDITATION: O that my failings might at least teach me humility, and convince me more effectually how frail I am.[152]   *Diary*, 22 January 1755

SERMON: MATTHEW 5:3 [2/3]

Test yourself

'Blessed are the poor in spirit: for theirs is the kingdom of heaven.'
Matthew 5:3
SUGGESTED FURTHER READING: Esther 5:9–7:10

Would you know if this is your state or how far you have advanced? Attend to the effects. So far as you are poor in spirit, you will find:

(i) a resignation to the will of God, for you will not only believe that his appointment is best, but you will see everything is better than you deserve.

(ii) you will not be easily angry. A knowledge of your own heart will teach you to make allowance for others. And from a sense of your debt of 10,000 talents to God, you will be ready to forgive a few pence to man.

(iii) you will not be over-confident. To be poor in spirit is to be sensible that you are weak, fallible and know but little, and this will keep you diffident of your own judgement.

(iv) you will not aim to stand high in the opinion of others, any more than a beggar will try to pass for a rich man.

(v) especially, you will most gladly renounce your own righteousness and count all things but dung for the excellency of the knowledge of Christ Jesus the Lord.

But what do I say? Shall I unchristian all my hearers and myself too? Many, I am afraid, can in no degree stand this trial, but these gracious tempers must be formed in you, if you would be saved. These are the mind that was in Christ, and if any man have not the Spirit of Christ he is none of his. What can those who live in pride, anger, peevishness—impatient of the least contradiction—say to this? O may the Lord convince you and stir you to seek for pardon and grace for Jesus' sake while it is to be found. And those of us who believe have need to be ashamed and humbled into the dust. How much do we feel contrary to these tempers!

FOR MEDITATION: Bless God for an Advocate—admire rich grace and trust to it. If he has begun the work, he will finish. And even now you are blessed, for yours is the kingdom. The kingdom of grace is yours. Grace is glory begun.[153] Glory is grace perfected. Watch, pray and strive for an increase of this poverty of spirit, that your light may shine to the glory of your Father which is in heaven.

SERMON: MATTHEW 5:3 [3/3]

The Israel of God

'Happy art thou, O Israel: who is like unto thee, O people saved by the LORD, the shield of thy help, and who is the sword of thy excellency! and thine enemies shall be found liars unto thee; and thou shalt tread upon their high places.' Deuteronomy 33:29

SUGGESTED FURTHER READING: Deuteronomy 33:26–29

Happy indeed are the people who are in such a case, yea blessed are the people who have the Lord for their God. As we observed lately,[154] no God like the God of Israel, so no people like the Israel of God. The believers are called *Israel,* because, like Jacob of old, they are children of the covenant and have obtained a new name by faith and prayer. They are a *saved* people. Saved from guilt, wrath and Satan, and saved of the Lord—therefore their salvation is honourable and sure. As they are called to war, they are well provided. The Lord is their *shield*, to defend them in all perils. The Lord is their *sword*, he fights for them; it is by laying hold of his arm that they are victorious. Therefore opposition shall be vain. Their *enemies shall be liars*. Satan despises and threatens us, but all shall be liars. There is help in God even to the uttermost. Their warfare shall end in complete victory. They shall *tread upon the high places* of sin (of long habit, of general custom—see Daniel 3), of sins that plead necessity (as a right hand or right eye) and of Satan (unbelief, terror, presumption). And when they are thus made more than conquerors, they shall enter into Canaan—that blessed rest which remaineth for the people of God.

FOR MEDITATION: [specially written to be sung after this sermon]

With Israel's GOD who can compare?	Upheld by everlasting arms,
Or who, like Israel, happy are?	Thou art secured from foes and harms!
To people saved by the LORD,	In vain their plots, and false their boasts!
He is thy shield and great reward.	Our refuge is the LORD of Hosts.[155]

Pray for your ministers

'Brethren, pray for us.' 1 *Thessalonians* 5:25
SUGGESTED FURTHER READING: 1 Thessalonians 5:12–28

The Apostle, though eminent in grace and experience, often entreats the prayers of the Lord's people. His dependence was upon the Lord himself, but he knew he who has promised to do great things has said, I will be enquired of to do them, and therefore expected success in proportion as prayer should be engaged. Good reason then have succeeding ministers to make the like request. If you pray for us, you will strengthen our hands and thereby draw down blessings upon yourselves. This entreaty can only be effectually complied with by those whose hearts are in some measure alive and earnest for gospel causes. To pray for ministers, the people must be able to love them principally and chiefly as his ministers. If they have a just sense of the importance of the gospel message, they will love and pray for the messengers. This kindness they owe to them all. Stated ministers, if they really value their people's prayers, will endeavour to deserve a personal and special affection. Next to the supports and comforts they receive immediately from the Lord, they find their chief consolation in the affections of their people and the most interesting proof of this is their prayers. There are those who will sometimes plead and dispute and almost fight for their minister and labour to set him above others. But they are the best friends who strive most earnestly in prayer for them.

FOR MEDITATION: [for the New Year sermon 1778]

O Thou, at whose almighty word
The glorious light from darkness sprung!
Thy quickening influence afford,
And clothe with power the preacher's tongue.

As when of old, the water flowed
Forth from the rock at thy command;
Moses in vain had waved the rod,
Without thy wonder-working hand.

Though 'tis thy truth he hopes to speak,
He cannot give the hearing ear;
'Tis thine, the stubborn heart to break,
And make the careless sinner fear.

Now, while we hear thy word of grace,
Let self and pride before it fall;
And rocky hearts dissolve apace,
In streams of sorrow at thy call.[157]

SERMON: 1 THESSALONIANS 5:25 [1/6]

Empathize with your ministers

'Brethren, pray for us.' 1 *Thessalonians* 5:25
SUGGESTED FURTHER READING: 2 Corinthians 6:1–13

To pray for ministers the people must be able to feel for them. Here there is a difference. We know most of your exercises, because we share them with you in common. But you are not proper judges of ours. You do not stand in our place; we must tell you what we feel to engage your pity, but we can never tell you all. I need your prayers, and to engage them, I am desirous at this time a little to open my mind to you upon the subject of our trials. As to myself, if I had only to get through an hour in the pulpit, though I should prize your love and your prayers, I should have no very strong claim to your compassion. My outward trials are neither many or heavy, considering the usual lot of human life. But preaching is not all, and even in preaching, if the Lord has given us a love to our work and to our hearers, we have often, when we seem to speak with liberty, very painful feelings. Had we this desirable liberty always and nothing painful mixed with it, we should soon forget ourselves. This the Lord knows, and finds ways to make us remember what we are, which though necessary, are often very sharp. And though we are supported for public service and some persons may be ready to think we lead happy lives, we could (at least I could) often address you in the words of Job, *Have pity upon me, O my friends, for the hand of God has touched me* [Job 19:21].

FOR MEDITATION:

Chief Shepherd of thy chosen sheep,
From death and sin set free;
May every under-shepherd keep
His eye, intent on thee!

With plenteous grace their hearts prepare,
To execute thy will;
Compassion, patience, love and care,
And faithfulness and skill.

Inflame their minds with holy zeal
Their flocks to feed and teach;
And let them live, and let them feel
The sacred truths they preach.[158]

The trials of a minister

'Brethren, pray for us.' 1 *Thessalonians* 5:25
SUGGESTED FURTHER READING: 2 Timothy 4:1–8

We are tried in private. I should be happy indeed, if I always felt the comforts of those truths which I trust at times comfort many of you when I set them forth here. But if any of you know what it is to groan under the power of unbelief and indwelling sin, deadness in prayer and even unwillingness to pray, coldness and confusion in reading the Scripture, be assured that preaching with some earnestness and apparent pleasure, at times, does by no means secure us from these groanings. One of my greatest trials is the difference between what I may seem to be in public, and what I feel myself to be in private, which has made me often ready to compare myself to a player on a stage. We are tried in the pulpit: a consciousness of the weakness and unskilfulness of our best attempts, the evils that beset us in our most solemn services, a conviction how far we fall short ourselves of what we propose to you, and sometimes a straitness and dryness of spirit when we must speak, though we know not what we can say. If private believers are not in a frame of mind to speak they may keep silence, but ministers are like post horses— when the hour comes, they must set out, whatever disadvantages attend the journey.

FOR MEDITATION: The afternoon service approaches. Do thou give me wisdom and a blessing. There is great cause for humiliation and prayer amongst us. In vain shall I try to teach their hearts, unless thou art pleased to work.[159]

Diary, Sunday 23 June 1776
[immediately prior to preaching this sermon]

Ah, my Lord, I seem to be something when among my fellow creatures, but am nothing in thy sight—a poor heartless worm. I had words to speak at the Great House,[160] but to myself—words without feeling. I am beset with evils, which, like the canker upon a tree, keep me low. O Lord, put forth thy power—blow with thy wind, dissolve the ice and cause the waters to flow.[161]

Diary, 4 June 1776

A Shepherd's heart

'Brethren, pray for us.' 1 *Thessalonians* 5:25
SUGGESTED FURTHER READING: Isaiah 49:8–23

We are, we must be, sharply tried by the cases of our hearers.

With respect to the congregations at large, I must have a heart like a stone if I could look seriously round this congregation without being affected. To see so many who are stumbling in the broad day, still under the power of sin, after long enjoying such uncommon advantages as the Lord has been pleased to favour this town with. To see them from week to week, from year to year, still careless and hardening under the means of grace. … often I shrink at the thought lest I am unfaithful. I fear I am not faithful, earnest or importunate enough, though I seem not to know how to be more so. I am a debtor to all, I bear a love to every soul that hears me.

But there are among you a number who not only hear but profess the truth; to these I bear a more immediate relation. I am more acquainted with them, I feel more for them. I may say without boasting, the Lord has given me, at least in a little measure, the heart of a shepherd. I feel for the distresses of many. As I am much among the people, I know a good deal of their personal and their family troubles. My heart sinks at the trials of some here before me and of others whose afflictions detain them at home. Perhaps no one in the parish knows so much of these things as I do. And I could relate cases which would, I am persuaded, draw tears from many eyes. I know likewise something of the spiritual distresses of those whom I endeavour to comfort but cannot.

FOR MEDITATION: My time and thoughts much engrossed today by an affecting and critical dispensation at *Orchard Side* [William Cowper attempted suicide]. I was sent for in the morning early and returned astonished and grieved. Could hardly attend to anything else.[162]

Diary, 2 January 1773

The first temptation the enemy assaulted him with was to offer up himself as Abraham his son. He verily thought he ought to do it. We were obliged to watch with him night and day. I, my dear wife and Mrs Unwin with whom he lived, left him not an hour for seven years.[163]

John Newton's Funeral Sermon for William Cowper, May 1800

SERMON: 1 THESSALONIANS 5:25 [4/6]

Where is their zeal?

'Brethren, pray for us.' 1 *Thessalonians* 5:25
SUGGESTED FURTHER READING: Galatians 6:1–10

I feel for the declensions of many. I will lay no stress upon my own personal concern. It is trying to flesh and blood to see any who once professed a warm regard, look shy and cold, and when one loves and studies to show it, to be misapprehended and misrepresented. Blessed be the Lord, if I have something of this kind to complain of, the instances are not many. And were it not for the cause, the effect would sit light upon me. But how many do I know who have carried it unkindly to the Lord, if not to me. O where is their zeal, where is their first love, where is the value they once put upon ordinances, where is that gospel conversation they once aimed at? Once they loved to assemble with the Lord's people, now they may be often seen with the drunkards. *Brethren, pray for me.* I fear lest the Lord should be displeased. Would it be believed if I should tell it in London, where I am going,[164] that in such a place as they suppose Olney to be and where there are so many people and where the gospel has been so many years, it should sometimes be difficult to find one man present to set the psalm before sermon on a Thursday evening? I well remember when it was far otherwise.

FOR MEDITATION:

Thus saith the LORD to Ephesus,
And thus he speaks to some of us;
'Amidst my churches, lo, I stand,
And hold the pastors in my hand.

'Thy works, to me, are fully known,
Thy patience, and thy toil, I own;
Thy views of gospel truth are clear,
Nor can'st thou other doctrine bear.

'Yet I must blame while I approve,
Where is thy first, thy fervent love?
Dost thou forget my love to thee,
That thine is grown so faint to me?

'Recall to mind the happy days
When thou wast filled with joy and praise;
Repent, thy former works renew,
Then I'll restore thy comforts too.

'Return at once, when I reprove,
Lest I thy candlestick remove;
And thou, too late, thy loss lament;
I warn before I strike, Repent.'

Hearken to what the Spirit saith,
To him that overcomes by faith;
'The fruit of life's unfading tree,
In paradise his food shall be.'[165]

SERMON: 1 THESSALONIANS 5:25 [5/6]

Pray for a fresh anointing

'Brethren, pray for us.' 1 *Thessalonians* 5:25
SUGGESTED FURTHER READING: Galatians 5:16–26

I feel for the congregation's heart-burnings and grudgings one towards another. Alas, when a little word inadvertently spoken shall be sufficient foundation for a quarrel. When there is a readiness to give offence, a readiness to take offence, a backwardness to reconciliation—these things throw two things in a minister's way. He cannot but consider them as a sign that grace is low, and a means of keeping it so—that to such persons he is little useful at present and, unless the Lord interpose, he has but a poor hope of being more so. Some or other of these trials are always present to my mind and of late they have brought another troublesome thought upon me. I had not been a month in Olney before the Lord gave me such a regard for the people that it has ever since been the place of my choice. I have ever laboured to decline and avoid what the world calls advantageous offers and at this moment you are upon my heart to live and die with you, if the Lord please. But I am not my own master. And if the gospel should come to be greatly neglected and slighted and a form of godliness take place of that power which once was known here, will there not be some reason to fear lest the Lord should show his displeasure by removing it?

Brethren, pray for us. Pray for me and for yourselves—that the Lord may take away our iniquities, pour a fresh anointing upon minister and people, that I may be strengthened and owned in the work and you may know and prize and improve the privileges you enjoy.

FOR MEDITATION: [for New Year's Evening 1775]

Preachers may, from Ezekiel's case,	Like him, around I cast my eye,
Draw hope in this declining day,	And oh! what heaps of bones appear!
A proof like this, of sovereign grace	Like him, by JESUS sent, I'll try,
Should chase our unbelief away.	For he can cause the dead to hear.

When sent to preach to mouldering bones,	Hear, ye dry bones, the Saviour's word!
Who could have thought he would succeed?	He, who when dying, gasped, 'Forgive',
But well he knew, the LORD from stones	That gracious, sinner-loving LORD,
Could raise up Abram's chosen seed.	Says, 'Look to me, dry bones, and live.'[166]

SERMON: 1 THESSALONIANS 5:25 [6/6]

Reverent joy: his greatness, our unworthiness

'Rejoice with trembling.' Psalm 2:11
SUGGESTED FURTHER READING: Psalm 2:1–12

This psalm is a prophecy of the establishment of the Redeemer's kingdom in defiance of all the opposition raised against it. God had declared the decree and therefore the heathens and people, the Jews and Gentiles, kings and rulers, raged against it—as without just cause, so without effect. The Redeemer is seated in heaven and has his enemies in derision. Their resistance is to no purpose and, if persisted in, can only issue in their own ruin. They are therefore in mercy exhorted to submit and humble themselves before him. This, if they rightly know the nature of his kingdom, is their interest and would be their happiness. His subjects have good ground for joy—but a joy tempered with reverence. They may well rejoice, for he is able and engaged to bless those who put their trust in him. At the same time his greatness and their unworthiness, the dangers and snares they are exposed to, the evil within them and the enemies around them, are suited to inspire an awe and a jealousy. They are exhorted to rejoice, but with trembling. I think these words may be accommodated to enforce that temper of mind which becomes us all on the present occasion, when we professedly meet to offer our thanks to him who has the supreme government of all things, for putting an end to the late calamitous war. We have reason to rejoice and we have still reason to tremble.

FOR MEDITATION: Oh that our great men and statesmen rightly considered that the Lord reigneth—that they would seek wisdom from him to plan their enterprises and depend upon his blessing for their success. The finest spun schemes of men on earth may be compared to a spider's web. One unforeseen contingence is sufficient to derange and sweep them away. Many proofs we have had in the course of this unhappy war[168] that no human counsels or prospects can stand against the Lord. It is not Britannia, as our boasting song pretends, but the Lord who rules the waves, and them who sail upon them.[169]

John Newton to William Wilberforce, 30 March 1796

SERMON: PSALM 2:11 [1/3] [END OF AMERICAN WAR OF INDEPENDENCE]

A great and undeserved mercy

'Rejoice with trembling.' Psalm 2:11
SUGGESTED FURTHER READING: Isaiah 2:1–5

Rejoice that during the war we were favoured with peace at home. I have nothing to say either of the grounds of the war or the terms of the peace in a political view. I believe sin kindled the war and mercy gave us peace. But that when we were gradually drawn into a war with so many formidable powers, we should be preserved in peace, guarded by the providence of God, and that no attempts should be permitted to be formed, or at least to succeed against these kingdoms, is, in my view, a great and undeserved mercy. Especially as the effects of the war, so far as we felt them or suffered by them abroad, had no visible influence to bring us to humiliation and repentance, but rather, as a nation, the increase of dissipation and wickedness and contempt of God kept pace with the increase of our distresses and dangers. We count it a successful war when the enemy's fleets and armies are destroyed and when islands and provinces are added to our dominion. But no increase of riches or domain can make war properly successful. No conquest can be worth the lives that are sacrificed to obtain them. All the wealth of both the Indies would be a poor equivalent for the havoc and slaughter of the last war. It will be found so at last. Let us rejoice then that this horrid evil is suspended. Nor is it a prevention of the loss of lives only. The death of one person often deeply affects many persons. The parent has perhaps lost a child, by the same stroke a child is deprived of a parent, the wife becomes a widow. The griefs, the woes, the pressures, that have been brought upon individuals and families by the late war, cannot be fully conceived. If there are any hearts so hard and unfeeling as to rejoice in public calamity, if their private wealth is increased by it, yet I hope *we* can sincerely rejoice that God has sheathed the devouring sword and made wars cease to the ends of the earth.

FOR MEDITATION: Rejoice that we are still favoured with religious liberty and gospel light. God has not taken his mercy and truth from us. He is still carrying on his work, increasing the number of faithful ministers and, thereby, as we hope, adding to the number of his people and of those for whose sakes we are preserved from utter desolation.

SERMON: PSALM 2:11 [2/3] [END OF AMERICAN WAR OF INDEPENDENCE]

Cause for trembling

'Rejoice with trembling.' Psalm 2:11
SUGGESTED FURTHER READING: Hosea 11:1–11

While we rejoice let us remember the causes we still have as a nation to tremble.

(i) God has a controversy with this land. It seems indeed, with respect to a great part of the kingdom and especially of those who are in most estimation for rank, wealth or human wisdom, an undecided point whether the Lord be God, whether he be the Governor and Judge of all the earth or not. Therefore he has withdrawn his blessing. Divisions in our counsels, disappointment in our undertakings followed. But he is merciful and restores us peace. We, alas, are still hardened—the point is not yet acknowledged and there is reason to fear it must be brought to a new trial. And why should it not? Who that loves the Lord can wish that he should desert his cause, and wickedness and infidelity triumph with impunity?

(ii) The actual state of affairs at present: the accumulated burdens on the state, the violence of parties, the generally acknowledged want of public spirit. It is not necessary that we should be destroyed by earthquake, famine or pestilence. It is enough to ruin us if the Lord does not in an extraordinary manner interpose to prevent our destruction. If he leave us to ourselves, we are going, we are gone.

If you speak of the glory and honour of Great Britain as a nation among the nations, you may write *Ichabod* upon it—the glory is departed [1 Samuel 4:21]. But what is this? The influence of our pride and oppression will not be so severely and extensively felt abroad—nor the profligacy and luxury be so great at home. Perhaps if we were enclosed within the walls of our island, which may possibly be the case, we may become a more temperate and moral, and therefore a more happy, people. I am not sure that these are upon the whole bad times. It is the best time when the best cause prospers most. The truth, I hope, spreads. The kingdom of our God and Saviour is upon the increase.

FOR MEDITATION: This kingdom is not of this world, nor dependent upon kingdoms of the earth. It cannot be shaken. They who belong to it may rejoice, and so far as they live to their Lord, need not tremble, though the earth itself were moved and the mountains cast into the midst of the sea.

SERMON: PSALM 2:11 [3/3] [END OF AMERICAN WAR OF INDEPENDENCE]

Children of his grace

'And in process of time it came to pass, that Cain brought of the fruit of the ground an offering unto the LORD. *And Abel, he also brought of the firstlings of his flock and of the fat thereof. And the* LORD *had respect unto Abel and to his offering: but unto Cain and to his offering he had not respect. And Cain was very wroth, and his countenance fell.' Genesis 4:3–5*
SUGGESTED FURTHER READING: Genesis 4:1–7

From the Fall of man, the Scripture proceeds to an exemplification of the effects of sin, the manifestation of grace, and the opposition foretold between the seed of the serpent and those who by faith belonged to him who was revealed as the hope of sinners, by the name of the seed of the woman. These are the chief points insisted on through the whole Bible. The first remarkable instance in which they are confirmed is the history of Cain and Abel. It seems that Eve had great joy in the birth of Cain, nay some from the manner of her expression think that she supposed Cain was the promised Messiah. If so, she was greatly disappointed. Parents usually receive children with joy—but if God has given you children, pray that they may be the children of his grace; if not, rejoice with trembling. If the Lord is not honoured by them, you will have small comfort in them. You know not what they may come to. And this should be a quieting thought when the Lord has taken away children while young. We are informed that Cain was a wicked man, yet he was not without a form of religion. Cain himself would probably pass for a saint if he were alive now, in comparison with many who are not only destitute of the life and power of godliness, but despise and renounce the very appearance of it. But his religion was vain—the Lord had respect to Abel and his offering and not to Cain's.

FOR MEDITATION: Give my love to all your children, particularly to the little stranger [baby 'John Newton' Coffin]. I am duly sensible of the honour you have done me in incorporating my name with your own. May the name of Newton be to him as a lighthouse upon a hill as he grows up, to warn him against the evils I ran upon in my youth, and on which (without a miracle of mercy) I should have suffered a fatal shipwreck.[170]

John Newton to James Coffin, 29 September 1792

SERMON SERIES: GENESIS, NO. 11 [1/4], GENESIS 4:3–5

Sovereign grace

'And in process of time it came to pass, that Cain brought of the fruit of the ground an offering unto the LORD. *And Abel, he also brought of the firstlings of his flock and of the fat thereof. And the* LORD *had respect unto Abel and to his offering: but unto Cain and to his offering he had not respect. And Cain was very wroth, and his countenance fell.' Genesis 4:3–5*
SUGGESTED FURTHER READING: 1 Samuel 16:1–13

If any say, 'Is God then a respecter of persons?' I answer, God respects not persons of men so as to be influenced by any outward differences between one man and another, which is the proper sense of the word. He does not prefer the rich to the poor, the wise to the ignorant, or the mighty to the mean. The cry of a beggar will enter the ear of the Lord of hosts and obtain a gracious answer as soon as the cry of a king. Yet in the dispensation of his grace he is sovereign, he gives what none has a right to demand, to whom he pleases. Cain and Abel were both born in sin. He might have rejected them both, and in preferring one to the other he exercised his undoubted right to do what he will with his own. This is mortifying doctrine to the pride of man—but as it gives all the glory of salvation to the Lord, so it provides the surest ground of peace to an awakened soul, when taken in connection with the rest of his Word. When you know yourselves, you will soon see that if it was not thus you could not be saved at all.

Observe: though the ways of God are sovereign, they are just and equal. Though he gives not a full account of his matters, yet he reveals enough not only to silence our cavils but to satisfy our doubts.

FOR MEDITATION: 'What shall we say then? Is there unrighteousness with God? God forbid. For he saith to Moses, I will have mercy on whom I will have mercy, and I will have compassion on whom I will have compassion. So then it is not of him that willeth, nor of him that runneth, but of God that sheweth mercy … Thou wilt say then unto me, Why doth he yet find fault? For who hath resisted his will? Nay but, O man, who art thou that repliest against God? Shall the thing formed say to him that formed it, Why hast thou made me thus? Hath not the potter power over the clay, of the same lump to make one vessel unto honour, and another unto dishonour?' (Romans 9:14–16, 19–21).

SERMON SERIES: GENESIS, NO. 11 [2/4], GENESIS 4:3–5

A more excellent sacrifice

'And in process of time it came to pass, that Cain brought of the fruit of the ground an offering unto the LORD. *And Abel, he also brought of the firstlings of his flock and of the fat thereof. And the* LORD *had respect unto Abel and to his offering: but unto Cain and to his offering he had not respect. And Cain was very wroth, and his countenance fell.' Genesis 4:3–5*
SUGGESTED FURTHER READING: Matthew 26:17–30

Let us consider Cain's offering a little more attentively and we shall perhaps see that in the nature of things it was utterly impossible that such an offering and such a worshipper could be accepted by a God of truth and holiness. For we read that God clothed our first parents with the skins of beasts—and here, of Abel's sacrifices. Bloody sacrifices were doubtless instituted when God gave the promise of a Saviour, and his death was shown forth in type till he appeared in the flesh to put away sin by the sacrifice of himself. That *without shedding of blood there is no remission* [Hebrews 9:22], was a truth taught fallen man from the beginning. To this Abel conformed, and therefore is said by faith to have offered *a more excellent sacrifice* than Cain, who seems to have made light of the divine appointment of blood and to have presented his offering rather as a natural homage to God as his Creator, than to come in a prescribed way as a poor sinner to plead for mercy. This should be well considered. We have too many like Cain, who affront God while they pretend to worshipping, making light of the prescriptions of his Word; putting a slight upon the blood of Jesus, they presume to serve him with inventions of their own. God will accept nothing from us, but what has the sanction and warrant of his own Word.

FOR MEDITATION: 'By faith Abel offered unto God a more excellent sacrifice than Cain, by which he obtained witness that he was righteous, God testifying of his gifts: and by it he being dead yet speaketh' (Hebrews 11:4).
'And he took the cup, and gave thanks, and gave it to them, saying, Drink ye all of it; For this is my blood of the new testament, which is shed for many for the remission of sins' (Matthew 26:27–28).

Heart failure

'And in process of time it came to pass, that Cain brought of the fruit of the ground an offering unto the LORD. *And Abel, he also brought of the firstlings of his flock and of the fat thereof. And the* LORD *had respect unto Abel and to his offering: but unto Cain and to his offering he had not respect. And Cain was very wroth, and his countenance fell.' Genesis 4:3–5*
SUGGESTED FURTHER READING: Acts 5:1–11

You see, Cain's religion was a bargain. He thought it no small matter that he would submit to bring a little of the fruit of the ground to the Lord. He expected to be highly commended and rewarded for it. And when he found that the Lord did not think so well of him as he did of himself, he was wroth, as if some great injury had been done. He disdained that Abel should be preferred to him, and upon this account he hated him and at length embraced his hands in his blood. You see then, under the appearance of Cain's religion there was hid disobedience and pride in the sight of God, and hatred and malice against his brother. What wonder then, that it should be said of the Lord, who searcheth the heart, that to Cain and his offering he had not respect. This is the very picture of the spirit of self-righteousness in all ages—thus it acts towards God, opposing his will and yet expecting his favour—and thus it acts towards man, who dare not offer a service or allow themselves in a hope, but through the blood and mediation of Jesus. Be assured that the principles of Cain and Abel divide this assembly. If you are of Cain's religion you have Cain's spirit—you never found comfort in *your* way, and you are angry with those who hold to it in another way. Therefore you despise, perhaps revile, and probably if all restraints were taken away, you would think to do God service by putting those to death whom he loves.

But happy are you who are seeking salvation in Abel's way, by blood—the blood of Jesus. It *cleanseth from all sin* [1 John 1:7]. *He is able to save to the uttermost* [Hebrews 7:25]. *Believe and you shall be saved* [Luke 8:12].

FOR MEDITATION:

The sacrifice the Lord ordained
In type of the Redeemer's blood,
Self-righteous reasoning Cain disdained,
And thought his own first-fruits as good.

Yet rage and envy filled his mind,
When, with a sullen, downcast look,
He saw his brother favour find,
Who GOD's appointed method took.[171]

SERMON SERIES: GENESIS, NO. 11 [4/4], GENESIS 4:3–5

A murderous heart

'And Cain talked with Abel his brother: and it came to pass, when they were in the field, that Cain rose up against Abel his brother, and slew him.'
Genesis 4:8
SUGGESTED FURTHER READING: Genesis 4:8–16

We have here the first effort of Satan to manifest his enmity against the servants of God. It is a specimen, or sample, of the religious history of mankind from the beginning to this day. We have the murder of Abel, the cry of his blood, the judgement of Cain.

The murder. *Cain talked with Abel.* The subject of the converse is not recorded. If we may conjecture from what we hear with our own ears, it is not improbable that Abel was reproached as a hypocrite, despised as an enthusiast and a bigot, and that Abel's humble joy in the Lord's acceptance and his steadfastness in preferring sacrifices with blood, together with the free and faithful advice he gave his brother to acquaint himself with God and be at peace, provoked Cain to slay him. Something like this may perhaps be inferred from the Apostle's account of the cause (1 John 3:12). Now from hence we may observe for our own instruction the desperate wickedness of the heart. The carnal mind of Cain was enmity against God. He thought himself injured and affronted because Abel was preferred. His Maker was out of his reach and therefore he wreaked his displeasure against his faithful servant. Thus it is with all persecutors in whatever degree they are permitted to act. *For thy sake we are killed* [Romans 8:36]. If a person does not show any sign of the fear, love and image of God, he shall pass unnoticed; but if he does, he will be sure to meet with opposition.

FOR MEDITATION: We have likewise to encounter with the spirit of the world that knows not God, and cannot well bear with those who serve him according to the gospel. Through mercy we are exempted from those heavy sufferings by stripes, imprisonment and death, which many believers have been called to. Yet in one way or other, we experience what the Apostle says, that all who will live godly in Christ Jesus shall suffer persecution. Unkindness and opposition we shall be sure to meet with, and often from our dearest friends (Matthew 10:35–36).[172]

John Newton to William Wilberforce (the MP's uncle), 4 July 1771

SERMON SERIES: GENESIS, NO. 12 [1/4], GENESIS 4:8

'Consequences'

'And Cain talked with Abel his brother: and it came to pass, when they were in the field, that Cain rose up against Abel his brother, and slew him.'
Genesis 4:8
SUGGESTED FURTHER READING: 1 Samuel 18:1–30

Observe the progress of sin: Cain first indulged anger and then proceeded to murder. One is the seed, the other the fruit. Therefore, whoever hateth his brother is a murderer in the sight of God [Matthew 5:21–22]—if he was not restrained by his providence he would proceed to the outward act. Take heed of indulging dislike and ill will—it may lead you farther than you are aware, to do injury, if not to touch the life. However, the law of God will condemn you, even for evil thoughts.

Note the nature of a religious profession and what it will expose you to: look through the whole Bible—you may trace the same spirit. Isaac, the child of the promise, was mocked by Ishmael. This the Apostle calls persecution [Galatians 4:29]. The life of Jacob was sought by Esau because God gave him the blessing. So David was hunted like a partridge upon the mountains. Christ and his apostles were despised and opposed even to the death. Marvel not if the world hate you. And see the necessity of a continual dependence upon grace, that you may not fear them who can kill the body but can do no more. For if you are strengthened by faith in him who is invisible, you will dare to obey God rather than man.

What we owe to the providence and goodness of God in restraining the wrath of man! The same spirit is always awake, but he who rules the stormy wind and the raging waves of the sea, keeps it within bounds. Especially in our land and day, we have reason to be thankful.

FOR MEDITATION: If therefore you meet with some unkind reflections and misrepresentations from men of unfeeling and mercenary spirits, you will bear it patiently when you think of him who endured the contradiction of sinners against himself.[173]

John Newton to William Wilberforce, 4 August [1793]
[during the struggle to abolish the slave trade]

The blood of a martyr

'And Cain talked with Abel his brother: and it came to pass, when they were in the field, that Cain rose up against Abel his brother, and slew him.'
Genesis 4:8
SUGGESTED FURTHER READING: Matthew 23:27–39

Think it not strange that the Lord did not protect Abel. By death he entered into life and had the honour to be the first martyr of the truth. Thus God confirmed the belief of a future state, otherwise it would appear a dangerous thing to please God. But it was not overlooked—his blood cried for vengeance [verse 10]. What a dreadful account will the wicked world have to make for the blood of believers they have shed. Yea, all their sufferings and all their tears shall be had in remembrance. When he maketh inquisition he will not forget. The Lord's people are now, to an eye of sense, left destitute and exposed, as if everyone was at liberty to use them ill with impunity, but a change will soon take place. But there is blood *that speaketh better things than the blood of Abel* [Hebrews 12:24]. Jesus was slain like Abel, but his blood calls for pardon and mercy upon the poor sinners who spilt it, and upon those who by their wicked deeds have crucified him afresh. *Only believe and you shall be saved* [Luke 8:12].

FOR MEDITATION:

By Cain's own hand, good Abel died,
Because the LORD approved his faith;
And, when his blood for vengeance cried,
He vainly thought to hide his death.

Like him the way of grace we slight,
And in our own devices trust;
Call evil good, and darkness light,
And hate and persecute the just.

Such was the wicked murderer Cain,
And such by nature still are we,
Until by grace we're born again,
Malicious, blind and proud, as he.

The saints, in every age and place,
Have found this history fulfilled;
The numbers all our thoughts surpass
Of Abels, whom the Cains have killed.

Thus JESUS fell—but oh! his blood
Far better things than Abel's cries:
Obtains his murderers' peace with GOD,
And gains them mansions in the skies.[174]

SERMON SERIES: GENESIS, NO. 12 [3/4], GENESIS 4:8

A hardened heart

'*And the* LORD *said unto Cain, Where is Abel thy brother? And he said, I know not: Am I my brother's keeper?*' Genesis 4:9
SUGGESTED FURTHER READING: Zechariah 7:1–14

Cain did not escape. The Lord called to him. By his answer you may perceive how sin had hardened his heart. What ignorance to think his way hid from the Lord. What insolence in asking, *Am I my brother's keeper?* But he was soon silenced, the fact pressed home upon his conscience and, though he was suffered to live, his life was a burden. He was driven from the presence of the Lord, from his ordinances and the society of his people, and made, for a season at least, a terror to himself. If he afterwards recovered his spirits, he seems to have done it by getting the better of his conscience and to have been given up judicially to an impenitent mind. This is the greatest punishment on this side hell, when a man has been convinced and distressed for sin and yet afterwards finds a way, without the application of the blood of sprinkling, to make himself whole, and can busy himself for the rest of his time with a worldly life, till at length his hour comes and he falls with all his sins unpardoned into the hands of the living God.

FOR MEDITATION: 'Wherefore (as the Holy Ghost saith, Today if ye will hear his voice, Harden not your hearts, as in the provocation, in the day of temptation in the wilderness: When your fathers tempted me, proved me, and saw my works forty years…) Take heed, brethren, lest there be in any of you an evil heart of unbelief, in departing from the living God. But exhort one another daily, while it is called Today; lest any of you be hardened through the deceitfulness of sin. For we are made partakers of Christ, if we hold the beginning of our confidence steadfast unto the end; While it is said, Today if ye will hear his voice, harden not your hearts, as in the provocation (Hebrews 3:7–9,12–15).

A great salvation

'How shall we escape, if we neglect so great salvation ...?' Hebrews 2:3
SUGGESTED FURTHER READING: Hebrews 1:1–2:4

The love of God towards sinners is most amazing and wonderful. When they deserved death and misery, he revealed unto them *a great salvation*. The wonders of his grace afford a wonderful proof of man's depravity. This salvation, so great, so necessary, so undeserved, has been, and is, too generally neglected. Consider the danger of this neglect. How shall we escape? You may observe a comparison between the Jewish and the gospel dispensation in the preceding verses. The Israelites had seen the Lord's salvation—he freed them from bondage, maintained them in the wilderness, gave them his covenant, and placed them in Canaan. Yet many of [them] neglected their salvation, despised the word given by angels, and were for their disobedience destroyed. And all that happened to them was written for our instruction (1 Corinthians 10:11). Their salvation was typical of ours, but fell short in every respect—so that this is emphatically called *a great salvation*:

(i) with respect to the objects: miserable sinners, who might justly have been left to perish, groaning under worse than Egyptian bondage, upon the very brink of hell, as brands in the burning (Romans 5:6,8).

(ii) with respect to the means: the deliverance from Egypt was only a display of divine power, but this salvation was the price of blood, the blood of God (Acts 20:28; Revelation 5:9). He saved others, himself he could not save.

(iii) the application of this salvation to a sinner's heart is a *great* work, compared to *creation* (2 Corinthians 4:6), raising the dead (Ephesians 2:5; Colossians 2:13).

(iv) with respect to the end. What is a temporal Canaan, if compared with spiritual blessings—children of God here and heirs of glory hereafter?

FOR MEDITATION: I recommend it as *a great salvation*—sufficient to pardon the greatest sins (Isaiah 1:18); sufficient to save the greatest sinners— instance in Paul, Mary Magdalene, the malefactor. We are assured by our Lord himself in John 6:37, Isaiah 45:22 and Matthew 11:28. Do not think it humility to say, My sins are too great to be forgiven. It is unbelief, pride and a direct affront to the truth and power of Christ.

SERMON: HEBREWS 2:3 [1/1]

The all-sufficient God

'And when Abram was ninety years old and nine, the LORD *appeared to Abram, and said unto him, I am the Almighty God; walk before me, and be thou perfect.' Genesis 17:1*
SUGGESTED FURTHER READING: Psalm 89:1–18

The Lord's appearance to Abraham in the former chapter was some time before the birth of Ishmael; this was thirteen years after his birth. Abraham had some special visits of love but his ordinary walk was, I suppose, by faith and dependence—the Lord did not appear to him every day. The time was not yet at hand when Isaac should be born and now the covenant is again confirmed. This text is of general application. We have the Lord's character and his people's duty [see 2/2].

The Lord's character: *God Almighty*, or All-sufficient. O who can expound the fullness of this glorious name? Happy are his people who know him in Christ. This name is applicable to all their circumstances. In him they have an all-sufficiency:

(i) of righteousness—so the songs in Isaiah 12 and Psalm 27. They are accepted and no charge shall be heard against them. Herein they may glory all the day long (Psalm 89:16).

(ii) of strength—and that both in them and for them. In them: to enable them for suffering and for service (2 Corinthians 12:9), so that they shall not faint, but shall endure to the end. Their strength is not in themselves, but is renewed by waiting upon him. For them: to control and subdue all their enemies. Herein is their safety. Many fight against them, but cannot prevail, for *if God be for us* ... (Romans 8:31).

(iii) of happiness. He is their portion, all-sufficient—in time—affording by his presence such a joy as the world cannot give—and he will be their portion for ever.

FOR MEDITATION: 'And he said unto me, My grace is sufficient for thee: for my strength is made perfect in weakness ...' (2 Corinthians 12:9).

Strange and mysterious is my life,	The rule of grace, the power of sin:
What opposites I feel within!	Too often I am captive led,
A stable peace, a constant strife,	Yet daily triumph in my Head.[175]

SERMON SERIES: GENESIS, NO. 35 [1/2], GENESIS 17:1

With a single eye

'And when Abram was ninety years old and nine, the LORD *appeared to Abram, and said unto him, I am the Almighty God; walk before me, and be thou perfect.' Genesis 17:1*
SUGGESTED FURTHER READING: 1 Peter 1:13–25

His people's duty and aim, in consequence of his all-sufficiency, is:

(i) to *walk before him*; that is, as in his sight, importing acting from a principle of love and reverence, with a view to his glory, and in a spirit of dependence. O the honour, the comfort, the excellence of such a walk.

(ii) to *be perfect*. This means not a sinless perfection, but sincerity. This includes a single eye, in opposition to all mean and selfish views, and a universal respect to all his commandments.

The knowledge of God as all-sufficient will influence us to such a walk and it is impracticable upon any other principle. Whatever is short of this is but a poor pretence, a lifeless shadow of religion.

FOR MEDITATION: How shall I speak with that reverence which becomes an ambassador of God, with that earnestness which is suitable to the case of perishing souls, with that faithfulness as to deliver my own soul and be pure from the blood of all men, with that wisdom as to avoid unnecessary offences and not lay obstacles in my own way, with that steadiness as not to be disconcerted by smiles or frowns, by temptations or afflictions, by men or devils? The servant of God will not be deterred by these considerations, because he knows the Lord whom he serves is able to deliver and support him, but it seems impossible he should be unaffected with them.[176]

Miscellaneous Thoughts, Thursday 29 June 1758

Oh, may it please thee, that now in the evening of life, I may not dishonour my profession, or lose the testimony of a good conscience. But that my sun may set without a cloud, and that I may be a testimony to thy goodness for the encouragement of those around me, with my latest breath or so long as I am able to speak. Amen.[177]

Diary, 21 March 1794

SERMON SERIES: GENESIS, NO. 35 [2/2], GENESIS 17:1

Lifted up to die

'And I, if I be lifted up from the earth, will draw all men unto me. This he said, signifying what death he should die.' John 12:32–33
SUGGESTED FURTHER READING: John 12:20–36

When our Lord spoke these words, the season of his passion was approaching. His holy soul was troubled at the prospect of that woeful hour in which, for sins not his own, he was to sustain the curse of the law in all its horrors. But his purpose was fixed, his love was unalterable. In another view he rejoiced, he saw of the travail of his soul and was satisfied. The thought of the salvation of innumerable sinners made him willingly obedient to the death of the cross. The phrase *lifted up* may be applied to his suffering upon the cross, to his exaltation in his kingdom, to his being set forth in the preaching of the gospel. The former sense is particularly intended here, as is plain by his own words, though the others are not to be excluded—for the Spirit is given in consequence of his ascension, and if he was not preached he could not be known. He was *lifted up*—that is crucified—as the brazen serpent in the wilderness. This death was to the last degree painful; it was ignominious, being only the punishment of slaves and the vilest malefactors. And in the eye of the law it was an accursed death (Galatians 3:13 [*Christ hath redeemed us from the curse of the law, being made a curse for us: for it is written, Cursed is every one that hangeth on a tree*]).

FOR MEDITATION:

'Father, forgive (the Saviour said)
They know not what they do':
His heart was moved when thus he prayed
For me, my friends, and you.

He saw, that as the Jews abused
And crucified his flesh;
So he, by us, would be refused,
And crucified afresh.

Through love of sin, we long were prone
To act as Satan bid;
But now, with grief and shame we own,
We knew not what we did.

We knew not the desert of sin,
Nor whom we thus defied;
Nor where our guilty souls had been,
If JESUS had not died.

But JESUS all our guilt foresaw,
And shed his precious blood
To satisfy the holy law,
And make our peace with GOD.

My sin, dear Saviour, made thee bleed,
Yet didst thou pray for me!
I knew not what I did, indeed,
When ignorant of thee.[178]

SERMON: JOHN 12:32–33 [1/2]

Drawn through the cross

'And I, if I be lifted up from the earth, will draw all men unto me. This he said, signifying what death he should die.' John 12:32–33
SUGGESTED FURTHER READING: John 6:35–51

If … I will draw all men unto me. On this clause a few remarks—much is implied in it:

(i) that men are by nature at a distance from God (for in drawing to himself he draws to God—there is no other way to the Father). We are far from the knowledge of God, from his love, from communion with him.

(ii) that men are unable to come to God of themselves—they must be drawn, as in Song of Solomon 1:4; unable in every sense, but especially because unwilling—their carnal hearts are enmity.

(iii) the knowledge of Christ crucified is the effectual and only effectual means to draw sinners to God. The heart will stand it out against every other motive and argument, but not against this, which is spiritually revealed.

(iv) multitudes who call themselves Christians, though they know as a fact that Christ was crucified, yet have not the knowledge of it aright, because they are not drawn to him.

(v) the Lord's people are drawn, that is, made willing; they do not serve him by constraint. Their hearts are won by the display of love, wisdom and grace manifested in his lifting up upon the cross. This gives them right views of God, of sin, of themselves.

(vi) they whom Christ draws, he draws to himself. This precious promise looks not only to the beginning, but the accomplishment of the work. His love will persevere till it has drawn them safe through all dangers and difficulties and brought them home to his kingdom.

FOR MEDITATION: The expression *all men* denotes not all universally, but some of all sorts—not the Jews only, but Gentiles also—young and old, rich and poor, of many nations, in various circumstances—so that none who feel their need of him and look to him as lifted up, have reason to think themselves excluded. They are invited without exception, with an assurance that he will in no wise cast them out.

SERMON: JOHN 12:32–33 [2/2]

Prayer from the heart

'*And Abraham said unto God, O that Ishmael might live before thee!*'
Genesis 17:18
SUGGESTED FURTHER READING: Genesis 17:1–22

The Lord was now confirming his covenant to Abraham and assuring him of the promised son, in whom he should be a father of many nations. But he had another son, and embraces the occasion of speaking for him likewise.

Observe from the occasion: faith takes encouragement, when much is given or promised, to ask the more. So he gains upon the Lord, as it were, in the next chapter, every time he speaks. We are not straitened in the Lord; were we not in ourselves, we should see great things. What lies near the heart will be spread before the Lord in prayer in an hour of liberty. It is our duty to pray—and too often believers have little else to prompt them to it. Their spirits are dry, and they deal mostly in generals, but there are favoured seasons when the soul comes near to the Lord and then can open all its particular desires. These are golden hours; one such is preferable to a thousand. The sun in its course beholds nothing more honourable than this: a worm of dust holding conference with the great God.

And dost thou say, 'Ask what thou wilt'? More of thy presence, LORD, impart,
LORD, I would seize the golden hour; More of thine image let me bear;
I pray to be released from guilt, Erect thy throne within my heart,
And freed from sin and Satan's power. And reign without a rival there.[179]

FOR MEDITATION: *He that spared not his own Son, but delivered him up for us all, how shall he not with him also freely give us all things?* Go then with this promise to the throne of grace—pray first to know your own state and wants and to have your desires moulded by his Word and will, and then be careful about nothing but in everything by prayer and supplication make your request known unto God. And you shall not pray in vain. He that spared not his own Son will freely give you every thing else—*grace*, peace, wisdom, provision and protection.[180]

Sermon on Romans 8:32, *The Searcher of Hearts*

Practise hospitality

'Let a little water, I pray you, be fetched, and wash your feet, and rest yourselves under the tree: and I will fetch a morsel of bread and comfort ye your hearts; after that ye shall pass on: for therefore are ye come to your servant. And they said, So do, as thou hast said.' Genesis 18:4–5
SUGGESTED FURTHER READING: Genesis 18:1–16

We may briefly note Abraham's hospitality and the reward he found it. The apostle refers to this and to the case of Lot (in Hebrews 13:2) where he says, *Be not forgetful to entertain strangers: for thereby some have received angels unawares*. It seems Abraham did not at first know his guests, but it was his usual custom to welcome strangers. We are not bound to open our doors to all, nor would it be prudent, but we should be hospitable and kind, especially to the Lord's people. We know not what a blessing they may bring with them. The kindness we show to the meanest of his, he will accept as done to himself. These three men were three angels, or rather, one of them was the angel of the covenant, the Lord, who afterwards assumed a real body on behalf of his people. This was a greater honour and happiness to Abraham, but such honour have all his saints. He still walks with them and dwells in them.

Observe the simplicity of the times. Abraham was a great man, he lived in plenty. But the idle pomp and luxury of aftertimes was not then practised. His entertainment was plain. And he and Sarah, though they had many servants, were not above a concern in it. Abraham fetched the calf and Sarah made the cakes. So we find Rebecca drawing water. I do not say it is necessary or would even be proper for persons of rank and destination to employ themselves so with us. But the pride and vanity which grows in our times as people are raised a little above the lowest state of life, appears doubly contemptible when compared with the manner of Abraham's living, whose wealth, honour and influence were very great, and yet he had no regard to the things of the world, but for their real use.

FOR MEDITATION: 'Offer hospitality to one another without grumbling. Each one should use whatever gift he has received to serve others, faithfully administering God's grace in its various forms' (1 Peter 4:9–10, NIV).

SERMON SERIES: GENESIS, NO. 37 [1/4], GENESIS 18:14

The promise confirmed

'Is anything too hard for the LORD? At the time appointed I will return unto thee, according to the time of life, and Sarah shall have a son.'
Genesis 18:14
SUGGESTED FURTHER READING: Psalm 145:1–21

The design of this visit [by the three men] was to give a final confirmation to the promise, which was now near to an accomplishment and took place the next year. Abraham and Sarah were now both old and Sarah expressed her unbelief in a manner which showed she thought it was now impossible. For this she was reproved and weakly attempted to deny what she had said. The words of my text are added to satisfy both Abraham and Sarah that it should surely be so.

The observation that offers is this: the consideration of the power of God to make good his promises, is the great stay and support of faith under all difficulties. This was actually the support of Abraham. He *staggered not* because he considered that *he who had promised was able also to perform* [Romans 4:20–21]. And most of the fears and mistakes of the Lord's people are owing to their not knowing or not considering the Scriptures and the power of God. Our expectations from the Lord's power must, however, be limited by his promises, or we shall surely be disappointed. We are often so inconsistent that while we give up the hope of what is promised, we are looking for what is not. Some disquiet themselves because they cannot attain to such a complete deliverance from the effects of indwelling sin as the Scripture does not warrant us to look for. Some expect to be led just in the way they think others are led, or else suppose they cannot be right. But where has the Lord promised this as to particulars? Let us then notice how the promises run, how objections rise against them, and how we should arm ourselves with the question in my text.

FOR MEDITATION:

Yes! since God himself has said it,
On the promise I rely;
His good word demands my credit,
What can unbelief reply?
He is strong and *can* fulfil,
He is truth and therefore *will*.

As to all the doubts and questions,
Which my spirit often grieve,
These are Satan's sly suggestions,
And I need no answer give;
He would fain destroy my hope,
But the promise bears it up.[181]

Is *anything* too hard?

'Is anything too hard for the LORD*? At the time appointed I will return unto thee, according to the time of life, and Sarah shall have a son.'*
Genesis 18:14
SUGGESTED FURTHER READING: Isaiah 40:27–31

Convinced souls are hard to be persuaded of forgiveness. Yet they have a sure ground to wait for it. The promises are many and explicit. But the nature of their sins, and the views they have of his justice and holiness, make them question, if not for others, yet for themselves. It is observable the mercy of God is spoken of in connection with his power—he is mighty to save, he shall come with a strong hand. Consider what the power of God has done in giving his Son, raising him from the dead, pardoning the vilest—such as Manasseh and the thief upon the cross. In the conflict with indwelling sin, some are so sorely beset, they are ready to give up hope; but read Isaiah 40:28–31. He can uphold, and he will, and show himself strong in behalf of the upright of heart. Some are distressed about their own conversion. 'How long have I heard, how many have I seen called before me? I sometimes think, if the gospel was quite new to me, surely I should not sit so stupid under it. But I have attended so long, that it seems a thing of course.' Come, take courage and listen again—it is a hard thing, but not *too hard for the Lord*. He can yet make the desert a fruitful field. Others are distressed for their friends. 'I have prayed and hoped for my child—for my husband—but the prospect grows darker; they seem more hardened, more obstinate. Formerly the Word seemed to touch them, but now they are sermon-proof.'

FOR MEDITATION: Fear not—he will not despise the day of small things or quench the smoking flax. All things shall work together for your good. Your love to him shall sweeten all your difficulties, his love to you shall enable you to hold out, make you more than conquerors in the end and bestow on you the crown of life which the Lord has promised to them that love him and wait for his appearing.[182]

Sermon on Romans 8:28, *The Searcher of Hearts*

SERMON SERIES: GENESIS, NO. 37 [3/4], GENESIS 18:14

Something more

'Is anything too hard for the LORD? At the time appointed I will return unto thee, according to the time of life, and Sarah shall have a son.'
Genesis 18:14
SUGGESTED FURTHER READING: Revelation 2:1–7

I know there are some evidently fed and strengthened; they grow in knowledge and in grace. And now and then when I am ready to faint, my heart is a little revived by hearing of a new enquirer. If I could be content with some liberty of speech and with the respect and kindness which my hearers in general show me, I might sit down quiet and be satisfied with my situation. But indeed this does not content me—I want something more. Though I am not opposed and persecuted, yet my heart is often grieved. I see many who, though they hear me patiently, yet hear in vain. I see believers who once bid fair to be pillars in the church and lights in the world, evidently declining from bad to worse, and I am daily trembling lest things which at present are confined to the knowledge of a few should break forth and become public offence and scandal. If conscience suggests to any of you, 'Now he means me', I am content you should think I do, though what I am speaking concerns more than one or two or three. My heart bears me witness that the Lord enables me to be in some measure fruitful to you, at least in public. Yet alas, I come short; I ought to follow you to your houses, to stop you in the streets, to break in upon you in those places and at those seasons when you would least choose to see me, and to entreat you *with the affection of Christ Jesus* [Philippians 1:8, NIV] to consider what you are doing—to ask you, Where is that blessedness you once spoke of?[183] There is something in my temper that makes this an hard, an almost impossible, service. When I would speak, my mouth is stopped. But *is anything too hard for the LORD?*

FOR MEDITATION: And this word is for the comfort of believers under outward troubles. The promises respect the life that now is, but providences often seem to cross them. Remember Israel, they were hungry and thirsty, and saw nothing but rocks and deserts—but the Lord brought water from the rocks and gave them food out of the clouds. His arm is not shortened. He is still the same.

SERMON SERIES: GENESIS, NO. 37 [4/4], GENESIS 18:14

Sending the Word to them, or them to the Word

'Believe on the Lord Jesus Christ, and thou shalt be saved, and thy house.'
Acts 16:31
SUGGESTED FURTHER READING: Acts 16:11–40.

The context of this passage which we were just now reading affords us an instructive view of the Lord's directing hand in disposing of his ministers and gospel according to his own good pleasure, and how he overrules the designs of his enemies to accomplish his own purposes in favour of his people. He knows them that are his, and when and where to find them. He knows how to send the Word to them or to send them to the Word, and one or the other he will do, when his time is come. Many who now believe and see what a dreadful case they must have been in if they had died in their sins, are often struck with wonder when they reflect on the first occasions that brought them to the knowledge. Some wonder that the gospel should be brought to them, rather than to the people of another town and parish, who were not more undeserving of it. Others wonder at the circumstances which first engaged them to hear it, for they can remember when they accounted it a burden and offence, and were ready to throw stones at any man that would trouble them with it. But it is his Word, he has promised that it shall not return void. He has a people in his eye, whom he designs to make *willing in the day of his power* [Psalm 110:3]—and all outward circumstances are ordered and disposed for their sakes.

FOR MEDITATION: O my Lord. What a series of wonders is my history! Wonders of mercy on thy part. Wonderful proofs of depravity on mine. Surely no one who reads this letter can surmise how far and how often I returned thee evil for good. I remember my faults and follies this day and fain would I praise thee for thy long-suffering and forbearance exercised for so many years towards a most undeserving creature![184]
Annotated Letters to a Wife, 4 August 1794

Believe in Him

'Believe on the Lord Jesus Christ, and thou shalt be saved, and thy house.'
Acts 16:31
SUGGESTED FURTHER READING: Luke 12:1–12

*And on the Sabbath we went out of the city by a river side, where prayer was
wont to be made...* [Acts 16:13]. In the meantime there was a poor sinner
who perhaps had never been at a place of prayer in his life, nor knew what
prayer meant—he was a stranger to the Apostle and the Apostle to him.
How should they be brought together? To effect this the Lord permitted
Satan to rage—a great mob and clamour was made, Paul and his
companions beaten and delivered to the charge of this very jailer. He little
thought these men were come to show him the way of salvation—he gladly
executed his charge and put them in the dungeon. But at midnight while
they prayed and sang, there was an earthquake, the prison doors were
thrown open, and the jailer, awaking in surprise, thinking the prisoners
were escaped and fearing to be punished, was going to kill himself. Paul,
though he saw him not, was informed of his intention and cried out, *Do
thyself no harm.* All these circumstances concurred to awaken his
conscience; fears of another kind took [hold] of him, his heart smote him for
his sins, particularly for the abuse offered to the servants of God. He sprang
in trembling and cried out, *Sirs, what must I do?* My text is the answer to this
question.

The means by which God awakens sinners are various, but all lead to this
enquiry. I hope some of you are earnestly concerned about it; to you
especially I address myself, *Believe.*

FOR MEDITATION:

A Believer, free from care,	Suddenly the prison shook,
May in chains, or dungeons, sing,	Open flew the iron doors;
If the LORD be with him there;	And the jailer, terror-struck,
And be happier than a king:	Now his captives' help implores:
Paul and Silas thus confined,	Trembling at their feet he fell,
Though their backs were torn by whips,	'Tell me, Sirs, what must I do
Yet possessing peace of mind,	To be saved from guilt and hell?
Sung his praise with joyful lips.	None can tell me this but you.'[185]

SERMON: ACTS 16:31 [2/4]

Who is Jesus Christ?

'Believe on the Lord Jesus Christ, and thou shalt be saved, and thy house.'
Acts 16:31
SUGGESTED FURTHER READING: Hebrews 8:1–13

Believe on the Lord Jesus Christ. But lest any of you are ready to say with the blind man, *Who is he?* [John 9:36] I shall speak something of him. The little I can speak of the LJC [Lord Jesus Christ] may be summed up in two particulars: his person and his office.

(i) His person: he is God, blessed for ever (Romans 9:5; Isaiah 9:6; John 12:41). He is man (1 Timothy 3:16) here, or named Emmanuel (Matthew 1:23). This is the great mystery of Godliness; we can see but little of the wisdom, condescension and love. The angels cannot fathom. God alone can reveal it. For this the Holy Spirit is given, that we may know the mystery of God, of the Father, and of Christ *in whom are hid all the treasures of wisdom and knowledge.* (Colossians 2:2–3).

(ii) His office: in general, Mediator (1 Timothy 2:5). There is no other (John 14:6). This includes his whole undertaking. We may consider:

(a) What he did as Mediator upon earth, summed up in his obedience unto death. He fulfilled the law for us—he made atonement for our sins.

(b) Now he is in his kingdom he acts the Mediator's part, applying the benefits of his righteousness to those who believe: as a Prophet, a Priest, a King.

FOR MEDITATION: The doctrine of Jesus Christ crucified: I believe to insist much upon the great essential points of the glories of his person and offices, his wonderful love and condescension, his power, faithfulness and readiness to save, the grandeur of his works, the perfection of his example, his life, passion, death and resurrection. I say thus to enlarge much on the Names, properties, and so on, of our dear Redeemer, as it is undoubtedly the most pleasant set of topics, so the most useful and effectual, to rouse a hatred against sin, to feed the springs of grace into the heart, to animate and to furnish every believer for his spiritual warfare.[186]

Miscellaneous Thoughts, Friday 4 August 1758

SERMON: ACTS 16:31 [3/4]

Just what we could wish for

'Believe on the Lord Jesus Christ, and thou shalt be saved, and thy house.'
Acts 16:31
SUGGESTED FURTHER READING: Song of Solomon 2:1–17

All that I have already said on the Lord Jesus Christ may be applied to this as a ground, warrant, encouragement. His power as God, his nearness, sympathy as man, the suitableness of his offices to our case—he is just what we could wish, and has all we could want. Add to this his promises (Matthew 11:27–28), the examples of others (whom did he ever refuse that called upon him?) and that this was the express design of all (1 Timothy 1:15).

To *believe* implies a persuasion that he is able to save and he only (John 6:68), and a dependence on him (2 Timothy 1:12). The chief evidences are love (1 John 4:19) and obedience (1 John 2:6).

Fear not poor soul. Do not listen to Satan and unbelief. Continue waiting and you shall grow.

Let none dare to build upon another foundation.

It is said, *Thou and thy house*. Not that they should be saved for his faith, but to show the blessing open to all who seek. Have you obtained it? Go then, as you have opportunity, to your friends and neighbours; tell them what great things the Lord has done for you, and invite them to taste—see how gracious he is.

FOR MEDITATION:

'Look to JESUS,' they replied,
'If on him thou canst believe;
By the death which he has died,
Thou salvation shalt receive':
While the living word he heard,
Faith sprung up within his heart;
And released from all he feared,
In their joy his soul had part.

Sinners, CHRIST is still the same,
O that you could likewise fear!
Then the mention of his name
Would be music to your ear:
JESUS rescues Satan's slaves,
His dear wounds still plead, 'Forgive!'
JESUS to the utmost saves;
Sinners, look to him and live.[187]

Walking with God

'And Enoch walked with God: and he was not; for God took him.'
Genesis 5:24
SUGGESTED FURTHER READING: Genesis 5:18–24

To *walk* with God imports:

(i) acceptance by faith (Hebrews 11:6). This is through Christ the Saviour, to whom believers of old looked as he who was to come. The dispensation under which they lived was different, but their faith and its object the same.

(ii) obedience—a devotedness to God in the way of his commandments, for *how can two walk together except they are agreed?* [Amos 3:3]. Therefore none can walk with God who have not experienced a change of heart and views.

(iii) communion—in which the sweetness and comfort of religion consists. The desires, affections and secret prayers of the soul rising towards God, and God manifesting his light, love and peace to the soul. This is chiefly maintained on our parts by a humble attendance on the means of grace. They who thus walk with God experience his direction, protection and support. Examine what you know of this subject.

FOR MEDITATION: [written for 23 July 1775]
With him sweet converse I maintain,
Great as he is I dare be free;
I tell him all my grief and pain,
And he reveals his love to me.

Some cordial from his Word he brings,
Whene'er my feeble spirit faints;
At once my soul revives and sings,
And yields no more to sad complaints.[188]

Perseverance

'And Enoch walked with God: and he was not; for God took him.'
Genesis 5:24
SUGGESTED FURTHER READING: Jude 12–25

The beginning of Enoch's walking with God seems to be marked out (verse 22) from the time when he begat Methuselah, when he was about sixty-five years old. But whether it is so or not, we are sure there always must be a beginning, for as we are born in sin and under the law, we have neither skill nor power to walk with God. He is found of them that seek him not. He *walked with God* 300 years. So as long as he remained in the world, he persevered in this good way. He was not weary but endured to the end. Of too many it may be said that, according to outward appearance and in the judgement of men, they walked with God—some a month, some a year, some several years—but sooner or later they gave it up, and have outlived their profession. This is mournful. May the Lord revive, restore, recall all such wanderers, or their end will be dreadful. Enoch maintained his course of walking with God in the midst of a crooked and perverse generation. This I think may be gathered from the fallen state of mankind and from Jude 14–15. Enoch was a prophet and, like other prophets, surrounded by those who hated him because he testified of their evil deeds. The natural course of Enoch's abode upon earth was manifestly shortened. He lived upon the earth not half the time the rest of the patriarchs did before the flood. So the best of men are frequently cut short.

FOR MEDITATION: Enoch's removal was:
   (i) a mercy to himself. His eyes and ears and heart had been pained long enough—the world was growing worse and worse and he was taken from the evil to come.
   (ii) in judgement to others. They had abused and resisted his testimony, therefore they shall hear no more. It is a dark sign upon a place or people when the Lord takes away his servants and ministers from them. But he often deals so when his Word is accounted a burden.

Walking in glory

'And Enoch walked with God: and he was not; for God took him.'
Genesis 5:24
SUGGESTED FURTHER READING: Hebrews 11:1–7

Enoch was dismissed from his warfare. *He was not*—no more seen upon earth. But *God took him* to walk with him in glory (Hebrews 11:5). He saw not death. He felt not the painful separation between soul and body. Some think his enemies were about to kill him and the Lord thus interposed to deliver him. It is probable. Thus it was with Elijah—the only instances afforded amongst the many millions of Adam's posterity. In them God was pleased to give new evidence of an invisible state, and they were in that circumstance types of the ascension of the Lord Jesus.

Yet he was translated. Flesh and blood cannot see the kingdom of God. Therefore, says the Apostle, speaking of those who shall be on earth when the Saviour returns and shall be caught up to meet him in the air, *We shall not all die, but all must be changed*, the vile mortal body made conformable to Christ's glorious body [1 Corinthians 15:51–54].

God took him—took him for his own, took him to dwell with him in heaven, to fill him with happiness and glory. O happy end of a life spent in walking with God. Then his desires were answered, his sorrows removed, his labours and trials rewarded.

Life is compared to a journey—each of you is walking, but are you walking *with God*? If not, where are you going? (John 12:35). O that you might, by the example of others, be made wise to consider your latter end.

FOR MEDITATION:

By faith in CHRIST I walk with GOD,
With heaven, my journey's end, in view;
Supported by his staff and rod,
My road is safe and pleasant too.

Though snares and dangers throng my path,
And earth and hell my course withstand;
I triumph over all by faith,
Guarded by his Almighty hand.

I travel through a desert wide
Where many round me blindly stray;
But he vouchsafes to be my guide,
And will not let me miss my way.

I pity all that worldlings talk
Of pleasures that will quickly end;
Be this my choice, O LORD, to walk
With thee, my Guide, my Guard, my Friend.[189]

SERMON SERIES: GENESIS, NO. 13 [3/3], GENESIS 5:24

The desire of all nations

'And I will shake all nations, and the desire of all nations shall come: and I will fill this house with glory, saith the LORD of hosts.' Haggai 2:7
SUGGESTED FURTHER READING: Micah 4:1–5

A character of the Messiah: *the desire of all nations.* He is called *the desire of all nations* because the rumour of the prophecies spread abroad had awakened the expectations and desires of many, in different nations, that some great deliverer and friend of mankind was at hand. The sense of many prophecies of the Messiah, though misapplied, is remarkably expressed in a short poem of Virgil written a few years before our Saviour's birth, and of which we have a beautiful translation in the English language by Mr Pope.[190] It affords a sufficient proof that the heathens had an idea of some great personage who would shortly appear and would restore peace, prosperity and the blessings of their fancied golden age to mankind. On this account he was *the desire of nations.*

But, the need all the nations had of such a Saviour is sufficient to establish his right to this title, though they had no knowledge of him. If a nation was involved in the darkness of night, though they had no previous notion of light, yet light might be said to be their desire—because the light, whenever they should enjoy it, would put an end to their calamity, would answer their wants, and therefore accomplish their wishes; for if they could not directly wish for light, they would naturally wish for relief. The heathens were miserably bewildered—they had desires after happiness which could not be satisfied—they had fears and forebodings of conscience, but knew no remedy. They paid a blind devotion to idols because they were ignorant of the true God. When the Messiah came, as he was the Glory of Israel, so he was a Light to the Gentiles. He, therefore, who came purposely to bless the nations and turn their darkness into light, might justly be called their *desire*, though before his appearance they could form no just conception of him. What a nation was ours at the time of his birth—how evil, how wretched! And what a change has his gospel wrought!

FOR MEDITATION: Is *the desire of all nations* the object of your desire?

SERMON SERIES: MESSIAH, NO. 3 [3/5], HAGGAI 2:6–7

Sought out and not forsaken

'And they shall call them, The holy people, The redeemed of the LORD: and thou shalt be called, Sought out, A city not forsaken.' Isaiah 62:12
SUGGESTED FURTHER READING: Isaiah 62:1–12

Sought out—a city not forsaken. These are names of the church of God applicable to each of his people. They speak comfort to believers, and display the glory of their Redeemer. He is the Alpha and the Omega. He begins to make known his purposes in their favour, and he also will make an end. The first of these names excludes all boasting, the other forbids fear. The Lord's people are possessed of great privileges: they are near to him and he is all that to them which he was to Israel in the wilderness, but in a higher sense—their guide, their guard and their glory. If you enquire how they attained to this, the answer is grace, free grace; their name is *sought out—* not that they loved him but that he loved them, and it pleased the Lord notwithstanding all hindrances, to make them his people.

Consider them in another view, as beset with snares and enemies, as exposed to the rage of the powers of darkness, as weak and helpless in themselves, and, what is worse, too frequently unfaithful, backsliding and provoking the Lord on whom they depend. It seems natural to ask by whom shall these rise? How shall they stand? Will they not at last be a prey to the teeth of their enemies? No, he that sought them out will keep them—this is their name: *not forsaken.* They are liable to many changes but they are safe, for they have an unchangeable Saviour, who fainteth not nor is weary.

FOR MEDITATION: Surely mercy and goodness have followed me all my days. He has been my guard and my guide; he found me in a waste howling wilderness, in the most helpless state of sin and misery—but in consequence of his everlasting purpose and love, he was pleased to deliver me from ruin, to call me by his grace, to give me a name and place amongst his children, and amongst his ministers. O to grace how great a debtor,[191] daily I'm constrained to be![192]

John Newton to John Thornton, 4 August 1770

SERMON: ISAIAH 62:12 [1/3]

The Lord who seeks

'And they shall call them, The holy people, The redeemed of the LORD: and thou shalt be called, Sought out, A city not forsaken.' Isaiah 62:12
SUGGESTED FURTHER READING: Exodus 3:1–10

The Lord seeks his people. Hence they are compared:

(i) to stones in a quarry which must lie in that state, till they are selected and removed from the rest (Isaiah 51:1 [*Hearken to me, ye that follow after righteousness, ye that seek the LORD: look unto the rock whence ye are hewn, and to the hole of the pit whence ye are digged*]).

(ii) to wandering sheep (Luke 15) who never can find the way to the fold of themselves.

(iii) to people in the dark who cannot tell where to set a foot (Matthew 4).

It is true that in time they all seek him, but not till he has found them first (Psalm 27). Till then they know not the two chief motives of seeking:

(i) for pardon of sin. They are insensible of the nature, abounding and desert of sin, till he shows them. And therefore he is to them as a physician to them who are in health.

(ii) for happiness. This indeed they desire and seek but not from him, till he puts it into their hearts. In this sense the world is their God. But he seeks them. He gives them light, he gives them a heart to pray, he teaches, leads them to a throne of grace, then he reveals himself and says, Behold me.

This to be insisted on:

(i) for the humiliation of believers and the praise of his grace.

(ii) for the encouragement of seekers.

(iii) for encouragement of ministers to preach the gospel to sinners. The Lord knows them that are his.

FOR MEDITATION: [for New Year's Evening 1771]

Let us adore the grace that seeks	Though filled with awe, before his throne
To draw our hearts above!	Each angel veils his face;
Attend, 'tis GOD the Saviour speaks,	He claims a people for his own
And every word is love.	Amongst our sinful race.[193]

SERMON: ISAIAH 62:12 [2/3]

Look up with hope

'And they shall call them, The holy people, The redeemed of the LORD: *and thou shalt be called, Sought out, A city not forsaken.' Isaiah 62:12*
SUGGESTED FURTHER READING: 1 Samuel 30:1–6

Not forsaken. This may be argued from his purpose, his covenant, his promise, and is to be pleaded against:

(i) Satan. He often threatens like Rabshakeh before Jerusalem.

(ii) unbelief. This musters and magnifies the difficulties in the way and says, 'Ah, what shall we do?' But infinite wisdom, power and love will not be disappointed.

(iii) guilt. For sin the Lord will often hide his face and permit dark clouds to hang over us. Yet we must not give way. We cannot recover ourselves but by believing. To keep at a distance and despond makes bad worse. So David encouraged himself when greatly distressed (1 Samuel 30:6 [*And David was greatly distressed; for the people spake of stoning him, because the soul of all the people was grieved, every man for his sons and for his daughters: but David encouraged himself in the* LORD *his God*]). So also 12:20–22. Let the poor backslider look up with hope—he knew what his poor people would prove. Let this subject lead us to admire Jesus for his love, his power, his patience—praise him and trust him.

FOR MEDITATION: Tonight I attended an eclipse of the moon. I thought, my Lord, of thine eclipse. The horrible darkness which overwhelmed thy mind when thou saidst, *Why hast thou forsaken me?'* Ah, sin was the cause—my sin.[194]   *Diary,* 30 July 1776 [prompting the following hymn]

Fain would my thankful heart and lips
Unite in praise to thee;
And meditate on thy eclipse,
In sad Gethsemane.

Thy people's guilt, a heavy load!
(When standing in their room)
Deprived thee of the light of GOD,
And filled thy soul with gloom.

Dark, like the moon without the sun,
I mourn thine absence, LORD!
For light or comfort have I none,
But what thy beams afford.

But lo! the hour draws near apace,
When changes shall be o'er;
Then shall I see thee face to face,
And be eclipsed no more.[195]

SERMON: ISAIAH 62:12 [3/3]

A Star in sight

'I shall see him, but not now: I shall behold him, but not nigh: there shall come a Star out of Jacob, and a Sceptre shall rise out of Israel, and shall smite the corners of Moab, and destroy all the children of Sheth.' Numbers 24:17
SUGGESTED FURTHER READING: Revelation 22:7–21

How useless to the believer—gifts without grace! Judas an apostle, Balaam a prophet, etc. In the words we have:

(i) his certainty—*I see, I behold*. What the Lord reveals is clear and sure.

(ii) an interval—*not now*, or *nigh*, but through a series of ages. From his character, we may consider the words as spoken without personal hope—not as Job, *I know my Redeemer liveth* [Job 19:25]. Uncomfortable thought to see him, as the rich man saw Lazarus—afar off.

It is Christ called *a Star*—not a conducting star as Matthew 2, but the bright morning star whose approach brings on the day. The Day Star, the Sun, the Light of the Gentiles, the Glory of Israel—he shall arise and shine. Jesus is the Sun, the source of life, light and comfort, the light and life of the world.

His *Sceptre*—his rule and government of his kingdom, of which there shall be no end.

His victories—He *shall smite the corners of Moab*. Moab and Edom are types of all adversary and antichristian powers.

Sheth perhaps was some place in Moab. Some understand it of men in general and the word may be rendered 'to subdue'.[196] He will conquer all his enemies, and all by nature are his enemies—the hearts of his people are a stronghold till he forces and wins them. This Scripture was fulfilled in type in David who conquered Moab. Jesus subdues by love, but those that finally resist he will destroy.

FOR MEDITATION: Have you seen this Star? Has he shined into your hearts? If so, be thankful. Rejoice that he came into the world. If asked, how knew you he was born today?—no matter, you may keep Christmas all the year round. If not, remember you must see him (Revelation 1). Have you submitted to his Sceptre? Surely yes, if you have indeed seen him. But remember, he must and will rule. He will be glorified in you either in mercy or subjection.

SERMON: NUMBERS 24:17 [1/1]

Instruments for his service

'And Melchizedek king of Salem brought forth bread and wine: and he was the priest of the most high God.' Genesis 14:18
SUGGESTED FURTHER READING: Hebrews 7:1–28

In the remaining part of this chapter we have two things worthy of note: Abraham's interview with Melchizedek and his conduct to the king of Sodom. We may be sure the account of Melchizedek is recorded with a view to our instruction, since it is so largely commented on in Hebrews 7 with reference to the gospel. Yet the subject has its difficulties and has given rise to a variety of uncertain conjectures concerning this person. He was a *priest of the most High God*, a servant of the God of Abraham, though not of Abraham's family. Canaan was then inhabited by idolaters whose posterity were to be destroyed before Israel. That there was such a man in such a place at such a time may teach us:

(i) that the Lord can raise up instruments for his service and glory when and where he pleases.

(ii) that a person in the character of a priest of God and a signal type of Christ, at the same time the promises were made to Abraham, was a pledge and intimation of the call of the Gentiles.

FOR MEDITATION: What a phenomenon has Mr Wilberforce sent abroad! *Such* a book, by *such* a man, and at *such* a time! A book which must and will be read by persons in the higher circles, who are quite inaccessible to us little folks; who will neither hear what we can say, nor read what we may write. I am filled with wonder and with hope. I accept it as a token for good, yea as the brightest token I can discern in this dark and perilous day. Yes, I trust that the Lord, by raising up such an incontestable witness to the truth and power of his gospel, has a gracious purpose to honour him as an instrument of reviving and strengthening the sense of real religion where it already is, and of communicating it, where it is not.[197]

John Newton to Charles Grant, 18 April 1797
[on the publication of *A Practical View of Christianity* by William Wilberforce[198]]

King of righteousness and peace

'*For this Melchisedec, king of Salem, priest of the most high God, who met Abraham returning from the slaughter of the kings, and blessed him; to whom also Abraham gave a tenth part of all; first being by interpretation King of righteousness, and after that also King of Salem, which is, King of peace; without father, without mother, without descent, having neither beginning of days, nor end of life; but made like unto the Son of God; abideth a priest continually.*' Hebrews 7:1–3
SUGGESTED FURTHER READING: Titus 3:3–8

Melchizedek was king of Salem, most probably Jerusalem, though commentators are divided. This city was governed by a priest and servant of *the most High God*, afterwards possessed by the Jebusites, then the seat of the temple of God, at length totally destroyed and lays waste to this day. Thus the Lord is not confined to places. Thus we should learn not to depend upon outward privileges—they may be soon taken away—nor to give up hope of any because dark at present, for he can soon command the light to shine. The Apostle takes notice of the names—*Melchizedek: Melchi Salem—King of Righteousness* and *King of Peace*. Under these characters we have a type of Jesus:

(i) he is *King of Righteousness*, the perfector of righteousness in himself (Psalm 45:6), the author of righteousness to his people (Jeremiah 23:5).

(ii) he is *King of Peace* (Isaiah 9:6; Ephesians 2). To him poor sinners are to look for those needful blessings. He can justify the ungodly and fill the troubled mind with peace surpassing all understanding.

His characters—*without descent*—show that he was a proper type of Christ's priest office as distinct from the Levitical priests. They were registered, their genealogies carefully kept, and otherwise they could not be received—a stated time was appointed for their entrance on their office and their discharge—but he was without beginning of days or end of time.

FOR MEDITATION: 'And he hath on his vesture and on his thigh a name written, KING OF KINGS, AND LORD OF LORDS' (Revelation 19:16).

'I am Alpha and Omega, the beginning and the ending, saith the Lord, which is, and which was, and which is to come, the Almighty' (Revelation 1:8).

SERMON SERIES: GENESIS, NO. 28 [2/3], GENESIS 14:18–19

Jesus our Great High Priest

'And Melchizedek king of Salem brought forth bread and wine: and he was the priest of the most high God. And he blessed him, and said, Blessed be Abram of the most high God, possessor of heaven and earth: and blessed be the most high God, which hath delivered thine enemies into thine hand. And he gave him tithes of all.' Genesis 14:18–20
SUGGESTED FURTHER READING: Hebrews 6:13–20

Observe:

(i) Melchizedek *came forth* to meet Abraham. Believers, like Abraham, are called to a warfare. Jesus their King and High Priest teaches them to fight and conquer and often *comes forth* to meet them, as Melchizedek.

(ii) he brought *bread and wine*. Thus the Lord refreshes, strengthens his warriors—he comes forth in the ordinances.

(iii) he *blessed* him in the name of God. Jesus had obtained the blessing and he blesses all his people; yea, and they shall be blessed.

(iv) *Abraham gave him tithes of all*—as an acknowledgement to the Lord by his priest. And thus believers render to God their services and sacrifices of praise, by Jesus Christ.

Happy are the subjects of this King, the people who have such a great High Priest—no enemy shall hurt them, no weapon formed against them prosper, no charge to their prejudice be received. But what must become of those who reject his mediation and will not have him reign over them?

FOR MEDITATION:

But JESUS invitations sends,
Treating with rebels as his friends;
And holds the promise forth in view,
To all who for his mercy sue.

Too long his goodness I disdained,
Yet went at last and peace obtained;
But soon the noise of war I heard,
And former friends in arms appeared.

Weak in myself for help I cried,
LORD, I am pressed on every side;
The cause is thine, they fight with me,
But every blow is aimed at thee.

With speed to my relief he came,
And put my enemies to shame;
Thus saved by grace I live to sing,
The love and triumphs of my King.[199]

More to come

'After these things the word of the LORD *came unto Abram in a vision, saying, Fear not, Abram: I am thy shield, and thy exceeding great reward.'*
Genesis 15:1
SUGGESTED FURTHER READING: Psalm 18:1–19

When we meet with the words *After these things* it leads our thoughts backwards:

(i) *after* the general call and promise (chapter 12). After Abraham had made many a journey, reared many an altar, the Lord manifests himself further and confirms his faith with brighter tokens of his favour. The believer's progress is from strength to strength. Be thankful for what you have received but count not that you have attained—there is still more behind. The tendency of grace is to mount higher and higher and it is the Lord's purpose to answer the hungerings and thirstings which he has put in the soul.

(ii) *after* the victory he had lately obtained. No doubt this success was pleasing to Abraham, but it was not the great thing. Believers are thankful for the mercies of the present life, but these are not their treasure and their joy. A gracious visit from the Lord, an application of the promises, is more to them than the joy of harvest or of them that divide the spoil.

Thanks to thy name for meaner things.
But these are not my God.[200]

As if the Lord had said, 'Temporal blessings are but the tokens and earnests of my favour. You have more than this to rejoice. *I myself am your shield and reward.'*

FOR MEDITATION: 'For he looked for a city which hath foundations, whose builder and maker is God' (Hebrews 11:10).

'One thing I do: Forgetting what is behind and straining toward what is ahead, I press on toward the goal to win the prize for which God has called me heavenward in Christ Jesus' (Philippians 3:13–14, NIV).

Fear not

'After these things the word of the LORD *came unto Abram in a vision, saying, Fear not, Abram: I am thy shield, and thy exceeding great reward.'*
Genesis 15:1
SUGGESTED FURTHER READING: Psalm 56:1–13

After these things:

(i) *after* Abraham's conduct towards the king of Sodom, proving the disinterestedness of his spirit and the strength of his faith. He would accept nothing, though offered all. He would not tarnish his good action by admitting selfish views, nor be beholden to a king when he was at God's keeping. Now the Lord shows him that he shall be no loser.

(ii) It seems to intimate that Abraham, though honoured and successful, had intervals of fear. We find it so now and have reason to think it has been so always. Believer, though in the Lord's strength you have gained many a battle, you know you cannot live by past experiences. Unless the Lord says again, *Fear not*, your fears will return like an armed man. And what he said to Abraham in a vision, he says to you, *Fear not....*, for this promise belongs not to Abraham only, but to all who partake of his faith (as Joshua 1:5; Hebrews 13:5–6).

FOR MEDITATION:

When the wounded spirit hears
The voice of JESUS' blood;
How the message stops the tears
Which else in vain had flowed:

Pardon, grace, and peace proclaimed,
And the sinner called a child;
Then the stubborn heart is tamed,
Renewed, and reconciled.

Oh! 'twas grace indeed, to spare,
And save a wretch like me!
Men or angels could not bear
What I have offered thee.[201]

Jesus our shield

'After these things the word of the LORD *came unto Abram in a vision, saying, Fear not, Abram: I am thy shield, and thy exceeding great reward.'*
Genesis 15:1
SUGGESTED FURTHER READING: Romans 5:1–11

The promise expresses the believer's safety: the Lord is his *shield* (Psalm 18:2).²⁰² Many images denote the safety and security of those who put their trust in him—none more comfortable or suitable than this of a shield:

(i) against the demands of the law and justice of God. Too many would shelter themselves with a refuge of lies—self-righteousness, false notions of God's mercy—repentance, promises and purposes are all they have to trust to. But this is like trusting to a cobweb to shield us from a cannonball. Jesus is the only shield. He bore the wrath for his people and keeps it from them. Under his wing they are safe and the swift sword that justice draws, flaming and red, shall pass them by.

(ii) from Satan. This is the shield of faith. Faith itself is not properly our shield, but Christ is the shield which faith opposes to the enemy, and thus his fiery darts are quenched. As one said, 'Trouble not me Satan, I am a weak and sinful woman, but go to Jesus—he shall answer you.' So the Apostle (in Romans 8:34) looks round and challenges his enemies, *Who shall condemn?* Then he takes up his shield, *It is Christ that died.* With this shield in hand, we cannot be greatly hurt.

FOR MEDITATION:
Heavy charges Satan brings
To fill me with distress;
Let me hide beneath thy wings,
And plead thy righteousness:
Lord, to thee for help I call,
'Tis thy promise bids me come;
Tell him thou hast paid for all,
And that shall strike him dumb.²⁰³

Shielded from evil

'After these things the word of the LORD *came unto Abram in a vision, saying, Fear not, Abram: I am thy shield, and thy exceeding great reward.'*
Genesis 15:1
SUGGESTED FURTHER READING: Psalm 91:1–16

Consider the believer's safety from the evil that is in the world, whether affliction or opposition. He is shielded:

(i) by his providence. We are liable to many harms and dangers continually, by night and by day, abroad and at home, and have need of a defence from wicked men. We see too many who love to practise mischief, and they have a secret grudge at the Lord's people. Why are they preserved? Because he is their *shield* and sets a hedge about them. It is true the Lord protects careless sinners likewise. It is because some of them, though not yet called, shall live to know his name. Others, though tares, grow among the wheat and are preserved for the wheat's sake. The preservation of others is a judgement. They are suffered to go on to add sin unto sin. But the protection he affords his own people is of special grace and he enables them to see, own and rejoice in it as such.

(ii) by his Spirit. When he suffers affliction to touch them, he interposes his grace to take away the evil of it and to support them under it. The sting, the curse, is taken away and they are strengthened with strength in their souls, with patience, resignation and peace, so that often the heaviest blows are hardly felt.

FOR MEDITATION: Ask yourselves, my friends, what you think of this shield. You need one. And if not conscious of it now, you will be hereafter when death comes with his dart and the summons of judgement shall be sounding in your ears.

An exceeding great reward

'After these things the word of the LORD *came unto Abram in a vision, saying, Fear not, Abram: I am thy shield, and thy exceeding great reward.'*
Genesis 15:1
SUGGESTED FURTHER READING: Habakkuk 3:17–19

The promise expresses the believer's happiness: *thy exceeding great reward.* On this ground faith rejoices and says, *The Lord is my portion* [Lamentations 3:24].

Thy reward: this does not import any desert on our parts. The smallest mercy is of undeserved grace—much more when he gives us himself. But it is a *reward*, a full amends:

(i) for all we leave for him. To be the Lord's will cost us something. Some sacrifices must be made. But O how are those overpaid who have him. They are all of St Paul's mind and count everything loss and dung that they may win Christ [Philippians 3:7–8].

(ii) for all we can suffer for him. The world may hate and despise. It may cost a man his life for his attachment to Jesus. But to lose our life in this cause is to save it.

Exceeding great. What words can express it? Happy soul who hast the Lord for thy portion. You may rejoice with Habakkuk in the God of your salvation, though everything else is blasted and comfortless around you [Habakkuk 3:17–18]. Rejoice in your privileges. He will guide you while here with his counsel, refresh you with his presence, support you with his arm. Hereafter, he shall receive you to his glory, wipe away all your tears, exceed all your desires, seat you near himself, and so you shall be with him for ever. Was Thomas filled with rapture and love when he saw him return from the grave? What then will you say when you shall see him as he is, when he shall own your worthless name before assembled worlds and say, *Come ye blessed* [Matthew 25:34]?

FOR MEDITATION: You that see your need of an Almighty Shield, that be happy with nothing less than the Lord himself: fear not—he that has begun the good work will increase it. Pray him to bless the means which he has appointed to strengthen your weak faith. By and by you shall be enabled to say, *My beloved is mine and I am his* [Song of Solomon 2:16].

SERMON SERIES: GENESIS, NO. 29 [5/5], GENESIS 15:1

Bless the Lord, O my soul!

'And Abram said, Lord GOD, what wilt thou give me, seeing I go childless, and the steward of my house is this Eliezer of Damascus?' Genesis 15:2
SUGGESTED FURTHER READING: Psalm 103:1–22

These words sound very strange from the father of the faithful. Was this a suitable answer to the promise he had just received? If we take them in their first and immediate sense, they answer to what many believers have felt and what I suppose Abraham himself was not wholly free from: a spirit of impatience and unbelief, which makes it well for us that the grace of God is free and his love unchangeable, or we might expect to be cast off for our perversity. The psalmist charges his soul, *forget not all his benefits* [Psalm 103:2]. There are seasons when we are liable to forget not only one or a few, but to forget them all, as:

(i) in a time of sharp affliction. Then too often a believer is like other men. The Lord has saved him from hell and appointed him to glory, but the trouble so fixes the attention that everything else seems forgot.

(ii) when the heart is keenly set upon creature good. O then a depraved nature shows itself. If we cannot have what we want, all that we have seems useless and tasteless and the sun shines upon us in vain.

From hence we may observe that a constant meditation upon the mercies of God to us, especially to our souls, is an excellent means to keep our hearts in a right frame, to make trouble sit easy and to teach us how to seek or to use the good things of this world as becomes Christians

FOR MEDITATION:
His love in time past
Forbids me to think
He'll leave me at last
In trouble to sink;
Each sweet Ebenezer
I have in review,
Confirms his good pleasure
To help me quite through.[204]

All upon the wing!

'But thou, O LORD, *art a shield for me; the glory and the lifter up of mine head.' Psalm 3:3*
SUGGESTED FURTHER READING: Psalm 42:1–11

The Lord ... our *shield*. This is a glorious word, yet some other things are wanting to give us full comfort in it. The soul will desire:

(i) his presence and the light of his countenance: if it be so, why go I mourning?

(ii) power over sin: I cannot rejoice in my portion while I feel so many things in me contrary to thy will.

(iii) a lively spirit for his service: I am a debtor not to the flesh to live after the flesh. O give me so to feel my privileges, that I may be all upon the wing to show forth thy praise.

These and the like are petitions surely agreeable to his will. And it is a proof of sincerity not to rest satisfied with any comforts or experiences we have received, but to thirst after a fuller accomplishment of what he has bid us hope for. Too many fall sadly short here. They have been in distress for sin and the Lord has given them a hope in his mercy. They believe he has accepted them, and, by degrees, set down easy and contented, though there is little liveliness in their spirits, much amiss in their tempers, and a prevalent cleaving to the world in their conversation. Though their profession is known by little more than an outward attendance upon ordinances, they satisfy themselves with looking back to past times, when they think it was better with them, and rest in a doctrinal notion of his unchangeableness and the sure perseverance of his people. This is a bad sign. If such are the children of God, they may expect something to rouse them from their security.

FOR MEDITATION: Alas, I teach others but cannot teach myself. Thou knowest a want of taste for thy Scripture is one of my chief burdens. How often it is to me as a sealed book, How often do I read it as a mere task. How defective am I in searching into this inestimable mine and how seldom is it the medium of real intercourse between thee and my soul. O send forth thy light and shine upon thy truth that I may not only judge but taste it to be more sweet and desirable than my necessary food.[205]

Diary, 16 October 1775

SERMON SERIES: GENESIS, NO. 30 [2/2], GENESIS 15:2

To him we can appeal

'O send out thy light and thy truth: let them lead me; let them bring me unto thy holy hill, and to thy tabernacles.' Psalm 43:3
SUGGESTED FURTHER READING: Psalm 43:1–5

This psalm was probably penned by David in some time of trouble. He met with much injustice and trouble from men, but the Lord was his God. To him he could appeal as a righteous Judge that would in good time plead his cause. He was sometimes driven from the sanctuary below and the public worship, but he could not be cut off from immediate communion with him who is not confined to temples made with hands. His sixty-third psalm we are expressly told was made in the wilderness; perhaps likewise this—and we see how full of spiritual and divine breathings he is when cut off from the ordinances. For no matter where we are driven, if the Lord goes with us, nor what we are deprived of, if he is our God, and is pleased to manifest his presence. Let men do their utmost; though I am confined to a desert, yet thou art all-sufficient. *O send forth thy light.* These words express the desires of an awakened soul. By nature we can neither understand or form such a wish as this. Many of you have perhaps often repeated them in the service without knowing what you meant, but I am persuaded there are some amongst you who can heartily join with them; they express the very language of your souls. May our present meditations on them be made a means to add new life to your desires and strength to your faith.

FOR MEDITATION:

Kindle, Saviour, in my heart
A flame of love divine;
Hear, hear, for mine I trust thou art,
And sure I would be thine:
If my soul has felt thy grace,
If to me thy name is known;
Why should trifles fill the place,
Due to thyself alone?

'Tis a strange mysterious life
I live from day to day;
Light and darkness, peace and strife,
Bear an alternate sway;
But when CHRIST, my LORD and Friend,
Is pleased to show his power;
All at once my troubles end,
And I've a golden hour.[206]

SERMON: PSALM 43:3 [1/5]

The emptiness of the 'enchanted places'

'O send out thy light and thy truth: let them lead me; let them bring me unto thy holy hill, and to thy tabernacles.' Psalm 43:3
SUGGESTED FURTHER READING: Ecclesiastes 2:1–11

Here we observe what is implied: a conviction of the emptiness and vanity of the present state. This world and all that is in it may be compared to what some writers have fancied of enchanted places.[207] It has been supposed that by the power of a sorcerer people have been surprised with fine sights, noble buildings, pleasant gardens, entertained with music and feasting, till by and by the charm has been broke; all these gay things have vanished, and they have found themselves disappointed and alone. Such an enchantment is the world. Such a magician is the devil. He deceives the sight and stupefies the mind of sinners. They think themselves in a world of delights. They propose nothing but pleasure and joy. They look no farther than the present life. But when the Word of God comes powerfully to the heart, then the enchantment is broke—all those fine things are gone at one. The soul is like a hungry man that has been dreaming of eating, and now it awakes and finds itself empty. Then it sees and feels this cannot be its rest. It can no longer feed upon the wind. It wants something more substantial. How have I been seeking the living among the dead, expecting to enjoy peace and happiness in a state of sin and misery! But now I see I never can be happy unless the mighty God vouchsafes to be my portion—not until I arrive at his heavenly hill, the place of his holiness. No happiness for me till guilt is pardoned, sin subdued and Satan trampled under my feet.

FOR MEDITATION:

Blinded in youth by Satan's arts,
The world to our unpractised hearts,
A flattering prospect bows;
Our fancy forms a thousand schemes,
Of gay delights, and golden dreams,
And undisturbed repose.

But while he listens with surprise,
The charm dissolves, the vision dies,
'Twas but enchanted ground;
Thus if the Lord our spirits touch,
The world, which promised us so much,
A wilderness is found.[208]

Helplessness stirs us to prayer

'O send out thy light and thy truth: let them lead me; let them bring me unto thy holy hill, and to thy tabernacles.' Psalm 43:3
SUGGESTED FURTHER READING: Psalm 61:1–8

A conviction of helplessness and insufficiency is implied. When an awakened sinner has seen the world to be what indeed it is and has obtained some apprehensions of heavenly things, still it is at a distance and much darkness lies upon the way to obtain. Only in this the soul is satisfied and certain: that it has no strength and wisdom of its own whereby to escape deserved evil or to obtain the desired good. It stands in need of assistance and this stirs it up to prayer, even the prayer of my text, for there is likewise implied some beginnings of knowledge that our help is in the name of the Lord—that if he does it not, it can never be done. We are not brought to this at once. When we first begin to open our eyes, we are very prone to seek deliverance by our own arm, by confessions, resolutions and outside services. We begin to attempt a reformation, to set about a new life and perhaps go on so very quietly for a while. Our great enemy loves to see us busied in building a house upon the sand and may suffer us to carry it on to a good height, for he knows that he is able with one puff of temptation to blow it down again. Then when we think it strong, he is suffered to come to try our work and soon it falls before him. After many such disappointments, we at last see how poor and helpless we are and cry to the Lord, *O send forth thy light and thy truth*.

FOR MEDITATION: The resolutions I made seem to be still good and the means of peace and happiness, but I fear I have broken every one. I am willing to think I stand till I am really fallen, and then, by presuming to rise by my own strength, I lie grovelling long before I can be persuaded of my insufficiency. I would endeavour to guard more against this error for the future and make it a particular point of my prayers … so I may more fully than ever feel the reality and necessity of his assistance; and that when I say that I can do nothing good without him, can forbear nothing evil without him, nor hope for any peace or pardon without him, I may speak entirely from my heart and that this absolute dependence upon him only, may be the ruling principle of my life. Amen.[209]

Diary, 1 February 1752

SERMON: PSALM 43:3 [3/5]

Send forth thy light and thy truth

'*O send out thy light and thy truth: let them lead me; let them bring me unto thy holy hill, and to thy tabernacles.' Psalm 43:3*
SUGGESTED FURTHER READING: John 7:37–44

What is expressed: every word is emphatical and full of meaning.

Send forth. From whence? From Jesus. He is the Fountain, the Sun, the Treasury of all grace. This sending forth is the fruit of his intercession. He has received gifts, even the Holy Spirit, to teach, comfort and seal every seeking soul.

Thy light. All light and knowledge is from God, but natural and common light, the light of reason, books, or education, will not do—therefore the soul prays *thy light*, that which is peculiarly thine, and which none partake of but by special favour. Light signifies knowledge, as in Psalm 119:130, and comfort, as in Micah 7:9. Both these, the heart which God has touched seeks from him alone.

And thy truth. This is already revealed or sent forth in the Word, but the meaning of the prayer is that the promises, which are true in themselves, may be sent forth in their power and sweetness and applied to the heart. Two things the soul wants to know of God's truths: their extensive meaning and fullness and its own interest in them.

FOR MEDITATION: I labour under a thousand difficulties in my ways to goodness, my heart is wicked and deceitful, my affections corrupted, my hopes and fears misplaced, and all my faculties unhappily bent toward evil; the world, the flesh and the devil in many different forms and circumstances strive to draw me from my duty. These things are to me insuperable but they are not so to thee. If thou but speak the word, all obstacles shall vanish. That powerful word which cleansed the lepers and raised the dead can in one moment purge my soul from all the defilements it has contracted and raise me up to newness of life. Lord I believe, help thou mine unbelief, for thy name's sake, for thy promise' sake, for the sake of that precious sacrifice thou didst once offer up for all.[210]

Diary, 1 July 1752

SERMON: PSALM 43:3 [4/5]

Heaven as your home

'O send out thy light and thy truth: let them lead me; let them bring me unto thy holy hill, and to thy tabernacles.' Psalm 43:3
SUGGESTED FURTHER READING: Psalm 27:1–14

Let them lead me. The question is asked somewhere, *Who shall lead me into the strong city?* [Psalm 60:9]. And here the soul is taught an answer—I indeed am dark and weak, I cannot see my way, nor walk in it by my own strength, but let the truth of God support me and his light shine upon my paths and I shall go on well.

And bring me. Here is the humble confidence of faith—that what God begins shall not miscarry and those whom he leads shall not be lost. I know that my path is full of snares and dangers—if left to myself I should soon stumble and fall and be snared and broken—but thy light and truth shall lead me in safety to the end. I am faint and apt to tire, but these shall revive me in the way and at length bring me to the end, and in safety.

To thy holy hill. The soul is sick of earth and longs for heaven; this is the place where it would be. It is described:

(i) as a *hill*, in allusion to Mount Zion (Revelation 14:1): perhaps to signify the difficulty of the way (it is an uphill road)—the security and safety (it is high out of the reach of all enemies)—and its eminence (it cannot be hid: it is set on a hill and attracts the hearts and views of all the children of God. They are all looking to this prize of their calling).

(ii) as a *holy* hill. No unclean thing shall enter. When the everlasting gates are lifted up to receive my poor unworthy soul, I shall leave all my sins and sorrows behind me.

(iii) *thy tabernacles.* This is the crowning circumstance: our Lord Jesus dwells on this holy hill. There we shall see him as he is and love him as we ought. There we shall cast our crowns at his feet. We shall go up to his altar with exceeding joy, to sing his praise on harps of gold for ever.

FOR MEDITATION: If you choose heaven as your home, and God's light and truth as your way, your prayer shall be answered. Fight against your unbelief as David does in verse 5: *Why art thou cast down, O my soul? And why art thou disquieted within me? Hope in God: for I shall yet praise him, who is the health of my countenance, and my God.*

SERMON: PSALM 43:3 [5/5]

The fear of man

'The fear of man bringeth a snare: but whoso putteth his trust in the LORD *shall be safe.' Proverbs 29:25*
SUGGESTED FURTHER READING: Proverbs 29:1–27

All opposition to the ways and people of God are originally from the devil. To this purpose he bestirs himself more or less as he is permitted so soon as a soul begins to seek salvation by Jesus. Many can witness what they have suffered from his suggestions because they would no longer live in his service. Some are more harassed in this way by his own immediate influence. Against others, or against the same person at other times, he employs his great instrument—the world—and with but too much success, because the fear of man is a principle deeply rooted in our human nature. We are departed from God and are naturally prone to serve, love, trust and fear the creature more than the Creator. The heart of man is so at enmity against God, that whoever will be the Lord's servant, will on that account stand exposed to the resentment and displeasure of men.

The fear of man bringeth a snare. This hurries many on in a course of sin. It is not so much for the pleasure they find, as that they are influenced by others. They depend upon their favour, or are afraid of their frown. This keeps many from confessing the truth, who are convinced of it in their hearts (as in John 12). This draws many away from the people of God who had for a season joined them. They are afraid of their anger, afraid of their reviling. If it cannot be maintained without breaking the peace of their families, endangering their worldly interest, or exposing them to suffer, they will give it up.

A snare. It works secretly and gradually—leads to a train of vain reasoning. People do not give up all at once, but, by endeavouring to keep fair with God and the world together, they grow worse and worse. Therefore take heed of beginnings. Every compliance will lead you farther.

FOR MEDITATION:

When any turn from Zion's way,
(Alas! what numbers do!)
Methinks I hear my Saviour say,
'Wilt thou forsake me too?'

What anguish has that question stirred,
If I will also go?
Yet, LORD, relying on thy word,
I humbly answer, No![211]

SERMON: PROVERBS 29:25 [1/2]

Safety in trusting the Lord

'The fear of man bringeth a snare: but whoso putteth his trust in the LORD *shall be safe.' Proverbs 29:25*
SUGGESTED FURTHER READING: Daniel 3:1–30

Here is the remedy for the fear of man: *Whoso putteth his trust in the* LORD. If you have God and conscience on your side, none can prevail against him—but this implies knowledge and sincerity.

See how safe were:

(i) Shadrach, Meshach and Abednego—they would not worship [Daniel 3].

(ii) Daniel—he would pray [Daniel 6].

(iii) Yea Stephen—safe though slain [Acts 7].

Consider:

(i) God has all hearts in his hand.

(ii) He can give you better—even in temporals, but especially in spirituals.

(iii) Soon these things will be at an end and then, O to be owned by him.

How awful the case of those who endeavour to entice or affright believers from their duty. There is no safety but in putting your trust in the Lord.

No voice but thine can give me rest,
And bid my fears depart;
No love but thine can make me blest,
And satisfy my heart.[212]

FOR MEDITATION: This is a confused world, and this seems to be an eventful period. But the Lord reigns, and he will manifest his wisdom by overruling apparent evil for real good. All things shall ultimately contribute to the enlargement and establishment of his church and kingdom. In the meantime, they who serve him have nothing to fear. He will enable them to acknowledge him here, and he will acknowledge them when he shall appear in glory.[213]

John Newton to William Wilberforce, 4 August [1793]

Accounted righteous

'And he brought him forth abroad, and said, Look now toward heaven, and tell the stars, if thou be able to number them: and he said unto him, So shall thy seed be. And he believed in the LORD; and he counted it to him for righteousness.' Genesis 15:5–6
SUGGESTED FURTHER READING: Luke 19:1–9

Two things affirmed of Abraham:

(i) *he believed in the Lord.* The Lord had before given him the promise—of a child and a numerous seed—on which Abraham rested, not without some solicitude when the accomplishment was so long delayed. The Lord now confirmed his hope; he bid him look at the stars and said, *So shall thy seed be.*

(ii) *it was accounted to him for righteousness.* He was dealt with upon the footing of a sinner who had nothing of his own to plead and was justified by a righteousness accounted, or imputed, to him.

The question is, what was imputed to him for righteousness? Or, in what was his believing or his faith so imputed? We are assured that the seed emphatically promised to Abraham was Christ, or the Messiah, who was to be born of his family according to the flesh (Galatians 3). And we are assured that he so understood, for our Lord says, *Abraham rejoiced to see my day* [John 8:56]. The promise of numerous children of Abraham—compared to the stars—was not merely applicable to the posterity which should spring from his loins, but especially respected the company of believers who should partake of Abraham's faith. Thus Zacchaeus was a son of Abraham by believing [Luke 19:9], and the woman of Canaan, though a Gentile and not a Jew by birth, proved to be one of the lost sheep of the house of Israel [Matthew 15:24]. The Jews, though they boasted that Abraham was their father [John 8:39], were strangers to the true commonwealth of Israel. And John the Baptist told them that God was able to raise up children to Abraham in their room, from the very stones [Matthew 3:9].

FOR MEDITATION:

When a guilty sinner sees him,
While he looks his soul is healed;

Soon this sight from anguish frees him,
And imparts a pardon sealed.[214]

True justifying faith

'And he brought him forth abroad, and said, Look now toward heaven, and tell the stars, if thou be able to number them: and he said unto him, So shall thy seed be. And he believed in the LORD*; and he counted it to him for righteousness.' Genesis 15:5–6*
SUGGESTED FURTHER READING: Romans 3:21–31

Answerable to Abraham's faith is the way of justification now, by faith in the same object, and upon the same ground. The object is Christ. No other name is given, no other name is desired or regarded by those who are truly convinced of sin. He is appointed of God and proposed to them and set before them as wisdom, righteousness, and so forth. The Holy Spirit who has convinced them of sin, convinces them of righteousness, the necessity of it—that it is not in themselves and that it is in Jesus.

The ground (or warrant) is the promise, and that under no less outward discouragements than Abraham had to encounter. The guilt of sin, the power of corruption, the stress of temptation, the delay of comfort—by these things the soul is sometimes startled and put almost to a stand. But faith prevails and reasons, as Abraham, 'God has promised and is able also to perform—therefore I will hope against hope' [Romans 4:18].

We conclude then that a venturing upon Jesus from the invitation of gospel promises is true, justifying faith. To such, his righteousness is accounted as their own, and, notwithstanding all their fears and infirmities, they are accepted in the beloved; their state is safe. O blessed are ye of the Lord that are seeking salvation in this way. But this faith in the lowest degree, if but as a grain of mustard seed, will have fruits: love, desire, obedience. Though in many things they come short, they will be pressing forward.

FOR MEDITATION: Two sorts of persons then are in a dangerous state:
(i) they who seek salvation by the works of the law. If they can be saved in their present way, Christ has died in vain.
(ii) they who talk of faith and are utterly destitute of its fruits, who have a form without the power. This is the proper description of a corpse. So James says the faith of such is dead [James 2:26].

Plucked as a brand out of the fire

'And he said unto him, I am the LORD *that brought thee out of Ur of the Chaldees, to give thee this land to inherit it.' Genesis 15:7*
SUGGESTED FURTHER READING: Zechariah 3:1–10

In this passage we have the Lord's word to Abraham by way of remembrance: *I brought thee from Ur of the Chaldees*—from idolaters, plucked thee as a brand out of the fire [Zechariah 3:2]. Thus he reminds all his people. It is said the night when Israel left Egypt was a night much to be remembered [Exodus 12:42]. Believers surely will never forget the mercy which called them. It was a special mercy. Many [were] left when Abraham was called. How many of your companions have been left? Some of you were brought from places at a great distance, like Abraham, and it was a foundation mercy—how much depended upon it. As it is farther said: *to give thee this land*—a type of the heavenly Canaan. The Lord did not call Abraham to leave him by the way. If you are called out of sin and the world, brought to Jesus, it is because the Lord designs to give you the good land— for his gifts and callings are without repentance.

FOR MEDITATION:

With Satan, my accuser near,
My spirit trembled when I saw
The Lord in majesty appear,
And heard the language of his law.
In vain I wished and strove to hide
The tattered filthy rags I wore;
While my fierce foe, insulting cried,
'See what you trusted in before!'
Struck dumb, and left without a plea,
I heard my gracious Saviour say,
'Know, Satan, I this sinner free,
I died to take his sins away.
'This is a brand which I in love,
To save from wrath and sin design;
In vain thy accusations prove,
I answer all, and claim him mine.'

At his rebuke the tempter fled;
Then he removed my filthy dress;
'Poor sinner take this robe,' he said,
'It is thy Saviour's righteousness.
And see, a crown of life prepared!
That I might thus thy head adorn;
I thought no shame or suffering hard,
But wore, for thee, a crown of thorn.'
O how I heard these gracious words!
They broke and healed my heart at once;
Constrained me to become the Lord's,
And all my idol-gods renounce.
Now, Satan, thou hast lost thy aim,
Against this brand thy threats are vain;
Jesus has plucked it from the flame,
And who shall put it in again?[215]

An atoning sacrifice

'And he said, Lord GOD, whereby shall I know that I shall inherit it? And he said unto him, Take me an heifer of three years old, and a she goat of three years old, and a ram of three years old, and a turtledove, and a young pigeon.' Genesis 15:8–9
SUGGESTED FURTHER READING: Hebrews 12:1–3

We have Abraham's request—he wanted a sign:

(i) for the confirmation of his own faith. When we believe, there is still unbelief in us.

(ii) for the sake of his posterity. What the Lord put now in Abraham's heart to ask, was recorded in his Word for those who should come after. Believers of old had but few footsteps to follow, but we have a beaten path before us—the advantage of their experiences.

In the Lord's command we may observe a sacrifice and a sign.

(i) A sacrifice. The animals mentioned were the same as were principally used after Moses. The death of Christ was thus set forth from the beginning to intimate that without shedding of blood there is no remission. All the promises of God are made and confirmed in the death of Christ. Here is our only right to them, and in this way they are sure.

(ii) A sign. The division of the beasts was the customary form of a covenant (Jeremiah 34:18–19). And between these the smoking furnace and the lamp afterwards passed.

FOR MEDITATION:

The GOD who once to Israel spoke
From Sinai's top, in fire and smoke,
In gentler strains of gospel grace
Invites us, now, to seek his face.

The holy Moses quaked and feared
When Sinai's thundering law he heard;
But reigning grace, with accents mild,
Speaks to the sinner, as a child.

He wears no terrors on his brow,
He speaks, in love, from Zion, now;
It is the voice of JESUS' blood
Calling poor wanderers home to GOD.

Hark! how from Calvary it sounds;
From the Redeemer's bleeding wounds!
'Pardon and grace, I freely give,
Poor sinner, look to me, and live.'[216]

SERMON SERIES: GENESIS, NO. 32 [2/3], GENESIS 15:7–11

Birds of prey

'And he took unto him all these, and divided them in the midst, and laid each piece one against another: but the birds divided he not. And when the fowls came down upon the carcases, Abram drove them away.' Genesis 15:10–11
SUGGESTED FURTHER READING: 2 Peter 2:1–22

We note *the birds came down*—an emblem:

(i) of the attempts that would be made to frustrate the covenant—by men and by Satan. This is the *vain thing* that is always imagined from age to age [Psalm 2:1]. But as Abraham drove the birds away, so the Lord himself will protect his church and his people and keep them as the apple of his eye.

(ii) of the evil thoughts and imperfections that accompany our holy things. Alas, we cannot attempt a sacrifice to the Lord our God, but the birds of prey are ready to devour it. Of this the Apostle complains, *When I would do good evil is present with me* [Romans 7:21]. There are wandering thoughts, which insensibly catch our minds away till we forget almost where we are. And still worse, for there are wicked thoughts, such as would be wicked in any time or place, and are therefore doubly so when they mix with our sacrifices. The true believer, like Abraham, is grieved on this account and labours to drive them away. But formal worshippers regard them not. If they go through the outward duty they are satisfied.

(iii) May I not compare these birds to false believers? They would avail themselves of Christ's sacrifice while they live and remain unclean, but they shall be driven away.

FOR MEDITATION: The Apostle was well acquainted with the Christian warfare, how fiercely the soul that loves Jesus is sure to be assaulted—he was well acquainted with the heart of man, how weak, deceitful and prone to wander. Yet, says he with a holy triumph, *Who shall separate us from the love of Christ?* [Romans 8:35]… While Jesus is the foundation, root, head and husband of his people, while the Word of God is yea and amen, while the counsels of God are unchangeable, while we have a Mediator and High Priest appointed of God, while the Holy Spirit is willing and able to bear witness to the truth of the gospel, while God is wiser than men and stronger than the devil, so long, the believer in Jesus is, and shall be, safe.[217]

Sermon on Romans 8:30, *The Searcher of Hearts*

SERMON SERIES: GENESIS, NO. 32 [3/3], GENESIS 15:7–11

Delivered from bondage

'*And when the sun was going down, a deep sleep fell upon Abram; and, lo, an horror of great darkness fell upon him. And he said unto Abram, Know of a surety that thy seed shall be a stranger in a land that is not theirs, and shall serve them; and they shall afflict them four hundred years; and also that nation, whom they shall serve, will I judge: and afterward shall they come out with great substance.' Genesis 15:12–14*
SUGGESTED FURTHER READING: 1 Kings 8:54–61

The Lord, in this chapter, confirmed his covenant with Abraham by repeated promises and by signs—suited to establish his faith, and likewise for the instruction of his church in succeeding times. A deep sleep fell upon him (his bodily senses were overpowered, but his soul was awake to the visions of God) and a horror of darkness—an emblem of the afflictions his posterity was to meet with and of the dispensations of the law they were to be subject to.

Here Abraham is informed of:

(i) their trouble. They were to possess the land but first they were to suffer in bondage. When the time of the promise drew nigh he found them in misery and slavery—thus he made himself known as their deliverer. So it is with all the Lord's people. He has appointed them an inheritance, but they are for a season in the enemies' hands.

(ii) God's vengeance on their enemies: *I will judge them.* The Lord will plead his people's cause and then they shall come forth with victory and honour.

FOR MEDITATION:
JOHN NEWTON, CLERK,
Once an Infidel and Libertine,
A servant of slaves in Africa,
Was, by the rich mercy of our Lord and Saviour
JESUS CHRIST,
Preserved, restored, pardoned,
And appointed to preach the Faith
He had long laboured to destroy.[218]

Epitaph, by John Newton

SERMON SERIES: GENESIS, NO. 33 [1/2], GENESIS 15:17

The furnace of affliction

'And it came to pass, that, when the sun went down, and it was dark, behold a smoking furnace, and a burning lamp that passed between those pieces.' Genesis 15:17
SUGGESTED FURTHER READING: Job 23:1–10

The whole [incident] was closed by a sign—a smoking furnace and a burning lamp—a type of the state of the church.

(i) *The furnace* of affliction. Here, says he, *I have chosen thee* [Isaiah 48:10]. Here he first finds them and we may say of the furnace—as of the Apostle, of the stream of the Rock—it follows them all the way through the wilderness [1 Corinthians 10:4]. This is to refine them. They are compared to silver—the precious metal of his grace is in them, but mixed with much dross. Therefore they stand in need of continual refining. Self-will, self-dependence, the affections cleaving to the dust. Affliction shows them what they are, what the world is, and makes them look upward and long for their rest. The furnace is also to manifest his power and faithfulness.

(ii) *The burning lamp*: a token of God's presence with them in their affliction. *To the upright there ariseth light in darkness* [Psalm 97:11]. The wicked are all darkness—they have no knowledge, true comfort or hope. But his people have light by which they see the hand that appoints their trials: *I was dumb—because thou didst it* [Psalm 39:9]. His design is not to consume them but to do them good. *When he has tried me, I shall come forth as gold* [Job 23:10]. So Romans 8:28. They know that the fruit shall be to take away sin. They see an end. The lamp throws a light beyond the grave. I shall not always suffer thus. *These light afflictions, which are but a moment, shall issue in a far more exceeding and eternal weight of glory* [2 Corinthians 4:17]. They have therefore comfort. Sometimes the lamp shines so bright that they can glory in tribulation.

FOR MEDITATION: The Lord's people are sure of afflictions. If any of them are favoured with earthly comforts, yet trials are their daily lot and they groan, being burdened [2 Corinthians 5:4]. Have you light in your afflictions or do you suffer in vain? Let the redeemed of the Lord praise him. You have found him thus far faithful and he will be with you to the end.

The brightest rainbow on the darkest cloud

'And it shall come to pass, when I bring a cloud over the earth, that the
bow shall be seen in the cloud.' Genesis 9:14
SUGGESTED FURTHER READING: Genesis 9:8–17

The rainbow is promised in the cloud and in due time it shall appear. This
may signify:

(i) that their troubles shall be moderated. 'I will correct thee in measure,
but will not make a full end of thee.' The degree and the duration of their
trials are limited and have bounds beyond which they cannot pass. He
remembers their frame and considers they are but dust.

(ii) they are supported. They wonder how it is possible, but they find they
do hold out. Had they been told what they were to go through, they would
have sunk at the thought, but they are brought through the storm, because,
though his face may be hid, his arm is underneath them.

(iii) they are at last comforted. The rainbow does not usually appear in
the cloud at first, but rather when the rain is going off. And as the brightest
rainbow is painted upon the darkest cloud, so their greatest distresses are
often accompanied or succeeded by their brightest and sweetest
consolations.

Remember therefore when you see the rainbow, that it is a witness for the
truth of God's promise—that he will not contend for ever, that all shall
work together for good, that though weeping may endure for a night, joy
shall come in the morning. But to sinners, out of Christ, the rainbow gives
you but small comfort as a pledge that you shall not be destroyed by a
deluge. Yet the rainbow signifies to you that the day of God's grace and
patience is not yet ended; it encourages you to seek him for pardon and
salvation.

FOR MEDITATION:

When the sun, with cheerful beams,	Thus the Lord's supporting power
Smiles upon a lowering sky;	Brightest to his saints appears,
Soon its aspect softened seems,	When affliction's threatening hour
And a rainbow meets the eye:	Fills their sky with clouds and fears:
While the sky remains serene,	He can wonders then perform,
This bright arch is never seen.	Paint a rainbow on the storm.[219]

Bound to obey

'*Children, obey your parents in the Lord: for this is right. Honour thy father and mother; (which is the first commandment with promise;) that it may be well with thee, and that thou mayest live long on the earth.*'
Ephesians 6:1–3
SUGGESTED FURTHER READING: Proverbs 4:1–27

The duty and obligation of children is to obey and honour. This is a precept of the moral law, and the first, and indeed the only, command to which there is a special promise annexed. It partly is founded upon natural obligation. We came into the world in a helpless, pitiable state; and what would become of us in infancy when our wants are so many, when we occasion so much trouble, if God had not put a natural affection into our parents? Though a child is brought into the world with pain and danger to the mother, yet as soon as it is born she forgetteth her sorrow for joy that she is the mother of a living child. And an affection which is quite a new feeling takes place in the father also. And what care have parents while their offspring are in a state of childhood, and afterwards for their comfortable settlement in life. Thankful as they are if the Lord has quickened their own souls, they know not how to be satisfied unless their children are saved too. They tremble at the thought of seeing them hereafter at the left hand of the judgement seat. It shall be no trouble to them then, yet they know not how to think of it now. On these accounts children are surely bound to love and obey their parents.

FOR MEDITATION: It is more than sixty years since my mother died. I was then younger than you are now, but I can still remember that some people stroked my head and said, Poor child, he does not know what he has lost! Indeed I could not know the value of a good mama at that time, but I felt the want of her afterwards. For, Miss Jean, we are all such creatures, even when we are young, that we find it difficult to learn what is good; but that which is evil and wicked is so well suited to our inclinations, that we can learn it quickly, even without a teacher. Remember, my dear, in the first place, to love and honour your parents. If you do your utmost, you can never fully requite your obligations to them. You are bound to show your gratitude to them by your love, respect and obedience in all things.[220]

John Newton to Jean Coffin (aged 10), 28 September 1792

SERMON SERIES: RELATIVE DUTIES, NO. 3 [1/5], EPHESIANS 6:1–3

The duty of obedience

'Children, obey your parents in the Lord: for this is right. Honour thy father and mother; (which is the first commandment with promise;) that it may be well with thee, and that thou mayest live long on the earth.'
Ephesians 6:1–3
SUGGESTED FURTHER READING: Deuteronomy 5:1–22

The duty of children to obey their parents is also founded on the authority of God. It is his command. When he gave but ten commandments this was one, which shows its importance, and there is a promise—which literally was in some sense peculiar to the Old Testament dispensation, but in general it expresses that obedient children have reason to hope for his blessing, and that disobedience exposes to his displeasure. Under the law, such were subject to the same punishment as blasphemers, and there is severe threatening (Proverbs 30:17). In effect we see that those who are disobedient to their parents are usually marked by the providence of God—some meet the same return from their own, and if you enquire of them who are brought to an untimely end by the law of the land, many or most of them will confess disobedience to parents was their first fatal step that led them into the way of mischief.

This duty of obedience is also founded on the example of Jesus, who, though Lord of all, yet when he humbled himself for our sakes, was subject to his parents during his private life.

FOR MEDITATION:

Dear Myra, hear the Saviour speak,
He speaks this day to thee,
Renounce the world (he says), and seek
Your happiness in me;
The world will flattering baits present,
But 'tis delusion all,
And you can only find content,
By yielding to my call.

Devote to me your early days—
Can you too soon be blessed?
And I will guide you by my grace,
To an eternal rest;
The object of my care and love,
You then shall walk in peace,
And rise to higher joys above,
When this frail life shall cease.[221]

John Newton to Miss Sarah Myra Gardiner
on the anniversary of her birthday

SERMON SERIES: RELATIVE DUTIES, NO. 3 [2/5], EPHESIANS 6:1–3

Honour your parents

'Children, obey your parents in the Lord: for this is right. Honour thy father and mother; (which is the first commandment with promise;) that it may be well with thee, and that thou mayest live long on the earth.' Ephesians 6:1–3
SUGGESTED FURTHER READING: Genesis 46:26–47:12

Reverence or *honour*. It might be hoped that a sense of obligation might make children love their parents, yet this is not always the case, and where there is not a total want of love, there is often a great want of respect. But what shall we say of those who despise their parents, can make a jest of their infirmities and, instead of submitting as they ought, to bear with their temperaments, fly as it were in their faces. I must say, as I said before—it is a sad sign, a presumptuous contempt of God, which, unless they are partakers of his mercy by faith in Christ, will expose them to his curse both here and hereafter. When parents are old and in the decline of life, it is the duty of their children to behave to them with the greatest tenderness and care—patiently to bear with their infirmities and, if necessary and so far as in their power, to provide for them. It is to be feared there is wickedness in many hearts secretly to wish their deaths, to look upon them as a burden, especially if on the one hand they have money to leave behind them, or on the other they contribute more or less to their maintenance. All sharp language and unkind behaviour to them at such a time is not only a breach of the command but barbarous, base and ungrateful. May nothing of this be found amongst us, especially amongst those who profess to fear God. I hope such will always ... study how to make the little remainder of their parents' lives as comfortable as may be. The pains and infirmities of old age are hard enough to bear, without this addition of unkindness from those who are most obliged to them.

FOR MEDITATION: I hope often to pray that this child and all your children may be taught of God, and that if he is pleased to prolong their lives, they may grow up like olive branches around your table, may be an honour and a comfort to their parents, and when their parents shall be removed to a better world, their children may fully supply their places as members of his *true* church, and instruments in his hand of much good and usefulness in civil life![222]
John Newton to William Wilberforce, 21 December 1802
[on the birth of Robert Isaac]

SERMON SERIES: RELATIVE DUTIES, NO. 3 [3/5], EPHESIANS 6:1–3

Children of unbelieving parents

'Children, obey your parents in the Lord: for this is right. Honour thy father and mother; (which is the first commandment with promise;) that it may be well with thee, and that thou mayest live long on the earth.'
Ephesians 6:1–3
SUGGESTED FURTHER READING: 2 Kings 5:1–14

Let me add a word on the case of children who fear the Lord and have the trial of parents who treat them harshly upon that account. You are to obey your parents in the Lord. When their will is inconsistent with the will of God, you stand excused. If they will reproach you for your profession you must pray for grace not to be frightened out of it. If they would persuade or force you with the practices of the world you must not comply. But even in these things you must remember that they are your parents, and endeavour to behave with all meekness and patience. Your disobedience, if they will call it such, must be confined to such points in which you are sure you have the express warrant of Scripture on your side. In all other respects you are still bound, and if you would not prejudice them against the truth, endeavour to let them see that the knowledge of the gospel has strengthened the ties of duty and made you more observant, obliging and respectful than you were before. We are all concerned in this subject. We all stand or have stood in this relation. May the Lord lead you to reflect how you have behaved in it.

FOR MEDITATION:

If to JESUS for relief
My soul has fled by prayer;
Why should I give way to grief,
Or heart-consuming care?
Are not all things in his hand?
Has he not his promise past?
Will he then regardless stand
And let me sink at last?

While I know his providence
Disposes each event;
Shall I judge by feeble sense,
And yield to discontent?
If he worms and sparrows feed,
Clothe the grass in rich array;
Can he see a child in need,
And turn his eye away?[223]

Growing in meekness

'Blessed are the meek: for they shall inherit the earth.' Matthew 5:5
SUGGESTED FURTHER READING: Micah 7:7–10

Meekness arises from the poverty of spirit mentioned in verse 3. It is the temper of a soul convinced of the guilt and misery of sin, and seeking salvation by the blood of Jesus. Hence it is wholly a grace of the gospel, and accordingly the heathen philosophers, who said many fine things of their moral virtues, never once thought of putting meekness into their catalogues. It stands opposed to pride, self-will, impatience and resentment, and its trial and exercise lies both towards God and man. Where there is true humiliation begun in the heart, the Lord's dealings are often suited to try and exercise this grace:

(i) in spirituals. In waiting for manifestation of pardon. This is wearisome work to the flesh, when the arrows of the Almighty stick fast and one or another obtains or seems to obtain pace before us. The meek soul, amidst a thousand fears and discouragements, sees it has no right to complain (reasons as in Lamentations 3:26, Micah 7:9), and is grieved at every rising of a contrary spirit. And so under all backslidings and desertions.

(ii) in temporals. In a time of affliction. See it in Job 1, in Hezekiah (Isaiah 38), acknowledging that all is less than he has deserved. Contentment with the situation of life. It is this temper makes the precept practicable—*in everything give thanks*—and checks our spirits when they would repine and be seeking great things for ourselves. While in all these things, the carnal unrenewed heart is impatient and tosses like a wild bull in a net.

FOR MEDITATION:

I asked the Lord that I might grow
In faith and love and every grace;
Might more of his salvation know,
And seek, more earnestly, his face.

'Twas he who taught me thus to pray,
And he, I trust, has answered prayer;
But it has been in such a way,
As almost drove me to despair.

Lord, why is this, I trembling cried,
Wilt thou pursue thy worm to death?
''Tis in this way,' the Lord replied,
'I answer prayer for grace and faith.

These inward trials I employ,
From self and pride to set thee free;
And break thy schemes of earthly joy,
That thou may'st find thy all in me.'[224]

SERMON: MATTHEW 5:5 [1/2]

Meekness towards others

'Blessed are the meek: for they shall inherit the earth.' Matthew 5:5
SUGGESTED FURTHER READING: 2 Samuel 16:5–14

Meekness is daily exercised in our conversation with men:

(i) in lowliness of mind, if the providence of God has favoured us with any outward distinction. *The meek* person is not lifted up, but knows that he is unworthy of bread and water, much more of so many comforts. Hence he knows how to condescend to men of low estate.

(ii) *the meek* are not stiff and stubborn in their temper and manners. They speak with diffidence of themselves, are sensible that they are fallible and prone to mistake, therefore will hear reason. A want of this is often observable in religious disputes.

(iii) *the meek* are not easily angry. They remember that the Lord is concerned, let who will be the instrument, so David in the affair of Shimei [2 Samuel 16:11].

(iv) *the meek* are easily reconciled. They owe 10,000 talents and therefore dare not stand out for a few pence.

(v) *the meek*, as they are not hasty in taking offence, so they are desirous to avoid giving offence. What they feel in their own hearts makes them unwilling to lay provocations in the way of others, or to do anything which they themselves would dislike from others in their own case.

How is the promise to be understood, when in fact we see little of the earth comes to the share of such? They shall have as much as the Lord sees good; and meekness, as I have hinted, cuts short the desire of more. What they have, they have with the Lord's blessing, and this makes a little go a great way, and every sweet sweeter. They are freed from those hurrying passions which, when unrestricted, spoil the relish of every situation in life. They have an inheritance on high, of which every good here is an earnest. Here is a ground of examination for all, of humiliation for the best, yet, I hope, of comfort to many. If these things are begun, you are blessed of the Lord, and you shall be blessed.

FOR MEDITATION: Thou wert meek and lowly; O let this mind be also in me.[225]

Miscellaneous Thoughts, Monday 3 July 1758

SERMON: MATTHEW 5:5 [2/2]

Peace shaken

'Behold, for peace I had great bitterness: but thou hast in love to my soul delivered it from the pit of corruption: for thou hast cast all my sins behind thy back.' Isaiah 38:17
SUGGESTED FURTHER READING: Job 1:1–22

One of the chief differences observable in the experience of the Lord's people is with regard to the season and means of their establishment in the faith. Some, after their first convictions, go mourning for years, tried by the Lord but fettered by Satan, and, though secretly supported, have little sensible comfort, but are perhaps still expecting to perish at last. At length the Lord's time of deliverance comes, and afterwards they have generally a smoother part; and though they may continue to meet with many difficulties, they are seldom brought to question the foundation any more. Others pass through but little trouble at first; the Lord draws them by love, gives them liberty soon, and continues their peace till they are ready to think they shall see no changes. But by and by they are suddenly brought into darkness and depths, are at their wits' end, and can hardly be persuaded they were ever right. They find things both within and without so different from what they were aware of. Job was an instance of this. We have the best evidence (the testimony of God himself) that he was a gracious man before his troubles—but how rudely was he shaken—not in outward things only, but his joy and peace in believing was taken away.

Then to his saints I often spoke; Of what his love had done;
But now my heart is almost broke, For all my joys are gone.[226]

He had only the root of faith left—the exercise was gone, so that in the anguish of his spirit he cursed the day of his birth. But when the Lord returned, Job came out of the furnace purified like gold. He had seen more of his own heart, more of the power and majesty of God, than ever he had done before.

FOR MEDITATION: O Lord, what shall I say? I am the very wretch that was once an outcast in Africa; how dost thou comfort and honour me on every side, though I am still most ungrateful.[227]

Diary, 19 July 1774

SERMON: ISAIAH 38:17 [1/2]

The effect of peace

'Behold, for peace I had great bitterness: but thou hast in love to my soul delivered it from the pit of corruption: for thou hast cast all my sins behind thy back.' Isaiah 38:17
SUGGESTED FURTHER READING: Isaiah 38:1–22

[Contd from 1/2] Another instance [of being at their wits' end] is Hezekiah in this chapter. He had feared the Lord from his youth and been an instrument of great public service, yet perhaps he never thoroughly knew himself till this sickness. We see something of a self-righteous spirit in his prayer—see verse 3. He speaks more of what he had done for the Lord than of what the Lord had done for him. But this sickness cured him. It was accompanied with sharp exercises of mind which gave him a deeper sense of sin and showed him greater abominations in his heart than he was aware of. See how he speaks—verses 13–14. And thus he was taught to speak of gospel grace. He no more says, 'See how I have walked', but, 'See how gracious the Lord has been to me, *in love to my soul* ...' This passage is similar to Psalms 40 and 41. When the Lord delivers his people from the pit, and sets their feet upon a rock, it puts a new song in their mouths. They love to look back and to speak of his mercy. And these things are written to encourage others who are yet in distress. The Lord's arm is not shortened— he is able to save you likewise.

FOR MEDITATION:

They often murmured by the way,
Because they judged by sight;
But were at length constrained to say,
The Lord had led them right.

The way was right their hearts to prove,
To make God's glory known;
And show his wisdom, power and love,
Engaged to save his own.

Just so the true believer's path
Through many dangers lies;
Though dark to sense, 'tis right to faith,
And leads us to the skies.[228]

SERMON: ISAIAH 38:17 [2/2]

A well of salvation

'Now the God of peace, that brought again from the dead our Lord Jesus, that great shepherd of the sheep, through the blood of the everlasting covenant, make you perfect in every good work to do his will, working in you that which is well pleasing in his sight, through Jesus Christ; to whom be glory for ever and ever. Amen.' Hebrews 13:20–21
SUGGESTED FURTHER READING: John 4:4–14

There is an analogy between the works and the Word of God. If we consider the creation, the vastness of the whole and the unsuitableness and violation of the several parts strike us with an impression of his immensity and his manifold wisdom. At the same time his hand is seen and acknowledged by an attentive mind in the smallest of his works. The more we examine them, the more we discover of the finger of God. Not only the glory of the sun, but the structure of a plant or an insect bear the impression of divine power and wisdom which may well fill us with astonishment and reverence. So his wisdom is displayed not only in the whole compass and connection of the Scripture, but there is a fullness and a beauty often in a single text, which the application of our utmost industry to the end of our lives, could not fully discover if we were to attend to nothing else. It is our duty and great advantage to aim at a comprehensive knowledge of the whole. At the same time he has favoured us with many summaries of the gospel doctrine, which in a few verses, sometimes in a few words, comprise the substance of all that we are taught more largely elsewhere—as it were, in miniature. This is a condescension to our weakness and should be a spur to our meditation. Of this kind is the prayer in my text, which shows us not only the fullness of the Apostle's heart, but the fullness of the Scripture phrase. A close examination of these two verses might lead us to speak of everything relative to the faith, experience and practice of a Christian, and furnish a minister with subjects to the end of his life. I do not mean to treat it in such an extensive view, but neither shall I be able to confine what I may offer from it within the compass of a single sermon. I may say this is one of the wells of salvation; may the Lord open it for us, enable us to drink of the water of life freely.

FOR MEDITATION: '… Christ; In whom are hid all the treasures of wisdom and knowledge' (Colossians 2:2–3).

SERMON SERIES: HEBREWS 13:20–21, NO. 1 [1/3]

The God of peace

'Now the God of peace, that brought again from the dead our Lord Jesus, that great shepherd of the sheep, through the blood of the everlasting covenant, make you perfect in every good work to do his will, working in you that which is well pleasing in his sight, through Jesus Christ; to whom be glory for ever and ever. Amen.' Hebrews 13:20–21
SUGGESTED FURTHER READING: Isaiah 9:1–7

The title by which God is addressed: *the God of peace*. Many of the Lord's titles are taken from the effects of his goodness to his creatures. So he is called the God of grace, of comfort, of hope. The ground of reason is the same in all. He is the author and fountain of all grace, hope and comfort, and so likewise of peace. He designed the plan and provided the means of our peace, according to his eternal purpose. There is no peace to the wicked, that is, not in themselves, not while under the influence of the carnal mind. Yet we are all by nature wicked. But it was the Lord's pleasure that rebels should obtain peace. This was the song and the wonder of angels, *on earth, peace* [Luke 2:14]. For this purpose:

(i) he gave his Son. He is our peace.

(ii) he sends his gospel—the gospel of peace. It intimates the full and complete satisfaction of God in the work of Christ, reconciling the world unto himself: every demand satisfied, every perfection glorified, and such an abundance opened for goodwill to mankind, that now he takes his title from hence and is revealed as *the God of peace*. You that are seeking him by Christ need not be afraid. He is *the God of peace*, more ready to receive than you to come.

FOR MEDITATION:

As the serpent raised by Moses	Hear his gracious invitation,
Healed the burning serpent's bite;	'I have life and peace to give,
JESUS thus himself discloses	I have wrought out full salvation,
To the wounded sinner's sight:	Sinner, look to me and live.'[229]

Peace with God and conscience

'*Now the God of peace, that brought again from the dead our Lord Jesus, that great shepherd of the sheep, through the blood of the everlasting covenant, make you perfect in every good work to do his will, working in you that which is well pleasing in his sight, through Jesus Christ; to whom be glory for ever and ever. Amen.*' *Hebrews 13:20–21*
SUGGESTED FURTHER READING: Philippians 4:4–9

He bestows peace: I create the fruit of the lips; peace to him that is afar off [Isaiah 57:19]; and only he can do it. He gives peace by faith: Romans 5:1 [Therefore being justified by faith, we have peace with God through our Lord Jesus Christ]. Let us consider the branches:

(i) *peace* with God. By nature we are at war, he with us and we with him. All the evils and miseries we feel and fear are tokens of his displeasure, and our spirits and conduct show our enmity, especially when he touches us closely either by his Word or providence. Now this war ceases when we believe. He is at peace with us: no more condemnation, though perhaps the comfort of it is not yet known. He then supports and teaches, and blesses the soul with spiritual blessings. The enmity on the sinner's part is ended and he is made willing to serve and love the Lord.

(ii) *peace* of conscience. Many are in a safe state before they know it assuredly in themselves—but in due time he will show it them. From hence flows:

(a) a *peaceful* frame of mind. Where sin is pardoned, all is well. Not that there will be no exercises and distresses, but there is a ground of peace in the heart, and in proportion as faith and grace grow, it has power to rule in the heart, as is expressed [in] Colossians 3:15 [*And let the peace of God rule in your hearts, to the which also ye are called in one body; and be ye thankful*].

(b) a disposition of *peace* towards others. The Lord's peace sweetens the spirit and subdues selfishness. By nature we are hateful and hating one another.

FOR MEDITATION: Try yourselves by these things. Sinners, can you be content to remain at war with *the God of peace*?

SERMON SERIES: HEBREWS 13:20–21, NO. 1 [3/3]

That great Shepherd of the sheep

'Now the God of peace, that brought again from the dead our Lord Jesus, that great shepherd of the sheep, through the blood of the everlasting covenant, make you perfect in every good work to do his will, working in you that which is well pleasing in his sight, through Jesus Christ; to whom be glory for ever and ever. Amen.' Hebrews 13:20–21
SUGGESTED FURTHER READING: Psalm 23:1–6

That great Shepherd of the sheep. This name is precious to his sheep and it comprehends his whole role. Their safety depends on his being their Shepherd, and their consolation on their knowing that he is so.

Let us speak of *the sheep.* They are a great multitude which no man can number, but their number is determinate and known to their Shepherd. When they are assembled at his right hand on the great day, not one will be missing. They are the remnant, which the sovereign wisdom and grace of God purposed from everlasting to save out of the ruin which sin had brought upon mankind. As such, they were given as a trust and as a gift by the Father to the Son. He accepted them as a charge, and rejoices in them as his portion, in whom he will be admired, in time and eternity. They are born in sin, and live for a longer or shorter space in vanity and ignorance even as others, but he who has loved them with an everlasting love, in due time draws them to himself. Till that hour comes, he watches over them by his providence, and then he makes himself known as a Shepherd—rules, leads, guides and guards them, till they arrive in glory. The proof of their relation to him lies in their effectual calling by the power of his Word and Spirit. And here we must begin if we desire to know whether we are his sheep or not. Whoever receives the gospel report, feels the need of a Shepherd, and seeks to him and him alone, is undoubtedly one, for he says, *My sheep hear my voice* [John 10:27].

FOR MEDITATION: [for Sunday, 6 September 1778]

The Saviour calls his people sheep,	The bull can fight, the hare can flee,
And bids them on his love rely,	The ant, in summer, food prepare;
For he alone their souls can keep,	But helpless sheep, and such are we,
And he alone their wants supply.	Depend upon the Shepherd's care.[230]

None like him

'*Now the God of peace, that brought again from the dead our Lord Jesus, that great shepherd of the sheep, through the blood of the everlasting covenant, make you perfect in every good work to do his will, working in you that which is well pleasing in his sight, through Jesus Christ; to whom be glory for ever and ever. Amen.' Hebrews 13:20–21*
SUGGESTED FURTHER READING: John 10:1–18

Let us speak of the *Shepherd*. Jesus the Son of God, Christ the anointed, is the *Shepherd*. Herein we may notice:

(i) condescension. The Lord of angels, undertaking to be the Shepherd of sinners.

(ii) love. For his sheep were in a ruined state and must have perished, unless he had paid the redemption price. He is the Good Shepherd who laid down his life for the sheep.

(iii) authority. Anointed, sent and empowered for this purpose, and having done all in their behalf, he has a right to give them eternal life.

He is the *great* Shepherd. That *great*—emphatical—there is none like him, there is no other. He has many under-shepherds, his ministers, by whom as instruments he works, but whatever is effectually done is done by him. He fully and truly answers to the Shepherd's character. This title is applied to him very early (Genesis 49 [verse 24]). The ancient patriarchs were mostly shepherds, Jacob in particular. He calls the Lord his Shepherd—the Shepherd of Israel. O how happy are his people! The welfare of the flock depends upon the ability and care of the *Shepherd*. None can shadow forth his qualifications.

FOR MEDITATION:

JEHOVAH is our Shepherd's name,	Dear LORD, if I am one of thine,
Then what have we, though weak, to fear?	From anxious thoughts I would be free;
Our sin and folly we proclaim,	To trust, and love, and praise, is mine,
If we despond while he is near.	The care of all belongs to thee.[231]

His eye is upon them

'Now the God of peace, that brought again from the dead our Lord Jesus, that great shepherd of the sheep, through the blood of the everlasting covenant, make you perfect in every good work to do his will, working in you that which is well pleasing in his sight, through Jesus Christ; to whom be glory for ever and ever. Amen.' Hebrews 13:20–21
SUGGESTED FURTHER READING: Ezekiel 34:11–16

The Shepherd seeks the sheep out while wandering upon the dark mountains and brings them into his fold. Not one shall be lost or overlooked. When they know him, then they shall experience:

(i) his care. Though his flock is large and widely dispersed, he has his eye upon them all at once and every moment. He never slumbers nor sleeps, and is as present to each one as if he had but that one. *I am with you* in all places.

(ii) his tenderness. O this good Shepherd has an especial regard to the weak and wounded of the flock (Isaiah 40:11 [*He shall feed his flock like a shepherd: he shall gather the lambs with his arm, and carry them in his bosom, and shall gently lead those that are with young*]).

(iii) his bounty. He provides well for them. *The eyes of all wait upon him; he gives them their food in due season* [Psalm 145:15]. He leads them to green pastures, living waters, promises, ordinances, manifestations, so that they are satisfied as with marrow and fatness.

(iv) his power. He shall stand and feed in the majesty of the Lord. He is able to protect them in the midst of wolves and cruel enemies. Once when the wolf came, because they were his own sheep, he laid down his life for them, but now he dieth no more, but lives to save them to the uttermost.

O that I could commend him to sinners. The fold is not full, the Shepherd is waiting—yet there is room. Unless Jesus is your Shepherd the wolves of hell will prey upon your souls forever. You that are seeking, take courage—think of his tenderness. Let his people look to him and rejoice in him continually.

FOR MEDITATION:

When Satan threatens to devour,	There, 'midst the flock the Shepherd dwells,
When troubles press on every side;	The sheep around in safety lie;
Think of our Shepherd's care and power,	The wolf, in vain, with malice swells,
He can defend, he will provide.	For he protects them with his eye.[232]

Because he lives ...

'*Now the God of peace, that brought again from the dead our Lord Jesus, that great shepherd of the sheep, through the blood of the everlasting covenant, make you perfect in every good work to do his will, working in you that which is well pleasing in his sight, through Jesus Christ; to whom be glory for ever and ever. Amen.*' *Hebrews 13:20–21*
SUGGESTED FURTHER READING: 1 John 1:5–2:2

The act ascribed to the God of peace: *brought* him *from the dead*. This does not mean merely his resurrection by power, but his restoration and exaltation by authority, as Philippians 2:9 [*Wherefore God also hath highly exalted him, and given him a name which is above every name*]. These are two affecting thoughts of his people, that:

(i) he was dead. Such was his love he willingly died for his sheep. And they remember how he died—not in peace with his friends about him, but upon the cross.

(ii) he is alive. Hereby their justification is confirmed; they have a pledge of their own resurrection; they have an Advocate and Protector, and because he lives they shall live also.

To sinners I would hint:

(i) he is now exalted—therefore not to be trifled with. *See that ye refuse not him that speaketh from heaven* [Hebrews 12:25].

(ii) he is exalted to save. There is forgiveness with him. He can pardon and sanctify the vilest. To faith in his name, all things are easy.

FOR MEDITATION: When believers look unto Jesus, the representative of his people, as rising from the grave on their behalf, they are enlightened and strengthened and comforted. They find his promise, *because I live you shall live also* [John 14:19], sweetly and wonderfully fulfilled in their souls. What is your hope with respect to your present and final acceptance before God? Is it founded on what Jesus did and suffered in the flesh, and in the glorious testimony God gave to his obedience in raising him from the dead? This is the only plea which the Scripture affords or which will be accepted in the great day.[233]

Church Catechism, Lecture 22, 12 January 1766

The blood of the everlasting covenant

'*Now the God of peace, that brought again from the dead our Lord Jesus, that great shepherd of the sheep, through the blood of the everlasting covenant, make you perfect in every good work to do his will, working in you that which is well pleasing in his sight, through Jesus Christ; to whom be glory for ever and ever. Amen.' Hebrews 13:20–21*
SUGGESTED FURTHER READING: Hebrews 9:11–28

The manner—*by the blood of the everlasting covenant*. This covenant is the 'covenant of grace,' that better covenant of which Jesus is the Mediator. When the covenant of works was rendered useless, a new one is provided in which the Lord undertakes to do all (see 8:10). And this is *everlasting* and not that of Sinai. And the blessings are not temporal but everlasting blessings. *The blood* is the blood of Jesus, whereby the covenant is confirmed and valid. This blood is the foundation of all God's dealings in a way of mercy. All the blessing shall be bestowed, because it is a *covenant* of blood. This blood is the sinner's encouragement; it is, like the rainbow, a token of peace. Let us not fear to draw nigh, for though we are unworthy, we have the blood speaking for us. Herein is the apostle's meaning. The value and efficacy of the blood was complete. Thereby the whole will of God was fully accomplished—the types and ceremonies of the old covenant fulfilled, a perfect atonement made for sin, and Christ having in and by his death done all. In virtue of his blood he is released from the grave, declared to be the Son of God and Saviour of men with power, and, as such, solemnly received and seated at the right hand of the Majesty on high.

FOR MEDITATION: These truths speak to his people:
   (i) love: O how should we think of him.
   (ii) security: He ever lives to plead for and protect his own.
   (iii) gratitude: What shall we render! How shall we praise.

Let us *love* and *sing* and *wonder*,   He has quenched Mount Sinai's flame:
Let us *praise* the Saviour's name!   He has washed us with his blood,
He has hushed the Law's loud thunder,   He has brought us nigh to GOD.[234]

Put in tune

'*Now the God of peace, that brought again from the dead our Lord Jesus, that great shepherd of the sheep ... make you perfect in every good work to do his will...' Hebrews 13:20–21*
SUGGESTED FURTHER READING: Psalm 40:1–8

Make you perfect in every good work. First, it is not an actual perfection intended—the word signifies to make you meet or fit, to give a right disposition, and might be applied to an instrument of music when it is put in tune. So David says, *My heart is fixed* [Psalm 57:7; 108:1]—made ready or in tune. It is of the Lord to give to his people this habitual disposition or meetness for his will. It consists of such things as these:

(i) humility, or a due sense of our own weakness and imperfections. Without this we cannot be rightly disposed for the exercise of duty.

(ii) faith—laying hold of the strength, grace and promise of the Lord Jesus. To know that we can do nothing will sink us in despondency, unless we can rely upon him to perfect his strength in our weakness.

(iii) love—that feeling his peace, and considering the means by which we obtain it, we may be animated to cheerful obedience.

Without these principles it is impossible to aim at any good work in an acceptable manner.

The object of this disposition is universal obedience. *Every good work* may be distributed as respecting: (i) the Lord—his worship, his will (ii) the church—walking in love (iii) the world—in the exercise of integrity, truth.

FOR MEDITATION: Methinks I may compare myself to a harpsichord—how often in tuning, how seldom in tune, and how soon put out of tune again. My imagination in particular is as an instrument which seems not in my own power. Happy am I when it is under a gracious influence. But at times it seems as if an evil genius had command of the keys. Then I am tortured with a medley of folly, discord and confusion, from which I cannot run; nor can I stop my ears against it for it is within me. Wonderful is the grace that can cause the voice of joy and melody to be heard when, but a little before, all was disorder and distress. If the Lord appears, the storm is hushed and calm succeeds.[235]

John Newton to William Wilberforce, 15 November 1786

SERMON SERIES: HEBREWS 13:20–21, NO. 4 [1/2]

A continual supply of the Spirit

'Now the God of peace, that brought again from the dead our Lord Jesus, that great shepherd of the sheep, through the blood of the everlasting covenant, make you perfect in every good work to do his will, working in you that which is well pleasing in his sight, through Jesus Christ; to whom be glory for ever and ever. Amen.' Hebrews 13:20–21

SUGGESTED FURTHER READING: Ephesians 1:15–2:10

Make you perfect in every good work. Besides his disposing and preparing us for his service, there is working in us by an immediate and effectual operation. The first is grace in habit; this second petition is grace in exercise. The instrument, though tuned, will yield no music of itself. We need a continual supply of the Spirit, without which we can do nothing—this is needful as wind to the ship, or water to the mill.

The words *through Jesus Christ* may be understood: (i) that he is the medium of communication of grace. Of his fullness alone can we receive. Or, (ii) that all which is wrought in us is only acceptable through him and for his sake.

From hence observe:

(i) how entirely all is of grace—that we can will and that we can do and that when we have done we can find acceptance—all is of grace.

(ii) what encouragement for those who find they have nothing and can do nothing. Here is all provided and engaged for.

(iii) how great the sin and ingratitude of those who refuse this *great Shepherd* and the assistance of his grace.

FOR MEDITATION: *The power of grace*

Happy the birth where grace presides
To form the future life!
In wisdom's paths the soul she guides,
Remote from noise and strife.

Thy wondering saints rejoice to see
A wretch, like me, restored,
And point, and say, 'How changed is he,
Who once defied the Lord!'

O thou whose voice the dead can raise,
And soften hearts of stone,
And teach the dumb to sing thy praise,
This work is all thine own!

Grace bid me live, and taught my tongue
To aim at notes divine;
And grace accepts my feeble song,
The glory, LORD, be thine![236]

Plead for all this

'Look thou upon me, and be merciful unto me, as thou usest to do unto those that love thy name.' Psalm 119:132
SUGGESTED FURTHER READING: Psalm 119:129–144

This prayer is like a letter with a direction. It was used by one who loved the Lord's name, and had nothing else to plead, and it is recorded for the use of all who are like-minded.

The character: they *love thy name*, that is, his person, revelation and *will*—all that by which he is known—and it expresses the manner of their affection: they love him so that they love his very name. Conversation or preaching that is not seasoned with his name is unpleasant to them.

How the Lord *used to* deal with such: he looks upon them with an eye of favour, they are accepted in the beloved, having protection, Psalm 91:14 [*Because he hath set his love upon me, therefore will I deliver him: I will set him on high, because he hath known my name*] and compassion. He is merciful to them, in pardoning their sins, accepting their poor services, supplying their wants, preparing a kingdom.

Now if you love the name of Jesus you may, you ought, to expect and plead for all this. He has not excepted you. Why should you except yourself?

Shall I tell you how the Lord *'used to do'*[237] to those who love not his name, when his gospel is preached? He warns them. It is seldom but he strives with them for a season by his Word, Spirit and providence. He bears a while with them, he endures them with much patience and longsuffering. At length he punishes, either by leaving them to the hardness of their own hearts and Satan, and then how awful they turn out, or cutting them off with stroke. In either case they fall into his hands. Terrible thought.

FOR MEDITATION:

I'll cast myself before his feet,
I see him on his mercy-seat,
('Tis sprinkled with atoning blood)
There sinners find access to God:

Ye burdened souls approach with me,
And make the Saviour's name your plea;
Jesus will pardon all who come,
And strike our fierce accuser dumb.[238]

Crowned with his goodness

'For she did not know that I gave her corn, and wine, and oil, and multiplied her silver and gold, which they prepared for Baal.' Hosea 2:8
SUGGESTED FURTHER READING: Deuteronomy 32:1–18

The exceeding goodness, patience and bounty of God cannot be rightly conceived unless we compare it with the returns and provocations he meets with from sinful, rebellious man. Observe his carriage to Israel of old. He found them *in the waste howling wilderness* [Deuteronomy 32:10],[239] he guarded them there, and at last placed them in a good land. There he was an enemy to their enemies, and blessed them with abundant increase. But what was their behaviour towards him? Always rebellious and disobedient from their first settlement. In the prophet's time they were like their fathers. They are here charged with two great evils: insensibility—they knew not he gave them their good things; ingratitude—in abusing his gifts that he afforded them and intended as bonds of gratitude upon their souls; they misemployed to the worst purposes—they prepared them for Baal. But was Israel the only people who acted thus? Rather they were a sample of all mankind. In what respect can it be said we are better than they? I have chosen this as a proper subject for the present season. The Lord has crowned this year with his goodness, removed the threatening appearances which were against us some time ago, and favoured us with seasonable weather for gathering the fruits of the earth. There has been a general satisfaction amongst us that the harvest is happily closed. But against how many does this double charge lie—that they *know not*, consider not, the hand of God in giving them corn—and that they are disposed and determined to abuse his bounties by consuming them on their lusts?

FOR MEDITATION: 'Oh that men would praise the LORD for his goodness, and for his wonderful works to the children of men! For he satisfieth the longing soul, and filleth the hungry soul with goodness' (Psalm 107:8–9).

'Blessed be the Lord, who daily loadeth us with benefits, even the God of our salvation' (Psalm 68:19).

SERMON: HOSEA 2:8 [1/2]

The Lord, the Giver

'*For she did not know that I gave her corn, and wine, and oil, and multiplied her silver and gold, which they prepared for Baal.*' Hosea 2:8
SUGGESTED FURTHER READING: Psalm 65:1–13

It is the Lord that *gives corn*. How many plough and sow and reap without lifting up their hearts to him either in prayer or in praise. It is looked on as a thing of course. We think there is some necessary connection between sowing and reaping, but it all depends upon the Word and blessing of God who has appointed our provision to come this way. The clouds would drop down food for us as for Israel if the Lord should command, and without his command the earth could no more yield corn than the water. The dispensation of the weather is in his hand. He causes his sun to shine and sends his rain, and this he manages in such proportion that the end is generally answered. This likewise depends upon his promise, and mercy it was to make such a promise to those who are so unworthy of any good thing (Genesis 8:22). It is dangerous—who can tell how soon he may be provoked to punish? He commandeth the sun and it shineth not. He restraineth the rain. He has hailstorms and lightning at his beck. What havoc these have sometimes made in other places, we have heard. I am almost afraid to say what he can do, lest he should see fit to confirm the word by giving you a mournful proof that his ministers do not speak lightly of them when they warn you of the error of your ways.

FOR MEDITATION:

While I view the plenteous grain
As it ripens on the stalk;
May I not instruction gain,
Helpful, to my daily walk?
All this plenty of the field
Was produced from foreign seeds;
For the earth itself would yield
Only crops of useless weeds.

Let the praise be all the Lord's,
As the benefit is ours!
He, in seasons, still affords
Kindly heat, and gentle flowers:
By his care the produce thrives
Waving o'er the furrowed lands;
And when harvest-time arrives,
Ready for the reaper stands.[240]

SERMON: HOSEA 2:8 [2/2]

Make him your fear and dread

'And I saw a great white throne, and him that sat on it, from whose face the earth and the heaven fled away; and there was found no place for them. And I saw the dead, small and great, stand before God; and the books were opened: and another book was opened, which is the book of life: and the dead were judged out of those things which were written in the books, according to their works.' Revelation 20:11–12
SUGGESTED FURTHER READING: Revelation 20:1–15

The vanity and weakness of man is remarkably manifested by comparing the fears he is most frequently perplexed with, with their proper grounds and causes. There are very few who are not troubled with some fear or other which the slightest reasoning will show to be unnecessary and vain. Some who are bold and daring enough when in company (as if numbers could protect them from the deserts of their sins) yet tremble at the thoughts of being alone. Some are courageous in the daytime, but cannot bear the thoughts of being in the dark. Some are all life and spirits in settled weather, but a single clap of thunder at a distance will damp their mirth and spoil their spirits at once. Some can brave it out in noise and riot in a public house and yet dare not set their foot in a churchyard after dark. Some are afraid of seeing a spirit, yet are not alarmed at the thought that they must enter into the world of spirit. In a word, many who are ready to start at their own shadows or the fall of a leaf, can hear without concern of the great solemnity my text speaks of, though they profess to believe that it will certainly be so, and they are deeply interested in the consequences. May the Lord help you to improve [make good use of] the subject now before us, to sanctify the Lord God in your hearts, to make him your fear and your dread. So shall you be delivered from the vain fears which have hitherto detained you and be enabled to stand before him with boldness in the great day of his appearing.

FOR MEDITATION:

John in vision saw the day	Dead and living, small and great,
When the Judge will hasten down;	Raised from the earth and sea;
Heaven and earth shall flee away	At his bar shall hear their fate,
From the terror of his frown:	What will then become of me?[242]

SERMON: REVELATION 20:11–12 [1/6][243] [EASTER MONDAY EVENING]

The awesome Judge

'And I saw the dead, small and great, stand before God; and the books were opened: and another book was opened, which is the book of life: and the dead were judged out of those things which were written in the books, according to their works.' Revelation 20:12
SUGGESTED FURTHER READING: Luke 21:25–36

There is something awful and solemn in a day of Assize.[244] The news of the judge coming to town awakens a general concern for the unhappy prisoners who are to stand their trial. But especially the prisoners themselves, those who have been guilty of some capital crime and know that the law is against them. How are they affected! How dejected do they appear in earnest—they know their facts will be proved and that the forms of law to which they must be present will issue in their condemnation. The concourse of people, too, adds something to their distress, but especially when they hear their sentence read, how do their hearts fail, their limbs fail, and their eyes flow—they cry for mercy, but in vain. The judge cannot, the law will not, afford it, and the small remainder of life is spent in a comfortless expectation of their sentence. Most of the circumstances I have hinted at are borrowed in Scripture to remind us of the great and terrible day of the Lord, when all who ever lived upon the face of the earth shall stand before the Judge, the One Lawgiver who alone is able to save and to destroy. But the concourse, the solemnity, the event of the most important cases that come before a human judicature, are mere shadows and children's sports compared to that tremendous judgement which we must see and hear, each one for ourselves.

FOR MEDITATION: I visited the prisoners under sentence of death on Friday morning and again on Saturday. I spoke amongst them with all the earnestness and affection that I could—told them my own story, and that I was sent to them as a proof that Christ Jesus came into the world to save sinners. Poor men! I suppose this morning launched them into an eternal unchangeable state. The wealthy, the proud, the gay, and even many who are benevolent and useful in their connections, are likewise to be pitied—some, because though they have a religious character, and are in some respects exemplary, they do not effectually receive the record which God has given of his Son.[245]

John Newton to William Wilberforce, 1 July 1789

SERMON: REVELATION 20:11–12 [2/6] [EASTER MONDAY EVENING]

The majestic Judge

'And I saw a great white throne, and him that sat on it, from whose face the earth and the heaven fled away; and there was found no place for them. And I saw the dead, small and great, stand before God; and the books were opened: and another book was opened, which is the book of life: and the dead were judged out of those things which were written in the books, according to their works.' Revelation 20:11–12
SUGGESTED FURTHER READING: Daniel 7:9–14

A throne: intimating the King himself will preside in person. An appeal lies from the judge, but not from the throne. A criminal may sometimes escape by the favour of the judge, or through some defect in the law, or for want of sufficient proof, but nothing of these can happen then. The King is Judge—he of whom it is said, *His eyes are a flame of fire* [Revelation 1:14; 19:12]—he whose presence none can avoid, whose knowledge none can deceive, whose power none can resist, whose sentence none can revoke. If the pomp and solemnity of an earthly assize is suited to impress an awe upon the spectators, what heart can conceive the terror and majesty of this Judge? My text in one single sentence expresses more than any exposition can reach: before him *the heaven fled away*.

Can the solemnity be heightened by numbers? See what a concourse—all that ever lived, *small and great*. The greatest not excused, the least not overlooked. But of all this immense assembly, not one will be a mere spectator, but all parties—every one has a cause of his own, a cause for eternity, before this Sovereign Judge.

FOR MEDITATION:
Can I bear his awful looks?
Shall I stand in judgement then,
When I see the opened books,
Written by the Almighty's pen?
If he to remembrance bring,
And expose to public view,
Every work and secret thing,
Ah, my soul, what canst thou do?[246]

SERMON: REVELATION 20:11–12 [3/6] [EASTER MONDAY EVENING]

Open books

'...*And the books were opened: and another book was opened, which is the book of life: and the dead were judged out of those things which were written in the books, according to their works.*' Revelation 20:12
SUGGESTED FURTHER READING: Joshua 1:1–9

When the Judge is seated, and the multitude assembled, the trial will begin. *The books were opened*—this you will understand is spoken after the manner of men. The Lord needs no book, but it is to represent to us the exactness of his knowledge and the impartiality of his proceedings. But what are these books? There is:

(i) the statute book, the book of the law. Some of you perhaps have this in your houses and it lies by shut up from week to week. You think it not worthy your notice, but it will be opened then and you must hear its contents.

(ii) the book of God's remembrance. Because he exercises longsuffering now, poor blinded sinners think he regards them not. They say in their heart, at least, Psalm 73:11 [*How doth God know? and is there knowledge in the most High?*]. But what says the Lord? Jeremiah 23:24 [*Can any hide himself in secret places that I shall not see him? saith the* LORD. *Do not I fill heaven and earth? saith the* LORD]; Psalm 50:21 [*These things hast thou done, and I kept silence; thou thoughtest that I was altogether such an one as thyself: but I will reprove thee, and set them in order before thine eyes*]. Then they will find it so.

(iii) the book of conscience. Sinners strive to keep it shut now and too often prevail; they get but a little glance of its contents—they cannot bear to read it—but it is filling every day and O how will they be astonished when they are fully acquainted with its contents! When all their secret sins, their wicked works and words, are revealed to their view. Then they will be struck dumb.

FOR MEDITATION:

When the list shall be produced
Of the talents I enjoyed;
Means and mercies, how abused!
Time and strength, how misemployed!

Conscience then, compelled to read,
Must allow the charge is true;
Say, my soul, what canst thou plead
In that hour, what wilt thou do?[247]

SERMON: REVELATION 20:11–12 [4/6] [EASTER MONDAY EVENING]

The book of life

'And I saw a great white throne, and him that sat on it, from whose face the earth and the heaven fled away; and there was found no place for them. And I saw the dead, small and great, stand before God; and the books were opened: and another book was opened, which is the book of life: and the dead were judged out of those things which were written in the books, according to their works.' Revelation 20:11–12
SUGGESTED FURTHER READING: Matthew 25:31–46

How dreadful when they shall be found sinners against the law, and judgement given against them according to these books. What is the sentence? Read Matthew 25. But will this be the end of all mankind, seeing all have sinned against God? This is what we have all deserved, but we are told of another book: the book of life. What is this, but the revelation of God's love and mercy by Jesus Christ and his purpose to pardon and accept and bless all who are found believers in his name.

Be not afraid, you that have fled to Jesus for refuge. He, your Saviour, will be your Judge—and he himself will with strict justice overrule every charge against you. It will then appear, and you will not be backward to own it, that you have been great sinners, great debtors, but Jesus will put in a plea in arrest of judgement, and say, *Deliver them from going down to the pit, I have found ransom* [Job 33:24]. The more you think of the terrors of that, you will see the more cause to bless and praise him.

FOR MEDITATION:
But the book of life I see,
May my name be written there!
Then from guilt and danger free,
Glad I'll meet him in the air:
That's the book I hope to plead,
'Tis the gospel opened wide;
Lord, I am a wretch indeed!
I have sinned, but thou hast died.[248]

How willing Jesus is to save

'And I saw the dead, small and great, stand before God; and the books were opened: and another book was opened, which is the book of life: and the dead were judged out of those things which were written in the books, according to their works.' Revelation 20:12

SUGGESTED FURTHER READING: John 5:16–30

Think how Jesus has loved you. You might have been cut off in your sins. You might (and would, had not he prevented you with his grace) have gone on hardened and blinded till you perished with a lie in your right hand [Isaiah 44:20]. But now you have hope and can think of this great day without dismay—or if you feel a fear, you know it is your infirmity (2 Timothy 1:12, *Nevertheless I am not ashamed: for I know whom I have believed, and am persuaded that he is able to keep that which I have committed unto him against that day*).

But this, I fear, is not the case of all. Perhaps you have never thought of this before. See you take warning now. I hope some are thinking, *How shall we escape?* [Hebrews 2:3]. I direct you to that other book—the Gospel. There you may read and learn how able, how willing, Jesus is to save. He came into the world, he suffered, he died, he rose again, for this very purpose. Beware you do not stifle these thoughts. Perhaps vain company are waiting for you, or will seek you, to spend the rest of the evening in folly. But will you destroy your own soul? Will you sin against the light? Break from them as from a house where you expect to meet the plague. Consider you have a soul to be saved. Will you trifle upon the pit's brink? Rather, humble yourself before the Lord, pray for pardon, grace, and his Holy Spirit, that you may with him here stand with boldness in judgement and be received into his kingdom to dwell with him for ever.

FOR MEDITATION:

Now my soul knows what to do;	If thou help a foolish worm
Thus I shall with boldness stand,	To believe thy promise now;
Numbered with the faithful few,	Justice will at last confirm
Owned and saved, at thy right hand:	What thy mercy wrought below.[249]

SERMON: REVELATION 20:11–12 [6/6] [EASTER MONDAY EVENING]

Deliverance comes from God

'Zebulun and Naphtali were a people that jeoparded their lives unto the death in the high places of the field.' Judges 5:18
SUGGESTED FURTHER READING: Judges 5:1–18

War, with all its calamities, is the effect of sin. Relief and deliverance from those calamities are to be ascribed to the will and the mercy of God. He ruleth over the nations of the earth. He is the God of battles, the God of victory, and to him it is equally easy to save by many or by few. His favoured people Israel were often brought low by their iniquities, but when they were humbled, he pitied and delivered them. Sometimes he wrought salvation by his own Almighty Arm. When he destroyed Pharaoh and his army at the Red Sea and the army of Sennacherib, the people had only to stand still and see the mighty works of the Lord. At other times he commanded and animated them to attempt their own deliverance, but the success was from himself. We have an account of Barak being commissioned for such a service when Israel had groaned under the yoke of Midian. The tribes were all called upon, the army raised, the battle fought, the victory complete, their liberty restored, their enemies destroyed. This chapter is a hymn of praise to God who made them conquerors. The indolence of some of the tribes is reproved, the zeal and activity of others commended. And particular notice is taken of Zebulun and Naphtali who at such a time cheerfully hazarded their lives in the common cause. I would accommodate this passage to the present occasion. A noble design has been formed to furnish the navy and army with Bibles; it has been graciously supported, encouraged by the approbation of many of our officers, and received with thankfulness by many of our sailors and soldiers. I am appointed to recommend it today to this respectable auditory and I recommend it under this consideration, that is, in behalf of those who hazard their lives for us, even unto death, to defend us from our enemies.

FOR MEDITATION: [for the Fast Day, 27 February 1778]

When Moses' hands through weakness dropped,	A people, always prone to boast,
The warriors fainted too;	Were taught by this suspense,
Israel's success at once was stopped,	That not a numerous armed host,
And Am'lek bolder grew.	But God was their defence.[250]

SERMON: JUDGES 5:18 [1/4] [FOR THE BIBLE SOCIETY AT ALDGATE[251]]

A claim on our gratitude

'Zebulun and Naphtali were a people that jeoparded their lives unto the death in the high places of the field.' Judges 5:18
SUGGESTED FURTHER READING: 2 Corinthians 1:3–11

As it respects us, who under God owe our safety to the exertions of those who make jeopardy of their lives for us, I address your sensibility—perhaps you will allow me to say, your gratitude. Perhaps what is entreated of you as a favour might be justly claimed as a debt. In a state of war, at home we enjoy hitherto the same—the security, the blessings—as in a time of profound peace. We read indeed of abounding desolations and calamities which have overwhelmed multitudes of our fellow creatures, but we only hear of them, and therefore, alas, are too little affected by them, and therefore perhaps too faintly consider how much we are indebted to the bravery and the sufferings of those who hazard their lives for us.

Of the hardships and dangers peculiar to what we call the military line, I am no competent judge; of those to which our seamen in the King's service are exposed, I know something more than I could have learnt merely from description. Both the one and the other are called to wake when we sleep, to hunger and thirst while we live in plenty, are separated from their families, relatives and homes, many of them to return no more. They endure hardships of which few of us can properly conceive, from the changes of climates and seasons, and such like; for us they receive wounds not to be healed without much pain and length of time, and often wounds which admit no cure. When a war is ended, how many do we see deeply scarred or grievously marred, and see them perhaps reduced to beg their bread, being disabled from procuring it by honest industry. But a large number never return to tell their mournful tale. We only hear of the event from the cries and distresses of their widows and orphans. Have not those who thus venture for us, a claim upon our sensibility and gratitude? All I ask for them is that they may be furnished.

FOR MEDITATION:

While Joshua led the armed bands   The armed bands had quickly failed,
Of Israel forth to war;   And perished in the fight;
Moses apart with lifted hands   If Moses' prayer had not prevailed
Engaged in humble prayer.   To put the foes to flight.[252]

SERMON: JUDGES 5:18 [2/4] [FOR THE BIBLE SOCIETY AT ALDGATE]

A nation's secret strength

'Zebulun and Naphtali were a people that jeoparded their lives unto the death in the high places of the field.' Judges 5:18
SUGGESTED FURTHER READING: Nehemiah 1:1–11

This war is complicated.[253] Never before perhaps was the nation opposed by so powerful a combination of enemies—we feel the disparity and it is no dishonour in our situation to feel it. Except the Lord of hosts be on our side, there is but little hope of our standing long in so unequal a contest. We are brought to a crisis and our possessions, our civil and religious liberties, are all eminently at stake. Next to the prayers of those who fear God, our grand resource is in our fleets and armies. How desirable is it that the men to whom we commit our cause should be such as know to whom they should look for success. We may well wonder that the Lord of hosts should so often give us victory by such instruments as who, far from improving his blessing, or rendering him praise, disown his authority and in a manner defy him to his face. Could this insensibility and presumption be removed, we might hope that one might chase a thousand and five put ten thousand to flight—and that though millions were engaged against us, yet the Lord of hosts would be for us and preserve us. As things stand at present, they who really believe there is a God that governs the earth, can place but small dependence upon our warlike preparations when he is so little acknowledged either by those who plan our enterprises, or by those who undertake to carry them into execution. They know not what they do. Put the Bible into their hands, and who can tell but it may be in many instances the happy means of teaching them their sin, their dangers, their need of salvation and the worth of a Saviour. This would habituate them to obedience and subordination more than the strictest discipline without it. This will inspire them with a courage founded in principle; this would give strength to their arms and edge to their weapons, when lawfully called forth to plead the cause of their country.

FOR MEDITATION:

We now of fleets and armies vaunt,	Yet, Lord, we hope thou hast prepared
And ships and men prepare;	A hidden few today;
But men like Moses most we want,	(The nation's secret strength and guard)
To save the state by prayer.	To weep, and mourn, and pray.[254]

The value of a soul

'Zebulun and Naphtali were a people that jeoparded their lives unto the death in the high places of the field.' Judges 5:18
SUGGESTED FURTHER READING: Romans 10:1–15

Methinks I have a still more important and prevailing argument to excite your benevolence to provide Bibles for those who make jeopardy of their lives in fighting our battles, if we consider their situation as it respects themselves. They hazard their lives, they rush into danger—they fight, they die—cut off in a moment, they launch into an invisible, an unchangeable state—who can estimate the consequence? *Blessed are the dead that die in the Lord* [Revelation 14:13]; though they should fall by sword, pestilence or famine, they are blessed. The righteous hath hope in his death, but hope, to deserve the name, must be built by faith on the Word of God. How shall they believe in him of whom they have not heard? Indeed they often hear of the name of Jesus, but it is only when they hear it blasphemed. If they knew the dignity of his person, the greatness of his love to sinners, the nature and design of his sufferings—if they knew the greatness of his power and the riches of his grace—surely they would blaspheme him no longer. Furnish them with the means of this knowledge. Procure them Bibles and accompany your gift with your prayers. Whenever you succeed, you will be instrumental in saving a soul from death. This is an endeavour worthy of your ambition. To save a soul from death is of more real importance than to save a kingdom, or many kingdoms, from temporal ruin. Can you estimate the value of a soul? It is beyond the reach of natural members to express. It consists chiefly in two things—an immense capacity—an endless duration. Capable of possessing the power of God, or of being filled with an exquisite sense of his wrath, and that, for ever. It is not only the bodily life, but the precious soul is exposed to jeopardy in the high places of war. *What shall it profit a man if he gain the whole world and lose his own soul? What shall he give in exchange for his soul?*

FOR MEDITATION: 'For every living soul belongs to me …' (Ezekiel 18:4). '… and he who wins souls is wise' (Proverbs 11:30, NIV).

SERMON: JUDGES 5:18 [4/4] [FOR THE BIBLE SOCIETY AT ALDGATE]

Dying daily

'I protest by your rejoicing which I have in Christ Jesus our Lord, I die daily.' 1 Corinthians 15:31
SUGGESTED FURTHER READING: 1 Corinthians 15:12–34

This is a very lively and animated expression, especially in the original, where the words stand differently from our version: *by your rejoicing which I have*—that is, by our mutual rejoicing—*I die daily*. The Apostle uses these words as one proof of his faith in the doctrine of the resurrection and its influence to bear him above the troubles of life. They may be understood either to express the hazards and designs he was continually exposed to from the world, as a Christian and a preacher, or as the habitual experience and frame of his mind, from a conviction of the vanity of this life and the importance of the next. In this latter sense, the words suggest a subject which seems not unsuitable to our entrance on a new year.

Diary, 20 January 1755:
   As merchants begin their books with an inventory of stock, so would I in a brief manner set down my present state for my future government. I trust that the Lord has caused more of his goodness to pass before me this year than I ever before experienced; I hope particularly he has taken me more off my own bottom, and given me to see more of the necessity and the sufficiency of the Lord Jesus Christ in his office of Saviour of his people, and has made me more willing to depend upon his righteousness only. I trust he has enabled me to see more clearly the truth and comfort of those particular doctrines of the glorious gospel which in these days are by many either denied, or explained away. On the other side, I labour under weakness, I am wearied with a body of sin and death; often when I would do good, evil is present with me, my affections are cold and wavering, my faith weak and interrupted. Thus I find my life to be a continual warfare. But blessed be God for the hopes of final victory over sin and corruption, through Jesus Christ our Lord, by whom I hope I can in a low degree say the world is crucified unto me and I unto the world.[256]

FOR MEDITATION: Every believer should follow the Apostle's steps here, so as to be able to say, *I die daily*.

SERMON: 1 CORINTHIANS 15:31 [1/6]

Work at dying!

'I protest by your rejoicing which I have in Christ Jesus our Lord, I die daily.' 1 Corinthians 15:31
SUGGESTED FURTHER READING: 1 Corinthians 15:50–58

What is it to die daily? It is a believer's work and his only. It is not merely to entertain frequent thoughts of death—to converse much with funerals and tombstones and to repeat often to ourselves that we are all mortal. Many things of this kind may be done with much formality. A friend of mine has told me that when he first began to have serious thoughts, he proposed a great advantage to himself: he could daily think of death. And for this purpose he procured a skull out of a churchyard, which for a time he had always lying upon his chamber table that he might look at it night and morning and say, 'This is what I must come to.' For a few days this seemed to affect him, but a little use took off the impression and it was no more to him than the table it lay upon. In fact, we see that few people are more hardened to the thoughts of death than many whose business calls them to be much employed about dying or dead people. Nothing of this kind will truly affect the heart, but so far as we understand the influence of the light of faith.

I shall mention two things. Firstly, to *die daily* is constantly to resign ourselves into the hand and will of God with respect to the time and manner of our death, an event which we are sure must soon take place, and we are uncertain when [for the second point see 5/6].

FOR MEDITATION: We are now going down the hill of life. Oh, my Lord, cast us not off in our old age, forsake us not when our strength faileth. But do thou strengthen us according to our day! I trust thou wilt. Into thy gracious hands I commend myself and her [Polly, his wife]. I rejoice that future events, to us unknown, are under thy direction. There I would leave them. I pray that we may live with thee from day to day without anxiety. Help us to redeem the time, to fill up the uncertain remainder in a manner more suitable to thy will and our obligations than we have yet done. And when the summons shall at length arrive, may it find us waiting, willing, longing to leave all below, that we may see thee as thou art and be with thee for ever.[257]
Diary, 12 February 1784

SERMON: 1 CORINTHIANS 15:31 [2/6]

Non-accidental death

'I protest by your rejoicing which I have in Christ Jesus our Lord, I die daily.' 1 Corinthians 15:31
SUGGESTED FURTHER READING: Acts 20:17–24; 21:7–14

We have but very faint apprehensions of that unseen world which lies beyond the moment of death. We know we must then be separated from all we have seen or known here below, and enter upon an unchangeable state. And we cannot tell how soon the summons may reach. Perhaps the disease that is to remove us may be just at the door—or we may be snatched away without notice by some of those innumerable events which the world, who know not God, call accidents—but though they are accidental to us, with respect to any power we have to foresee or prevent them, they are, in the disposal of God, as fixed and determinate as the rising or the setting of the sun. What then is our wisdom in this situation, while surrounded with so much darkness on every side? Happy they who are enabled to *die daily*.

John Newton to John Ryland, 26 March 1791, after Mrs Newton's death:
I hope from henceforth I shall be a pilgrim and a stranger upon earth. The world is too poor to repair my loss. It is a wound which can only be effectually healed by him that made it. And faithful indeed are the wounds of such friend! But what is the death of a fellow worm, however beloved, to the death of Jesus! This is the thought which ought to wean us from the world and to crucify us unto it, and, indeed, which alone is sufficient for the purpose! May we die daily. May we live for ever. Amen.[258]

FOR MEDITATION: Her [Polly's] patience was wonderful. No complaining or impatient word was heard from her lips. She still found something to be thankful for; that she was preserved from extreme pain, that she could use her hands, though she could not move her body. Her natural spirits were good and cheerful to the last. ... Excuse me, I could still run on upon a subject so near my heart. Her sufferings are now over; her tears, I trust, wiped away, and she shall weep no more. She is gone a little before I am following her. Blessed be God, I am satisfied. ... if I may but live to him and be enabled to make full proof of my ministry, till his appointed time shall come.[259]
John Newton to William Wilberforce, 24 December 1790

SERMON: 1 CORINTHIANS 15:31 [3/6]

An unnatural death

'I protest by your rejoicing which I have in Christ Jesus our Lord, I die daily.' 1 Corinthians 15:31
SUGGESTED FURTHER READING: Psalm 31:1–24

To *die daily*: that is, to resign ourselves daily to God in a believing consideration of his adorable attributes such as:

(i) his sovereignty. This sweetly allays all difficulties, fears and objections. So David, *My times are in thy hand. Thou art my God*, therefore *into thy hands I commend my spirit* [Psalm 31 verses 15 and 5. As a dying person commits his dearest concerns, the care of an only child perhaps, to his best friend, so to die daily is to commit our soul to God as our rightful, sovereign disperser, and to leave all future events to him.

(ii) his power. I am speaking of an act of faith. It is easy to acknowledge the power of God in words, but O to say upon good grounds, *'I am persuaded he is able to keep'* [2 Timothy 1:12]. This gives an habitual readiness to depart.

(iii) his faithfulness, with an especial view to his promises—to venture our all upon his word. For his sovereignty is to his people a sovereignty of grace. He has told them it shall be well with them in time and to eternity.

You see these things are not in the natural power of man. If you would *die daily* you must have faith in the Lord Jesus Christ and some degree of good hope that your sins are forgiven for *his name's sake*.

FOR MEDITATION: Lord grant that the uncertain remnant of my days may be devoted to thee, and that the prayer which thou hast permitted me to offer for many years, that my close of life may be without any stain unsuitable to my character as a Christian and a minister, may be answered! Preserve me from pride, envy, jealousy, impatience, and every wrong and hurtful temper. Let me retire as a thankful guest from a full table and rejoice that others are coming forward to serve thee (I hope better) when I can do no more. For the rest, I leave all to thee. Into thy hands I commend my spirit, for thou hast redeemed me, O Lord God of Truth! Thou hast done and wilt do all things well![260]

Diary, 21 March 1804 (aged 78)

'Very much better'

'I protest by your rejoicing which I have in Christ Jesus our Lord, I die daily.' 1 Corinthians 15:31
SUGGESTED FURTHER READING: 2 Corinthians 5:1–10

The second meaning [for the first, see from 2/6] of to *die daily* is practically to improve [grasp more fully] the doctrines of faith, to weaken and overcome the natural reluctance we have to death. The soul has a natural unwillingness to leave the body because it has hitherto been the instrument of all its operations. The bodily senses are the inlets of perception to the soul, therefore the thoughts of parting with them seem strange. There is nothing like this union in all the works of God. From death to the resurrection, only one part of our nature shall act. This is a great mystery. Now these difficulties must be opposed [withstood] by faith. To *die daily* is to consider the death of Jesus; this throws light upon darkness. We follow him. But O how different his death from ours! For a believer, to *die* is to be with Christ. Is not this far better? To *die* is to cease from sin. Cannot some of you say, 'This alone would make me willing to depart?' To *die* is to be free from all grief and infirmity. What can the coward flesh plead against such arguments as these? This is to *die daily.*

FOR MEDITATION: In short, only the man who upon scriptural grounds is prepared to die, is properly qualified to enjoy the life that now is. A sense of the evil of sin and of his own heart once greatly distressed him, till he was able to approve and accept God's method of saving sinners by faith in the Son of his love. He has seen, with the eye of his mind, the necessity and the efficacy of the Saviour's obedience unto death, even the death of the cross. Weary and heavy laden, he has complied with his gracious invitation to come to him for rest, and he has found it. And if sudden danger appears, he has a sure hiding place, and is warranted not to be afraid for himself, though the earth should be removed and the mountains cast into the sea. Thus he is glad to live while the Lord has any employment for him, and he is glad to think he shall not live here always, but in due time depart to be with Jesus, which is πολλῷ μᾶλλον κρεῖσσον [very much better].[261]

John Newton to William Wilberforce, 2 October 1794

SERMON: 1 CORINTHIANS 15:31 [5/6]

O look to Jesus

'I protest by your rejoicing which I have in Christ Jesus our Lord, I die daily.' 1 Corinthians 15:31
SUGGESTED FURTHER READING: Psalm 33:1–22

The advantages of dying daily:

(i) it has an immediate tendency to maintain in our souls a constant reverence of God, which is the spring and life of all true obedience. If you daily resign yourself to him as if you were going immediately into his presence, and do so sincerely, it will have an habitual effect upon the frame of your mind.

(ii) it teaches that moderation in all earthly things which becomes our profession [of faith]. From whence come our eager pursuits, our anxious fears, our liftings up and our castings down, our anger, impatience, disputes and jars? Alas, are not these plain proofs [that as] yet we are but little acquainted with this heavenly art of dying daily? Yea, may we not all take shame and say, *'Teach us so to number our days'* [Psalm 90:12]?

(iii) it will animate to a faithful and diligent discharge of present duty. *What thy hand finds to do*, do it now, and do it with all thy might [Ecclesiastes 9:10].

(iv) it will prepare us for dying comfortably. This many desire. I will not limit the Lord, but in the way of means, we can hardly expect to die comfortably *unless* we *endeavour to die daily*.

I am afraid some of you understand but little of this subject. Yet die you must. And will you be thoughtless about it? If you had but a journey or a voyage before you, you would be often enquiring about it, asking questions, making provision. And *can* you be careless about your last journey?

FOR MEDITATION: I am now far advancing in my seventy-fourth year, and should be thankful for whatever the Lord sends to remind me that I cannot be long here … I see little here worth living for, but my Christian profession and my ministry. I hope to be willing to live my appointed time; and I hope and pray that when the Lord shall call me hence, he will make me willing to go. Without him I can do nothing. Without the promised support of his grace, I am neither fit to die nor fit to live. I am to yield all up to him, and to say, 'What and when and how thou wilt.'[262]

John Newton to Mrs Barbara Wilberforce, 28 November 1798

SERMON: 1 CORINTHIANS 15:31 [6/6]

From strength to strength

'And the LORD *said, Shall I hide from Abraham that thing which I do?'*
Genesis 18:17
SUGGESTED FURTHER READING: Genesis 18:17–33

The farther we proceed in the history of Abraham, we find his privileges and blessings still increase. When the Lord called him, he went forth not knowing whither; he had only a general promise and was to wait the Lord's time and way for the rest. The Lord showed him more from time to time. The promise was frequently repeated and always (as we have observed in going through the preceding chapters) with a farther enlargement. In the seventeenth chapter the Lord informed him what should be the state of his posterity after his decease. In this chapter he fixed the precise time when his son Isaac should be born. Having thus satisfaction in what more immediately concerned him himself, the Lord now admits him, as it were, into his counsel, and intimates an unwillingness to execute his judgments against Sodom without acquainting his servant Abraham with what he was about to do. Thus he was led on from strength to strength. His path was like the shining light advancing more and more in nearness and communion with the Lord whom he served [Proverbs 4:18].

FOR MEDITATION:

Poor, weak, and worthless though I am,
I have a rich almighty friend;
JESUS, the Saviour, is his name,
He freely loves, and without end.

He ransomed me from hell with blood,
And by his power my foes controlled;
He found me, wandering far from GOD,
And brought me to his chosen fold.

He cheers my heart, my wants supplies,
And says that I shall shortly be
Enthroned with him above the skies,
O! what a friend is CHRIST to me.[263]

SERMON SERIES: GENESIS, NO. 38 [1/4], GENESIS 18:17–19

For our instruction

'And the LORD *said, Shall I hide from Abraham that thing which I do?'*
Genesis 18:17
SUGGESTED FURTHER READING: 2 Peter 3:1–18

How unspeakable the condescension of this expression, *Shall I hide ...?*
Would not Abraham have sufficient cause of thankfulness if he himself was
spared, though he had known nothing of the destruction of Sodom till he
afterwards saw the smoke of the country ascending like the smoke of a
furnace? But it was the Lord's pleasure to honour him. The case of Abraham
is not to be so far drawn into a precedent for all believers as to give us
expectations that he will give us a prophetical view of his providential
dispensations before they come to pass, but only in general, that he will hide
nothing from them that fear him and walk humbly before him, in which
their good and his glory is concerned—though by a careful attention to the
Word of God and what the Scripture calls the signs of the times, perhaps a
clearer view of the Lord's hand and design in his providences is attainable
than what we are ordinarily aware of. It was upon several accounts desirable
that Abraham should know of the Lord's purpose against Sodom before it
took place. It was to be an unusual judgement such as had never before been
heard of. And his people may expect that in very extraordinary
dispensations he may appear in an extraordinary way for their support. So
our Lord gave his disciples notice of the approaching destruction of
Jerusalem and I doubt not but there are many prophecies as yet unfulfilled
that, when the time of their accomplishment draws nigh, will give his people
a light into his proceedings, though at present they seem dark to us. The
Lord's notice likewise was designed to engage Abraham's intercession,
which was to be recorded for our instruction to teach us how we should be
affected when the judgements of God are in the earth.

FOR MEDITATION: *On the commencement of hostilities in America*
[written for 11 June 1775]

Ye saints, unite in wrestling prayer;	May we, at least, with one consent,
If yet there may be hope;	Fall low before the throne;
Who knows but Mercy yet may spare,	With tears the nation's sins lament,
And bid the angel stop?	The church's, and our own.[264]

SERMON SERIES: GENESIS, NO. 38 [2/4], GENESIS 18:17–19

He sees from beginning to end

'And the LORD *said, Shall I hide from Abraham that thing which I do; seeing that Abraham shall surely become a great and mighty nation, and all the nations of the earth shall be blessed in him?' Genesis 18:17–18*
SUGGESTED FURTHER READING: Psalm 139:1–18

Leaving what is specially applicable to Abraham, let us inquire what observations we may draw for our own use from the reasons the Lord himself gives, why he would not hide this thing from Abraham. The reasons are two: the one suited to confirm our faith, the other [see 4/4] to animate us in our duty.

The first is, *seeing that Abraham* ... The Lord had in view all that he had intended to do for and by Abraham from the first. He was present to the Lord's mind from the time of his calling, yea long before his birth, as the father of many nations, the father of the faithful. And he makes the full and final good he intended for him, an argument for the favour he was about to show him, that is to say, 'This is not too much for the man whom I delight to honour.' I believe some of you will easily perceive how this thought may be applied to the comfort of believers in general. When first awakened, they seem at an uncertainty, come to the Lord upon a peradventure, and meet with many a perplexing hour afterwards—but all this while the Lord sees the whole of their course from beginning to end, sees them as they will stand accepted before him in glory. He has given them his Son and appointed them a kingdom. Having designed them to such an end, what shall he withhold from them by the way (Romans 8:32)? [Do you] think you hear the Lord saying, 'Shall I refuse that person bread, or leave him to sink in trouble, seeing he shall ere long see my face in glory?' If he suffers you to meet with many trials, it is not for want of care, or power or compassion, because he has chosen you and designed great things for you; he will surely deliver you and you shall glorify him.

FOR MEDITATION: 'He who did not spare his own Son, but gave him up for us all—how will he not also, along with him, graciously give us all things?' (Romans 8:32, NIV).

SERMON SERIES: GENESIS, NO. 38 [3/4], GENESIS 18:17–19

Faithful in teaching others

'*For I know him, that he will command his children and his household after him, and they shall keep the way of the* LORD, *to do justice and judgement; that the* LORD *may bring upon Abraham that which he hath spoken of him.' Genesis 18:19*
SUGGESTED FURTHER READING: Deuteronomy 6:1–25

[One] reason the Lord assigns to why he would not hide this thing from Abraham is much to the honour of Abraham, and in this we are called upon to imitate him: *I know him, that he will teach.* May he give like grace to all who have families, to be wise and faithful in teaching, warning and ruling their children and servants. All who know and fear the Lord, whether parents or children, masters or servants, have a talent committed to you— some opportunities of speaking to those whom you love or who love you, or with whom you are acquainted or connected, concerning the things of God. Entreat the Lord to give you a concern for souls, for the honour of his name, and to teach you to speak in meekness a word in season [Isaiah 50:4]. To him that hath shall be given [Mark 4:25]; in attempting to water others you shall be watered also yourself. And if you have little opportunity in other ways, be careful of your conduct and example. By this, through the blessing, you may be greatly useful to win upon others; if you let your light shine before men, it shall be to the glory of God and to your own comfort.

FOR MEDITATION: When I am in the pulpit, perhaps I am about to preach my last sermon; and it is almost certain that there are those present who come to hear me for the last time. Some of these are probably ignorant of God and themselves, standing upon the brink of the pit, and regardless of their danger. If I miss this opportunity of warning and rousing them, I shall not have another. I would therefore bend my whole strength to this point, and not drop a word to draw the attention to anything else. I endeavour to do the same in the parlour. If what I say has no tendency to impress eternal concerns upon my friends and acquaintances, I had better hold my tongue. Why should I encumber myself and them with many things, when I profess to believe that *one thing is needful?* It will be a poor plea for me, to say at last, While thy servant was busy here and there, *the man was gone.*[265]
John Newton to John Ryland, 15 March 1794

SERMON SERIES: GENESIS, NO. 38 [4/4], GENESIS 18:17–19

Sin cries out

'And the Lord *said, Because the cry of Sodom and Gomorrah is great, and because their sin is very grievous; I will go down now and see whether they have done altogether according to the cry of it, which is come unto me; and if not, I will know.' Genesis 18:20–21*
SUGGESTED FURTHER READING: Isaiah 59:1–20

This is one of the many passages in which the Lord speaks after the manner of men. He is present in all places, and knows all things. But it intimates the exactness of his judicial proceedings, that he will not punish without cause, and that he exercises such forbearance and patience as will leave sinners without excuse. Sin has a voice, a cry. It cries for vengeance, like the blood of Abel. It is opposite to the perfections of God. His holiness, justice, truth and authority are called upon, provoked and defied by sin. Though he spare long, his honour would suffer if he did not at length take notice of it. Ah my friends, you little know what you do, when you allow yourselves in a course of sin against the great God who *has power to destroy both soul and body in hell*.[266]

FOR MEDITATION:

Ah, what can I do,
Or where be secure!
If justice pursue
What heart can endure!
When God speaks in thunder,
And makes himself known,
The heart breaks asunder
Though hard as a stone.

With terror I read
My sins heavy score,
The numbers exceed
The sands on the shore;
Guilt makes me unable
To stand or to flee,
So Cain murdered Abel,
And trembled like me.

And must I then go,
Forever to dwell
In torments and woe
With devils in hell?
Oh where is the Saviour
I scorned in times past?
His word in my favour
Would save me at last.

Lord Jesus, on thee
I venture to call,
Oh look upon me
The vilest of all!
For whom didst thou languish,
And bleed on the tree?
Oh pity my anguish,
And say, ''Twas for thee'.[267]

SERMON SERIES: GENESIS, NO. 39 [1/3], GENESIS 18:20–21

Learning from very grievous sin

'*And the* LORD *said, Because the cry of Sodom and Gomorrah is great, and because their sin is very grievous; I will go down now and see whether they have done altogether according to the cry of it, which is come unto me; and if not, I will know.*' *Genesis 18:20–21*
SUGGESTED FURTHER READING: Romans 1:18–32

The cry of some sinners and in some places is louder than others. The cry and sin of Sodom was great and grievous. Let us see what might concur to increase the cry, that we may learn what are those circumstances and aggravations which make sin particularly provoking to the Lord and expose the sinner to sudden and exemplary vengeance. Observe their height of sinning. A particular instance of wickedness (not to be named without horror) is remarked in the course of their history, as likewise afterwards was found among the Benjamites in Gibeah (Judges 19). But this proves a course of abandoned sinning in other respects. When sinners do not like to retain God in their knowledge, he sometimes righteously gives them up to a reprobate mind to do those things which are not convenient[appropriate] and many who have cast off his fear have sunk far below the level of the beasts that perish. It is to be feared, or rather there is too much ground to speak positively, that there was no abomination practised in Sodom which is not committed in our Christian country. The heart of man under the power of Satan is capable of abominations which cannot with propriety be insisted on in a public discourse, and which charity would hope may be safely omitted here. The great God, to whom the night shineth as the day, knoweth all things, and there is *an hour cometh* when the secrets of all hearts shall be disclosed. O the blasphemy, the drunkenness, the whoredom, the adultery, under which our land groans.

FOR MEDITATION: 'Do you not know that the wicked will not inherit the kingdom of God? Do not be deceived: Neither the sexually immoral nor idolaters nor male prostitutes nor homosexual offenders nor thieves nor the greedy nor drunkards nor slanderers nor swindlers will inherit the kingdom of God. And that is what some of you were. But you were washed, you were sanctified, you were justified in the name of the Lord Jesus Christ and by the Spirit of God' (1 Corinthians 6:9–11, NIV).

SERMON SERIES: GENESIS, NO. 39 [2/3], GENESIS 18:20–21

The Lord takes notice

'And the LORD *said, Because the cry of Sodom and Gomorrah is great, and because their sin is very grievous; I will go down now and see whether they have done altogether according to the cry of it, which is come unto me; and if not, I will know.' Genesis 18:20–21*
SUGGESTED FURTHER READING: Numbers 12:1–15

The Lord takes notice of these things. He comes down to see. He has a book of remembrance for his people—so likewise for sinners. There is an awful account kept against them. And he makes his coming down known: to some in a way of providence, visiting them with such rebukes as they may read their sin in their punishment; to some by the power of his convincing Spirit, impressing them with fears which they cannot always shake off, which seize them not only under hearing, but perhaps in the midst of their frantic mirth, or however, find them out when they are by themselves and make them feel that he is angry with them. But let it be remembered that the Lord once came down upon the account of sin, not to destroy, but to save. Let us not speak wholly of the cry of sin, but attend likewise to the cry of the Saviour's blood. We are not yet in the case of Sodom—there is a respite, there is forgiveness. Sin has abounded, but grace much more abounds [Romans 5:20]. A free salvation is published. Believe—and *though your sins have been as scarlet they shall be white as snow* [Isaiah 1:18].

FOR MEDITATION: Some of you are like Abraham. The Lord reveals to you how he will deal with impenitent sinners, but you have fled to Jesus and are accepted. It is your part to intercede like Abraham for others—to mourn for sin and to stand in the breach while there is yet hope.

To others like Lot, the Lord has sent a gracious warning. O be thankful, and make good use of the mercy; flee to the hope set before you; have no more fellowship with the wicked—whether they will hear or forbear, do you be mindful of yourselves. And then fear not—he has not called you to disappoint the hopes he has raised in you.

Asleep on duty

'But Peter and they that were with him were heavy with sleep …' Luke 9:32
SUGGESTED FURTHER READING: Matthew 26:36–46

They were heavy with sleep. If this had not been recorded we should have little expected that, on such an affecting and extraordinary occasion, the disciples should be overpowered with sleep. These same persons were afterwards chosen to be witnesses of his agony, and then they slept again. Though they loved their Lord, yet they could not watch with him when he took them to be spectators of his glory and of his sufferings. We may consider this as a proof of their infirmity. The flesh is weak. Perhaps they were weary with their journey and in want of rest. The natural imperfections of our frame, and which are not sinful as we usually understand the word, greatly indispose and hinder us from the due improvement of our spiritual opportunities. It is the case with many. Their love to the ordinances and a desire to obtain some glimpse of the Lord, makes them glad to appear in his courts, and perhaps they come from a considerable distance. But when there, they are heavy to sleep. If this is mourned over, and striven against, people should not be so distressed for it, as if they had committed a sin. Yet it is a cause of humiliation. It is the fruit and effect of that sin which has defiled and enfeebled us in every part. We did not come thus, heavy, languid and stupid, out of the hands of our Maker at first. But now the believer finds the body a clog and an impediment in his best opportunities of waiting upon the Lord.

FOR MEDITATION: Alas! the many instances I can recollect in which I dallied and trifled with dangerous temptations, so that if thy mercy had not watched over me when I was sleeping in the midst of my enemies, they had surely prevailed and triumphed over me.[268]

Annotated *Letters to a Wife*, 4 August 1794

Lost opportunities

'But Peter and they that were with him were heavy with sleep: and when they were awake, they saw his glory, and the two men that stood with him. And it came to pass, as they departed from him, Peter said unto Jesus, Master, it is good for us to be here: and let us make three tabernacles; one for thee, and one for Moses, and one for Elias: not knowing what he said.' Luke 9:32–33

SUGGESTED FURTHER READING: Ephesians 6:10–20

Perhaps Satan had some influence here. He is desirous to spoil our worship and to rob us of our comfort as much as he can. And many attentive observers of themselves think they know something of his practising upon their bodily indispositions in order to distract their minds. It is our wisdom in all our approaches to God, and particularly when we wait upon him in public, to pray against his wiles, and that the Lord may keep us wakeful and attentive to what we are engaged in.

This bodily weakness will have influence when we have the greatest seeming advantage to help us against it. I believe sometimes when people are drowsy they are ready to charge it upon the preacher—and indeed we have not much to say for ourselves. We wish we could speak with an earnestness and power suitable to the great subjects of our ministry, then surely we should command more attention. However, the disciples could not charge their drowsiness upon any defect in means, for Jesus was transfigured before them, and Moses and Elijah were visible in glory, yet they slept. It is therefore a deep-rooted evil which lies in our very nature and of which every spiritual worshipper must be more or less aware.

FOR MEDITATION: Though this example of the disciples, and our Lord's gracious condescension to their weakness, affords sincere souls some encouragement under the infirmities which burden them, it gives no excuse to an allowed slothfulness. I observe at times some who sit so much at their ease and sleep with so much composure—as if they came to church for nothing else. This is shameful—I wish there was no occasion to speak of it. People should strive against it, and they who love the Lord will do so because they are losers—as the disciples were—they only awaked just in time enough to see the *glory* departing.

SERMON SERIES: ON THE TRANSFIGURATION, NO. 6 [2/3], LUKE 9:32–33

More trials, more conflicts, more victories

'And it came to pass, as they departed from him, Peter said unto Jesus, Master, it is good for us to be here...' Luke 9:33
SUGGESTED FURTHER READING: James 1:2–12

We have Peter's declaration: *it is good to be here.* He was struck with what he saw and wished for its continuance. We have from this verse more offers than we can well speak to at present.

(i) When he spoke—*as they were departing.* Till they were going, he slept, and then he said, *O it is good to be here.* Thus we usually prize our mercies most when we are just about to lose.

(ii) His judgement—*it is good to be here.* Such is the effect of a sight of the glory of Christ or a taste of his love: O that this frame, this ordinance, might continue long; O that I could bid the world adieu and come down from the mount no more. Such are the desires of the heaven-born soul. Though imperfect, they are sincere; their hearts are to the Lord, to his presence. Never do they find this sweet satisfaction in worldly goods, or in creature comforts—still there is something wanting, something amiss. But spiritual joys give full and sweet content.

But it must not be yet—you must come down—you must attend to the calling the Lord has placed you in, that your light may shine before men. You must have more trials, more conflicts, and these will open the way to more victories. Be thankful for tastes by the way. Ere long you shall arrive at the Fountainhead.

FOR MEDITATION: Your affliction, my dear Sir, did not spring out of the ground. The season, the measure, the event, are in the hands of him who so loved you, as to redeem you by his blood. To you it is now given, not only to believe in his name, but also to suffer for his sake. He calls you now to a post of honour. Many eyes are upon you; both your friends and your enemies have seen that the Lord has been wonderfully with you in your public life. You will now, I trust, burn and shine in a different situation, to the praise and glory of his grace, and to the increase of your experience and wisdom, power and faithfulness.[269]

John Newton to William Wilberforce, 30 September 1800
[on learning 'that dear Mrs Wilberforce was dangerously ill']

SERMON SERIES: ON THE TRANSFIGURATION, NO. 6 [3/3], LUKE 9:32–33

Bringing up children

'And ye fathers, provoke not your children to wrath: but bring them up in the nurture and admonition of the Lord.' Ephesians 6:4
SUGGESTED FURTHER READING: Psalm 78:1–8

There are doubtless many feelings in a parent's heart and many difficulties in the discharge of their duty, of which I, who have no child, can form but a very general notion. Observation must here, in part, supply the want of experience. But I shall endeavour to say no more than I have a warrant from the Word of God, and may he give his blessing. My text contains an express precept: *bring them up in the nurture and admonition of the Lord.* Consider:

(i) this is much insisted on in the Word of God (Deuteronomy 6:7).

(ii) because they have the charge of them while they are tender and fittest to receive impressions.

(iii) it is what God especially notices—instance in Abraham and in Eli.

(iv) let affections plead for them—think what a state they are in, and what a world they are going to. If you do not endeavour to check the seeds of evil, they will spring up to a plentiful harvest and end in ruin.

What then shall we say of parents who are so hardened against the will of God, so cruel to their children, as to neglect their instruction and suffer them to grow wild in ignorance and wickedness? The looks and language of too many of the youth too plainly show how they have been educated. As you sow, you will surely reap, unless grace prevent. If you bring them up in sin, very probably they will contribute to bring your grey hairs down with sorrow to the grave. And O, what a dreadful greeting—when they shall charge the loss of their souls at their parents' door.

FOR MEDITATION: 'Prayer for my dear Elizabeth on the Anniversary of her Birthday', 22 June 1800.

Dear Saviour, at thy feet I bow!	May she be recompensed by thee,
Bless my dear child, O bless her now;	For all her kind regard to me;
Fill her with light and love and peace,	And when my pilgrimage shall end,
May every year her grace increase!	Still be her Guard, her Guide, her Friend,
Renew her strength, suppress her fear,	Till she shall join with all thine own,
And lead her on from year to year:	In songs of praise before the throne!

Amen, and Amen[270]

SERMON SERIES: RELATIVE DUTIES, NO. 4 [1/4], EPHESIANS 6:4

Instruct children early

'And ye fathers, provoke not your children to wrath: but bring them up in the nurture and admonition of the Lord.' Ephesians 6:4
SUGGESTED FURTHER READING: Matthew 19:13–15

I must speak to those parents who have a sense of the worth of souls. I need say nothing to persuade you of the importance of this duty. I wish I was able to advise and assist in the discharge of it. It requires wisdom and steadiness. But be not discouraged. If any parent lacks wisdom for this service, let him ask of God and it shall be given. Three or four things I may mention from the text. Instruct your children early in the principles of religion. For this purpose catechisms have their good use. But teaching children a form of words by rote is not the main thing. Endeavour to converse with them. Children have curiosity, which is as a handle by which they may be led. Endeavour to impress them with a sense of the goodness of God, their dependence upon him for life, health and protection—his governing providence and the authority of his blessed Word. Pray for them, pray with them and put them upon praying for themselves.

FOR MEDITATION: Had my first meeting with the children at the Great House. Called one of them out to read Matthew 19:13–15, from whence I took occasion to speak of the condescension and love of the Lord Jesus and his gracious attention even to young children, having been once (for our sakes) an infant and a child himself. Gave to most of them Mason's Catechism[271] and explained a few of the questions and answers at the beginning. Cautioned them against the proofs of depravity which too soon appear in children: disobedience, lying, bad words, petty thefts, breach of the Sabbath, and such things. Amongst other things I directed them to attend at church. Accordingly the chief part of them came at the lecture and seated themselves before the pulpit in the middle aisle. It was a pleasing and affecting sight and moved me to pray for them before the congregation.[272]
Journal of children's meetings at Olney, Thursday 17 January 1765

Instruction begins at home

'And ye fathers, provoke not your children to wrath: but bring them up in the nurture and admonition of the Lord.' Ephesians 6:4
SUGGESTED FURTHER READING: 2 Timothy 3:1–4:5

Maintain your authority over your children and endeavour to restrain the workings of those irregular passions and desires which begin early to show themselves. A false tenderness in indulging their humours, is often called spoiling them, and the expression is significant. Many are so entirely spoilt that they are good for nothing afterwards. No care can change the heart, but the Lord works by means—and these evils may be restrained. If you suffer them to be self-willed when they are three or four years of age, they will ordinarily be much more so when they are fourteen or fifteen. Many good people are grieved and bowed down with the perverseness of their children's carriage as they grow up, but may not conscience say, *Hast thou not procured this unto thyself?* [Jeremiah 2:17] Be resolute in repressing them for, and restraining them from, things that are plainly sinful—the use of ill words, lying, pilfering, contempt of the Sabbath. Accustom them to a constant attendance upon the worship of God, and to a decent behaviour while they are there. It is a shame to think how many children are playing in the streets, or perhaps robbing orchards [or supermarkets?] instead of being in the house of God. And many come here who can hardly be kept from play in the church; it is a sign how little they are instructed at home.

Diary, 10 July 1777:
Met the children ... perhaps I never speak more to the purpose than when the bulk of my auditory is under ten, and many of them under six years of age. ... the power is thine also, therefore I may hope.[273]

FOR MEDITATION: My mother was a pious, experienced Christian. I have some faint remembrance of her care and instructions. She stored my memory, which was then very retentive, with many valuable pieces, chapters, and portions of Scripture, catechisms, hymns and poems. Further, my dear mother often commended me with many prayers and tears to God; and I doubt not but I reap the fruits of these prayers to this hour.[274]

Narrative, 1764, Letter 2 [Newton's mother died when he was six]

SERMON SERIES: RELATIVE DUTIES, NO. 4 [3/4], EPHESIANS 6:4

Don't provoke your children

'And ye fathers, provoke not your children to wrath: but bring them up in the nurture and admonition of the Lord.' Ephesians 6:4
SUGGESTED FURTHER READING: 2 Corinthians 1:23–3:6

Provoke them not to wrath, lest they be discouraged. God has given you a great power over them. I have said do not be remiss in using it, but you must likewise beware of the other extreme. Let your children be guards upon your own conduct. Avoid all passionate [volatile] behaviour and harsh language—all severity. And if correction is necessary, let it be accompanied with reasonings, persuasions and endeavour to show them that it is not to gratify your own passions, but from a regard to their welfare. Consider they are but children, therefore especially while they are unawakened, lay not too much upon them. Some good people have wearied their children by expecting conduct from them as if they were experienced Christians, and have thereby given them a disgust and distaste for religion, and made them look upon it as a burden. If you can keep them from sinful ways, and in attendance upon the means of grace, you have reason to be thankful. For the rest—a little advice now and then, always in a spirit of love and not too much at a time, is the best course. They must, they will, have something to engage their thoughts till the Lord shall be pleased to open the eyes of their minds. In a word, parents ... I must say of your duty as of my own, *Who is sufficient for these things?* [2 Corinthians 2:16].

FOR MEDITATION: The other day I was at Deptford and saw a ship launched... my thoughts turned from the ship to my child. It seemed an emblem of your present state: you are now, as it were, in a safe harbour; but by and by you must launch out into the world, which may well be compared to a tempestuous sea. I could even now almost weep at the resemblance; but I take courage; my hopes are greater than my fears. I know there is an infallible Pilot, who has the winds and the waves at his command. Under his care I know you will be safe; he can guide you, unhurt, amidst the storms, and rocks, and dangers, by which you might otherwise suffer, and bring you, at last, to the haven of eternal rest. I hope you will seek him while you are young, and I am sure he will be the friend of them that seek him sincerely.[275]

John Newton to his niece [adopted daughter], 15 October 1782

SERMON SERIES: RELATIVE DUTIES, NO. 4 [4/4], EPHESIANS 6:4

A taste for heavenly things

'And it came to pass, as they departed from him, Peter said unto Jesus, Master, it is good for us to be here: and let us make three tabernacles; one for thee, and one for Moses, and one for Elias: not knowing what he said.'
Luke 9:33
SUGGESTED FURTHER READING: Mark 9:2–13

Peter's desire was from a good principle. Grace had changed his heart and given him a taste for heavenly things. He loved his Saviour, and when he saw him transfigured and had a specimen of the glory of heaven in the appearance of Moses and Elijah, he would willingly have bid the world adieu. He wanted to *build tabernacles*. His motive was right, but his proposal was wrong, and proceeded from ignorance and fear—*not knowing what he said, for he was afraid*, as is added by Mark [9:6].

His proposal was inconsistent with the design of Christ's coming. He had been offended at the mention of his cross before (Matthew 16:22). Now he seems quite to forget it. But Peter's soul and all his hopes depended upon his Master's not staying there, but returning to his state of humiliation. This is the appointed, both for Head and members, to enter into glory through sufferings. He knew but little of the state of glorified spirits when he thought of tabernacles for Moses and Elijah. It is so with us. We are apt to form low and earthly notions of heavenly things—indeed we can form no others, having no ideas but what we have received by our senses. When we strive to go beyond this, we are soon lost. Peter was ignorant of the design of his own calling. He was not to live upon the mount but to be a fisher of men, to do and to suffer for Christ and to glorify God in the world.

FOR MEDITATION: There is no school like the school of the cross. There men are made wise unto salvation, wise to win souls. In a crucified Saviour are hidden all the treasures of wisdom and knowledge. And the tongue of the truly learned, that can speak a word in season to them that are weary, is not acquired like Greek and Latin by reading great books—but by self-knowledge and soul exercises. To learn navigation by the fireside will never make a man an expert mariner. He must do his business in great waters. And practice will bring him into many situations of which general theory could give him no conception.[276]
John Newton to John Ryland jnr, 26 March 1791

SERMON SERIES: ON THE TRANSFIGURATION, NO. 7 [1/5], LUKE 9:33

A steady, habitual exercise of grace

'And it came to pass, as they departed from him, Peter said unto Jesus, Master, it is good for us to be here: and let us make three tabernacles; one for thee, and one for Moses, and one for Elias: not knowing what he said.'
Luke 9:33
SUGGESTED FURTHER READING: 1 Kings 3:5–14, 28

Peter was afraid, surprised and confused, so that he forgot himself and spoke without thought and, as it were, *without being aware of what he said.* Perhaps this is one reason why perceptible manifestations are so sparingly vouchsafed, considering the weakness of our animal frame; they would too much engage and swallow up our thoughts, indispose for the services of common life, and deprive us of the power of sedately using our judgements. Several observations may be made upon this passage applicable to our general use and especially to young converts. Peter here seems to judge, talk, feel and mistake, as many since his time have done in what is called their first love. We may note therefore that the growth and attainment of a Christian is not to be estimated by perceptive comforts and manifestation. Peter was warm hearted and lively; he was happy for the season, and if he had been at leisure could have told a wonderful story of his experience. Yet at this time he knew but little experimentally either of himself or his Saviour, in comparison of what he knew afterwards. Some poor souls are apt to be discouraged when they see others comfortable and taken up upon the mount, and ready to say, 'O that I was so'—but there is a difference between pleasant frames and a steady, habitual exercise of grace.

FOR MEDITATION: ['to a favourite tune of Mrs Newton's—in Arne's Opera of *Eliza'*, Liverpool 1763].

When my Saviour, my Shepherd is near,	By these changes I often pass through,
How quickly my sorrows depart!	I am taught my own weakness to know;
New beauties around me appear,	I am taught what my Shepherd can do,
New spirits enliven my heart:	And how much to his mercy I owe:
But alas! what a change do I find,	It is he who supports me through all,
When my Shepherd withdraws from my sight?	When I faint he revives me again;
My fears all return to my mind,	He attends to my prayer when I call,
My day is soon changed into night.	And bids me no longer complain.[277]

Build upon the Word of God

'And it came to pass, as they departed from him, Peter said unto Jesus, Master, it is good for us to be here: and let us make three tabernacles; one for thee, and one for Moses, and one for Elias: not knowing what he said.'
Luke 9:33
SUGGESTED FURTHER READING: Judges 8:22–27

A person's being in a lively state of mind and near the Lord will not exempt him from the danger of making great mistakes in what they would propose and determine to do in such a state. Some people are ready to think that any purpose that comes into their minds, when their spirits are lively and they have liberty in prayer, must therefore be right and proper. They will say, I trust the Lord was surely with me when I purposed it, and therefore it must doubtless be from him. The Lord was surely and sweetly with Peter at this time, but he did not put it into his heart to build tabernacles. Satan may be near at such a time likewise and many plausible motions may arise from Self. If we would be wise builders, we must build not upon feelings and suggestions, but upon the Word of God. Is your spirit quickened by a taste of his love and a glimpse of his glory? Then to the law and the testimony to learn his will concerning you, and do not think your human temperament will warrant you to do anything which you are not directed to by the Scripture. Innumerable enthusiasms and offences have arisen from a want of caution in this respect. The zeal of young converts is very apt to spend itself in singularities and things not commanded.

FOR MEDITATION:

Once I thought my mountain strong,
Firmly fixed no more to move;
Then thy grace was all my song,
Then my soul was filled with love:
Those were happy golden days,
Sweetly spent in prayer and praise.

When my friends have said, 'Beware,
Soon or late you'll find a change';
I could see no cause for fear,
Vain their caution seemed and strange:
Not a cloud obscured my sky,
Could I think a tempest nigh?

Little, then, myself I knew, Little thought of Satan's power;
Now I find their words were true, Now I feel the stormy hour!
Tell him, since I know thy name, Though I change thou art the same.[278]

SERMON SERIES: ON THE TRANSFIGURATION, NO. 7 [3/5], LUKE 9:33

Making allowances

'...As they departed from him, Peter said unto Jesus, Master, it is good for us to be here: and let us make three tabernacles; one for thee, and one for Moses, and one for Elias: not knowing what he said.' Luke 9:33
SUGGESTED FURTHER READING: John 21:15–25

A want of experience makes us very apt to mistake and misapply the cordials the Lord gives us by the way. Peter did not say, 'Now we have seen his glory, let us take courage and be willing to do and suffer for him, for he is worthy. Let us improve the remembrance of this to make us more earnest in pleading with our friends or obstinate countrymen to believe on him.' Friends, neighbours, services and sufferings, were all forgot, and he only thought of building tabernacles and having his present comforts continued. There is much selfishness in our hearts, often when they seem best disposed. St Paul was better taught—he had been caught up into the third heaven, yet though he had an earnest desire to depart and be with Christ, he was willing to wait for his happiness, for the sake of being useful to his church.

We may observe our Lord's gracious compassion to the weakness of his people. He accepted Peter's willing mind according to his light, and though what he said showed ignorance, rashness and selfishness had too much place in him, we do not find he rebuked him upon this occasion. He knows our frame, he remembers we are but dust. He does not teach us all at once, but with patience and tenderness, as we are able to bear it. We should learn of him. If we advise (as we ought to do) young believers of what is amiss in their first joy, let us do it with candour and gentleness and make allowances for those mistakes which can only be corrected by experience. Fruit is not ripened as soon as it is formed, but it is not to be thrown away because it is yet green. If good in its kind, allow it time and it will come to maturity.

FOR MEDITATION: Methinks the Apostle strongly intimates the deep depravity of our nature, when he says, *Ye have need of patience* ... We are selfish, ungrateful creatures, and if the Lord crosses us in one thing, we are prone to forget our many calls for thankfulness. ...Notwithstanding all we know, and the fine things we can say to others upon the subject, we are liable to toss like a wild bull in a net, or to sink into despondency.[279]

John Newton to John Ryland, 30 August 1790

SERMON SERIES: ON THE TRANSFIGURATION, NO. 7 [4/5], LUKE 9:33

Keep watchful and humble

'And it came to pass, as they departed from him, Peter said unto Jesus, Master, it is good for us to be here: and let us make three tabernacles; one for thee, and one for Moses, and one for Elias: not knowing what he said.'
Luke 9:33
SUGGESTED FURTHER READING: 1 Peter 5:8–11

Let not those who are upon the mount depend upon their present warm desires and resolutions, but rather, pray to the Lord to keep them watchful and humble. The enemy is upon his watch and he gained great advantage of Peter after this and terrified him to a denial of his Master. It is written for our instruction.

But some are not concerned with these things. Instead of building tabernacles upon the mount with Peter, their hearts go more with the rich man in the Gospel, who would pull down his barns and build them larger and enjoy the good things of the world for many years. Alas, this, if you could have it, would be a poor portion. You must die and leave all, and what will the world be to you then? O that you may be wise in time and *seek the things that are above, where Christ sitteth at the right hand of God* [Colossians 3:1].

FOR MEDITATION:

'Simon, beware!' the Saviour said,
'Satan, your subtle foe,
Already has his measures laid
Your soul to overthrow.

'He wants to sift you all, as wheat,
And thinks his victory sure;
But I his malice will defeat,
My prayer shall faith secure.'

Believers, tremble and rejoice,
Your help and danger view;
This warning has to you a voice,
This promise speaks to you.

But JESUS lives to intercede,
That faith may still prevail,
He will support in time of need,
And Satan's arts shall fail.

Yet, let us not the warning slight,
But watchful still be found;
Though faith cannot be slain in fight,
It may receive a wound.

While Satan watches, dare we sleep?
We must our guard maintain;
But, LORD, do thou the city keep,
Or else we watch in vain.[280]

SERMON SERIES: ON THE TRANSFIGURATION, NO. 7 [5/5], LUKE 9:33

The pre-eminence and dignity of Jesus

'*While he yet spake, behold, a bright cloud overshadowed them: and behold a voice out of the cloud, which said, This is my beloved Son, in whom I am well pleased; hear ye him.*' Matthew 17:5
SUGGESTED FURTHER READING: Matthew 17:1–13

This is my beloved Son. The Greek is emphatic with a double article—This is that Son, that beloved Son of mine[281]—to distinguish him from all others and to show his pre-eminence and dignity. Believers are the sons of God, not by nature but by adoption. Jesus is his own, his only beloved Son. He is the brightness of the Father's glory, the express image of his person and the temple of his glory. If we speak of his divine nature, he is of the same essence with the Father, equal in power and glory. If we speak of his human nature, this is assumed into such an immediate and indissoluble union with the Divine, that in his whole person as Mediator and Head of his church reside all the characters and perfections of the Godhead. He is the true God and eternal life. There are mysteries in this subject which cannot be truly understood by any who are not taught of God, and cannot be fully comprehended by the most exalted creatures, for *none knoweth the Son but the Father* [Matthew 11:27]. Enough, however, is revealed for faith to build and feed upon—enough to point him out to sinners as the ground of their hope and the object of their supreme love, trust and adoration. If you would know this great mystery of godliness aright, you must pray the Father to reveal the Son to you and in you. According to the views you have of Jesus, in the glory of this character, the *beloved Son* of God, such will be your knowledge of the other great truths of the gospel which are derived from this and depend upon it.

FOR MEDITATION: The disciples not only saw the cloud, but they heard a voice directing them to Christ. This is a sure mark: whatever seems extraordinary in our experience, any manifestation or comfort that does not lead us to Jesus and tend to make him glorious in our eyes and precious to hearts, may be justly suspected. The Word of God, the ordinances, the teachings of the Spirit, all concur with this voice to glorify Jesus. Let us now attend to this voice from the excellent glory, which still speaketh to us also. May the Holy Spirit impress it powerfully upon all our hearts.

SERMON SERIES: ON THE TRANSFIGURATION, NO. 9 [1/4][282]

God's love known only in Christ

'*And there came a voice out of the cloud, saying, This is my beloved Son: hear him.*' Luke 9:35
SUGGESTED FURTHER READING: Ephesians 3:1–21

This is my beloved Son. By this you must learn to estimate the love of God to sinners. When St Paul is speaking of this love, he often labours for words, though he exhausts the power of language. His expressions are strictly true, or rather too low and faint to do justice to the subject, upon a supposition that Jesus is that excellent and glorious person, the *beloved Son* of God; but upon any other scheme his language must appear excessive, hyperbolical and idolatrous. But St Paul's views were right, and therefore we can easily conceive why the holy angels looked down with wonder, and learn the brightest discoveries of God in his dealings with his church. For he has so loved it as to give his only begotten Son to redeem it from ruin. That God is good may be easily proved from his works of creation, of providence—but his love is only to be known in Christ. They who refuse to give Jesus the glory due to his name, can never entertain due apprehensions of the love of God. On the other hand, if this love of God in this unspeakable gift does not affect you with wonder and draw forth your love to him, though you may have been brought up with right notions and may confess Christ in words, be assured you have not as yet received the true knowledge of him.

FOR MEDITATION:

My guilt is cancelled quite, I know,	The love I owe for sin forgiven,
And satisfaction made;	For power to believe,
But the vast debt of love I owe,	For present peace, and promised heaven,
Can never be repaid.	No angel can conceive.

That love of thine! thou sinner's Friend!
Witness thy bleeding heart!
My little all can ne'er extend
To pay a thousandth part.[283]

A right knowledge of sin

'And there came a voice out of the cloud, saying, This is my beloved Son: hear him.' Luke 9:35
SUGGESTED FURTHER READING: Revelation 5:1–14

On the knowledge of this character of Christ depends the right knowledge of the sinfulness of sin. Conceive of him for a moment as he stood transfigured in glory upon the mount and attested by a voice from heaven. And then follow him in your thoughts to those sufferings which he soon after endured. Think of him in his agony in the garden—see him the sport of servants and soldiers, see him buffeted and spit upon and at last hanging upon the cross, surrounded with his enemies who mocked his torments. Would any of you, being evil, treat a son, a *beloved son*, in this manner, or permit him to be so treated, if it was in your power to prevent it? And can you think that the great God would deliver up his only Son, who had always pleased him, to endure such things without an important reason? O sin, how exceeding sinful, when viewed in this light. He had, of his enormous love, given his Son to stand for sinners, and when sin was found charged upon him, though he was the *beloved Son*, he was not spared. Here let me drop a word:

(i) to you who go on in your sins. If God spared not his own Son, can you presume that he will spare you?

(ii) to you that are seeking to establish your own righteousness. Are you prepared to meet this holy God, who dealt thus with his own Son? Will you reject this atonement to trust to the work of your own hands?

(iii) to believers. You know there is much evil in your natures and many temptations and snares in the world. See here your best preservative against sin. The Lord help you the next time you are in danger, to remember what your sins cost Jesus. Sure, if this had not been out of your thoughts, you would not have given way in one or another instance, the remembrance of which now fills you with shame.

FOR MEDITATION: Yes, my soul, for thee, wretched sinner, a vile miserable apostate, did this wonderful Saviour leave the fullness of all glory and happiness to redeem thee from destruction, and took upon him the form of a servant, that thou mightest receive the adoption of a son.[284]

Diary, Sunday 1 July 1752

SERMON SERIES: ON THE TRANSFIGURATION, NO. 9 [3/4]

The Beloved Son of God

'And there came a voice out of the cloud, saying, This is my beloved Son: hear him.' Luke 9:35
SUGGESTED FURTHER READING: Isaiah 45:15–25

Except you conceive aright of Jesus as the *Beloved Son* of God, all your professed dependence upon him as a Saviour, is presumption and idolatry. You may learn from Isaiah 45:21 and 43:11 that there is but one Saviour, and that he is the Lord Jehovah. He is jealous of his glory and will not give it to another, nor could he, consistent with his honour and holiness, command all men to honour the Son as they honour the Father, if he was not the proper object of our supreme adoration and love. Your making mention of the name of Jesus, being baptized in it, and concluding your prayers with it, will not make you a Christian, except you are enlightened to receive him as he is revealed in the Word.

Here is comfort for believers and all who are truly seeking salvation. That name in which you are directed to trust is above every name—he on whom your help is laid is mighty, all-mighty. As the *Beloved Son*, he exercises all power in heaven and earth and is therefore able to save unto the uttermost.

What think you of Christ? If he is the *Beloved Son*, what will be the end of those who despise him, live in rebellion against him and say in their hearts, *We will not have this man to reign over us* [Luke 19:14]?

FOR MEDITATION:

What think you of CHRIST? is the test
To try both your state and your scheme;
You cannot be right in the rest,
Unless you think rightly of him.
As JESUS appears in your view,
As he is beloved or not;
So GOD is disposed to you,
And mercy or wrath are your lot.

If asked what of JESUS I think?
Though still my best thoughts are but poor;
I say, he's my meat and my drink,
My life, and my strength, and my store,
My Shepherd, my Husband, my Friend,
My Saviour from sin and from thrall;
My hope from beginning to end,
My Portion, my LORD, and my All.[285]

A heart to know me

'And I will give them an heart to know me, that I am the LORD: *and they shall be my people, and I will be their God: for they shall return unto me with their whole heart.' Jeremiah 24:7*
SUGGESTED FURTHER READING: Jeremiah 24:1–10

This was an encouraging word concerning the people that should return from Babylon—but not confined to them. It is repeated within some variety of expression more than once by this prophet, by Ezekiel, and applied by the Apostle to the Hebrews as a summary of the blessings of the New Testament dispensation. It is an encouraging word likewise to me and my hearers. I am to speak more especially to young people. Many of you are yet unsettled, undetermined. How can I expect to prevail on you, or what can you expect from me? But the gospel I preach is a gospel of grace. The Lord undertakes to do all. It is a word of sovereignty and power—*they shall*, and *I will*. However, he that does all, works by means. The means of his own appointments to which he has annexed his blessing, are now in our hands. He will do it, but he will be enquired of by us to do it for us. I therefore enter upon the service with hope, with a cheerful expectation that neither my preaching nor your hearing shall be in vain. I mean not to be large in what is usually called a doctrinal way. Young persons have usually warm passions, lively imaginations. The world is opening upon them with pleasing prospects—and their want of experience makes them too ready to mistake its shadows and delusions for realities. I must endeavour, if you will allow the expression, to outbid the world. This I shall effectually do if the Lord the Spirit is pleased to enable me to open the meaning of this promise, and to accompany what I shall say, with the life, light and influence of his Spirit.

FOR MEDITATION: *I will give them a heart to know me*—this is all that is wanting. Lord give them this, and the rest will follow. Ignorance of God is the root of every sin, and is the source of every misery.

SERMON: JEREMIAH 24:7 [1/4] [FOR THE YOUNG PEOPLE]

Pray for a new heart

'And I will give them an heart to know me, that I am the LORD: *and they shall be my people, and I will be their God: for they shall return unto me with their whole heart.' Jeremiah 24:7*
SUGGESTED FURTHER READING: Ezekiel 36:22–32

God is known by his Word. Though you doubt not there is a God, you do not *know* him unless you know him from Scripture—and especially in Christ. His outward signs give some idea of his wisdom, power and goodness, but too faint to impress the heart. His holiness and justice, his grace and love, are revealed in the work of redemption. God is in Christ revealing himself to the world and reconciling the world to himself. Yea, you may have some outward knowledge of all this, and yet not know the Lord. He must give you a heart, a new heart—the heart of stone cannot come to him. Here we must begin. Pray for a heart of flesh. Oh that moment when a divine light shines into the dark heart! Should that favoured moment be now to any of you, you will say with Jacob, *The Lord is in this place* [Genesis 28:16]. They shall *know me.* While ignorant of God, we cannot know ourselves. We are separated from him, degraded and blinded. And therefore though our souls are immortal, our capacities too great to be filled with anything short of himself, we are seeking the living among the dead, hewing out cisterns, and regardless of the fountain. This state is sinful. For he made us, and we are his property. His will should be our rule, our law, his power our life, his glory our end.

FOR MEDITATION: It is possible to approve and profess the gospel, and yet to be quite strangers to that change of heart, that new birth, that hidden and spiritual life of faith in the Son of God, which are essentially necessary to the character of a true Christian. If profession does not spring from the root of a broken and contrite spirit, a solid conviction of sin, and such a sense of the wretched, ruined state of a sinner as makes the Saviour precious and all in all to the soul, and leads to a renunciation of self in every view, and a separation from the spirit of the world—though it may seem to flourish for awhile, sooner or later, it will wither, and come to nothing. The true Christian is like a river where the stream, though not always of the same depth or rapidity, yet always runs, because it is fed from an unfailing spring.[286]
John Newton to William Wilberforce, 1 July 1789

SERMON: JEREMIAH 24:7 [2/4] [FOR THE YOUNG PEOPLE]

The supreme desire of our souls

'And I will give them an heart to know me, that I am the LORD: and they shall be my people, and I will be their God: for they shall return unto me with their whole heart.' Jeremiah 24:7
SUGGESTED FURTHER READING: Hosea 14:1–9

When we know the Lord we therefore come to him for pardon and for liberty. Both are in Christ—they who believe are accepted and made free. He becomes their God. They return to their allegiance and rest. They own and feel their dependence. They devote and yield themselves to him, and thus are restored to their proper rank and state as his intelligent creatures, under additional obligation of being bought with blood. Now they say—What have I to do any more with idols? He is their refuge; we are weak, defenceless, exposed, but Psalm 146:5 [*Happy is he that hath the God of Jacob for his help, whose hope is in the LORD his God*]; Deuteronomy 33. There is our sap. The Lord is their tower and their shield. He is their portion, their happiness. The supreme desire of their souls is to him; they have fellowship with him—and for ever. They are his people, interested in all his attributes, perfections, promises and providences.

FOR MEDITATION: I doubt not many of thy children think highly of me, but what I really am thou only knowest, and well it is for me. Thou canst bear with me, but could my fellow creatures see me as I appear in thy sight, surely they would flee from me. Thou, Lord, knewest what I would be. Thou knowest that I desire to love thee, yea, that I do love thee, above all. Thou art the foundation of my hope and chief object of my soul's desire. I trust there is nothing in heaven or upon earth that I hold in competition with thee. I seek my happiness only in thy favour and propose thy glory as the great end of my being.[287]

Annotated *Letters to a Wife*, 27 October 1794

SERMON: JEREMIAH 24:7 [3/4] [FOR THE YOUNG PEOPLE]

Heavenly minded

'*And I will give them an heart to know me, that I am the* LORD*: and they shall be my people, and I will be their God: for they shall return unto me with their whole heart.*' *Jeremiah* 24:7

SUGGESTED FURTHER READING: Philippians 3:12–4:1

His service, and the views under which his people engage in it, enables them. They no longer grovel. They are heavenly minded. Like the angels they behold his face and do his will. A dignity and grandeur is impressed upon the actions of common life—because done for him. They are faithful, diligent in all their callings. Devotedness to God inspires them with benevolence to man for his sake. Hence they are delivered from guilt, fear, anxiety, the dominion [of sin] and hurtful tormenting passions. They live with honour, they die with comfort, and then they ascend to dwell with him whom here they loved, trusted and served. May I not hope you are touched with the high ambition of being the Lord's? Some young people, I trust, have already chosen this good part; yea, I will hope others see it desirable. To both, permit me to offer a word of advice:

(i) prize and study the Scripture and ordinances

(ii) draw nigh to him by prayer

(iii) be careful of your company

(iv) beware of resisting conscience.

Tremble at the thoughts of rejecting this call. Life is uncertain. If you are not his people here, you will sink at death into the outward darkness, prepared for the devil. Your ruin will be aggravated.

[Newton made himself a note here to 'add a word to the aged' also.]

FOR MEDITATION: *They shall be my people, and I will be their God*. Now can the world promise anything like this? Will it give you comfort? Will it comfort you in trouble? Will it cheer your dying hours? Will its pleasures attend you into an eternal state?

The Lord my Helper

'Because thou hast been my help, therefore in the shadow of thy wings will I rejoice.' Psalm 63:7

SUGGESTED FURTHER READING: Psalm 63:1–11

Man is a helpless creature in himself, insufficient to his own happiness. The state of infancy is an emblem of his future life. From first to last he is unable to stand without support, and has wants and desires which he is not fully able to express. This weakness is felt by all and in our natural state, in the midst of our proudest boasts, we are seeking help from everything around us. But how many disappointments do we meet while we live without God in the world, and what a wilderness do we find ourselves in when awakened to see the world in a true light. Then we are stirred up to look for help in God. And blessed be his name, his Word warrants us so to do. He does not, as he might, send us to our idols—but he invites, he receives and he helps the unworthy. This is the acknowledgement and determination of an experienced soul—I have received a conviction that I can do nothing for myself, and that creatures cannot help me. *I sought the Lord and he heard me, therefore with him will I abide.* [Psalm 34:4; 2 Samuel 16:18]

My help. Here consider:

(i) to whom God is a help: those who know that they in themselves are helpless, that see and approve his way, his covenant in Jesus, that plead his promises for help.

(ii) when he helps: always, particularly in conviction, temptation, affliction, duty.

(iii) what a help he is: free and gracious, a present help; Romans 10: a seasonable help, a sufficient help.

FOR MEDITATION:

When Hannah pressed with grief,
Poured forth her soul in prayer;
She quickly found relief,
And left her burden there:
Like her, in every trying case,
Let us approach the throne of grace.

When she began to pray,
Her heart was pained and sad;
But ere she went away,
Was comforted and glad:
In trouble, what a resting place,
Have they who know the throne of grace![288]

SERMON: PSALM 63:7 [1/2] [ALSO PREACHED 28 JAN. 1776 & 3 OCT. 1779]

Help and hope for the helpless and hopeless

'Because thou hast been my help, therefore in the shadow of thy wings will I rejoice.' Psalm 63:7
SUGGESTED FURTHER READING: Psalm 9:1–20

In the shadow of thy wings will I rejoice. Experience should determine us to David's determination. The *wings* refer either to the holy place or to the image of a hen over her young. And there to *rejoice*, considering his ability (Psalm 27:1 *my light... my salvation... the strength of my life*), and his constancy. He will not change. From hence consider the life of faith as safe (Psalm 9), pleasant, honourable—near the Lord. This is the gospel declaration: a tender of help and hope for the helpless and hopeless. How blind are sinners to put this from them. Who else can help you at death or judgement? This is a suitable meditation to take to the Lord's table. Think of the help you have found—of the mercy seat between the cherubim. Offer your praise and make your vows.

Diary, 28 January 1776:

Ah! I feel my weakness; how much have I said and written concerning dependence and resignation, but alas! how hard, how impossible, to practise what I know and teach, any farther than thou art pleased to strengthen me. Lord I believe, help thou my unbelief.[289]

FOR MEDITATION:

When first before his mercy-seat,
Thou didst to him thy all commit;
He gave thee warrant, from that hour,
To trust his wisdom, love and power.

Did ever trouble yet befall,
And he refuse to hear thy call?
And has he not his promise past,
That thou shalt overcome at last?

Like David, thou may'st comfort draw,
Saved from the bear's and lion's paw
Goliath's rage I may defy,
For GOD, my Saviour, still is nigh.

He who has helped me hitherto,
Will help me all my journey through;
And give me daily cause to raise
New Ebenezers to his praise.

Though rough and thorny be the road, It leads thee home, apace, to GOD;
Then count thy present trials small, For heaven will make amends for all.[290, 291]

SERMON: PSALM 63:7 [2/2] [ALSO PREACHED 28 JAN. 1776 & 3 OCT. 1779]

Breaking through prejudices

'The same came to Jesus by night, and said unto him, Rabbi, we know that thou art a teacher come from God: for no man can do these miracles that thou doest, except God be with him.' John 3:2
SUGGESTED FURTHER READING: Luke 11:14–28

Our Lord was indeed *a teacher sent from God*, and we who know his character are ready to wonder that he was not generally received. But his enemies who hated him had many plausible objections to discourage some from hearing and to divert others from attending to what he said. They rejected the supposed place of his birth, Nazareth, concerning which those who were not diligent to search out the truth might easily mistake, as his mother had lived there before he was born and returned while he was very young (John 7:52)—this stumbled Nathaniel for a season. They pretended that he broke the Sabbath. They urged the character and meanness of his followers, and so on. We may therefore wonder that Nicodemus could break through so many prejudices. We are here informed what prevailed on him— the works which Jesus did led him to think that, notwithstanding all his brethren could say, he must be an extraordinary person, for none could do such things *except God was with him*. He concluded that the works of Christ, such as to raise the dead, necessarily required a divine power. His enemies acknowledged them beyond the power of man, but would have thought he did them by the assistance of Satan. But this black, malicious charge was confuted by a single question: Is Satan divided against himself? How could the great enemy of mankind assist, if he had been able, in producing such wonderful acts of compassion and bounty? He concluded that as our Lord's miracles were wrought in confirmation of his character and doctrine, God would not have owned him by his power unless his doctrine had been true, and he a teacher sent from him as he professed. We are to apply this reasoning to our own circumstances.

FOR MEDITATION:

Now my search is at an end,	JESUS , source of excellence!
Now my wishes rove no more!	All thy glorious love reveal!
Thus my moments I would spend,	Kingdoms shall not bribe me hence,
Love, and wonder, and adore:	While this happiness I feel.[292]

SERMON: JOHN 3:1–2, NO. 2 [1/6]

The reproach of the gospel

'...*Rabbi, we know that thou art a teacher come from God: for no man can do these miracles that thou doest, except God be with him.*' John 3:2
SUGGESTED FURTHER READING: Acts 5:12–33

Our Lord foretold that his gospel, after his ascension, would meet with the same reception as his person, that those who preached in his name should do the same works which he did, or even greater, that they should be chiefly owned (as he was) by the poor and ignorant, and generally rejected by those who were in most esteem with the world for their seeming goodness, or their rank in life. We find his words fulfilled. As the scribes and the Pharisees, who professed great regard to the Scriptures, taught the people falsehood from truth, and opposed Christ, so in many countries called Christian there is a sort of doctrine generally taught which cannot be from God because it is attended with no mighty works, nor does it glorify Jesus, which is the great object of the Christian ministry. But here and there another sort of preaching prevails which tends to lay low the haughty looks of man, that the Lord alone may be exalted. It proclaims a feast of good things for the hungry, but sends those who are rich and wise in their own conceits empty away. But wherever this is heard the world is presently in an uproar. It is charged with licentiousness, folly and madness. The preachers and believers of it are loaded with reproach, and all who are disposed to hear it are either pitied as out of their wits, or opposed as if they had been guilty of some great crime. However there are such mighty effects attending it as lead some before they hear it to reason as Nicodemus—Surely it must be of God, or else how can these things be?

FOR MEDITATION: I conceive therefore, that an upright, conscientious man cannot, by the most circumspect and prudent behaviour, wholly avoid the censure and dislike of the world, so far as his religious principles are concerned, and he is determined to square his life according to the precepts and spirit of the gospel. He must expect to be misunderstood by some, and misinterpreted by others. For in a degree, and upon some occasions at least, all who will live godly in Christ Jesus must suffer persecution.[293]

John Newton to William Wilberforce, 1 November 1787
[in reply to advice sought as the MP set out to abolish the slave trade]

SERMON SERIES: JOHN 3:1–2, NO. 2 [2/6]

Gospel doctrine

'The same came to Jesus by night, and said unto him, Rabbi, we know that thou art a teacher come from God: for no man can do these miracles that thou doest, except God be with him.' John 3:2
SUGGESTED FURTHER READING: Galatians 2:15–21

Let us briefly speak of gospel doctrine. Its chief points are:
(i) to show that all mankind are by nature under the curse of the law.
(ii) that there is no deliverance from this curse but by Jesus.
(iii) that no work of man contributes in the least to their acceptance with God.
(iv) that true religion supposes an entire change in the soul and all its faculties and that without this change of the heart the most costly or painful services are of no value or acceptance before God.

This is what we mean by the gospel doctrine. The sum and substance of it is Jesus Christ and him crucified. This awakens the opposition and scorn of men, even as the appearance and preaching of Christ in the flesh did. But we are bold to say that by this doctrine as the means, such mighty works are wrought as necessarily declare the power of God does accompany it—such works as no other sort of preaching can effect, such works as in the spiritual sense are answerable to the miracles which our Lord wrought in the view of the Jews, and are equally sufficient to condemn those of obstinacy, who refuse to acknowledge the doctrine to be of God.

FOR MEDITATION: With regard to the work—I hope I am in some measure aware of its weight and importance and am willing to enter upon it accordingly, so as to make it the sole business of my life: to devote all my time, strength, talents and interest to the carrying it on; to allow myself in no engagement, converse, correspondence or study, which I cannot conscientiously pursue as subservient to this main point. Having a view of the pearl of great price, I am willing to part with all to receive it, and to take the apostle's resolution to know nothing but Jesus Christ and him crucified, that I may declare his unsearchable riches to sinners.[294]
Miscellaneous Thoughts, Monday 26 June 1758

These miracles

'...For no man can do these miracles that thou doest, except God be with him.' John 3:2
SUGGESTED FURTHER READING: Luke 7:11–23

Some of these works our Lord sums up as evidence of his mission to John's disciples (Luke 7:22).

(i) *The blind see.* This was a proof of the power of God, and so acknowledged in John 10:21. His ministers cannot indeed give bodily sight, but they are his instruments to open the eyes of the mind. All men are blind till the gospel gives them sight—stark blind to the things of God. They know not where they are going, they are insensible to danger, though they stand upon the brink of it. They know not God or themselves. But this foolishness of preaching opens the eyes of many. And they can say, *Whereas I was blind, now I see* [John 9:25]. Where this preaching is applied to the heart by the Spirit, those who were before ignorant are made wise. Yea, though they are of moderate capacities and of the lowest ranks in life, they soon outstrip such as have the greatest natural advantages, if they have not this likewise.

(ii) *The deaf hear.* God is often speaking to sinners—to their consciences by his Spirit, to their eyes and their ears by his providence—but they are deaf. Though his voice is in the city there is no man of wisdom to understand it, till the preaching of the gospel comes, then the ears of the deaf are unstopped, and...

(iii) *The dumb speak.* Men indeed are not dumb wholly. They have tongues which they think are their own. Words of blasphemy, cursing, lying and vanity they are free to speak, but with respect to the best use and purpose of speech they are as dumb as fishes, till the knowledge of sin and of a Saviour opens their mouths. Then they speak to God's praise and say, *Come and I will tell you what he hath done* [Psalm 66:16] [contd in 5/6].

FOR MEDITATION:

Sight, hearing, feeling, taste and smell,
Are gifts we highly prize;
But faith does singly each excel,
And all the five comprise.

It hears the mighty voice of GOD,
And ponders what he saith;
His word and works, his gifts and rod,
Have each a voice to faith.[295]

SERMON SERIES: JOHN 3:1–2, NO. 2 [4/6]

Till the Son makes them free

'...*For no man can do these miracles that thou doest, except God be with him.*' John 3: 2
SUGGESTED FURTHER READING: 2 Thessalonians 2:13–17

[contd from 4/6—evidence of our Lord's mission:]
(iv) *The lame walk.* There is inability for the service of God in us by nature, as much as in a cripple to run a race. So that when the conscience is a little alive, and a necessity is seen to forsake evil and practise that which is good, there is no power at all till the Son makes them free by the light of the preached gospel, and then they are free indeed.

(v) *The lepers are cleansed.* The leprosy was an emblem of sin as: a total pollution; such as separated a person from a communion in holy things; incurable to natural and ordinary means. In this disorder all helps and medicines were of no value. God alone could heal it. But Jesus cleansed the lepers, and by his gospel he cleanses from the leprosy of sin, and frees those who believe from its guilt and from its power.

(vi) *The dead are raised.* Devils are cast out and raging storms silenced by this powerful word. That is, those who were dead in trespasses and sins, habitually accustomed to evil, so led and governed and hurried on by Satan in his wicked service as to break through all restraints, like the man possessed with a legion, are made partakers of a new spiritual life, brought to their right minds and enabled to live according to the will of God, to be comfortable in themselves and useful, exemplary to those about them.

FOR MEDITATION: *Faith a new and comprehensive sense*

It feels the touch of heavenly power,
And from that boundless source,
Derives fresh vigour every hour,
To run its daily course.

It smells the dear Redeemer's name
Like ointment poured forth;
Faith only knows or can proclaim,
Its favour or its worth.

The truth and goodness of the LORD,
Are suited to its taste
Mean is the worldling's pampered board,
To faith's perpetual feast.

Till saving faith possess the mind,
In vain of sense we boast;
We are but senseless, tasteless, blind,
And deaf, and dead, and lost.[296]

Living witnesses for God and his truth

'...For no man can do these miracles that thou doest, except God be with him.' John 3:2
SUGGESTED FURTHER READING: Philemon 8–21

Now if you ask who or where are these extraordinary persons [who experienced miraculous healings], I acknowledge they are comparatively but few. The subjects of our Lord's miraculous power were but few likewise, and he has taught us to expect that his flock will be a little flock. I confess the best are subject to so many infirmities—so many things are still amiss (for this is but a begun work). I allow that too many are pretenders. This, likewise, we are taught to expect. But there are some, and not hard to be found and known ... who are living witnesses for God and his truth, who are not ashamed of the gospel, nor a shame to it, but have found and do evidence that it is the power of God unto salvation, and whose lives and conversations too prove that they are different from what they once were, and from the generality of those about them.

On the other hand, we challenge any to produce instances of the same effects wrought by any other doctrine. How much is said and written to tell people what they should be and what they should do, yet where the gospel principles are not enforced there is nothing done, nothing attempted, beyond a formal round of dull and heartless service—a little something like religion on Sundays: to go to church when the bell tolls, to repeat words because other people do, to hear without attention and then to run full swing into the world again.

Or if here and there a person is truly touched, where they have no better helps, the consequence always is that they renounce the things they held for truths, are brought into that way of thinking which is agreeable to the gospel preaching, and receive it gladly whenever it comes in their way.

FOR MEDITATION: He can call the most unworthy persons, and bring them from the most unlikely places, to labour in his vineyard. Had it not been so, you would never have heard of me. Consider what I was, and where I was (in Africa) and you must acknowledge that I am a singular instance of the sovereignty and the riches of his mercy![297]

John Newton to John Ryland, 29 November 1799

SERMON SERIES: JOHN 3:1–2, NO. 2 [6/6]

Compassionate prayer

'And he said, Oh let not the Lord be angry, and I will speak yet but this once: Peradventure ten shall be found there. And he said, I will not destroy it for ten's sake.' Genesis 18:32
SUGGESTED FURTHER READING: Matthew 5:43–48

When the Lord had intimated to Abraham his purpose concerning Sodom, it prompted Abraham to pray for the place. The occasion, the manner and the force of this prayer are very instructive. The occasion, or rather the motive, was compassion to sinners. No doubt Abraham thought of Lot, but he does not directly mention him. He knew Lot's character and hoped there were more like him. But he is not content to plead for the righteous only, but rather uses them as a plea for the preservation of the whole place. Though the men of Sodom were great sinners, Abraham prayed for them; though he was safe himself, he pitied them. This is a right spirit. May the Lord cause it to abound more in his people. We are by nature even as others and the grace that has saved us is able to save the vilest. We should not look on them with indifference, or give them up absolutely as reprobates. Secret things belong to the Lord, but it is our duty to pray and hope. We cannot be too much displeased with their sins; we cannot be too compassionate to their persons.

FOR MEDITATION: [for the Fast Day, Friday 13 December 1776]

His grace despised, his power defied,	The LORD, displeased, has raised his rod;
And legions of the blackest crimes,	Ah where are now the faithful few
Profaneness, riot, lust and pride,	Who tremble for the ark of GOD,
Are signs that mark the present times.	And know what Israel ought to do?

> LORD, hear thy people everywhere, Who meet to mourn, confess and pray;
> The nation and thy churches spare, And let thy wrath be turned away.[298]

O may a blessing be on this day's work throughout the kingdom. Lord, if thou awaken thy people to pray, thou wilt surely incline thy ear to hear. And we may expect more from the prayer of faith, than from fleets and armies, and all that politicians account wisdom.[299]

Diary, 13 December 1776

SERMON SERIES: GENESIS, NO. 40 [1/3], GENESIS 18:32

Ground for prayer

'Peradventure there be fifty righteous within the city: wilt thou also destroy and not spare the place for the fifty righteous that are therein? That be far from thee to do after this manner, to slay the righteous with the wicked: and that the righteous should be as the wicked, that be far from thee: Shall not the Judge of all the earth do right?' Genesis 18:24–25
SUGGESTED FURTHER READING: John 17:1–26

As to the manner of the prayer, observe the ground upon which Abraham went: *Shall not the Judge of all the earth do right?* He thought that the Righteous Judge would not destroy the righteous with the wicked. But was there not sin enough in the righteous to justify the Lord if he had suffered them to fall in the common calamity? Abraham was a believer; he did not trust in his own righteousness himself. He knew that strictly speaking there was not a righteous person upon earth. But those are righteous who are justified and accepted of God and who walk in his fear. As the threatened judgement was to manifest God's displeasure in a remarkable way upon daring sinners, Abraham humbly hoped that the Lord would make a difference between those who feared him and those who feared him not. And the Lord allowed this plea. Had he been strict to mark what is amiss, he might have left even Lot to perish, for taking up his abode in such a place as Sodom. But he is gracious, and showed himself disposed not only to spare those who feared him, but to spare Sodom likewise for their sakes, if they were found to be so many as Abraham was willing to hope. And yet these were few. Abraham himself could not hope there were more than fifty and this number he diminished till he brought it to ten.

We may observe how truly those who fear the Lord are the salt of the earth. I think we may infer that neither London or Olney would long stand if the Lord had not a remnant in them. The world think little of this, that they are indebted for their preservation to those whom they despise.

FOR MEDITATION: They who have access to God by Jesus Christ have more power and influence than the greatest monarch upon earth. Mighty things have been done by prayer; and however little thought of by statesmen, I believe … it is the only effectual bulwark of our sinful nation.[300]
John Newton to William Wilberforce, 2 October 1794

SERMON SERIES: GENESIS, NO. 40 [2/3], GENESIS 18:32

Access by faith in prayer

'And he said, Oh let not the Lord be angry, and I will speak yet but this once: Peradventure ten shall be found there. And he said, I will not destroy it for ten's sake.' Genesis 18:32
SUGGESTED FURTHER READING: Psalm 20:1–9

We may take notice of the issue:
(i) the Lord continued to answer, so long as Abraham continued to ask. It was his own Spirit encouraged and enabled Abraham to carry his suit so far. But he found no liberty to press it farther. Abraham could not but acknowledge the justice of the sentence against Sodom, if ten righteous persons could not be found in it. It may be right in us to pray far in such cases, when we cannot be sure what the Lord's purpose may be, but at length he will overrule and direct his people's desires so that they shall be brought to acquiesce in his will.

(ii) the Lord withdrew and Abraham returned humbled and thankful for the honour he had received. O it is wonderful—that dust and ashes should converse with the great God. Yet such honour have all his saints. This is the honour that cometh of God only—access by faith in prayer.

Abraham could not obtain mercy for Sodom. But there is One who by his intercession can prevail to save *to the uttermost* [Hebrews 7:25]. May the Spirit of the Lord enable poor sinners to put their cause into the hands of Jesus, so shall they be saved in the day of anger.

FOR MEDITATION: *Ask what shall I give thee*

Come, my soul, thy suit prepare,
JESUS loves to answer prayer;
He himself has bid thee pray,
Therefore will not say thee nay.

With my burden I begin,
LORD, remove this load of sin!
Let thy blood, for sinners spilt,
Set my conscience free from guilt.

Thou art coming to a King,
Large petitions with thee bring;
For his grace and power are such,
None can ever ask too much.

LORD! I come to thee for rest,
Take possession of my breast;
There thy blood-bought right maintain,
And without a rival reign.[301]

Secured by his mark

'And while he lingered, the men laid hold upon his hand, and upon the hand of his wife, and upon the hand of his two daughters; the LORD *being merciful unto him: and they brought him forth, and set him without the city.' Genesis 19:16*
SUGGESTED FURTHER READING: Genesis 19:1–14

As the cry of Sodom's sin, so the cry of Lot's prayers had been heard of the Lord. Judgement must take place, but a mark is set upon him. The angels were sent to deliver him. They found that though Lot dwelt in Sodom, he was not of it. To him they were welcome guests—but the inhabitants would have offered them violence. This filled up the measure of their iniquities. An observation or two from the verses before my text, I must not omit:

(i) the angel's question, *Hast thou here any besides?* Ah, some of the Lord's people who see the destruction of Sodom approaching will feel this. Was it proper for you to speak, what complaints should I hear from different parts—I have a rebellious child, or a parent growing old in sin—or a wife or a husband. Well, complain to the Lord—pray for them yet more earnestly.

(ii) Lot's endeavours to save his sons-in-law; but they would not be warned, and their wives, though the children of pious Lot, were equally hardened. Let those who have light, take care how they marry with the profane and wicked, lest they become like them.

FOR MEDITATION: The evening hymn on Sunday 11 June 1775, 'which I composed with a view to the present troubles in America, and gave a brief sketch of the past and present state of the nation, with a view to engage the people to attendance on our Tuesday morning meetings, by apprising them of the importance of the crisis.' [The 5am weekly Tuesday morning prayer meetings drew over a hundred people.][302]

The gathering clouds, with aspect dark,
A rising storm presage;
Oh! to be hid within the ark,
And sheltered from its rage!

The humble souls who mourn and pray,
The LORD approves and knows;
His mark secures them in the day
When vengeance strikes his foes.[303]

SERMON SERIES: GENESIS, NO. 41 [1/4], GENESIS 19:16

Linger no longer

'And while he lingered, the men laid hold upon his hand, and upon the hand of his wife, and upon the hand of his two daughters; the LORD *being merciful unto him: and they brought him forth, and set him without the city.' Genesis 19:16*
SUGGESTED FURTHER READING: Revelation 3:14–22

But my text leads me to speak of Lot himself. Is it not strange even Lot lingered? The passage is of general application. The world, like Sodom, lies in wickedness. Believers are like Lot—the Lord informs them of the consequences of sin and says, *Come out from among them, that ye be not consumed.* They hear and obey. Yet they are so faint, so half in earnest, so lingering, that the Lord's mercy is as much magnified in bearing with them after he has called them, as in calling them at first. However, he will not suffer them to perish, but employs various means by which he, as it were, takes hold of them by the hand and pulls them away by force. Let us speak to these things. The Lord's people are prone to linger. Perhaps some of you may wonder at Lot, and think that if you were sure this place was to be instantly destroyed, you would hasten as soon and as far from it as you could. But they who know their own hearts will wonder least at him. His life was given him for a prey, but he must leave his house, his substance, his children, behind him. His heart cleaved too much to these things and the command was sudden. Now to us all these things are transacted in a spiritual manner; the judgement is yet unsure and distant, and present objects strike powerfully upon the senses. We are not to leave the world absolutely, but to forsake it in our affections while we are yet in it. Here is a call for much self denial: to forgo the love of the world—its pleasures, its friendships—to endure its scoffs, to be accounted mockers and to suffer mocks and taunts and hard treatment. The Lord pity and pardon us, these things make too much impression upon our spirits and cause us strangely to linger.

FOR MEDITATION: Let us pray for grace to linger no longer—for a powerful sense of the truth of his Word, that we may believe, act and endure, as seeing him who is invisible.

SERMON SERIES: GENESIS, NO. 41 [2/4], GENESIS 19:16

The Lord's patience and mercy

'*And while he lingered, the men laid hold upon his hand, and upon the hand of his wife, and upon the hand of his two daughters; the* LORD *being merciful unto him: and they brought him forth, and set him without the city.*' Genesis 19:16
SUGGESTED FURTHER READING: Isaiah 1:9–20

To some of you, we seem as mockers; we can only repeat our message and leave it with your consciences, entreating the Lord to give a blessing, while we declare the danger and the remedy. That Lot escaped at last, is ascribed to the Lord's mercy. He might justly have been left to perish with the rest. O the patience of the Lord towards his own people. Indeed it is in some respects more wonderful than his long forbearance of the wicked. These know not what they do. But believers sin and trifle against knowledge and love and experience. On this account they may be said to be though scarcely saved. They have so often provoked the Lord, that if his mercy was not infinite, he would be weary of them and cast them off for ever.

Annotated *Letters to a* Wife, 4 August 1796, aged 70:
O my LORD! If I would recollect or recount thy mercies they are more in number than the sands! The best part of my childhood and youth was vanity and folly but before I attained the age of man I became exceeding vile indeed and was seated in the chair of a scorner in early life. Troubles and miseries I for a time endured, were my own. I brought them upon myself by forsaking thy good and pleasant paths and choosing the way of transgressors, which I found very hard. They led to slavery, contempt, famine and despair, but my recovery from that dreadful state was wholly of thee. How nice [precise] were the terms upon which my deliverance from Africa depended. Had the ship passed one quarter of an hour sooner I had died there a wretch as I had lived.[304]

FOR MEDITATION: We are passengers in a ship in which the Lord's cause and faithfulness are embarked with us, and therefore we need not fear sinking. The infallible pilot will guide us safely through the storms.[305]
John Newton to John Ryland, 28 January 1781

SERMON SERIES: GENESIS, NO. 41 [3/4], GENESIS 19:16

Rescued—taken by the hand

'And while he lingered, the men laid hold upon his hand, and upon the hand of his wife, and upon the hand of his two daughters; the LORD *being merciful unto him: and they brought him forth, and set him without the city.' Genesis 19:16*
SUGGESTED FURTHER READING: Jonah 1:17–2:10

The Lord takes believers by the hand and saves them in defiance of themselves. The usual means are:
(i) by his Word and ordinances. Here he meets them—sometimes with an alarming word that makes them tremble; sometimes a humbling word that makes them ashamed (as when he looked upon Peter); sometimes a reviving word, accompanied with a constraining force of his love. Then like Matthew and the sons of Zebedee they can forsake all and follow. O it is a blessing to have the ordinances.
(ii) by his conduct towards them. He hides his face. They lose the blessedness they once spoke of. He makes the heavens over their heads iron and the earth brass. They walk in darkness and mourn under deadness and dryness of spirit. Thus he makes them feel the evil of their way.
(iii) by his providence. He fills their mouths with ashes and makes the world bitter—pains, sickness, poverty, crosses, loss of friends and earthly comforts. He has many scourges of this kind.

FOR MEDITATION:

When thy loved presence meets my sight,   My sun is hid, my comforts lost,
It softens care, and sweetens toil;   My graces droop, my sins revive;
The sun shines forth with double light,   Distressed, dismayed, and tempest-tossed,
The whole creation wears a smile.   My soul is only just alive!

But ah! since thou hast been away,   LORD, hear my cry and come again!
Nothing but trouble have I known;   Put all mine enemies to shame,
And Satan marks me for his prey   And let them see, 'tis not in vain
Because he sees me left alone.   That I have trusted in thy name.[306]

The fear of the Lord

'Then they that feared the LORD *spake often one to another: and the* LORD *hearkened, and heard it, and a book of remembrance was written before him for them that feared the* LORD, *and that thought upon his name.'*
Malachi 3:16
SUGGESTED FURTHER READING: Malachi 3:6–18

The prophet Malachi lived as we do now at a time when the words of many were stout against the Lord. They counted his service a burden and spoke well of them whom he abhorred. The priests and the people were in general going backward with one consent, and many severe threatenings are denounced against them both. Yet the Lord has a remnant, a few secret ones, who would not follow a multitude to do evil. To these this comfortable passage relates, and it is equally applicable in all times. It is always the lot of the Lord's people to be comparatively a small number, and to live in the midst of those who are contrary to him and to them. It is both their duty and privilege to imitate these conscientious servants of God, to speak often one to another, and they have the same encouragement to hope the Lord will notice, accept and bless their communications.

Those who *feared*. This is a sufficient mark of distinction. Those who belong to the Lord fear him; those who truly fear him, assuredly belong to him, for if he had not put this fear in their hearts they would have continued regardless of him, as they were once. The general character of the unconverted is that there is no fear in God before their eyes. Their practice proves it. Observe them in their business, in their amusements, in their form of religion, in their common conversation (Luke 6:45). Those who are awakened and drawn by divine grace are different in all these respects. They have an habitual principle of the fear of God—not a slavish fear, though it begins perhaps with terror, but it grows brighter and clearer as their faith increases. It is connected with a hope in his mercy (Psalm 33:18). They are affected with a sense of his greatness, his goodness and their unworthiness.

FOR MEDITATION: 'The fear of the LORD is the beginning of wisdom: and the knowledge of the holy is understanding' (Proverbs 9:10).

SERMON: MALACHI 3:16–17 [1/5]

Speak often one to another

'Then they that feared the LORD *spake often one to another: and the* LORD *hearkened, and heard it, and a book of remembrance was written before him for them that feared the* LORD, *and that thought upon his name.'*
Malachi 3:16
SUGGESTED FURTHER READING: Hebrews 10:19–39

When those who are drawn by the Lord are brought to fear him, the world (who are stout against the Lord) will be stout against them. What then shall they do? Why, they are constrained to cry to the Lord in secret and they are glad, as opportunity offers, to speak often one to another. If your lot was settled in some distant part of the kingdom, and you were to meet one of your own townsfolk or old schoolfellows, you would be glad to speak to them upon that single account. If you were in some more distant country whereby you could not understand the language of the people, a man's having been born in England would recommend him to your regard. Thus it is with the Lord's people, they are strangers in a strange land—they talk a language which none can understand but themselves—and therefore when sin and Satan do not prevent, they are glad to run together and to speak often. This is their privilege. It happens sometimes that an awakened soul lives alone for a season before he has freedom or opportunity to make himself known to others. And this is usually a great hindrance. While they carry their sorrows within them they are burdened. Satan has advantage of them, perplexes them with fears and doubts and troubles—he knows that if they could freely communicate their case to those who have been in the same way, they would probably receive assistance, and therefore he labours all he can to stop their mouths. O rejoiced have some of you been, when you have been enabled to break through these snares, and the Lord has brought you to have sweet and free communion with his children. You have found that as iron sharpeneth iron, so you have been stirred up by friendly converse.

FOR MEDITATION: Bless God then for the privilege and be careful to improve it. Consider it is not only your pleasure, but your duty. It is amongst the means which he has appointed to bless for your comfort and usefulness (1 Thessalonians 5:14). It has been the practice of the saints in all ages (Psalm 66:16; Luke 24:34–35). Gratitude demands it (Psalm 28:7).

SERMON: MALACHI 3:16–17 [2/5]

The Lord hears

'Then they that feared the LORD *spake often one to another: and the* LORD *hearkened, and heard it, and a book of remembrance was written before him for them that feared the* LORD, *and that thought upon his name. And they shall be mine, saith the* LORD *of hosts, in that day when I make up my jewels; and I will spare them, as a man spareth his own son that serveth him.' Malachi 3:16–17*
SUGGESTED FURTHER READING: Isaiah 65:17–25

Methinks the principal motive I can urge for speaking often to one another should be that in my text: the Lord's gracious and condescending acceptance. He—*he!—hearkened* and *heard*. It is mentioned as giving him pleasure. Though encompassed with the songs of angels he does not disdain our poor remembrance of him. *A book was written.* This is spoken after the manner of men, who write what they would not have forgot. We forget what passes upon these occasions, but he will not. He acknowledges it as a mark of his children: *they shall be mine, says the* LORD. Surely if this will not stir us up, nothing will. The Lord hears our discourses and sees all intimacies. Let them trouble that spend their time in vain company and vain conversation. He has a book for you too, and it will be opened against you in the great day. Now you laugh and play, but then you shall mourn and weep. If you do not fear the Lord now, you will fear him then. Though you think not of his name at present, you will think of him when he calls you to give an account of every idle word.

FOR MEDITATION:

When sinners utter boasting words,
And glory in their shame;
The LORD, well-pleased, an ear affords
To those who fear his name.

They often meet to seek his face,
And what they do, or say,
Is noted in his book of grace
Against another day.

For they, by faith, a day descry,
And joyfully expect,
When he, descending from the sky,
His jewels will collect.

Assembled worlds will then discern
The saints alone are blest;
When wrath shall like an oven burn,
And vengeance strike the rest.[307]

SERMON: MALACHI 3:16–17 [3/5]

Advice to those weak in the faith

'Then they that feared the LORD *spake often one to another: and the* LORD *hearkened, and heard it, and a book of remembrance was written before him for them that feared the* LORD*, and that thought upon his name.'*
Malachi 3:16
SUGGESTED FURTHER READING: 1 Thessalonians 2:17–3:13

My chief business is at present with those who are awakened and seeking the Lord's salvation. I would earnestly advise you to be after speaking one to another. I address myself to those who are weak in the faith. You have many complaints, fears and troubles, but is not their increase and continuance owing to your fault? If you were to mix freely with the Lord's people you would find many helps which you now deprive yourselves of. You would find that the trials which you think peculiar to yourselves, are common to others. You would be helped by the advice and the prayers of those who know how to pity you. Many are kept by a false humility. They are deceived; there is much of self-will in it. Some are afraid of making a profession, but what a poor excuse is this—not intend, never, to make a profession! Surely you have not considered our Lord's words in Luke 12:8 [*Also I say unto you, Whosoever shall confess me before men, him shall the Son of man also confess before the angels of God*]. But perhaps you are afraid, lest after joining more publicly you should fall back and dishonour the gospel. I think a fear of bringing a reproach upon God's ways is a good fear and a good sign—but if you are really afraid of falling back you ought rather to join with those who might be helpful to you. Do you expect to be stronger or more comfortable by yourselves?

FOR MEDITATION:

Often thy public means of grace,
Thy thirsty people's watering place,
The archers have beset;
Attacked them in thy house of prayer,
To prison dragged, or to the bar,
When thus together met.

But we from such assaults are freed,
Can pray, and sing, and hear, and read,
And meet, and part, in peace:
May we our privileges prize,
In their improvement make us wise,
And bless us with increase.[308]

Watch over one another in love

'Then they that feared the LORD spake often one to another: and the LORD hearkened, and heard it, and a book of remembrance was written before him for them that feared the LORD, and that thought upon his name.'
Malachi 3:16
SUGGESTED FURTHER READING: Ephesians 4:1–16

To those who are stronger and more established: you remember the time when the conversation of the people of God was exceedingly helpful to you, and you were glad to be admitted among them. If you think you can do without it now, yet remember there are some at this time in the same state as you were then. Should not then a remembrance of your own case awaken your compassion and diligence to seek out and assist others? Again, when you used to have free communion with another, was it not good? Have you not often met a blessing and a comfort? Have not your minds been composed and refreshed and strengthened for every service you were called to? Why then is the habit discontinued? Why do any of you live alone, and to yourselves? Have you forgot that you are members one of another, and that you are not your own? Do you plead business and families? These things are to be attended to, but perhaps you had such engagements in times past and you did not neglect them, though you could find time to speak often one to another. If these are your hindrances it argues that all is not right. A ready and willing heart will find times and seasons and be content to suffer some inconveniencies for the sake of speaking often one to another. Take heed lest dryness and leanness insensibly steal upon your souls. What, shall it be said that the Lord hearkens and hears with pleasure, that he writes our conferences in his book? Has he given us so many causes to speak of his goodness and exhorted and charged us to watch over one another in love, and shall we like men in a storm shift each for ourselves, think we need no assistance from our brethren, or express no desire to be helpful to our faith? I hope this will not be the case. Away with our sinful backwardness and selfish excuses and let us join heart and hand; let us speak one to another— we have enough to talk of.

FOR MEDITATION: Let us exhort one another today, while it is called today, lest any of us be hardened through the deceitfulness of sin [Hebrews 3:13].

SERMON: MALACHI 3:16–17 [5/5]

A momentary glimpse within the veil

'And it came to pass, as they departed from him, Peter said unto Jesus, Master, it is good for us to be here: and let us make three tabernacles; one for thee, and one for Moses, and one for Elias: not knowing what he said. While he thus spake, there came a cloud, and overshadowed them: and they feared as they entered into the cloud.' Luke 9:33–34
SUGGESTED FURTHER READING: Acts 1:1–11

Peter and his companions awoke from their sleep but just in time to be eye-witnesses of their Lord's glory and of the appearance of Moses and Elias. They were about to depart when he cried out, being struck with what he saw. He cried out, *It is good to be here.* Presently after, the whole was withdrawn. Some of the Lord's people have been witnesses to happy moments when the veil seemed to be removing and they were upon the point, as it were, of getting a sight of things invisible, but they have hardly had time to recollect themselves and raise their expectations, before a cloud comes between and they are left at their former distance, convinced indeed that there were great realities, ready open to their view, but unable to recollect even to their own apprehensions what that wonderful impression was which so affected them. Something like this was the experience of the disciples; they were beginning to rejoice in what they saw, when *a cloud overshadowed them* and turned their joy into *fear.*

FOR MEDITATION:

A glance from heaven, with sweet effect,
Sometimes my pensive spirit cheers;
But, ere I can my thoughts collect,
As suddenly it disappears.
So lightning in the gloom of night,
Affords a momentary day;
Disclosing objects full in sight,
Which soon as seen, are snatched away.
But shall I murmur at relief?
Though short, it was a precious view;
Sent to control my unbelief,
And prove that what I read is true.

The lightning's flash did not create
The opening prospect it revealed;
But only showed the real state
Of what the darkness had concealed.
Just so, we by a glimpse discern
The glorious things within the veil;
That when in darkness, we may learn
To live by faith, till light prevail.
The LORD's great day will soon advance,
Dispersing all the shades of night;
Then we no more shall need a glance,
But see by an eternal Light.[309]

Under a cloud

'While he thus spake, there came a cloud, and overshadowed them: and they feared as they entered into the cloud.' Luke 9:34
SUGGESTED FURTHER READING: Exodus 20:18–21; Hebrews 12:18–24

There came a cloud and overshadowed them. Matthew [17:5] calls it *a bright cloud.* It was a token of God's presence and favour, as when the cloud filled the tabernacle [Exodus 24:16; 40:34]. It was not filled with blackness, darkness and tempest, like that from which the Lord spoke from Sinai, when he would impress Israel with the awe of his holy majesty and law, but suited to the voice which soon proceeded from it, bearing testimony to Jesus and his acceptance of sinners in the beloved. Consider the difference of these clouds out of which God spoke at different times to men: they are emblems of the different spirit of the law and the gospel. When the Lord first speaks to the sinner's conscience to convince him of his lost estate, it is as if he was brought to the foot of Mount Sinai; he speaks in thunder, his majesty is awful and terrible, and the poor worm trembles before him. But when he speaks peace by the blood of Jesus, though the majesty and authority are the same, and produces a holy awe and reverence upon the spirit, it is different from the former—light and comfort and peace by the voice which directs and enables the soul to fix by faith upon Jesus, the Beloved, in whom the Father is well pleased. Yet still it was a cloud, though a bright one. In all divine communications in this mortal state, the Lord, who knows our frame, softens his majesty with a cloud. We are not able to bear his presence without the interposition of a cloud.

FOR MEDITATION: I have been praying that tomorrow may be a day of power with you and with us, and with all that love Jesus in sincerity, that we may see his glory and taste his love in the sanctuary... For this I sigh and long, and cry to the Lord to rend the veil of unbelief, scatter the clouds of ignorance and break down the walls which sin is daily building up to hide him from my eyes. I hope I can say, *My soul is athirst for God* [Psalm 42:2], and nothing less than the light of his countenance can satisfy me.[310]

John Newton to Hannah Wilberforce, Saturday 9 June 1770

SERMON SERIES: ON THE TRANSFIGURATION, NO. 8 [2/5], LUKE 9:34

Above the clouds

'*While he thus spake, there came a cloud, and overshadowed them: and they feared as they entered into the cloud.*' Luke 9:34
SUGGESTED FURTHER READING: Revelation 4:1–11

The ordinances and means by which the Lord converses with his people are answerable to this *cloud*. They are bright compared with the dark things of this world, but they are dark and cloudy with respect to that full knowledge and view of his glory which shall shine upon his people when they are permitted to see his face. While in one sense they reveal him to us, in another they hide him from us. They are suited to our present state of weakness and imperfection, but we shall not be quite happy, the desires he has given us will not be perfectly satisfied, till we get above them all. In the meantime we have cause to be thankful:

(i) for the superior light and liberty we enjoy by the gospel above what was vouchsafed to the servants of God under the Old Testament dispensation. They saw our privileges afar off, and would have rejoiced to share in them (Matthew 13:17).

(ii) for the assurances we have that the best we now enjoy is exceedingly short of that full portion reserved for us hereafter. *It doth not yet appear what we shall be* [1 John 3:2]. There is not so much difference between a believer's darkest and brightest hours here, as between his sweetest enjoyments now and the glory that awaits him hereafter.

FOR MEDITATION: Mr Cowper was afflicted with what is called a nervous complaint to such a degree as might justly be called insanity. I have had hopes the Lord would remove his malady a little time before his death, but it continued. The last twelve hours of his life … he lay in a state of apparent insensibility. But I seem to think that while the curtains were taking [being taken] down in the tabernacle [of his body that was] removing,[311] glory broke in upon his soul. The Lord had set his seal upon him and though he had not seen him he had grace to love him. He was one of those who came out of great tribulation. He suffered much here for twenty-seven years, but eternity is long enough to make amends for all. For what is all he endured in this life, when compared with that rest which remaineth for the children of God?[312]
John Newton's Funeral Sermon for William Cowper, May 1800

Reverence and humility before God

'While he thus spake, there came a cloud, and overshadowed them: and they feared as they entered into the cloud.' Luke 9:34
SUGGESTED FURTHER READING: Job 42:1–6

The disciples *feared as they entered the cloud.* From hence I would take occasion to observe that the manifestations of the Lord's presence have a tendency to humble and abase the Lord's people, to convince them of their nothingness and unworthiness before him, and at the same time that they are comforted with a sense of his love, they are awed with the consideration of his glorious majesty. By this you may try your spirits. There is a confidence and liberty promised in the gospel—they who have access to God by Christ may come with boldness, they may draw near as children to a father, they may use a holy importunity in prayer—yet when faith is indeed in lively exercise and this liberty is most improved, there will be likewise great reverence and humiliation before God. When God dealt familiarly with Abraham and conversed with him as a friend, Abraham fell on his face before him. When the Lord appeared to vindicate Job and to comfort him after his sorrows, he abhorred himself in dust and ashes. That we can often approach the Most High God with a kind of indifference, as if it were a thing of course, is a proof rather of the hardness of our hearts, than of the strength of our faith. The angels are represented as hiding their faces before him—with what humility then should we poor, sinful dust and ashes take his holy name upon our polluted lips!

FOR MEDITATION: Give me a humbling sense of my sins, give me a humbling view of thy glory, give me a humbling taste of thy love, for surely nothing humbles like these. All my pride springs from ignorance. Grant me to know myself, to know thee, to know my relation to thee, and my dependence upon thee, my unprofitableness and insufficiency before thee; and the extent and importance of the mercies I continually receive from thee.[313]

Miscellaneous Thoughts, 1758

True comforts have a humbling nature

'*While he thus spake, there came a cloud, and overshadowed them: and they feared as they entered into the cloud.*' Luke 9:34
SUGGESTED FURTHER READING: Isaiah 6:1–7

By this you may try your comforts. Many sincere souls are fearful lest their spiritual comforts are not of the right kind. Such fears are often the fruit of unbelief. Yet it is a good sign to be cautious and unwilling to be deceived. There are such things as false comforts. One of the best marks of the true, is that they are of a humbling nature and tend to fill our hearts with a fear and reverence of the great God from whom they proceed. If people talk of the Lord's presence and display a light, trifling, self-confident and careless disposition of spirit, I confess I do not understand them. The stony-ground hearers had a joy [Mark 4:5], but it was not of the right sort; it was not accompanied with gracious fruits and soon came to nothing. But if when you have most comfort, the sense of your sin is lively and your heart is led to bemoan and abase yourself before the Lord and to rejoice only in Christ, then you need not fear. What thus leads us to him undoubtedly comes from him.

FOR MEDITATION: Since there was so wonderful, so precious and expensive atonement for sin provided by God, it follows that there can be no other, no more cheap or easy way under heaven by which man may be saved: whatever schemes people may propose to themselves, it will appear at length that all who refuse to build upon the rock of salvation, Jesus Christ, are only setting up empty notions in express opposition to the work of infinite wisdom: for if any inferior satisfaction could have been sufficient, our blessed Lord would never have been manifested in so extraordinary a manner, and made a spectacle to angels and to men. Lord, impress these thoughts effectually on me. …grant me humility, charity and faith; and enable me carefully to study the pattern thou didst set me upon earth, as the only method by which I can attain the happiness thou reservest in heaven for such as shall approve themselves thy real disciples. Make me rich in good work and poor in spirit, and whatever blessings or attainments thou bestowest on me, give me grace therewith to subscribe myself *less than the least of all thy mercies.*[314]

Diary, 1 February 1752

SERMON SERIES: ON THE TRANSFIGURATION, NO. 8 [5/5], LUKE 9:34

A precious promise

'Fear thou not; for I am with thee: be not dismayed; for I am thy God: I will strengthen thee; yea, I will help thee; yea, I will uphold thee with the right hand of my righteousness.' Isaiah 41:10
SUGGESTED FURTHER READING: Isaiah 41:8–20

This precious promise has been a fountain of consolation to the people of God at all times, and it is as full as ever, as necessary, as suitable, as sure to us, as it has been to others. May the Lord open it at this time, and satisfy every weary soul with his goodness. Let us enquire to whom it is made. The promise is made to Jacob, or Israel, the Lord's chosen (verse 8). We may understand it in a literal and confined sense—to the nation of Israel. That though they were brought low and had many enemies, yet they should not be overpowered, for the Lord would plead their cause and provide their deliverance. The great promises which chiefly respected gospel times and spiritual things were usually made in such a manner as to afford some comfort to hope to the people under their present distresses. But though it might have this meaning, this was far from being the whole or the chief. We may understand it as a covenant promise to the Mediator that he should be successful in the work of redemption against all obstacles. Though he was Lord of all, for us he humbled himself to the form of a servant, and as such he is in many places encouraged and strengthened by the promises of his God and Father. The intimate and near relation between the Lord Jesus and his people is such that many things said of him are applicable to them likewise. He is pleased to take their name of Jacob, and to allow them a part of his (1 Corinthians 12:12). In this sense I shall consider it: as a promise to the church of God in general, and consequently to each particular believer, to every soul that like Jacob is wrestling for the blessing of the new name.

FOR MEDITATION:

Of thy goodness of old when I read,	Thine arm is not shortened since then,
To those who were sinners like me,	And those who believe in thy name,
Why may I not wrestle and plead,	Ever find thou art Yea, and Amen,
With them a partaker to be?	Through all generations the same.[315]

When it comes to a pinch

'Fear thou not; for I am with thee: be not dismayed; for I am thy God: I will strengthen thee; yea, I will help thee; yea, I will uphold thee with the right hand of my righteousness.' Isaiah 41:10
SUGGESTED FURTHER READING: 2 Chronicles 20:1–17

This promise supposes that the people of God are subject to fears, or the admonition, *Fear not,* would be in vain. Their fears are many and often great, and indeed if the Lord did not interpose with his promises, would be very just likewise.

(i) For a season they are under legal fear of God (Job 23:15 [*Therefore am I troubled at his presence: when I consider, I am afraid of him*]).

(ii) They are afraid of their own hearts when they look within. They are amazed, and disheartened, and ready to say, 'Alas, this vile nature will be too hard for me at last.'

(iii) They are afraid of outward enemies: the world and Satan. Sometimes the world's frowns make them afraid; and they no less fear its smiles—they see it has prevailed over many and they fear for themselves. They are afraid of Satan. They know he is strong, cunning, watchful. He eyes them close, assaults them often, and they escape not always without a wound.

The promise supposes that they have no ability of their own, thus they feel and readily acknowledge, as Jehoshaphat in 2 Chronicles 20:12. And though they profess and desire to trust the Lord, yet when it comes to a pinch they find it not easy to keep their hold.

It supposes that those who have God on their side have no just cause for fear, be their discouragements or difficulties ever so many or great (Romans 8:31 [*What shall we then say ...? If God be for us, who can be against us?*]).

FOR MEDITATION:

Why should I fear the darkest hour,	Though sin would fill me with distress,
Or tremble at the tempter's power?	The throne of grace I dare address;
JESUS vouchsafes to be my tower.	For JESUS is my righteousness.

Against me earth and hell combine;
But on my side is power divine;
JESUS is all, and He is mine.[316]

Weakness no obstacle

'*Fear thou not; for I am with thee: be not dismayed; for I am thy God: I will strengthen thee; yea, I will help thee; yea, I will uphold thee with the right hand of my righteousness.*' Isaiah 41:10
SUGGESTED FURTHER READING: 2 Kings 6:8–23

The contents of this promise are fully answerable to all our fears, needs and distresses. 'Poor fearing soul,' the Lord says, '*Fear not. I am with thee.*' When Elisha's servant saw the chariots of fire, he thought himself safe, though surrounded with an army. But here is more: Psalm 27:3 [*Though an host should encamp against me, my heart shall not fear: though war should rise against me, in this will I be confident*]. He is not with you only in a way of common providence, but in a way of covenant mercy and special grace. *I am thy God.* If so, you are his people, and of such he has said in Zechariah 2:8, … *he that toucheth you toucheth the apple of his eye.*

Are you weak? He says, *I will strengthen you.* But his strength is made perfect in weakness. Say therefore with Paul, [*…for when I am weak, then am I strong*] (2 Corinthians 12:9–10). See the chapter before my text, verse 29 [*He giveth power to the faint; and to them that have no might he increaseth strength*]. Consider how weak others have been, and yet how strong the Lord has made them—Abraham, Peter.

To John Ryland, 13 March 1782:
Such of your trials as cannot be entrusted to paper I will not charge myself with… However, I am persuaded that the known and unknown, what you can write and what you could only whisper, taken all together shall not overwhelm you. Thy God whom thou servest continually is able to deliver you. Cheer up. The skill of the pilot is best evidenced in a storm—so is the Lord's wisdom and faithfulness towards his children, and so is the sincerity of their hearts towards him.³¹⁷

FOR MEDITATION:

In themselves as weak as worms,
How can poor believers stand;
When temptations, foes and storms,
Press them close on every hand?

Weak, indeed, they feel they are,
But they know the throne of grace;
And the GOD, who answers prayer,
Helps them when they seek his face.³¹⁸

SERMON: ISAIAH 41:10 [3/5]

Strengthened and upheld

'Fear thou not; for I am with thee: be not dismayed; for I am thy God: I will strengthen thee; yea, I will help thee; yea, I will uphold thee with the right hand of my righteousness.' Isaiah 41:10
SUGGESTED FURTHER READING: Haggai 2:1–9

Are you discouraged with the great difficulties of your Christian calling? See what the Lord says—*I will bless thee.* Though you can do nothing, yet if he helps, works in you and by you, you shall both do great things and also shall prevail. Are you afraid you shall not endure but give up at last? How can that be when the Lord has said, *I will uphold thee?* Sooner the stars shall fall to the earth, than you fall from your Christian course, if the Lord vouchsafes to uphold you. Farther, take notice of the manner in which the Lord strengthens, helps, upholds:

(i) *with the right arm.* This implies power (Psalm 89:13) and tenderness (Hosea 11:3; Deuteronomy 33).

(ii) *of my righteousness.* This shows the sure ground whereon our hopes are built. The righteousness of Christ as Mediator is the fountain of all our strength, sufficiency and comfort. So long as he continues the Righteous One, so long as his obedience unto death comes in remembrance, so long all these benefits shall be made over and continued to his people. It shows that his faithfulness and truth are engaged to make these things good to waiting souls. The word is gone out of his lips and his righteousness is bound for the performance.

FOR MEDITATION: This evening I preached a funeral sermon for my dearest earthly comfort,[319] who was removed (I trust) to a better world, on the 15th inst., from Habakkuk 3:17–18. How can I sufficiently praise thee for the supports thou hast in mercy afforded me through the course of this long trial, so painful at times to the feelings of the flesh! Blessed be thy name, that I can now say from my heart, *Thy will be done.* My times and all my concerns are in thy hands. There I desire cheerfully to leave them. I would not form a wish, but to be and to do as thou wouldst have me.[320]

Diary, Sunday 26 December 1790
[Newton's wife died on 15 December 1790]

SERMON: ISAIAH 41:10 [4/5]

Receive his help by grace alone

'Fear thou not; for I am with thee: be not dismayed; for I am thy God: I will strengthen thee; yea, I will help thee; yea, I will uphold thee with the right hand of my righteousness.' Isaiah 41:10
SUGGESTED FURTHER READING: Isaiah 30:15–21

Are some saying, 'These are good things indeed, but I fear not for me.' Why not? Where are you excepted? They are for you, if you truly desire them and will be content to receive them of grace, without money or price. They are freely given but cannot be bought. Do not expect that you must do a great deal for yourself, and that then the Lord will make up the rest. It is his own work and he will not suffer you to share the glory. But remember, none have a right to apply it who do not feel themselves empty, poor, blind and naked. Take notice it is not your holding with the truth and assenting to what others say, will make you a believer. There are some who will think well of themselves and when they hear of the troubles and fears of exercised souls are ready to say, 'I pity them, poor things, but for my part I dare not distrust the Lord'—when yet they never knew what it was to trust him. They affect to talk like the Lord's people, but every word betrays their ignorance. To such the Lord's word is not, *Fear not*, but, *Take heed lest you are deceived* [Luke 21:8]. Examine, there are many false pretenders—you are healed before you are wounded, lifted up before you ever were cast down—you talk of being filled when you have never been emptied. This is not the Lord's methods.

FOR MEDITATION: I know that I cannot make you truly religious, nor can you make yourself so. It is the Lord's work, and I am daily praying to him to bless you indeed. But he has a time; till then, I hope you will wait upon him according to your light, in the use of appointed means. I do not wish you to affect more of religion in your appearance than you are really conscious of. There is some danger of this in a family where a religious profession is befriended. Young people are apt to imitate those about them and sometimes (which is abominable) to put on a show of religion in order to please, though their hearts have no concern in it. I have a good hope that the Lord will teach you and guide you, and that the many prayers and praises I have offered on your behalf will not be lost.[321]

John Newton to his niece, Betsy Catlett, 17 October [1781?]

SERMON: ISAIAH 41:10 [5/5]

Precious is the death of his saints

'And Jacob called unto his sons and said, Gather yourselves together, that I may tell you that which shall befall you in the last days.' Genesis 49:1
SUGGESTED FURTHER READING: Genesis 48:1–49:2

Precious in the sight of the Lord is the death of his saints; the season and every circumstance is under the appointment of his wisdom and love. Our times are in his hands and to him we may cheerfully refer them. Some have an early dismission and perhaps are suddenly called away. These escape many a trouble and pain, and when the state is safe, and we are firmly assured of his interest in the covenant, we might be ready to say, if we think only of ourselves, 'May this be my lot'. But they likewise are highly honoured, who, after having borne testimony to the goodness and faithfulness of God in the sense of a long life, are enabled to administer to the edification and comfort of others in their dying moments. The sun in his noonday height does not behold a more glorious spectacle than that of an aged believer, strengthened in the close of life to declare his own full assurance of faith, and, under the influence of the Holy Spirit, advising and blessing his family and surrounding friends, and commending them with his latest breath to the care and keeping of his God and their God—which was good old Jacob's deathbed scene. In the presence of his children and dependants he expressed the confidence with which he waited for the Lord's salvation. And being endued not only with the Spirit of grace but of prophecy, he delivered in a few comprehensive words the future history of the twelve tribes.

FOR MEDITATION: Mr Webb³²³ is gone—fully ripe I doubt not, like a shock of corn in due season. I knew him chiefly as a Christian; as such I thought him eminent, solid, humble, spiritual, peaceful in himself, and of course a friend of peace. Grace reigned in his heart, and out of the abundance of his heart his mouth spoke. In his last illness he did not speak of any remarkable consolations, but expressed an edifying, encouraging example of a calm, unshaken confidence in Jesus Christ crucified, as the alone and sufficient ground of his hope. I have lost for a season a valuable friend, but I hope by and by to see him again. Blessed are the dead who die thus in the Lord, they rest from their labours and conflicts, and are now before the throne.³²⁴

SERMON: GENESIS 49:10–12 [1/3] [ALSO PREACHED CHRISTMAS 1780]

Till Shiloh come

'The sceptre shall not depart from Judah, nor a lawgiver from between his feet, until Shiloh come; and unto him shall the gathering of the people be. Binding his foal unto the vine, and his ass's colt unto the choice vine; he washed his garments in wine, and his clothes in the blood of grapes: His eyes shall be red with wine, and his teeth white with milk.'
Genesis 49:10–12
SUGGESTED FURTHER READING: Genesis 49:8–12

Among Jacob's dying words, the prophecy concerning *Judah* is the most eminent. The victories and the blessings of this tribe, as well as its perpetuity, are all applicable to the person here spoken of—who is the Messiah, the Lord Christ. The land of Judah was to be, and so it proved, fruitful in *wine* and *milk*, under which emblems the abundance of gospel blessings is set forth by the prophet Isaiah in chapter 55 [verse 1]. The time of his [Messiah's] appearance is marked out by the *Sceptre*, or, as the word signifies, the tribeship. Judah was a distinct tribe and had the government—till he appeared. Then, or very soon after, they were destroyed out of their land, and their genealogies were lost, so that none of the Jews at present or for many ages past, have been able to prove their descent from any particular tribe.

To him shall the gathering of the people be. This clause is expounded by John's exposition of what Caiaphas unwittingly delivered (John 11:52 [*And not for that nation only, but that also he should gather together in one the children of God that were scattered abroad*]). *The people* whom God had chosen for himself were not confined to the Jewish nation but dispersed; by the preaching of the gospel revealing his love, they should be called out of ignorance. Note he is *the desire of all nations.* Some of all people and languages, when they hear of him and feel their need of a Saviour, shall be enabled to look to him and put their trust in his name, renouncing every other (see Isaiah 45:14). Note also the efficacy of his love and grace: they shall not be overlooked or disappointed. Whatever difficulties are in the way, they shall be surely gathered unto him, and not one of them lost.

FOR MEDITATION: 'And one of the elders saith unto me, Weep not: behold, the Lion of the tribe of Judah, the Root of David, hath prevailed to open the book, and to loose the seven seals thereof' (Revelation 5:5).

SERMON: GENESIS 49:10–12 [2/3] [ALSO PREACHED CHRISTMAS 1780]

Our Deliverer

'*The sceptre shall not depart from Judah, nor a lawgiver from between his feet, until Shiloh come …*' Genesis 49:10
SUGGESTED FURTHER READING: Psalm 72:1–20

To apply the passage to ourselves, I shall speak a little concerning this name of the Redeemer, *Shiloh*. Many of the Hebrew words have various significations. So has this, and it will bear different translations that are applicable to Christ. And to help you judge for yourselves, I shall mention some suitable passages where the root occurs. The root signifies 'to loose' as in Exodus 3^{325} and may be taken more generally to release from any bond or confinement. Thus *Shiloh* signifies the Deliverer, he who was anointed with power and authority to break open the prison doors and set the prisoners free—to take the prey from the hand of the mighty and to deliver the lawful captive. It denotes a state of prosperity and success. Thus it is used, in Job 12, of the prosperity of the wicked. And the same word occurs in Psalm 122:6–7. Thus it is applicable to Christ in two senses:

(i) to intimate the success and prosperity of his undertakings on behalf of his people. He not only fought but conquered for them, and subdued his and their enemies under his feet, and now he reigns in peace.

(ii) He is the giver and author of peace, prosperity and success to his people. Happy and glorious is the change, when they are freed from the dominion of Satan, and translated under his mild and gracious government. From him they derive all comfort, and by his power they are made more than conquerors.

Believers, fix the eyes of your faith upon this glorious *Shiloh*.

FOR MEDITATION:

Fervent persevering prayers
Are faith's assured resource,
Brazen gates, and iron bars,
In vain withstand their force:

Glad the summons they obey,
And liberty desire;
Straight their fetters melt away,
Like wax before the fire:

He can break through walls of stone,
Sink the mountain to a plain;
They, to whom his name is known;
Can never pray in vain.

By the word of him who died,
Guilty prisoners to release;
Every door flies open wide,
And they depart in peace.[326]

SERMON: GENESIS 49:10–12 [3/3] [ALSO PREACHED CHRISTMAS 1780]

The coming of Christ

'The Son of man is come to seek and to save that which was lost.' Luke 19:10
SUGGESTED FURTHER READING: Matthew 9:9–13

Attentive observers of divine providence may often remark that very great events often arise from small and unthought-of occasions. What an important moment, when a soul is first converted to God. What a change then takes place, yet how suddenly, and as it were accidentally, is it brought about. We have here an occasion which has been often made successful—curiosity. Zacchaeus did not press through the multitude to Jesus; he only wanted to see him from the top of a tree as he passed by. But behold Jesus, whom he thought a stranger, looked up and called him by his name—divine power accompanies the word, grace reached his heart, and that day salvation came to his house. O that it may be so with some present. Our Lord was often reproached by the blind Pharisees for the mercy he showed to the unworthy, and probably upon this occasion, as the publicans, or tax gatherers, of whom Zacchaeus was a chief, were the objects of their scorn and hatred. It was perhaps to prevent or answer their usual objections that he intimates how agreeable his conduct to Zacchaeus was to his own character and the great design of his coming into the world, which was not to call the righteous, but sinners, to repentance—to seek and to save that which was lost.

FOR MEDITATION:

Zacchaeus climbed the tree,
And thought himself unknown;
But how surprised was he
When JESUS called him down!
The LORD beheld him, though concealed,
And by a word his power revealed.

His long forgotten faults
Are brought again in view,
And all his secret thoughts
Revealed in public too:
Though compassed with a crowd about,
The searching word has found him out.

'Tis curiosity
Oft brings them in the way,
Only the man to see,
And hear what he can say;
But how the sinner starts to find
The preacher knows his inmost mind.

While thus distressing pain
And sorrow fills his heart,
He hears a voice again,
That bids his fears depart:
Then like Zacchaeus he is blest,
And JESUS deigns to be his guest.[327]

SERMON: LUKE 19:10 [1/5]

Lost

'For the Son of man is come to seek and to save that which was lost.'
Luke 19:10
SUGGESTED FURTHER READING: Matthew 1:18–21

The return of this day has by long custom been observed as a commemoration of the coming of Christ in the flesh. But how is it observed by many—alas, as a time of riot and folly for the indulgement of those sins and follies, those works of the devil, which Christ was manifest to destroy— a little lip service and outward attendance at church and the rest of the day and many following days (which instead of holidays might rather be called sinning days) spent in dissipation. So I fear it is with many here and perhaps you are waiting to close this very evening as you might do if you thought, or were sure, that Christ came into the world to procure you a liberty of sinning without control. The Lord give you a better understanding of my text before you go from hence.

The state of mankind, which moved the pity of Jesus to come that he might seek and save them, is expressed fully and briefly by *that which was lost*—which may be considered either as a thing is lost, when the rightful proprietor is deprived of it, or as a person is said to be lost, when he is in a miserable, hopeless, state, so as to be beyond all ordinary means of assistance and recovery. Thus sinners are lost to God and lost in themselves.

FOR MEDITATION: Thus I was as miserable on all hands as could well be imagined. My breast was filled with the most excruciating passions; eager desire, bitter rage, and black despair … no hope of relief or mitigation; no friend to take my part, or to listen to my complaint: Whether I looked inward or outward, I could perceive nothing but darkness and misery. I was tempted to throw myself into the sea, which would put a period to all my sorrows at once. But the secret hand of God restrained me. Help me to praise him, dear Sir, for his wonderful goodness to the most unworthy of all his creatures.[328]   *Narrative*, April 1745

Jesus my Saviour, who has redeemed my lost title to the good things of both worlds.[329]

John Newton to David Jennings, 29 August 1752

SERMON: LUKE 19:10 [2/5]

Lost to God

'For the Son of man is come to seek and to save that which was lost.'
Luke 19:10
SUGGESTED FURTHER READING: Isaiah 1:2–8

A sinner may be described as *lost* to God. He made us and he made us for himself, for his own service, for his own glory, to know, love and honour him. But as it was said of the prodigal, *this my son was lost* [Luke 15:24], so God has lost the reverence, obedience and dependence due to him from his creatures. Speaking after the manner of men he expresses concern, and, as it were, disappointment upon this account (Isaiah 1:2 and 5:4). *In him we live and move and have our being* [Acts 17:28]. He gives us life and breath and all things, rain and fruitful seasons—a boundless capacity and an immortal duration. But what are the returns? How totally are we all lost to him by nature, and how totally are some of you lost to him still. May he give you to know it—instead of reverence, contempt and blasphemy. See how it is with angels and glorified spirits (Isaiah 6). But how is it upon earth? Ah, how is the holy arm of God profaned, his worship neglected. Instead of dependence upon him, self reigns in every heart. We trust in our own strength and live to our own ends (Daniel 5:23). Instead of obedience, the sinner has broken the bonds of God and cast off his yoke behind him. Which of his holy commandments is not transgressed wilfully, habitually, openly, without control and without remorse—as if it was, as indeed it is, a very principle of our vile nature to set our Maker at defiance? Consider each of you what part you have in these charges.

FOR MEDITATION:

The thief who near the Saviour hung
(In death, how happy he!)
Was answered when his dying tongue
Said, 'LORD remember me.'

I take my pattern from the thief,
I have no other plea;
For I of sinners am the chief,
Then LORD remember me.

My sins are not less black than those
Which brought him to the tree:
No thought can give my heart repose,
But LORD remember me.

The Lamb upon his glorious throne
As newly slain I see,
And trust he will not those disown
Who plead, 'remember me'.[330]

SERMON: LUKE 19:10 [3/5]

Lost in ourselves

'For the Son of man is come to seek and to save that which was lost.'
Luke 19:10
SUGGESTED FURTHER READING: Luke 15:1–32

If man is *lost* to God, is he not *lost* in himself also? Yes, he that sinneth against God wrongeth his own soul. The utmost meaning of the word *lost* in a worldly sense, falls far short of its meaning here. O think what you have lost and how are lost, if Christ has not saved you and repaired your breaches.

You have lost the image of God—all spiritual knowledge of righteousness and true holiness. This loss perhaps does not affect you—the loss of health or money would trouble you more, but it will not be always thus. If you do not lay it to heart sooner, you will at least in that solemn hour when you render up your soul to God.

You have lost his favour and communion. Do you pity a blind man? You have lost the eyes of your soul. Would you pity a man banished from all that comfort and do him good? While you remain in your natural state, you are in the case of Cain, driven from the presence of the Lord. Ah, poor blind, banished, wanderers, where can you go for good, if he that has made you will have no mercy upon you, if he that formed you will show you no favour? But still more:

You are lost under his curse—you are not only excluded from his presence, but exposed to his wrath. You hear not from him now, only in his ordinances and providences, but ere long you must see him face to face. He will reprove you and set your sins in order before your eyes. Think of that dreadful sentence (2 Thessalonians 1:9). Thus we are utterly lost except Christ seeks and saves us.

FOR MEDITATION:

Thou didst once a wretch behold,	Once a sinner near despair,
In rebellion blindly bold;	Sought thy mercy-seat by prayer;
Scorn thy grace, thy power defy,	Mercy heard and set him free,
That poor rebel, LORD, was I.	LORD, that mercy came to me.[331]

To seek and to save

'For the Son of man is come to seek and to save that which was lost.'
Luke 19:10
SUGGESTED FURTHER READING: Psalm 80:1–19

He came *to seek and to save*—to restore man to God and to restore life and peace and happiness to man. This magnifies his grace. He did not come to save those who, sensible from their misery, were imploring his compassion, but he must *seek* them as well as *save* them. It magnifies his power. Had not this ruin been under [his] hand, we must have been lost for ever. For none less than Almighty could save us. Nor could he save by speaking; it was necessary he should *come*, that is, take our nature upon him, take our sin upon him and stand in our place for obedience and atonement. He came for these purposes and he effectually fulfilled them. Thus he saves by price and redemption. Farther, he saves by power—this is the *seeking* spoke of. They are insensible of his love and their own misery—in seeking he employs his providence, Word, ordinances and Spirit. May I not hope that he has come thus here to seek and to save some of you tonight? When he saves, he saves completely, he removes the curse, restores access and power with God, renews the divine image upon the soul, and thus reclaims the rebel and teaches him to reverence, love and serve the God of his life.

The Lord is now seeking. O may you be willing to be found of him, or else you are lost for ever. And let those whom he has redeemed out of the hand of the enemy, praise and magnify his name and renew their engagements in his strength to serve him and walk before him in holy obedience all their days.

FOR MEDITATION:

Sinner, hear the Saviour's call,
He now is passing by;
He has seen thy grievous thrall,
And heard thy mournful cry.
He has pardons to impart,
Grace to save thee from thy fears,
See the love that fills his heart,
And wipe away thy tears.

Raise thy downcast eyes, and see
What throngs his throne surround!
These, though sinners once like thee,
Have full salvation found:
Yield not then to unbelief!
While he says, 'There yet is room;'
Though of sinners thou art chief,
Since JESUS calls thee, come.[332]

The God-Man … all in all

'And a man shall be as an hiding place from the wind, and a covert from the tempest; as rivers of water in a dry place, as the shadow of a great rock in a weary land.' Isaiah 32:2

SUGGESTED FURTHER READING: John 1:9–18

Nothing raises the wonder and disgust of the world more than the high regard believers pay to the Lord Jesus. If they would only speak seriously of God, his goodness and providence, they might be borne with—but so much of Christ is offensive. Those who know him, however, will never think they can say enough of him, and they have good reasons the others cannot understand them: what he is in himself and what he is and will be to them. With regard to the latter we have a comprehensive description in this verse, which speaks at once the dangers and difficulties in the believer's path, and the security he enjoys in the Redeemer. The person to whom these great and gracious properties are applied is called *a man*—and this is our comfort that our Redeemer is our 'Goel',[333] our near kinsman—he took upon him our flesh and blood and was made man. But was he not more than man, who could venture upon him for these great purposes? We may read it *the Man*—here we may be sure it means the God-Man—the Man that is God's fellow—the Word who was made flesh—and who in the nature wherein he suffered, now reigns over heaven and earth. You that are desirous to escape this evil world, see what lies before you—here is winds and floods, a barren wilderness and a burning sun. Be prepared, but be not discouraged, for here is a hiding place where you shall be safe. Here is a river of life to cheer you when all within and without is dry. And here is a shadow through which the heat cannot pierce to hurt. In a word—if you seek Jesus you will find him all in all.

FOR MEDITATION: [preached from on Sunday evening, 26 February 1775]

He who on earth as man was known,	His righteousness, to faith revealed,
And bore our sins and pains;	Wrought out for guilty worms,
Now, seated on the eternal throne,	Affords a hiding place and shield,
The GOD of glory reigns.	From enemies and storms.[334]

A hiding place

'And a man shall be as an hiding place from the wind, and a covert from the tempest ...' Isaiah 32:2
SUGGESTED FURTHER READING: Daniel 5: 1–30

Here is a *wind* spoken of and a *hiding place* provided. In fair weather a hiding place is not thought of, but when a storm arises, everyone is glad of a shelter. Sinners are like those servants of Pharaoh, who, when Moses threatened a tempest, made light of it, and even ventured their people and cattle in the fields. The wrath of God is denounced against sin, and yet sinners are secure. But when the Spirit convinces the heart, then all is found true. O when a charge does conviction make, and how welcome would a hiding place be then. This may be compared to a storm of wind for:

(i) suddenness: the storm often rises when little expected. So conviction comes upon a soul unawares. Such was Belshazzar's case [Daniel 5]—and such the jailer's, though a vessel of mercy [Acts 16].

(ii) violence: who can stand before the whirlwind? It is uncomfortable to face a storm, yet when a building is known to be weak, fear forces people into the air lest their shelter should fail and bury them in the ruins. Such is the sinner's case—he had a refuge before the storm came, some good works or good resolutions, but now he dares not trust—the storm forces him out—and though he cannot stand, he cannot flee or hide.

(iii) The wind is searching: it will find its way, as we say, through a crevice. So is the wind of the Spirit—it pierces the inner man, it reaches to the remembrance of past and long-forgotten sins. It lays open the soul.

(iv) The wind cannot be stopped or moderated by all the art or power of man. It will blow where it listeth.

FOR MEDITATION: [for the Fast Day 10 February 1779]

Happy they, who love his name!	Hark! his voice in accents mild,
They shall always find him near;	(Oh, how comforting and sweet!)
Though the earth were wrapped in flame,	Speaks to every humble child,
They have no just cause for fear.	Pointing out a sure retreat.[335]

Placed out of danger

'And a man shall be as an hiding place from the wind, and a covert from the tempest ...' Isaiah 32:2
SUGGESTED FURTHER READING: Isaiah 53:1–12

Am I speaking to some that are now in the storm? Behold—*a hiding place.* Look to the Man in my text, flee to him and you shall be safe. Faith in his name shall place you out of danger, and as faith grows, you shall be out of fear likewise. O flee for refuge to the hope set before you. Dreadful as this storm sounds in the sinner's ears, it is indeed a merciful dispensation, sent to urge him to flee to the ark before a more dreadful storm comes. Consider the person of Christ—how great and how near—as God and man (John 1:1, 14). Think of the storm he endured for our sakes (Matthew 26:36–46, Gethsemane). His office in heaven is to present and plead his own blood and righteousness for us (Romans 3:25) and to receive and dispense pardon, peace and grace and eternal life (Revelation 5:1–14). Remember his promises—and these are absolute without exception (John 10:28).

Let others remember there is a storm of unmixed wrath in reserve for those who refuse this salvation (Jeremiah 23:19).

FOR MEDITATION:

Incarnate GOD! the soul that knows
Thy name's mysterious power
Shall dwell in undisturbed repose,
Nor fear the trying hour.

In vain the fowler spreads his net,
To draw them from thy care;
Thy timely call instructs their feet,
To shun the artful snare.

Thy wisdom, faithfulness and love,
To feeble helpless worms;
A buckler and a refuge prove,
From enemies and storms.

No midnight terrors haunt their bed,
No arrow wounds by day;
Unhurt on serpents they shall tread,
If found in duty's way.[336]

Urge the testimonies of Scripture

'And as they came down from the mountain, Jesus charged them, saying, Tell the vision to no man, until the Son of man be risen again from the dead.' Matthew 17:9

SUGGESTED FURTHER READING: 1 Corinthians 2:1–16

The account of the Transfiguration closes with the former verse [*And when they had lifted up their eyes, they saw no man, save Jesus only*]. But this verse seems to belong to the subject, and I shall employ our present opportunity in some observations upon it. It contains an injunction of secrecy for a limited time, after which they were freely to declare what they had seen. May we humbly enquire why our Lord was pleased to forbid them to speak of it till he should have risen from the dead? It may afford us some instruction for our own conduct. I conceive there might be several reasons. One reason: on account of the people. They daily saw Jesus conversing among them as a common, yea, as a poor man. The scribes and Pharisees traduced him and treated him as an impostor. Now the doctrine and miracles of our Lord in public were suited to convince the unprejudiced that he was indeed a teacher sent from God—but his transfiguration was a point which, if it had been mentioned, must have depended on the testimony of the three disciples. Who would hardly have been believed [them], when they could only say and not prove! Afterwards, when he had declared his power and glory by rising from the dead, and sent down his Spirit to confirm the words of his servants, the case was different. The disciples might enlarge upon our Lord's public works and urge the testimonies of Scripture concerning him. But they were directed not to take notice of this; having no such proof as the world would call for to offer, their bare assertion of such an extraordinary event might bring their sincerity into suspicion. It seems still a good rule, when conversing with unawakened people with a view to their good, to keep to such things as we can plainly prove from the Scripture. And there may be some kinds of experiences which, for this reason, it would be improper to lay before worldly people, because, not being able to understand them, they would be more prejudiced against anything else we could say.

FOR MEDITATION: '... But to this man will I look, even to him that is poor and of a contrite spirit, and trembleth at my word' (Isaiah 66:2).

Caution in speaking of experiences

'And as they came down from the mountain, he charged them that they should tell no man what things they had seen, till the Son of man were risen from the dead. And they kept that saying with themselves, questioning one with another what the rising from the dead should mean.' Mark 9:9–10
SUGGESTED FURTHER READING: Mark 9:33–37

One reason for secrecy is on account of their fellow disciples, lest they should be grieved and discouraged, as they probably would have been, for they, as well as we, had a mixture of self and were often contending who should be the greatest. I have found such an evil in my heart, that when persons on whom I could depend have been speaking of comforts and manifestations beyond the line of my experience, I have felt for the time an anger and enmity against them, and a repining of spirit against the Lord. Besides, I knew not but they would have absolutely disbelieved the relation. It was perhaps upon one or both these accounts, that when St Paul had been caught up into the third heavens, he kept it a secret in his own breast for fourteen years, and it would probably have died with him, if he had not seen his duty to mention it for the sake of the Corinthians. We have cause to be glad that their conduct made it necessary for him to relate it. From whence I would observe in general that there is a wisdom and caution to be used in speaking of our experiences—perhaps not all things, nor to all persons. We should endeavour to suit what we tell them of ourselves to what we judge is their state and attainment, lest we discourage when we would comfort and offend when we would instruct. So there are depths of Satan in a way of temptation which are not so fit to be told to young converts, unless we know they are led something in the same way.

FOR MEDITATION: 'But take heed lest by any means this liberty of yours become a stumbling block to them that are weak' (1 Corinthians 8:9).

Spiritual pride: fuel to the fire

'*And as they came down from the mountain, he charged them that they should tell no man what things they had seen, till the Son of man were risen from the dead. And they kept that saying with themselves, questioning one with another what the rising from the dead should mean.*' Mark 9:9–10
SUGGESTED FURTHER READING: Acts 8:9–24

There is reason for enjoining secrecy: on their own account. Such a favour as they had lately received was very likely to open a door to spiritual pride, and if they had been suffered to speak of it, it would have been like adding fuel to fire. We know their graces were but weak. Now our Lord, by enjoining them silence, preserved them from a snare. It is right and our duty to declare upon proper occasions and within the bounds of prudence what God has done for our souls, but if he is pleased to lead us in an extraordinary way and to favour us with peculiar comforts, it is not always easy to preserve a right spirit where self is closely concerned.

Diary, 4 August 1789
[birthday and anniversary of dedication to the ministry, 1758]:
Thirty-one years have today elapsed since thou didst draw my heart solemnly to devote myself to thy public service. There was then but little visible probability that such an unworthy creature would ever be employed in thy vineyard. But in thy best times, mountains became plain—the door which to appearance was fast barred and bolted, flew open. Thou hast honoured me. Thou hast given me a tongue and a pen, many friends, hast made me extensively known among thy people, and, I have reason to hope, useful to many by my preaching and writings. *Totum muneris hoc tui est.*338 It is of thine own that I can serve thee. And if others speak well of me, I have no cause to speak well of myself. They see only my outward walk—to thee I appear as I am. In thy sight I am a poor, unworthy, unfaithful, inconsistent creature. There is pride in my humiliation, in my repentance; self in my most spiritual desires—all is wrong, but thou art gracious.339

FOR MEDITATION: 'But Mary kept all these things, and pondered them in her heart' (Luke 2:19).

Under the dispensation of the Spirit

'*And as they came down from the mountain, he charged them that they should tell no man what things they had seen, till the Son of man were risen from the dead. And they kept that saying with themselves, questioning one with another what the rising from the dead should mean.*' Mark 9:9–10
SUGGESTED FURTHER READING: John 16:5–18

The disciples were only restrained till Jesus should rise from the dead. In the meanwhile they understood not what he meant. You see they had an extraordinary privilege upon the mount, above anything that we can expect, and yet, in point of knowledge, they were below the lowest of us. Peter could not bear to hear of Christ's death, and none of them could conceive what was meant by his rising again. But the rising of Christ from the dead was properly the beginning of the gospel kingdom. Then he opened their understandings, gave them his Spirit and commanded them to proclaim, as on the housetops, the things which they had heard in secret. Under this state which was established at his resurrection, we live. Under the dispensation of the Spirit now, all things are made known to us—his transfiguration, his crucifixion, his resurrection, his ascension. What was once hidden from the apostles for a season is made known to us. Say not then, 'Though the love of the world now keeps me from professing the gospel, if I had lived then I should surely have followed Jesus.' If any perish here it will not be for want of evidence. If what you hear and say does not affect you, neither would you be persuaded though one should rise from the dead. Let not the troubled soul say, 'If I could have seen him and been permitted to touch him and cast myself at his feet, surely he would have bid me go in peace; I should have believed.' Nay, indeed you have in some respects greater advantage than those who saw him in the flesh. His Word is himself—when you hear the promises, you hear him speak. He is now in the midst of you. Lift up your heart to him. If his time is come, he will surely give you peace. If not, continue waiting, and you shall surely find. He never bid any seek him in vain.

FOR MEDITATION: 'But when the Comforter is come, whom I will send unto you from the Father, even the Spirit of truth, which proceedeth from the Father, he shall testify of me' (John 15:26).

Foundations under trial

'And a man shall be as an hiding place from the wind, and a covert from the tempest; as rivers of water in a dry place, as the shadow of a great rock in a weary land.' Isaiah 32:2
SUGGESTED FURTHER READING: Mark 4:35–41

If the first clause had stood alone, I might have considered it under many particulars, for, not only the first work of conviction, but many things that follow in a believer's path may be compared to a mighty wind from which they need a strong and safe hiding place and must perish without one. But here are four different views given of this Man, and the benefits derived from him by faith, and we may therefore with more exactness refer some things to one heading and some to another. In the English this seems much the same with the former—*a hiding place from the wind* and *a covert from the storm* are not very different, but there is a difference in the Hebrew. The word signifies properly a flood and is so rendered in 28:2 and Psalm 90:5. The wind tries the strength of the building, the flood tries the foundation, and threatens to sweep all before it. Now when a soul has felt the mighty wind of the Spirit and bows in conviction, and sought and found a hiding place in Jesus, the difficulties are not all over. It is not indeed easy to persuade those who are rejoicing in their first love that they shall ever be otherwise, but experience convinces them.

Believers will know more or less of two floods which, if the Lord permits, will make them cry out for a *refuge* or *covert*: indwelling sin and temptation.

FOR MEDITATION:

When, like a baneful pestilence,
Sin mows its thousands down
On every side, without defence,
Thy grace secures thine own.

The angels' LORD, himself is nigh,
To them that love his name;
Ready to save them when they cry,
And put their foes to shame.

Angels, unseen, attend the saints,
And bear them in their arms;
To cheer the spirit when it faints,
And guard the life from harms.

Crosses and changes are their lot,
Long as they sojourn here;
But since their Saviour changes not,
What have the saints to fear?[340]

A refuge from the floods of sin

'And a man shall be as an hiding place from the wind, and a covert from the tempest; as rivers of water in a dry place, as the shadow of a great rock in a weary land.' Isaiah 32:2
SUGGESTED FURTHER READING: Nahum 1:1–15

The workings and overflowings of indwelling sin may be compared to a flood.

(i) A flood comes upon places that had been dry—where a stranger would not expect it. Frequently the power of divine things is so strong at first that corruption seems dried up—but sin, though kept down, is not slain. When these views abate, it will show itself again.

(ii) A flood is a great quantity. Sin is a great flood. The soul can say as Psalm 40:12 [*For innumerable evils have compassed me about: mine iniquities have taken hold upon me, so that I am not able to look up; they are more than the hairs of mine head: therefore my heart faileth me*].

(iii) A flood is violent. Many know the resemblance here—how long and sore the conflict, and how carried quite off their feet.

FOR MEDITATION:

Though small the drops of falling rain,
If one be singly viewed;
Collected, they o'erspread the plain,
And form a mighty flood.

Thus sinners think their evil deeds,
Like drops of rain, are small;
But it the power of thought exceeds,
To count the sum of all.

The house it meets with in its course,
Should not be built on clay;
Lest, with a resistless force,
It sweep the whole away.

One sin can raise, though small it seems,
A flood to drown the soul;
What then, when countless million streams
Shall join, to swell the whole!

Though for awhile it seemed secure,
It will not bear the shock;
Unless it has foundations sure,
And stands upon a rock.

Yet, while they think the weather fair,
If warned, they smile or frown;
But they will tremble and despair,
When the fierce flood comes down!

Oh! then on JESUS ground your hope, That stone in Zion laid;
Lest your poor building quickly drop, With ruin, on your head.[341]

A refuge from the floods of temptation

'And a man shall be as an hiding place from the wind, and a covert from the tempest; as rivers of water in a dry place, as the shadow of a great rock in a weary land.' Isaiah 32:2
SUGGESTED FURTHER READING: 2 Corinthians 4:1–18

Temptation may be compared to a flood—so it is expressed in Isaiah 57 and 59:19 [*When the enemy shall come in like a flood...*]. Indeed it is by this influence the other flood rises so high. I shall not say much of this. It is not needful to those who have felt it, and would not be well understood by those who do not. But, as by all temptations Satan's aim is to overturn the foundation of faith, they may be compared to a flood. Now in these floods or storms Jesus is a covert or refuge.

With regard to sin: his atonement—there is forgiveness; his intercession (Luke 22:32); his power and promise (Isaiah 41:10).

So against temptation: his experimental sympathy (Hebrews 2:18 and 4:15); his gracious promise (Isaiah 43:2); his engagement to interpose, as set forth (Zechariah 3:2).

You that are setting out—be not secure, be not discouraged. You that have found him faithful—go on trusting him. You shall soon be out of reach of storms and floods. You that know him not are exposed to a flood of wrath.

FOR MEDITATION:

Unless the LORD had been my stay
(With trembling joy my soul may say)
My cruel foe had gained his end:
But he appeared for my relief,
And Satan sees, with shame and grief,
That I have an almighty Friend.

Loud in my ears a charge he read,
(My conscience witnessed all he said)
My long black list of outward sin;
Then bringing forth my heart to view,
Too well what's hidden there he knew,
He showed me ten-times worse within.

O, 'twas a dark and trying hour,
When harassed by the tempter's power,
I felt my strongest hopes decline!
You only who have known his arts,
You only who have felt his darts,
Can pity such a case as mine.

'Tis all too true, my soul replied,
But I remember JESUS died,
And now he fills a throne of grace;
I'll go, as I have done before,
His mercy I may still implore,
I have his promise, 'Seek my face.'[342]

SERMON SERIES: ISAIAH 32:2, NO. 2 [3/3]

Inimitable

'Therefore the Lord himself shall give you a sign; behold a virgin shall conceive, and bear a son, and shall call his name Immanuel.' Isaiah 7:14
SUGGESTED FURTHER READING: Isaiah 55:6–13

The Lord God has impressed a signature upon his works, which evidently distinguishes them from the feeble imitations of men. Not only the splendour of the sun, but the glimmering of the glow-worm proclaims his glory. The structure and growth of a blade of grass are the effects of the same power which produced the fabric of the heavens and the earth. In his Word likewise he is inimitable. He has a style and manner peculiarly his own. What he declares in Isaiah 55 is confirmed by the whole Scripture, *My thoughts are not your thoughts...* The superiority of his thoughts to ours causes a proportionable difference in his manner of operation. His ways are above, and often contrary to, our conceptions. He sometimes produces great effects by means which, to us, appear unsuitable and weak. Thus he gave Gideon a complete victory, not by providing him an army equal to that of the enemy, but by 300 men armed only with earthen pitchers and lamps.

We have but slight thoughts of holiness and therefore are but slightly affected by the evil of sin. But though he is rich in mercy, no wisdom but his own could have proposed an expedient by which the exercise of mercy towards sinners could be made to correspond with his justice and truth and the honour of his government. But infinite wisdom and infinite love provided a way in which mercy and truth meet together, and his inflexible righteousness is displayed in perfect harmony with the peace of those who have transgressed his holy laws, and God appears not only gracious, but just, in restoring rebels to favour. This is the greatest of all his works and exhibits the most glorious revelations of his perfections which creatures are capable of conceiving. The means are answerable to the grandeur of the design. ... *Behold*—attend, admire and believe—*a virgin shall conceive...*

FOR MEDITATION:

Salvation! what a glorious plan,	Truth, Wisdom, Justice, Power and Love,
How suited to our need!	In all their glory shone;
The grace that raises fallen man,	When JESUS left the courts above,
Is wonderful indeed!	And died to save his own.343

Perfectly Man and perfectly God

'Therefore the Lord himself shall give you a sign; behold a virgin shall conceive, and bear a son, and shall call his name Immanuel.' Isaiah 7:14
SUGGESTED FURTHER READING: Romans 5:12–21

This passage expressly and exclusively refers to the Messiah and is directly applied, as accomplished in him, by the evangelists Luke and Matthew. If sinners are to be saved without injury to his government and the honour of his law (and otherwise they must perish), two things are necessary: firstly, *A virgin shall conceive and bring forth a son* [for second point see 4/6]. The Mediator, the Surety, must be a man. Those whom he came to redeem were partakers of flesh and blood. He therefore took part of the same. Had not the Messiah engaged for us, a case would have occurred which I think we may justly deem incongruous to the divine wisdom—that while fire and hail, snow and vapour and the stormy wind fulfil the will of God—while the whole brute creation are faithful to the instincts planted in them by their Maker—a whole species of intelligent beings would have fallen short of the original law and design of their creation, and indeed have acted in direct and continual opposition to it. For the duty of man to live, serve and trust God with all his heart and mind, and to love his neighbour as himself, is founded in the very nature and constitution of things, and necessarily results from his relation to God and his absolute dependence on him as a creature. Such a disposition was doubtless as natural to man, before the Fall, as it is for a bird to fly, or a fish to swim. But sin degraded and disabled him, detached him from his proper centre, if I may so speak, and rendered both his obedience and happiness impossible. Neither Adam after his Fall, nor any of his posterity, have kept this law; but the Messiah fulfilled it exactly as a man, and the principles of it are renewed in all who believe in him. Though the best fall short, his obedience is accepted on their behalf, and he will at length perfectly restore them to the primitive order and honour of their creation. When they shall see him as he is, they shall be like him.

FOR MEDITATION: 'The first man was of the dust of the earth, the second man from heaven. And just as we have borne the likeness of the earthly man, so shall we bear the likeness of the man from heaven' (1 Corinthians 15:47,49, NIV).

SERMON SERIES: MESSIAH, NO. 5 [2/6], ISAIAH 7:14

Our nearest kinsman

'Therefore the Lord himself shall give you a sign; behold a virgin shall conceive, and bear a son, and shall call his name Immanuel.' Isaiah 7:14
SUGGESTED FURTHER READING: Hebrews 2:5–18

The Messiah must not only be a man, but partaker of our very nature. It had been easy to divine power to have formed the second Adam as he did the first, out of the dust of the earth. But, though in this way he might have been a true and perfect man, he would have been no more related to us than an angel. Therefore when God sent forth his Son to be made under the law, he was made of a woman. Thus he became 'Goel' [Hebrew for kinsman], our near kinsman. But farther, had he derived his human nature wholly in the ordinary way, from sinful parents, we see not how he could have escaped that inherent defilement which the fall of Adam has entailed upon all his posterity. But his body, that holy thing conceived and born of a virgin, was the immediate production of God. Therefore he was pure and spotless, qualified to be such a High Priest as became us, holy, harmless, undefiled, separate from sinners, who needed not, as the typical high priest of Israel, to offer up sacrifice, first for his own sins, and then for the sins of the people. These difficulties were obviated by a virgin's conceiving and bearing a son. Let us now praise and admire the wisdom of God. Let us adore his power. Thus he created a new thing upon earth.

FOR MEDITATION:
JESUS, who passed the angels by,
Assumed our flesh to bleed and die;
And still he makes it his abode,
As man, he fills the throne of GOD.

Our next of kin, our Brother now,
Is he to whom the angels bow;
They join with us to praise his name,
But *we* the nearest interest claim.344

He honoured the law

'Therefore the Lord himself shall give you a sign; behold a virgin shall conceive, and bear a son, and shall call his name Immanuel.' Isaiah 7:14
SUGGESTED FURTHER READING: Philippians 2:5–11

The wonder rises unspeakably—this son of the virgin, *shall be called Emanuel,*345 *God with* us. The human nature of Christ considered alone, was not sufficient for the great undertaking of reconciliation. Two things were requisite which exceeded the utmost capacity of any mere creature: dignity and power. As sinless and perfect, he might have yielded a complete obedience, but it could have been only for himself. The most excellent creature cannot exceed the law of his creation. He is bound to serve God with his all, and his obligations keep pace with his ability. An obedience acceptable and available for others, for thousands and millions, for all who plead it, must be performed by a nature not necessarily bound. It was therefore a divine person in the human nature who engaged for us. He who was before all, by whom all things were made, assumed the nature of man. The lawgiver himself submitted in this way to be under his own law. This gave a value and dignity to all that he did, to all that he suffered; thus he not only satisfied but honoured the law. We may boldly say the law and perfections of God were more honoured by the Messiah in his obedience, in submitting to the death of the cross, than it could have been by the unsinning obedience of all mankind to the end of time.

FOR MEDITATION:

He bears the names of all his saints,
Deep on his heart engraved;
Attentive to the state and wants
Of all his love has saved.

The blood, which as a Priest he bears
For sinners, is his own;
The incense of his prayers and tears
Perfume the holy throne.

In him a holiness complete,
Light and perfections shine;
And wisdom, grace, and glory meet;
A Saviour all divine.

In him my weary soul has rest,
Though I am weak and vile,
I read my name upon his breast,
And see the Father smile.346

Oh, lonesome me!

'And a man shall be as an hiding place from the wind, and a covert from the tempest; as rivers of water in a dry place, as the shadow of a great rock in a weary land.' Isaiah 32:2
SUGGESTED FURTHER READING: Psalm 143: 1–12

We have spoken of Jesus as the refuge from storm and rain—the sure and welcome retreat for every convinced, tempted soul. The next clause sets him forth in a very acceptable view. And here we may enquire what is meant by *a dry place*. The dry place signifies a wilderness, as Psalm 105:41. The believing soul is in a wilderness in a twofold state and must perish without these refreshing streams. Such is the prayer of David (Psalm 143:6). A wilderness is barren, lonesome, uncomfortable. Such a state is applicable:

(i) to the world: it does not appear to us so by nature—rather fruitful and pleasant, and the poor soul says as Psalm 132:14. But when the eyes of the mind are opened, the false appearance vanishes and it is all a wilderness. A right view of God and divine things puts us out of conceit with the world, and its poor pleasures are no longer pleasing. A Christian, except he has some believers with him, is alone in a multitude—as a man would be counted solitary if he had none of his own kind, but only wild beasts of the forest around him.

(ii) to the heart: this likewise is known to be a wilderness when known aright. It is indeed full of wickedness—full, as it were, of serpents and dragons, but nothing good or pleasant. By nature we think ourselves rich and increased in goodness, but, when awakened, we find ourselves poor and destitute.

FOR MEDITATION: I have little new to say of myself. My wanderings and wildness when I would attempt praying in secret, are beyond description and would seem impossible to be the lot of a heart in any degree right with God. And yet I am enabled still to hold by the promise, and to say, He is my God and in him will I trust.[347]

Diary, 24 November 1774

A refreshing stream

'And a man shall be as an hiding place from the wind, and a covert from the tempest; as rivers of water in a dry place, as the shadow of a great rock in a weary land.' Isaiah 32:2
SUGGESTED FURTHER READING: Isaiah 35:1–10

Why is he compared to *rivers of water*? The knowledge of Jesus produces a change as if one could turn [divert] a river of water into a wilderness; then the desert begins to flourish and blossom like the rose. It puts a new face upon the world, gives a sunshine, as it were, to every object, sanctifies and spiritualizes common employments, gives a double relish to every comfort, and even sweetens the bitter cup of affliction. Then we see the directing, disposing hand of our Redeemer at every turn. We have a friend near to help us in trouble, and act and suffer in a new manner when we are taught to do everything as for him who loved us. And so it is written in the heart. The knowledge of Jesus and communion with him is a refreshing stream, by which comfort will flow in spite of awkward things. This healing, fertilizing, life-giving stream is communicated in the means of grace. These are as pipes through which the water is received: promises, ordinances, prayer. The promises are such channels, when opened and applied by the Spirit. How do they revive in the time of drought! The ordinances: when all has been barren and discouraging within and without, how sweet to have the heart opened and watered by a blessing on the preaching. So at times in prayer. Perhaps by one hour's secret waiting upon God, yea, a few minutes, there is a change like from the depth of winter to the height of summer.

This knowledge of Jesus is compared to water on account of its refreshing qualities: because it is necessary (no life or growth without it) and because it is cheap (wine and milk must be bought but water is free. Isaiah 55:1). It is compared to a river because it is full and always flowing. A summer's brook may fail, but rivers are abiding. Such a river is Jesus.[348]

FOR MEDITATION: [for Easter Day, 16 April 1775]

See! the streams of living waters	Who can faint while such a river
Springing from eternal love;	Ever flows their thirst to assuage?
Well supply thy sons and daughters,	Grace, which like the LORD, the giver,
And all fear of want remove:	Never fails from age to age.[349]

The shadow of a great Rock

'And a man shall be as an hiding place from the wind, and a covert from the tempest; as rivers of water in a dry place, as the shadow of a great rock in a weary land.' Isaiah 32:2
SUGGESTED FURTHER READING: Isaiah 25:1–8

This text is a comment upon *Christ is all in all* [Colossians 3:11]. In him his people find *a hiding place* where they cannot be found, a foundation from which they cannot be shaken off, streams of life and refreshment which cannot be dried up, and a sweet repose when everything is unquiet about them.

The shadow of a great rock. The allusion seems to travelling or toiling in the heat of the sun—a welcome shadow to such who are faint and weary. The believer has many weary hours—weary of himself, of the world, of affliction, especially when afflictions are many, sharp, long-continued. Indeed this heat would be insupportable without a shade. But Jesus is a great rock through which the sun's beams cannot pierce—hence called a shield. But how?

(i) By the knowledge he gives of himself, in his characters and relations.

(ii) By putting power with the promises.

(iii) By sanctifying afflictions so that though not joyous but grievous, they yield the peaceable fruits of righteousness.

(iv) By enabling them to look forward to the end, as Revelation 2:10.

Now this [man] is compared to *the shadow of a rock* to show its closeness. In other respects he is compared to a tree, affording not only shade, but fruit (Song of Solomon 2:[3]). Those who dwell under this shadow shall revive.

Unbelievers are exposed to the heat. Their troubles meet them without support and leave them without a blessing, therefore miserable here, and lost hereafter—when the heat of the Lord's anger shall be as a burning oven.

FOR MEDITATION: *The Refuge, River, and Rock of the Church*

This land, through which his pilgrims go,   When troubles, like a burning sun,
Is desolate and dry;   Beat heavy on their head;
But streams of grace from him o'erflow   To this almighty Rock they run,
Their thirst to satisfy.   And find a pleasing shade.[350]

The blood of God

'Therefore the Lord himself shall give you a sign; behold a virgin shall conceive, and bear a son, and shall call his name Immanuel.' Isaiah 7:14
SUGGESTED FURTHER READING: Leviticus 16:6–22

The Messiah was not only to obey, but to expiate, to sustain and exhaust the curse due to sin (Galatians 3). In this attempt no mere creature could have endured. Nor could the sufferings of a creature have been proposed to the universe as a sufficient consideration to vindicate the righteousness of God in the remission of sin, after he had determined and declared that the wages of sin is death. Upon the same ground that the apostle tells us it is impossible for the blood of bulls and goats to take away sin, we may assert the same of the blood of man, or of angels, if angels could bleed. But the atoning blood is the blood of *Emmanuel*, the blood of God (Acts 20[:28])—of *God with us* [Matthew 1:23]. And no sinner obtains forgiveness in this way, but he obtains by it such a knowledge of the evil of sin, and of the displeasure of God against it, as teaches and disposes him from that hour to fear and forsake it.

Behold the character of the Messiah in this prophecy: a man, a God-Man, a divine person in the human nature, God manifested in the flesh, *God with us* [Matthew 1:23]. As fallen creatures we had lost the true knowledge of God and were unable to conceive of him to our comfort. His glory shines in the heavens and fills the earth, yet he is to us unknown and unnoticed. But he is known and found when the Messiah is known. To us his glory shines in the person of Jesus Christ the Messiah.

FOR MEDITATION:

That dear blood, for sinners spilt,
Shows my sin in all its guilt:
Ah, my soul, he bore thy load,
Thou hast slain the Lamb of GOD.

Farewell world, thy gold is dross,
Now I see the bleeding cross;
JESUS died to set me free
From the law, and sin, and thee!

He has dearly bought my soul
LORD, accept, and claim the whole!
To thy will I all resign,
Now, no more my own, but thine.[351]

SERMON SERIES: MESSIAH, NO. 5 [5/6], ISAIAH 7:14

God with us

'Therefore the Lord himself shall give you a sign; behold a virgin shall conceive, and bear a son, and shall call his name Immanuel.' Isaiah 7:14
SUGGESTED FURTHER READING: John 20:24–31

As fallen creatures, God is against us and we are against him. But in the Messiah he is reconciled—*God with us*. He is God in our nature still. He suffered as a man, and as a man he now reigns on the throne of glory, exercises all power and receives all spiritual worship both in heaven and upon earth. He is the head of principalities and powers, thrones and dominions, and has *a name above every name* [Philippians 2:9]. Thus man is not only saved but enabled, brought into the nearest relation to him that sitteth upon the throne, and can say, He is our Lord, our Shepherd, our Saviour, our Friend, *Emmanuel, God with us.*

What a cold assent is paid to this doctrine by many who profess to receive it as a truth! What a strong foundation for the faith and hope of those who have put their trust in him. How awful the state of those who reject him and say in their hearts, *We will not have this man to reign over us* [Luke 19:14]. He is now manifested as a Saviour—hereafter he will appear as a Judge. Embrace his golden sceptre, lest you are broken by his rod of iron!

FOR MEDITATION:

Sweeter sounds than music knows
Charm me, in Emmanuel's name;
All her hopes my spirit owes
To his birth, and cross, and shame.

Did the Lord a man become
That he might the law fulfil,
Bleed and suffer in my room,
And canst thou, my tongue, be still?

When he came the angels sung
'Glory be to God on high',
Lord, unloose my stammering tongue,
Who should louder sing than I?

No, I must my praises bring,
Though they worthless are, and weak;
For should I refuse to sing
Sure the very stones would speak.

O my Saviour, Shield, and Sun,
Shepherd, Brother, Husband, Friend,
Every precious name in one;
I will love thee without end.352

SERMON SERIES: MESSIAH, NO. 5 [6/6], ISAIAH 7:14

Born King

'Where is he that is born King of the Jews? For we have seen his star in the east, and are come to worship him.' Matthew 2:2

SUGGESTED FURTHER READING: 2 Peter 1:16–21

The Lord knows his people and will find means that they, however circumstanced, shall come to know him. Jesus is a King, King of all, and especially *King of the Jews*—the true Israel (Romans 2:29)—*born* a King by an original right, their Redeemer, the Holy One of Israel, before his birth—and came to his own (John 1:11).

The enquirers: *wise men of the East*—at a great distance, probably like those called Chaldeans in Daniel—we might say, philosophers. A principal study in the East was astronomy, but without this one star, the knowledge of all the rest would have left them miserable.

Their guidance: no common star, neither fixed star or planet—a light, in appearance *a star*, which they saw in their own country, and again at Bethlehem leading them to the very house. But there was more than this: certainly a divine revelation to their mind. How else should the sight of a new star lead their thoughts to Jesus? Here is an emblem of the work of grace: a light is seen, the heart drawn. This light is the gospel, written or preached—the Word is a light in a dark place—and the Holy Spirit.

Note their declaration, *we have seen*, expressing their own certainty to excite the attention of others, expecting information from a people who had the Scriptures—might they not wonder they went forward by themselves?

Their design: *to worship*. Jesus the proper object of worship, of admiration, praise, profession, love, trust and service. Are these your views of worship (Psalm 45:11)?

They are *come*. They who are apprised of his glory will come, will use diligence, wait, read, pray, hear. These came a long journey. Enquiring souls are busy in earnest.

FOR MEDITATION: Shall these wise men condemn us in judgement? You have seen the star, heard the message. Do you yet sit still? You that are indeed come to worship, admire his love, approach his table. He who once lay in the manger will be there.

An appeal from the heart

'They shall ask the way to Zion with their faces thitherward, saying, Come, and let us join ourselves to the LORD *in a perpetual covenant that shall not be forgotten.' Jeremiah 50:5*
SUGGESTED FURTHER READING: 1 Thessalonians 2:1–16

If ever a sense of the worth of souls is impressed upon my heart (and I hope it sometimes is), if ever I find myself willing to spend and be spent for you, if I can ever adopt with sincerity the Apostle's words, and say, *Being affectionately desirous of you, we were willing to have imparted unto you, not the gospel of God only, but also our own souls, because ye were dear unto us* [1 Thessalonians 2:8], it is peculiarly so at the return of this opportunity. To the most of you, I preach frequently and I have no new tricks to set before you now. Why then is my heart engaged on a New Year's evening more than at other times? Why do I stand up at these times with a solicitude as if I had never preached before, or as if I expected never to preach again? I have frequently entertained a hope upon this account, that my concern was a token for good, a token that the Lord was about to do great things for us, and that the seed I endeavour to sow among the young people should, in the course of the year, spring up abundantly and give us the prospect of a plentiful harvest. Painful experience has taught me my own insufficiency, that though I should address you with the greatest earnestness, though I should accompany every word with tears, though I could even weep blood, all my earnestness will be in vain, unless the Lord himself is pleased to take the work into his own hands and apply the word by his own power to your hearts. This has been my prayer, and from entreating the Lord, I now come to entreat and beseech you, that you would hear with attention and receive with meekness the word which, by his blessing, is able to save your souls—that I may not have to return again and say, *Lord, who hath believed our report?* [John 12:38].

FOR MEDITATION: [written to be sung before this sermon]

Now may fervent prayer arise	Bless, O LORD, the opening year
Winged with faith, and pierce the skies;	To each soul assembled here;
Fervent prayer shall bring us down	Clothe thy word with power divine,
Gracious answers from the throne.	Make us willing to be thine.353

SERMON: JEREMIAH 50:5 [1/7] [TO THE YOUNG PEOPLE]

Citizens of Zion

'They shall ask the way to Zion with their faces thitherward, saying, Come, and let us join ourselves to the LORD *in a perpetual covenant that shall not be forgotten.' Jeremiah 50:5*
SUGGESTED FURTHER READING: Psalm 87:1–7

Zion represents the church of God. It has two branches during the present state of things: the church in glory—that is, the heavenly state—and the church on earth. Heaven answers not to the idea of a carnal heart. It is the state and place where the redeemed of the Lord rejoice in his presence and love, freed from all their sins, troubles and enemies, to which they are exposed here. *Zion* likewise is the church upon earth. Not this or that particular church, or denomination, but it consists of all who know Jesus, and have peace and communion with God by him. These are said to come to Mount Zion, the city of the living God, and as sure as they belong to the church below, they belong to the church above, and shall in due time join. This then expresses the desire of awakened souls—they wish to be remembered with the power which the Lord bears to his people, in time and to eternity.

Now my dear friends, how stand you affected to this thought? What is Zion in your view? Have you no desire to be a citizen of Zion? They, and they only, are happy. Their sins are pardoned, their persons accepted, they have access to God, are under his immediate teaching, care, protection. His eye is upon them, his ear is open to them. How far is their portion preferable to the worldling's while here, and when they die they are blessed indeed, and enter upon a glorious immortality. If nothing of this engages you, if you die before you are united to the Head of the church by faith, then when they are admitted, you will be shut out and must take up your abode with devils.

FOR MEDITATION: [*Asking the way to Zion,* written to be sung after this sermon]

Zion! the city of our God,	Firm, against every adverse shock,
How glorious is the place!	Its mighty bulwarks prove
The Saviour there has his abode,	'Tis built upon the living Rock,
And sinners see his face.	And walled around with love.354

SERMON: JEREMIAH 50:5 [3/7] [TO THE YOUNG PEOPLE]

Asking the way to Zion

'They shall ask the way to Zion with their faces thitherward, saying, Come, and let us join ourselves to the LORD *in a perpetual covenant that shall not be forgotten.' Jeremiah 50:5*
SUGGESTED FURTHER READING: Psalm 119:33–40

They shall ask the way. This intimates:

(i) Their natural ignorance. Men in a state of nature know many things, but not one knows the way to Zion. Many never heard of it. And many who have heard much, know nothing aright. They walk in a way of their own, seek salvation by works, or think they are right because they follow a multitude. Christ is the way, but to know him as such we must be taught, for none can know him so as to choose him and walk in him, to love, trust and worship him, but by the Holy Spirit.

(ii) Their willingness to be taught. The Lord convinces them of their ignorance, and makes them desirous of instruction. They see they must perish unless they come to Zion, and this makes them teachable. They are afraid of leaning to their own understanding and being mistaken in a point of this consequence.

(iii) That the Lord has appointed means of directing enquiring souls, otherwise it will be in vain to ask. The Lord is the only effectual teacher, but he does not speak to them by an outward voice from heaven. For this purpose he has appointed:

(a) prayer. *Teach me thy* way [Psalm 27:11]. *If any lack this wisdom, let them ask of God* [James 1:5].

(b) the Word. This is given for a lamp to their feet and a light to their path.

(c) the ordinances. This is a great privilege when afforded, as likewise …

(d) the Lord's people. These are glad to help enquirers, by telling them how they have been led themselves.

FOR MEDITATION: [*Asking the way to Zion,* written to be sung after this sermon]

There, all the fruits of glory grow,	The gospel shines to give you light,
And joys that never die;	No longer, then, delay;
And streams of grace, and knowledge flow,	The Spirit waits to guide you right,
The soul to satisfy.	And JESUS is the way. 355

SERMON: JEREMIAH 50:5 [4/7] [TO THE YOUNG PEOPLE]

Set your faces Zion-ward

*'They shall ask the way to Zion with their faces thitherward, saying,
Come, and let us join ourselves to the* LORD *in a perpetual covenant that
shall not be forgotten.' Jeremiah 50:5*
SUGGESTED FURTHER READING: 1 Timothy 4:9–16

They ask, with their faces thitherward. Too many are content with talking
of the way, but they may talk themselves into hell, while they amuse
themselves with talking about Zion. They who are sincere will set their faces
Zion-ward. That is:

(i) they will give all diligence to make their calling sure, by attending to
the means.

(ii) they will abstain from the wicked ways in which they once walked.
While the perishing pleasures of sin are desired, and the company of the
ungodly chosen, people cannot be in earnest in asking the way to Zion.

(iii) though they meet (as they surely will) discouragements from within
and without, they will keep their faces the right way and dread the thoughts
of turning back.

Diary, Saturday 18 December 1773:
I desire to be kept from a party spirit but I hope I may and I think ought
endeavour to prevent the young ones of the flock from being staggered and
puzzled by fine words and artful speech, which are employed to turn them
out of the way in which the Lord has led them. Some of my leisure employed
in hymn making.[356]

FOR MEDITATION: [*Asking the way to Zion,* written to be sung after this
sermon]
Come, set your faces Zion-ward,
The sacred road enquire;
And let a union to the LORD
Be henceforth your desire! [357]

SERMON: JEREMIAH 50:5 [5/7] [TO THE YOUNG PEOPLE]

Joined to the Lord

'They shall ask the way to Zion with their faces thitherward, saying, Come, and let us join ourselves to the LORD *in a perpetual covenant that shall not be forgotten.' Jeremiah 50:5*
SUGGESTED FURTHER READING: 2 Timothy 1:1–14

The desire which animates and encourages them is *Let us join ... in a covenant.* This covenant is not the creature's engagement to the Lord, but a laying hold on the Lord's covenant engagement to the sinner. This is established in Christ. He engaged to fulfil all righteousness for those who come to him, and to work all their works for them and in them. Our part is to consent to it, to choose it, and to venture ourselves. All promises and resolutions of our own will come to nothing without this. But when this covenant is known, it draws the soul to a willing surrender. Then the sinner gives himself away, and commits himself to the Redeemer, as the Apostle speaks in 2 Timothy 1:12. By accepting, yielding, to this covenant, the soul is joined to the Lord—in one spirit, one interest. Then Christ dwells in the sinner and puts forth his life, power, and grace in the soul, and the sinner dwells in Christ as in a strong tower of defence. This covenant *shall not be forgotten.* The effects and purposes of it are abiding and unchangeable. The Lord will remember it in every turn of life, at the hour of death and the day of judgement. It will not be forgotten by the soul. The hour, the place, will usually be remembered, the surrender often renewed and ratified. O that this may be the hour and this the place with some of you—that the glory of this covenant may win your hearts before you go hence.

FOR MEDITATION: The anniversary of my great deliverance in 1748 calls for my grateful acknowledgement. ... I remember when I stood trembling, to appearance upon the brink of eternity, and thought it impossible I could live a quarter of an hour. Since that memorable day thou hast added twenty-eight years to my life... My time is shortening apace. O that the remainder may be spent for thee. Be my Shepherd, my Saviour, my all, and may all that I have and am be devoted to thee and employed for thee.358

Diary, 21 March 1776
[anniversary of John Newton's conversion in a storm at sea]

SERMON: JEREMIAH 50:5 [6/7] [TO THE YOUNG PEOPLE]

What do you choose?

'They shall ask the way to Zion with their faces thitherward, saying, Come, and let us join ourselves to the LORD *in a perpetual covenant that shall not be forgotten.' Jeremiah 50:5*
SUGGESTED FURTHER READING: Deuteronomy 30:11–20

Some of you I trust are thus minded. You have already, through grace, chosen Jesus as your way and are walking on *to Zion*. The Lord encourage and strengthen you. See what a blessed hope is set before you. The Lord will guide you and support you. Only remember your own weakness, the strength and power of your enemies, and watch and pray that you may walk answerable to your high calling, that the Lord may have the glory and you the comfort of your profession. I must take it for granted that some of you have long been hearers and have had the advantage of the advice, example and prayers of the godly. Perhaps they who watched for your soul's good are now gone to a better world. You will see them again. How will you rejoice to meet them if you walk in their way; if not, it will be a dreadful meeting. Some of you are to this hour breaking the hearts of those who wish well to your souls. Behold the Judge standeth at the door. If you still despise this salvation, sermons, friends, ministers, will all aggravate your condemnation. Some of you have been brought up in the neglect of means and under the unhappy influence of bad examples. What have too many parents to answer for! Yet your parents' sins will not excuse yours. You now hear for yourselves, and it is at the peril of your souls if you do not begin to *ask the way to Zion*. Say not you are young. How know you but the year you are now entering upon may be your last? And why delay? Why unwilling to be happy too soon? If it is high time for the young, what then for the aged? Let the grey-headed sinner hear—many years you have wasted. Great is the account you have to give for abused mercies. Yet if *you* will now in good earnest *ask the way to Zion*, you may find it. One year more the Lord has waited to be gracious. But the sentence, *Cut it down* [Luke 13:7], cannot be far distant. O today, while it is called today, hear his voice [Hebrews 3].

FOR MEDITATION: [*Asking the way to Zion,* written to be sung after this sermon]

O Lord, regard thy people's prayer,	And young and old, by grace prepare,
Thy promise now fulfil;	To dwell on Zion's hill.359

SERMON: JEREMIAH 50:5 [7/7] [TO THE YOUNG PEOPLE]

Endnotes

1   *Olney Hymns*, 1779, p. 53, Book 1, Hymn 41, *Faith's review and expectation*, 1 Chronicles 17:16–17, v 1. The hymn, *Amazing Grace*, was almost certainly written for this New Year's Day sermon.

2   Sermon Notebook, MS 2940, Lambeth Palace Library.

3   John Newton Diary, Princeton University, CO199, 1 January 1780.

4   *Olney Hymns*, 1779, p. 53, Book 1, Hymn 41, *Faith's review and expectation*, 1 Chronicles 17:16–17, vv 2–3.

5   *Olney Hymns*, 1779, p. 53, Book 1, Hymn 41, *Faith's review and expectation*, 1 Chronicles 17:16–17, vv 4–6.

6   In 1910 Edwin Othello Excell published *Amazing Grace* from *Olney Hymns*, but dropped the last two of Newton's verses and substituted an alien verse beginning, 'When we've been there ten thousand years' (which he purloined from a 70–plus verse American camp song, *Jerusalem, My Happy Home*). Happily, several modern hymn books are restoring Newton's original verses to *Amazing Grace*.

7   *Olney Hymns*, 1779, p. 278, Book 2, Hymn 81, *The book of creation*, vv 1–8.

8   The timing is taken as from the date of the sermon, 1769. Newton preceded his statement by saying, 'There are indeed many disputes and differences among the learned about settling this chronology exactly, but a very great nicety [exactness] is not necessary.'

9   *One hundred and Twenty-nine Letters from the Rev. John Newton … to the Rev. William Bull*, ed Thomas Palmer Bull, Hamilton, Adams & Co, 1847, pp. 32–33, 27 October 1778.

10   *Olney Hymns*, 1779, p. 288, Book 2, Hymn 89, *The thaw*, vv 2,3,7.

11   *Olney Hymns*, 1779, p. 277, Book 2, Hymn 80, *The old and new creation*, vv 1–2, 5–6.

12   *Olney Hymns*, 1779, p. 181, Book 2, Hymn 1 [New-year's Hymns] *Time how swift*, vv 1, 3, written for New Year 1774.

13   Bristol Baptist College, John Ryland letters, G 97B OS Box C, John Newton to John Ryland, 5 June 1781.

14   A quote from one of Newton's favourite hymns by his contemporary Joseph Hart, *How good is the God we adore* (Hart's original hymn, of which this is the last verse, was *No prophet, nor dreamer of dreams*, based on Deuteronomy 13:1ff).

15   John Newton Diary, Princeton University, CO199, 8 and 17 November 1755.

16   *Olney Hymns*, 1779, p. 1, Book 1, Hymn 1, *Adam*, Genesis 3:9, v 1.

17   *Olney Hymns*, 1779, p. 312, Book 3, Hymn 4, *Prepare to meet God*, v 5.

18   *Olney Hymns*, 1779, p. 413, Book 3, Hymn 88, *Man by nature, grace and glory*, vv 1–2.

19   Newton used this same text, 1 Chronicles 28:9, for his New Year's Evening service in London in 1782. We speak of New Year's Eve as being 31 December. In Newton's notes, New Year's Evening meant the evening of New Year's Day, i.e. 1 January.

20   *Olney Hymns*, 1779, p. 204, Book 2, Hymn 20 [After Annual Sermons] *David's charge to Solomon*, 1 Chronicles 28:9, vv 1, 3, written for New Year's Evening 1770.

21   *Miscellaneous Thoughts on entering the Ministry*, John Newton, 1758, Lambeth Palace Library, MS 2937, ed Marylynn Rouse for *The Complete Works of John Newton*, quoting from Friday 23 June.

22   *Olney Hymns*, 1779, p. 132, Book 1, Hymn 106, *The importunate widow*, Luke 18:1–7, vv 1, 3–4, 9.

23   John Newton Diary, Princeton University, CO199, 15 and 16 June 1776.

24   *Olney Hymns*, 1779, p. 349, Book 3, Hymn 33, *The benighted traveller*, vv 1, 3–7.

25   John Newton Diary, Princeton University, CO199, 5 July 1754. Captain Alexander Clunie was the first Christian Newton had met at sea in the six years since his conversion. Clunie

taught Newton about justification by faith, how to read the Scriptures, how to pray extempore, who to go and hear preach back in England, and warned him of the heresies of the day. From this moment on, Newton became established in an evangelical faith. It is interesting to note that, unknown to him at the time, it was also to mark the end of his career in the slave trade.

26 *Olney Hymns*, 1779, p. 75, Book 1, Hymn 60, *Zion, or the city of GOD*, Isaiah 33:20–21, v 4.

27 In 1766, Newton found himself nominated for Cottingham parish church. He was deeply troubled at the thought of leaving his flock in Olney. After several distraught days in prayer he went to London to discuss the matter with Lord Dartmouth and John Thornton, who released him from any expectation. Had it gone ahead, Newton thought he would have 'sunk under the weight of a broken heart'. On his joyful return to Olney he held a thanksgiving service, adding it to the special anniversaries he kept (his own and his wife's birthdays, their marriage day and the day of his conversion at sea).

28 *Olney Hymns*, 1779, p. 75, Book 1, Hymn 60, *Zion, or the city of GOD*, Isaiah 33:20–21, v 3.

29 *Journal of children's meetings at Olney,* Cowper & Newton Museum, 28 March 1765.

30 *Divine Songs Attempted in Easy Language for the use of Children*, Isaac Watts, 1715.

31 Mrs Elizabeth Aspray (neé Andrews) to the daughter of Mrs Sarah Talbot (neé Thompson), c 1842. The children's meeting, on a Thursday, was sometimes held at the Great House, belonging to Lord Dartmouth. Quoted by kind permission of Mrs Hilary Aspray. Elizabeth Andrews and Sarah Thompson are both listed in Newton's notebook as members of his children's meetings (Cowper & Newton Museum).

32 *Twenty-One Letters, written to a near relative at school*, John Newton, Religious Tract Society, 3 August 1780. Newton adopted his niece Betsy as his daughter.

33 John Newton Diary, Princeton University, CO199, 2 February 1801. For 'Eliza' (who died in 1785) read 'Betsy'. Both nieces (who were both adopted by the Newtons) were named Elizabeth. Eliza was the daughter of Mary Newton's sister Elizabeth, and Betsy the daughter of Mary's brother George.

34 *Miscellaneous Thoughts on entering the Ministry,* John Newton, 1758, Lambeth Palace Library, MS 2937, ed Marylynn Rouse for *The Complete Works of John Newton*, quoting from Monday 3 July, meditations on 1 Timothy 4:16.

35 The original manuscript reads 'those who only have only a right'.

36 *Olney Hymns*, 1779, p. 43, Book 1, Hymn 33 [*Ask what I shall give thee*], *Another,* 1 Kings 3:5, vv 1–4.

37 *Olney Hymns*, p. 103, Book 1, Hymn 83, *A sick soul*, Matthew 9:12, vv 1, 3–7.

38 *An Authentic Narrative*, John Newton, 1764, Letter 8.

39 After preaching this sermon on Sunday evening Newton wrote in his diary, 'I have not shed a tear in the pulpit before today for many months.' John Newton Diary, Princeton University, CO199, Sunday evening 13 February 1774.

40 Bristol Baptist College, John Ryland letters, G 97B OS Box C, John Newton to John Ryland, 14 February 1774. Betty Abraham had been a 'Mother in our Israel' in Olney, giving wise counsel and encouragement to young believers. Her death left only one other 'eminently qualified to help enquirers forward', but, as Newton observed, 'she looks like the full ripe corn in harvest, and perhaps will not be long behind'. With the loss of his 'curate' William Cowper the previous year to severe depression, after which Cowper never entered church again (though the two men were still inseparable), this must have been a severe blow indeed.

Endnotes

41 *Olney Hymns*, 1779, p. 87, Book 1, Hymn 70, *Humbled and silenced by mercy*, Ezekiel 16:6, vv 1–5.

42 John Newton Diary, Princeton University, CO199, Sunday evening 20 February 1774.

43 *Olney Hymns*, 1779, p. 86, Book 1, Hymn 69, *The LORD is my portion*, Lamentations 3:24, vv 1–2, written for 20 February 1774, prompted by some of the last words of Betty Abraham.

44 *Olney Hymns*, 1779, p. 86, Book 1, Hymn 69, *The LORD is my portion*, Lamentations 3:24, vv 3–6.

45 *Olney Hymns*, 1779, p. 125, Book 1, Hymn 101, *The heart taken*, vv 1–2, 5–6.

46 John Newton Diary, Princeton University, CO199, 15 December 1796 (aged 71).

47 Annotated *Letters to a Wife,* John Newton, Cowper & Newton Museum, 21 February 1795.

48 John Newton to William Cowper, 22 February 1770, *The Works of the Rev. John Newton*, London, 1808.

49 John Newton Diary, Princeton University, CO199, Newton's prayers for Thomas Scott, 9 May 1776, 2 September 1777, 11 December 1778. Thomas Scott, a neighbouring vicar, sought at first to provoke Newton into controversy. However, he was eventually converted, thanks to Newton's patient friendship and prayers.

50 *Thoughts upon the African Slave Trade,* John Newton, 1788. Newton subsequently gave evidence against the slave trade before the Privy Council.

51 *Olney Hymns*, 1779, p. 323, Book 3, Hymn 11 [Seeking, Pleading, Hoping] *The effort*, vv 2–4.

52 *The Life of William Wilberforce*, Robert Isaac Wilberforce and Samuel Wilberforce, London, 1838, vol 1, p. 96. Wilberforce met Newton secretly at his home in Charles Square on Wednesday 6 December. He records, 'After walking about the Square once or twice before I could persuade myself, I called upon old Newton—was much affected in conversing with him—something very pleasing and unaffected in him. When I came away I found my mind in a calm, tranquil state, more humbled, and looking more devoutly up to God.'

53 Bodleian Library, MS Wilberforce c.49, f1, John Newton to William Wilberforce, 22 December 1785. Wilberforce's Diary for 12 January 1786 reveals that he was spotted walking across the Common with Newton that day. By then his fears had gone, for he wrote, 'Expect to hear myself now universally given out to be a Methodist: may God grant it may be said with truth.'

54 Newton's morning sermon for the Fast Day of Friday 28 February 1794 was on Jonah 3:9. He published it [reprinted in Newton's *Works*].

55 *Olney Hymns*, 1779, p. 334, Book 3, Hymn 21, *The storm hushed*, vv 2,4,6–7.

56 'When the sun sets, beasts come forth,' a reference to Newton's hymn on forest beasts, *Olney Hymns*, 1779, p. 349, Book 3, Hymn 33, *The benighted traveller* [see 30 Jan.]. This spiritual point was first learnt by harsh practical experience, as related in his *Narrative*: 'Another time, at Cape Lopez, some of us had been in the woods, and shot a buffalo, or wild cow; we brought a part of it on board, and carefully marked the place (as I thought) where we left the remainder. In the evening we returned to fetch it; but we set out too late. I undertook to be the guide; but night coming on before we could reach the place, we lost our way. Sometimes we were in swamps, up to the middle in water; and when we recovered dry land, we could not tell whether we were walking towards the ship, or wandering farther from her. Every step increased our uncertainty. The night grew darker, and we were entangled in inextricable woods, where, perhaps, the foot of man had never trod before. That part of the country is entirely abandoned to wild beasts, with which it prodigiously abounds. We were, indeed, in a terrible case, having neither light, food, nor

arms, and expecting a tiger to rush from behind every tree. The stars were clouded, and we had no compass, to form a judgement which way we were going. Had things continued thus, we had probably perished; but it pleased God no beast came near us; and after some hours' perplexity, the moon arose, and pointed out the eastern quarter. It appeared then, as we had expected, that, instead of drawing nearer to the sea-side, we had been penetrating into the country; but by the guidance of the moon, we at length came to the water-side, a considerable distance from the ship. We got safe on board without any other inconvenience than what we suffered from fear and fatigue.'

57 Cowper & Newton Museum, Newton's sermon notebook, 714(30), Sermon on Revelation 19:13 [from Series on Revelation 19:11–16, begun 26 July 1777].

58 *Olney Hymns*, 1779, p. 398, Book 3, Hymn 76, *Sin's deceit*, vv 1–2.

59 *Olney Hymns*, 1779, p. 398, Book 3, Hymn 76, *Sin's deceit*, vv 3–6, 8.

60 *Olney Hymns*, 1779, p. 215, Book 2, Hymn 29, *How shall I put thee among the children?* Jeremiah 3:19, vv 1, 6.

61 *Olney Hymns*, 1779, p. 208, Book 2, Hymn 23, *Waiting at Wisdom's gates*, Proverbs 8:34–35, vv 1,3,5–6, written for New Year's Evening 1773.

62 *Olney Hymns*, 1779, p. 138, Book 1, Hymn 111, *The woman of Samaria*, John 4:28, vv 2–4.

63 Newton's sermon series on the Transfiguration was based on these texts: Matthew 17:1–9; Mark 9:1–9; Luke 9:28–35. In a letter to Joshua Symonds, pastor of Bunyan Meeting in Bedford, 25 January 1771, Newton writes, 'I now send you my notes on the transfiguration which I received from Mrs Wilberforce [Hannah, the MP's aunt] but last week.' (Cowper & Newton Museum). The notebook is No. 40 in Newton's series.

64 Sermon No. 1 in the Transfiguration series is based on Matthew 17:1 and Luke 9:28. Space did not permit this note to be included on the pages for 8–11 March.

65 *Olney Hymns*, 1779, p. 189, Book 2, Hymn 7 [Before Annual Sermons] *Prayer for a blessing*, vv 1–2, probably written for New Year's Evening 1770.

66 *Olney Hymns*, 1779, p. 235, Book 2, Hymn 45, *The Lord's day*, vv 1–2.

67 *Olney Hymns*, 1779, p. 235, Book 2, Hymn 45, *The Lord's day*, vv 5–6.

68 Bodleian Library, MS Wilberforce c.49, f105, John Newton to William Wilberforce, 30 September 1800.

69 *Olney Hymns*, 1779, p. 339, Book 3, Hymn 25, *Rejoice the soul of thy servant*, vv 1, 4, 6.

70 *Twenty-One Letters, written to a near relative at school*, John Newton, Religious Tract Society, p. 102, 23 October 1783.

71 *Twenty-One Letters, written to a near relative at school*, John Newton, Religious Tract Society, pp. 12–13, 22 October 1779.

72 John Newton Diary, Princeton University, CO199, 21 March 1773.

73 John Newton Diary, Princeton University, CO199, 21 March 1773.

74 *Miscellaneous Thoughts on entering the Ministry*, John Newton, 1758, Lambeth Palace Library, MS 2937, ed Marylynn Rouse for *The Complete Works of John Newton*, quoting Saturday 24 June 1758.

75 This charity sermon was probably for the benefit of Langbourne-Ward Charity School. Newton wrote that it was preached at St Mary Woolnoth before the Lord Mayor 'usually' as on this occasion the Mayor failed to come.

76 The original manuscript is 'discoveredly'.

77 Bodleian Library, MS Wilberforce c.49, f67, John Newton to William Wilberforce, 22 December 1795.

Endnotes

78 *Journal of children's meetings at Olney,* Cowper & Newton Museum, 24 January 1765.

79 Newton's contemporary William Hogarth, a governor of the Foundling Hospital in London, donated a large painting of Moses being handed over to the Egyptian princess while his distraught mother looked on. It may still be viewed there. The charity is now named the Thomas Corum Foundation.

80 John Newton Diary, Princeton University, CO199, 1 January 1783.

81 Newton wrote to his thirty-year-old friend Josiah Symonds, pastor of the Bunyan Meeting, Bedford, of a recent experience of drying up mid-sermon. As his letter was written on 29 September 1769, it would seem to refer to this same incident that he has recorded here in his notebook. The dates tie in with having begun the Genesis series in January that year. He wrote, 'I think I may say without vanity that if you had heard me preach last Sunday in the afternoon, you would have been edified. You have seemed to think I have such a facility in speaking, that I am in no danger of appearing to any considerable disadvantage in the pulpit. I hope I never seriously thought so myself, but the Lord only knows the deceitfulness of my heart, and how prone I am to give way to the temptations of Satan, who would *willingly* persuade me to pride and presumption. I hope it was in mercy, that he was pleased at the time I have mentioned to give both me and the people a proof how little I can do without him. I found myself very much straightened before I had got to the middle of my sermon, and was at length brought to a full stop. I had only power to make a public confession of my weakness, and that I was utterly unable to proceed. The Lord gave me however at the same time to hope that it might be good for me and for my people that I should be thus humbled, so that I was not much disconcerted, nor has it given me a moment's uneasiness ever since. Only I hope it will be an abiding *memento* to me to be afraid of leaning to my own understanding, and make me go up the pulpit steps for the future, with a deeper conviction both of my unworthiness and my inability. When I had prayed and given out a hymn, I spoke for a few minutes and told the people what I thought might be the meaning of such a dispensation, namely, that I might not think too highly of myself, and that they might not think too highly of me, as if I had anything of my own, and that both they and I might be encouraged to hope that if I had more liberty at any time, it was not because I had words at will, but because the Lord was graciously pleased to afford me his promised assistance. As to myself I had no right to complain, having been conscious of so much deadness and evil in my heart, and such a disparity between what I seemed in the pulpit and what I felt myself at other times, that I have often wondered my mouth has not been stopped before. O my friend, we often pray that the Lord would make us sensible that we are nothing and can do nothing of ourselves and keep us in a humble and dependent spirit, let us not then be grieved if he is pleased to answer our prayers, though he does it by such methods as are not pleasing to flesh and blood. I hope I can thank him for what has happened. And I see he dealt gently with me in permitting it to be at home. It might have been at Everton, or some of the places where he has opened me a door abroad. And perhaps my foolish heart would have made a harder struggle, to have had my poverty exposed amongst strangers. Here I had many to pray for me, and many more to pity me, and I hardly think there was a single person in the congregation disposed to triumph over me. We had a comfortable prayer meeting that evening, another on Tuesday, and last night the Lord permitted me to preach with my usual liberty. Help me to praise him' [ALS, Cowper & Newton Museum].

82 *Olney Hymns*, 1779, p. 402, Book 3, Hymn 79, *Not in word, but in power*, vv 5–7.

83 *Olney Hymns*, 1779, p. 38, Book 1, Hymn 29, *David's fall*, 2 Samuel 11:27, vv 1–2, 4.

84 *Olney Hymns*, 1779, p. 263, Book 2, Hymn 68, *On the earthquake*, 8 September 1775, vv 4, 6-8.

85 *Letters to a Clergyman*, ed John Newton Coffin, 1845, pp. 53–54, 27 June 1793.

86 Bodleian Library, MS Wilberforce c.49, f119, 19 October 1767.

87 *Olney Hymns*, 1779, p. 72, Book 1, Hymn 57, *The name of JESUS*, Solomon's Song 1:3, vv 3,5.

88 John Newton Collection, Princeton University, CO 192, John Newton to Thomas Haweis, May 1763.

89 *Olney Hymns*, 1779, p. 72, Book 1, Hymn 57, *The name of JESUS*, Solomon's Song 1:3, vv 1–2.

90 *Olney Hymns*, 1779, p. 72, Book 1, Hymn 57, *The name of JESUS*, Solomon's Song 1:3, v 4.

91 Mrs Barham was Dorothea Foster-Barham, born 26 March 1721, died 26 September 1781. She was the wife of Joseph Foster-Barham, a Moravian minister in Bedford whom Newton often visited. He was very fond of the family and sometimes stayed with them, taking family prayers and attending chapel.

92 *One hundred and Twenty-nine Letters from the Rev. John Newton … to the Rev. William Bull,* ed Thomas Palmer Bull, Hamilton, Adams & Co, 1847, p. 127, 13 October 1781.

93 Quoted from verse 2 of *When I survey the wondrous cross* by Isaac Watts. Watts was best friends with Newton's mother's pastor, David Jennings. In his preface to *Olney Hymns*, Newton states that many of Watts's hymns were 'admirable patterns' for his own.

94 *Olney Hymns*, 1779, p. 247, Book 2, Hymn 54, *CHRIST crucified*, vv 1–6.

95 *Olney Hymns*, 1779, p. 72, Book 1, Hymn 57, *The name of JESUS*, Solomon's Song 1:3, vv 6–7.

96 *Olney Hymns*, 1779, p. 144, Book 1, Hymn 116, *The resurrection and the life*, John 11:25, vv 1–2, 6–7.

97 *Olney Hymns*, 1779, p. 107, Book 1, Hymn 87, *Peter walking upon the water*, Matthew 14:28–31, vv 1, 8.

98 *The Searcher of Hearts*, John Newton, ed Marylynn Rouse, Christian Focus, 1997, pp. 21–22.

99 Bodleian Library, MS Wilberforce c.49, f75, 30 March 1797.

100 Bodleian Library, MS Wilberforce c.49, f75, 30 March 1797.

101 Indeed Thomas Scott, a neighbouring vicar, heard Newton for this very reason. But Newton's patient invitation, *Come,* eventually led to his conversion. Scott became the spiritual teacher of William Wilberforce, and the author of a much valued Bible Commentary.

102 In his original notes Newton wrote 'situate'.

103 John Newton Diary, Princeton University, CO199, 9 September 1773. Newton's brother Henry [1740–1797] was a 1st Lieutenant in the Royal Navy. He was on board HMS *Lizard,* which moored for several months in Boston, departing shortly before the infamous Boston tea party of 1773.

104 Richard Cecil, *The Life of John Newton*, ed Marylynn Rouse, Christian Focus, 2000, p. 20, citing *Sermons to Young People*, David Jennings, 1730.

105 *Olney Hymns*, 1779, p. 100, Book 1, Hymn 81, *The beggar*, Matthew 7:7–8, vv 1, 8.

106 *An Authentic Narrative*, John Newton, 1764, Letter 13. Newton is referring to Job Lewis, whom he took with him as 'Volunteer and Captain's Commander'. Lewis was so difficult that Newton felt obliged to purchase a ship for him and separate. Lewis succumbed to a fever a few days later and died (17 February 1754).

Endnotes

107 *Olney Hymns*, 1779, p. 373, Book 3, Hymn 53, *Peace restored*, vv 1–3, 7.

108 *Olney Hymns*, 1779, p. 16, Book 1, Hymn 12, *Joseph made known to his Brethren*, Genesis 45:3–4, vv 4a, 5.

109 This paragraph has parallels to the hymn, *Glorious things of thee are spoken, Zion city of our God* (*Olney Hymns*, 1779, p. 75, Book 1, Hymn 60, *Zion, or the city of GOD*), which was written for Easter Day, 16 April 1775.

110 *Olney Hymns*, 1779, p. 75, Book 1, Hymn 60, *Zion, or the city of GOD*, Isaiah 33:20–21 (incorrectly printed as 27–28 in some editions), v 1, written for Easter Day 16 April 1775.

111 Cambridge University, Thornton Papers, Add 7826/1/A, John Newton to John Thornton, 12 September 1776. *O to grace how great a debtor* was one of Newton's favourite hymn quotes. It comes from the hymn by his contemporary Robert Robinson [1735–1790], *Come thou fount of every blessing*.

112 *The Searcher of Hearts*, John Newton, ed Marylynn Rouse, Christian Focus, 1997, pp. 64–65.

113 *An Authentic Narrative*, John Newton, 1764, Letter 8.

114 *Olney Hymns*, 1779, p. 361, Book 3, Hymn 42, *The Pilgrim's song*, vv 3–6.

115 John Newton Diary, Princeton University, CO199, 16 October, 1775.

116 *Olney Hymns*, 1779, p. 411, Book 3, Hymn 87, *Praise to the Redeemer*, vv 1–4, 10.

117 *Olney Hymns*, 1779, p. 250, Book 2, Hymn 57, *Looking at the cross*, vv 2–7.

118 Cambridge University, Thornton Papers, Add 7674/1/A, John Newton to John Thornton, 18 May 1775.

119 *Olney Hymns*, 1779, p. 353, Book 3, Hymn 37, *I will trust and not be afraid*, vv 1, 5.

120 *Olney Hymns*, 1779, p. 268, Book 2, Hymn 72 [Funeral Hymns] *On the death of a believer*, vv 1, 3.

121 *Olney Hymns*, 1779, p. 374, Book 3, Hymn 54, *Hear what he has done for my soul!* vv 1–4.

122 *Letters to a Clergyman*, ed John Newton Coffin, 1845, p. 193, 19 February 1799.

123 *Olney Hymns*, 1779, p. 326, Book 3, Hymn 14, *Rest for weary souls*, vv 1, 4.

124 Cambridge, Thornton Papers, Add 7674/1/A, John Newton to John Thornton, 18 August 1774.

125 *Olney Hymns*, 1779, p. 35, Book 1, Hymn 27, *The milch kine drawing the ark: Faith's surrender of all*, 1 Samuel 6:12, vv 5–8.

126 *Olney Hymns*, 1779, p. 8, Book 1, Hymn 7, *The LORD will provide*, Genesis 22:14, vv 4,7.

127 Bristol Baptist College, John Ryland letters, G 97B OS Box C, Newton to John Ryland, 26 November 1796.

128 *Olney Hymns*, 1779, p. 379, Book 3, Hymn 58, *Home in view*, vv 1–6.

129 Bodleian Library, MS Wilberforce c.49, f14, 1 November 1787.

130 Cited in *The Life of John Newton*, Richard Cecil, ed Marylynn Rouse, Christian Focus, 2000, p. 186.

131 John Newton Diary, Princeton University, CO199, 7 July 1776.

132 *An Authentic Narrative*, John Newton, 1764, Letter 9.

133 Newton preached from Exodus 20:1–11 sometime between 14 July and 8 September 1776.

134 Newton's notes begin 'After a long intercession (near 20 month) I now [2 June 1771] return to my purpose of considering the historical parts of the Old Testament.'

135 *Olney Hymns*, 1779, p. 6, Book 1, Hymn 5, *Lot in Sodom*, Genesis 13:10, vv 1–4.

136 *Olney Hymns*, 1779, p. 6, Book 1, Hymn 5, *Lot in Sodom*, Genesis 13:10, vv 5–8.

137 *Olney Hymns*, 1779, p. 353, Book 3, Hymn 37, *I will trust and not be afraid*, v 7.

Endnotes

138 *Olney Hymns*, 1779, p. 172, Book 1, Hymn 139, *Philadelphia*, Revelation 3:7–13, vv 4–6.

139 Bodleian Library, MS Wilberforce c.49, f26, 2 April 1789.

140 Handel's *Messiah* was performed at Westminster Abbey in 1784. Newton's distress over more attention being paid to the music for entertainment's sake than to the words of salvation, led him to preach a series of sermons in St Mary Woolnoth, one from each number in the libretto. He published these in two volumes in 1786 as *Messiah: fifty expository discourses, on the series of scriptural passages, which form the subject of the celebrated oratorio of Handel.* He confided to his friend William Bull that he considered it 'my most important publication', as well as his last.

141 *Olney Hymns*, 1779, p. 324, Book 3, Hymn 12, *The effort—in another measure*, vv 1–6.

142 *Olney Hymns*, 1779, p. 320, Book 3, Hymn 9, *Encouragement*, vv 1–3.

143 Olney Hymns, p. 320, Book 3, Hymn 9, *Encouragement*, v4

144 John Newton Diary, Princeton University, CO199, 1 July 1752.

145 *Olney Hymns*, 1779, p. 31, Book 1, Hymn 24, *Sampson's lion*, Judges 14:8, vv 1–6.

146 Robert Lowth [1710–1787], Bishop of London from 1777, author of *A New Translation with a Preliminary Dissertation and Notes Critical, Philological, and Explanatory,* 1788.

147 *Letters and Conversational Remarks*, ed John Campbell, 1811, pp. 74–76, 18 July 1795.

148 *Olney Hymns*, 1779, p. 238, Book 2, Hymn 47 *[Gospel privileges] Another*, vv 1,3–7.

149 Alec Motyer comments: The Greek literally means 'the exalted (thing)', i.e. 'what is exalted', conveying a bad meaning of haughtiness, or arrogant pride. There seems to be a reference to Luke 16:15, *the exalted thing among men is abomination before God*].

150 *summum bonum*: Latin for 'highest good', a term used by Cicero and the Stoics.

151 Bodleian Library, MS Wilberforce c.49, f50, John Newton to William Wilberforce, 19 June 94.

152 John Newton Diary, Princeton University, CO199, 22 January 1755.

153 From verse 8 of *Come, we that love the Lord* by Isaac Watts:
The men of grace have found
Glory begun below,
Celestial fruits on earthly ground
From faith and hope may grow.

154 On Sunday morning 14 December 1777 Newton had preached on Deuteronomy 33:26, *There is none like unto the God of Jeshurun.*

155 *Olney Hymns*, 1779, p. 419, Book 3, Hymn 96, [Short Hymns After Sermon] Habakkuk 3:17–18, vv 1–2.

156 Later this evening Newton set out for Bedford to catch the next morning's coach to London for an assessment of a wen on his thigh. Joseph Warner, a leading surgeon at Guy's Hospital, recommended an operation, which was successfully performed a few months later.

157 *Olney Hymns*, 1779, p. 202, Book 2, Hymn 18 [Before Annual Sermons] *A prayer for power on the means of grace*, vv 1–6. This hymn was written for 1 January 1778, to be sung before the evening sermon preached to the young people from Acts 20:26–27. 'Thou hast seen how wickedness increases amongst us and how the work of conversion is apparently at a stand,' Newton entered in his diary before preaching that evening. 'O my Lord hear prayer for our youth. Go forth with me tonight, and while I am speaking to them cause thine own voice to be heard in their hearts. I pray for liberty, but especially that I may be useful—that some poor souls may be turned this night from darkness to light, and from the power of Satan to the knowledge of thy love… Let me not only seem, but be in earnest.'

He was able to come home after the service and continue, 'I thank thee that thou didst open my mouth, and enable me to speak fully and boldly in the evening. O command a blessing to follow. The congregation was large and attentive.' The morning sermon was from Psalm 71:9.

158 *Olney Hymns*, 1779, p. 242, Book 2, Hymn 50, *Prayer for ministers*, vv 1–3.

159 John Newton Diary, Princeton University, CO199, Sunday 23 June 1776.

160 The Great House belonged to Lord Dartmouth, who owned the living of Olney parish church. Dartmouth did not reside in Olney, and gave Newton the use of rooms for church meetings such as their Tuesday evening prayer meetings and Thursday evening lectures. Newton also escaped there early on a Sunday morning when possible for a time of prayer. The building has since been demolished, but the pillars at the entrance to the drive have been moved to the entrance to the church pathway.

161 John Newton Diary, Princeton University, CO199, Sunday 4 June 1776.

162 John Newton Diary, Princeton University, CO199, 2 January 1773.

163 Richard Cecil, *The Life of John Newton*, ed Marylynn Rouse, Christian Focus, 2000, p. 363, John Newton's Funeral Sermon for William Cowper, May 1800.

164 As mentioned above in Note 156, Newton went to London for an assessment of a wen on his thigh. It was operated on in October by Joseph Warner, an eminent surgeon at Guy's Hospital.

165 *Olney Hymns*, 1779, p. 169, Book 1, Hymn 136, *Ephesus*, Revelation 2:1,7, vv 1–6.

166 *Olney Hymns*, 1779, p. 198, Book 2, Hymn 15 [Before Annual Sermons] *Preaching to the dry bones*, vv 1–2, 4–5, written for New Year's Evening 1775.

167 An official British Thanksgiving Service to mark the end of the War of American Independence was held in St. Paul's Cathedral in London, England, on 29 June 1784. Newton dated his sermon '29 ~~August~~ July 1784'. Perhaps he might even have meant June.

168 Britain declared war on France in 1793.

169 Bodleian Library, MS Wilberforce c.49, f69, 30 March 1796.

170 *Letters to a Clergyman*, ed John Newton Coffin, 1845, p. 49, 29 September 1792.

171 *Olney Hymns*, 1779, p. 2, Book 1, Hymn 2, *Cain and Abel*, Genesis 4:3–8, vv 2–3.

172 Bodleian Library, MS Wilberforce c.49, f121, 4 July 1791, shortly after Elizabeth Wilberforce had hastily withdrawn her young son William (later to become the MP) from the evangelical influence of his aunt and uncle.

173 Bodleian Library, MS Wilberforce c.49, f43, 4 August [1793].

174 *Olney Hymns*, 1779, p. 2, Book 1, Hymn 2, *Cain and Abel*, Genesis 4:3–8, vv 4–8.

176 *Olney Hymns*, 1779, p. 161, Book 1, Hymn 130, *The inward warfare*, Galatians 5:17, v 1.

176 *Miscellaneous Thoughts on entering the Ministry*, John Newton, 1758, Lambeth Palace Library, MS 2937, ed Marylynn Rouse for *The Complete Works of John Newton*, quoting Thursday 29 June.

177 John Newton Diary, Princeton University, CO199, 21 March 1794

178 *Olney Hymns*, 1779, p. 136, Book 1, Hymn 109, *Father forgive them*, Luke 23:34, vv 1–4, 6–7.

179 *Olney Hymns*, 1779, p. 41, Book 1, Hymn 32 [*Ask what I shall give thee*] *Another*, 2 Samuel 3:5, vv 5–6.

180 *The Searcher of Hearts*, John Newton, ed Marylynn Rouse, Christian Focus, 1997, p. 133, on Romans 8:32.

181 *Olney Hymns*, 1779, p. 372, Book 3, Hymn 52, *Confidence*, vv 1–2.

182 *The Searcher of Hearts*, John Newton, ed Marylynn Rouse, Christian Focus, 1997, p. 60, on Romans 8:28.

183 Perhaps a quote from William Cowper's hymn, *O for a closer walk with God*, which was

probably written for an earlier sermon of Newton's based on Genesis 5:24 (Newton preached twice on this text):
Where is the blessedness I knew
When first I saw the LORD?
Where is the soul-refreshing view
Of JESUS, and his word?
What peaceful hours I once enjoyed!
How sweet their memory still!
But they have left an aching void,
The world can never fill.

184 Annotated *Letters to a Wife,* John Newton, Cowper & Newton Museum, 4 August 1794.
185 *Olney Hymns*, 1779, p. 153, Book 1, Hymn 123, *The trembling gaoler*, Acts 16:29–32, vv 1–2.
186 *Miscellaneous Thoughts on entering the Ministry,* John Newton, 1758, Lambeth Palace Library, MS 2937, ed Marylynn Rouse for *The Complete Works of John Newton*, quoting from Friday 4 August 1758.
187 *Olney Hymns*, 1779, p. 153, Book 1, Hymn 123, *The trembling gaoler*, Acts 16:29–32, vv 3–4.
188 *Olney Hymns*, 1779, p. 5, Book 1, Hymn 4 [*Walking with GOD*] *Another*, Genesis 5:24, vv 5–6. Newton's diary states, 'Sunday 23 July 1775: hymn 113, walking with God'. Cowper's hymn, *O for a closer walk with God*, may have been prompted by this sermon, or by the earlier sermon Newton refers to on the same text.
189 *Olney Hymns*, 1779, p. 5, Book 1, Hymn 4 [*Walking with GOD*] *Another*, Genesis 5:24, vv 1–3, 7.
190 *Messiah. A Sacred Eclogue, in Imitation of Virgil's Pollio*, Alexander Pope, 1712. An extract:
Rapt into future times, the bard begun:
A virgin shall conceive, a virgin bear a son!
From Jesse's root behold the branch arise,
Whose sacred flower with fragrance fills the skies:
All crimes shall cease, and ancient fraud shall fail;
Returning Justice lift aloft her scale;
Peace o'er the world her olive wand extend,
And white-robed Innocence from heaven descend
Hark! a glad voice the lonely desert cheers;
'Prepare the way! a God, a God appears':
'A God, a God!' the vocal hills reply,
The rocks proclaim the approaching Deity.
Lo, Earth receives him from the bending skies!
Sink down, ye mountains, and ye valleys, rise;
With heads declined, ye cedars, homage pay;
Be smooth, ye rocks, ye rapid floods, give way!
The Saviour comes! by ancient bards foretold:
Hear him, ye deaf, and all ye blind, behold!
The seas shall waste, the skies in smoke decay,
Rocks fall to dust, and mountains melt away;
But fix'd his word, his saving power remains;
Thy realm for ever lasts, thy own MESSIAH reigns!

Endnotes

Quite incidentally, Pope's father had previously owned a laundry at No. 1 Lombard Street, directly opposite St Mary Woolnoth, where Newton was rector at the time of preaching this sermon. The adjacent alleyway is still called Pope's Alley.

191 *Come thou fount of every blessing* appears to have been one of Newton's favourite hymns, from which he often quoted the line *O to grace how great a debtor.* It was reputedly written by his contemporary Robert Robinson [1735–1790] (though John Gadsby in *Memoirs of the Principal Hymn-Writers*, London, 1882, declared that it had 'beyond doubt, been proved to be Lady Huntingdon's'). The hymn was published by George Whitefield in 1757.

192 Cambridge University Library, Thornton Papers, Add 7826/1/A, John Newton to John Thornton, 4 August 1770.

193 *Olney Hymns*, 1779, p. 205, Book 2, Hymn 21 [After Annual Sermons] *The Lord's call to his children*, 2 Corinthians 6:17–18, vv 1–2, written for New Year's Evening 1771.

194 John Newton Diary, Princeton University, CO199, 30 July 1776.

195 *Olney Hymns*, 1779, p. 283, Book 2, Hymn 85, *On the eclipse of the moon.* 30 July 1776, vv 4–5, 7–8.

196 The meaning of Sheth, which appears here only in the Bible, has long been considered dubious, but is still held to be 'desolation'.

197 Bodleian Library, MS Wilberforce c.49, f125, John Newton to Charles Grant, 18 April 1797.

198 *A Practical View of the Prevailing Religious System of Professed Christians in the Higher and Middle Classes of this Country contrasted with real Christianity*, William Wilberforce, 1797 [annotated critical re-issue of the 1797 text, edited by Kevin Belmonte, Hendrickson, 1996, with introduction by Chuck Colson.

199 *Olney Hymns*, 1779, p. 27, Book 1, Hymn 21, *Gibeon*, Joshua 10:6, vv 5–8.

200 Fifth stanza from *My God, my portion, and my love,* by Isaac Watts:
To thee we owe our wealth, and friends,
And health, and safe abode;
Thanks to thy name for meaner [lesser] things,
But they are not my God.

201 *Olney Hymns*, 1779, p. 377, Book 3, Hymn 56, *Humiliation and praise* (Imitated from the German), vv 1, 2a.

202 The word in Genesis 15:1 is a *shield*; in Psalm 18:2 it is a *buckler*: a small shield for deflecting or turning aside the enemy's blows.

203 *Olney Hymns*, 1779, p. 377, Book 3, Hymn 56, *Humiliation and praise* (Imitated from the German), v 5.

204 *Olney Hymns*, p. 353, Book 3, Hymn 37, *I will trust and not be afraid*, v 3.

205 John Newton Diary, Princeton University, CO199, 16 October 1775.

206 *Olney Hymns*, 1779, p. 342, Book 3, Hymn 27, *Bitter and sweet*, vv 1, 2a, 4a.

207 In John Bunyan's *Pilgrim's Progress* he warns Christian of the enchanted places, comfortable places near their journey's end, 'to allure, if it might be, some of the pilgrims to take up their rest there when weary'. The caution was that they were likely to continue sleeping instead of pressing on. Newton began teaching from *Pilgrim's Progress* at his Tuesday night prayer meetings on 2 June 1767. At John Thornton's request, Newton wrote the preface to the 1776 edition of *Pilgrim's Progress*.

208 *Olney Hymns*, 1779, p. 301, Book 2, Hymn 100, *The inchantment dissolved*, vv 1, 3.

209 John Newton Diary, Princeton University, CO199, 1 February 1752.

210 John Newton Diary, Princeton University, CO199, 1 July 1752.

Endnotes

211 *Olney Hymns*, 1779, p. 143, Book 1, Hymn 115, *Will ye also go away?* John 6:67–69, vv 1, 7.

212 *Olney Hymns*, 1779, p. 143, Book 1, Hymn 115, *Will ye also go away?* John 6:67–69, v 6.

213 Bodleian Library, MS Wilberforce c.49, f43, 4 August [1793].

214 *Olney Hymns*, 1779, p. 96, Book 1, Hymn 78, *On one stone shall be seven eyes*, Zechariah 3:9, v 6.

215 *Olney Hymns*, 1779, p. 95, Book 1, Hymn 77, *A brand plucked out of the fire*, Zechariah 3:1–5, vv 1–8.

216 *Olney Hymns*, 1779, p. 200, Book 2, Hymn 17, *God speaking from Mount Zion*, vv 1–4.

217 *The Searcher of Hearts*, John Newton, ed Marylynn Rouse, Christian Focus, 1997, p. 116, on Romans 8:30.

218 Newton wrote his own epitaph, requesting that it be put up on a plain marble tablet near the vestry door of his church in London, St Mary Woolnoth. It is still there, though he and his wife were later re-interred in the graveyard of his former church, St Peter and St Paul, in Olney, where the same words are inscribed on their tomb. Their removal from St Mary Woolnoth was necessitated by the construction of the London Underground, particularly Bank tube station.

219 *Olney Hymns*, 1779, p. 280, Book 2, Hymn 82, *The rainbow*, vv 1–2.

220 *Letters to a Clergyman*, John Newton Coffin, 1845, pp. 227–229, 28 September 1792.

221 *Twenty-One Letters, written to a near relative at school*, John Newton, Religious Tract Society, p. 123. Sarah Myra Gardiner married Newton's nephew, Benjamin Nind. Sarah was baptized on 6 July 1776.

222 Bodleian Library, MS Wilberforce c.49, f112, 21 December 1802; the child was Robert Isaac Wilberforce [1802–1857], who became Archdeacon of East Riding before entering the Roman Catholic Church; he was co-biographer (with his brother Bishop Samuel) of his father William.

223 *Olney Hymns*, 1779, p. 356, Book 3, Hymn 38, *Questions to unbelief*, vv 1–2.

224 *Olney Hymns*, 1779, p. 352, Book 3, Hymn 36, *Prayer answered by crosses*, vv 1–2, 6–7.

225 *Miscellaneous Thoughts on entering the Ministry*, John Newton, 1758, Lambeth Palace Library, MS 2937, ed Marylynn Rouse for *The Complete Works of John Newton*, quoting from Monday 3 July, meditations on 1 Timothy 4:16.

226 *Olney Hymns*, 1779, p. 55, Book 1, Hymn 43, *Oh that I were as in months past*, Job 29:2, vv 5,7.

227 John Newton Diary, Princeton University, CO199, 19 July 1774.

228 *Olney Hymns*, 1779, p. 63, Book 1, Hymn 49, *He led them by a right way*, Psalm 107:7, vv 4, 7–8.

229 *Olney Hymns*, 1779, p. 77, Book 1, Hymn 61, *Look unto me, and be ye saved*, Isaiah 45:22, v 1.

230 *Olney Hymns*, 1779, p. 294, Book 2, Hymn 94, *Sheep*, vv 1–2. Newton wrote this hymn for the evening service of Sunday 6 September 1778, when he preached from it. He mentions this the following day in a letter to his friend William Bull, the Independent minister at the nearby town of Newport-Pagnell.

231 *Olney Hymns*, 1779, p. 294, Book 2, Hymn 94, *Sheep*, vv 3, 7.

232 *Olney Hymns*, 1779, p. 294, Book 2, Hymn 94, *Sheep*, vv 4, 6.

233 *Church Catechism*, Lecture 22, January 12 1766, Cowper & Newton Museum.

234 *Olney Hymns*, 1779, p. 405, Book 3, Hymn 82, *Praise for redeeming love*, v 1.

235 Bodleian Library, MS Wilberforce c.49, f12, John Newton to William Wilberforce, 15 November 1786.

Endnotes

236 *Olney Hymns*, 1779, p. 381, Book 3, Hymn 60, *The power of grace*, vv 1, 5–7.

237 The original manuscript is 'uses to do', probably intending to write 'usest to do' as in the AV.

238 *Olney Hymns*, 1779, p. 347, Book 3, Hymn 32, *Cast down, but not destroyed*, v 4.

239 Newton often declared his whole history was expressed in Deuteronomy 32:10.

240 *Olney Hymns*, 1779, p. 224, Book 2, Hymn 36, *Harvest*, vv 2, 4.

241 On the Easter Monday Fair Day of 12 April 1773, William Cowper was so distressed by the noise in Market Square immediately outside his window that he pleaded with Newton to be allowed to stay overnight at the vicarage. Newton willingly consented. However, his guest stayed fourteen months before he could face returning home! This particular sermon would have been preached either in 1765 or between 1768 and 1772.

242 *Olney Hymns*, 1779, p. 276, Book 2, Hymn 79 [Funeral Hymns] *The great tribunal*, Revelation 20:11–12, v 1.

243 Newton preached on Revelation 20:10–11 on Sunday 19 April 1767 at 'the old church' (St Nicholas), Liverpool.

244 The day of Assize was the day a court was assembled.

245 Bodleian Library, MS Wilberforce, c.49, f29, John Newton to William Wilberforce, 1 July 1789.

246 *Olney Hymns*, 1779, p. 276, Book 2, Hymn 79, *The great tribunal*, v 2.

247 *Olney Hymns*, 1779, p. 276, Book 2, Hymn 79, *The great tribunal*, v 3.

248 *Olney Hymns*, 1779, p. 276, Book 2, Hymn 79, *The great tribunal*, v 4.

249 *Olney Hymns*, 1779, p. 276, Book 2, Hymn 79, *The great tribunal*, v 5.

250 *Olney Hymns*, 1779, p. 260, Book 2, Hymn 66, *Moses and Amalek*, 27 February 1778, vv 3–4, referring to the battle in Exodus 17:8–16. In the morning of 27 February 1778, which was a nationally appointed Fast Day, Newton preached from Exodus 17:11, *And it came to pass, when Moses held up his hand, that Israel prevailed: and when he let down his hand Amalek prevailed*. In the afternoon he preached from Mark 13:36 and in the evening from Jeremiah 5:9 (he published this latter sermon under the title 'The guilt and danger of such a nation as this'). The day had begun with a very early morning prayer meeting at the Great House 'attended by many'. At the end of the day Newton recorded in his diary, 'O my Lord may it please thee to hear the prayers and bless the word of this day. Surely thou hast seen many of thy children sighing and mourning before thee, under a sense of sin, and from a prospect of judgements being at the door.'

251 Founded in 1780, with Newton as one of its earliest Vice Presidents, this Bible Society still exists as the Naval, Military and Air-Force Bible Society. The organization known today as the 'Bible Society', i.e. the British and Foreign Bible Society, was founded in 1804, with William Wilberforce being one of it earliest Vice Presidents and John Newton a founder member.

252 *Olney Hymns*, 1779, p. 260, Book 2, Hymn 66, *Moses and Amalek*, 27 February 1778, Exodus 17:9, vv 1–2.

253 When Britain finally signed a peace treaty with America in November 1782, the Franco–American alliance meant that it could not go into effect until Britain declared peace with France; but France had an alliance with Spain, who were demanding the return of Gibraltar before agreeing to peace with Britain. Meanwhile the Dutch had previously formed an alliance with America against Britain. As Newton says, 'This war is complicated.'

254 *Olney Hymns*, 1779, p. 260, Book 2, Hymn 66, *Moses and Amalek*, 27 February 1778, vv 5–6.

255 Either New Year's Morning 1770 or Sunday morning 31 December 1769. In his notebook

Newton had written his sermon notes for the Young People's service to be held on New Year's Evening (1 January 1770)—his most important service of the year—immediately before this sermon; it was followed by the sermon notes for Sunday afternoon 31 December 1769. However, the context of the sermon makes it more likely that this one was for New Year's Day, i.e. he prepared the sermons in reverse order.

256 John Newton Diary, Princeton University, CO199, 20 January 1755.

257 John Newton Diary, Princeton University, CO199, 12 February 1784.

258 Bristol Baptist College, John Ryland letters, G 97B OS Box C, Newton to John Ryland, 26 March 1791 (following the death of Ryland's wife).

259 Bodleian Library, MS Wilberforce c.49, f33, 24 December 1790, following the death of Newton's wife on 15 December 1790.

260 John Newton Diary, Princeton University, CO199, 21 March 1804.

261 Bodleian Library, MS Wilberforce c.49, f52, 2 October 1794.

262 Bodleian Library, MS Wilberforce c.49, f83, John Newton to Mrs Barbara Wilberforce, 28 November 1798. Barbara Wilberforce was the wife of the MP William Wilberforce.

263 *Olney Hymns*, 1779, p. 39, Book 1, Hymn 30, *Is this thy kindness to thy friend?*, 2 Samuel 16:17, vv 1–3.

264 *Olney Hymns*, 1779, p. 258, Book 2, Hymn 64, *On the commencement of hostilities in America*, vv 3, 8.

265 Bristol Baptist College, John Ryland letters, G 97B OS Box C, Newton to John Ryland, 15 March 1794.

266 Matthew 10:28.

267 *Olney Hymns*, 1779, p. 315, Book 3, Hymn 6, *The burdened sinner*, vv 1–2, 5–6.

268 Annotated *Letters to a Wife,* John Newton, Cowper & Newton Museum, 4 August 1794.

269 Bodleian Library, MS Wilberforce c.49, f105, 30 September 1800.

270 *Twenty-One Letters, written to a near relative at school*, John Newton, Religious Tract Society, p. 114.

271 *A Little Catechism, with Little Verses and Little Sayings, for Little Children*, John Mason, 1st edition 1692, 8th edition 1755. John Mason [1646?–1694] was Rector of Water Stratford, Buckinghamshire.

272 *Journal of children's meetings at Olney,* Cowper & Newton Museum, 17 January 1765.

273 John Newton Diary, Princeton University, CO199, 10 July 1777. Newton spoke to the children from Luke 9:18-27 on this day.

274 *An Authentic Narrative*, John Newton, 1764, Letter 2.

275 Twenty-one Letters written to a Near Relative at School, John Newton, Religious Tract Society, 15 October 1782.

276 Bristol Baptist College, John Ryland letters, G 97B OS Box C, John Newton to John Ryland jnr, 26 March 1791.

277 *Olney Hymns*, 1779, p. 345, Book 3, Hymn 30, *Why should I complain?*, vv 1a, 2a, 3. This hymn was written in Liverpool in 1763 'to a favourite tune of Mrs Newton's—in Arne's Opera of *Eliza*.' The first production of *Eliza* by Thomas Augustine Arne, composer of *Rule Britannia* and *God save the king*, was in 1754 at the Little Theatre, Haymarket.

278 *Olney Hymns*, 1779, p. 57, Book 1, Hymn 44, *The change*, Job, vv 3–4, 5ab, 6c.

279 Bristol Baptist College, John Ryland letters, G 97B OS Box C, Newton to John Ryland, 30 August 1790.

280 *Olney Hymns*, 1779, p. 134, Book 1, Hymn 108, *The believer's danger, safety, and duty*, Luke 22:31–32, vv 1–3, 5–7.

Endnotes

281 Alec Motyer comments, 'Newton overstates his case here insofar as he makes it depend on the repeated definite article, a standard Greek idiom. Nevertheless, to say "my Son, the beloved" rather than "my beloved Son" undeniably gives some prominence to the qualifying adjective.'

282 No. 9 of Newton's sermon series on the Transfiguration was based on Luke 9:35 and Matthew 17:5.

283 *Olney Hymns*, 1779, p. 389, Book 3, Hymn 67, *The happy debtor*, vv 3–5.

284 John Newton Diary, Princeton University, CO199, Sunday 1 July 1752.

285 *Olney Hymns*, 1779, p. 109, Book 1, Hymn 89, *What think ye of CHRIST?*, Matthew 22:42, vv 1, 5.

286 Bodleian Library, MS Wilberforce c.49, f29, 1 July 1789.

287 Annotated *Letters to a Wife*, John Newton, Cowper & Newton Museum, 27 October 1794.

288 *Olney Hymns*, 1779, p. 32, Book 1, Hymn 25, *Hannah; or the throne of grace*, 1 Samuel 1:18, vv 1–2.

289 John Newton Diary, Princeton University, CO199, 28 January 1776.

290 *Heaven will make amends for all*—a comforting thought which Newton often associated with Cowper's torments.

291 *Olney Hymns*, 1779, p. 358, Book 3, Hymn 40, *Why art thou cast down?*, vv 3–7.

292 *Olney Hymns*, 1779, p. 388, Book 3, Hymn 66, *True happiness*, v 2.

293 Bodleian Library, MS Wilberforce c.49, f14, written on 1 November 1787 in response to Wilberforce's discussion with Newton on Sunday 28 October 1787, the day on which Wilber entered in his diary, 'God Almighty has set before me two great objects, the suppression of the Slave Trade and the Reformation of Manners' [*The Life of William Wilberforce*, Robert Isaac Wilberforce and Samuel Wilberforce, 1838, vol 1, p. 149].

294 *Miscellaneous Thoughts on entering the Ministry*, John Newton, 1758, Lambeth Palace Library, MS 2937, ed Marylynn Rouse for *The Complete Works of John Newton*, quoting 26 June 1758, meditations on Luke 14:28.

295 *Olney Hymns*, 1779, p. 362, Book 3, Hymn 43, *Faith a new and comprehensive sense*, vv 1, 3.

296 *Olney Hymns*, 1779, p. 362, Book 3, Hymn 43, *Faith a new and comprehensive sense*, vv 4–7.

297 Bristol Baptist College, John Ryland letters, G 97B OS Box C, Newton to John Ryland, 29 November 1799.

298 John Newton Diary, Princeton University, CO199, Friday 13 December 1776 (a national Fast Day).

299 *Olney Hymns*, 1779, p. 259, Book 2, Hymn 65 [Fast-Day Hymns] *Confession and prayer*, 13 December 1776, vv 4, 6–8. The Fast Day began with a prayer meeting at the Great House from 7am to 9am. Congregations at church throughout the day were 'larger than usual and very attentive', though Newton lamented that what he preached was 'set lightly by'. He preached from Luke 8:22–26 in the morning, Jonah 3:9 in the afternoon and 1 Samuel 4:13 in the evening. The afternoon text was preached from again on the Fast Day of Friday 28 February 1794 at St Mary Woolnoth in London. That sermon was published, under the title of 'The imminent danger and only sure resource of this nation', *Works*, vol 5.

300 Bodleian Library, MS Wilberforce c.49, f52, John Newton to William Wilberforce, 2 October 1794.

301 *Olney Hymns*, 1779, p. 40, Book 1, Hymn 31, *Ask what I shall give thee*, 1 Kings 3:5, vv 1–4.

Endnotes

302 John Newton Diary, Princeton University, CO 199, Sunday 11 June 1775.
303 *Olney Hymns*, 1779, p. 258, Book 2, Hymn 64, *On the commencement of hostilities in America*, vv 1,9.
304 Annotated *Letters to a Wife*, John Newton, Cowper & Newton Museum, 4 August 1796, aged 70.
305 Bristol Baptist College, John Ryland letters, G 97B OS Box C, Newton to John Ryland, 28 January 1781.
306 *Olney Hymns*, 1779, p. 346, Book 3, Hymn 31, *Return, O Lord, how long*, vv 2, 4–6.
307 *Olney Hymns*, 1779, p. 99, Book 1, Hymn 8, *They shall be mine, saith the Lord*, Malachi 3:16–18, vv 1–3, 6.
308 *Olney Hymns*, 1779, p. 418, Book 3, Hymn 95 [from Short Hymns Before Sermon], vv 1–2.
309 *Olney Hymns*, 1779, p. 282, Book 2, Hymn 84, *Lightning in the night*, vv 1–2, 4–7.
310 Cowper & Newton Museum, ALS, John Newton to Hannah Wilberforce, Saturday 9 June 1770. Hannah Wilberforce was the aunt of William Wilberforce, MP and slave trade abolitionist.
311 For the image of the tabernacle of one's body being taken down, see for instance 2 Peter 1:14; 2 Corinthians 5:1; Isaiah 33:20–21.
312 Mr Newton's Account of Mr Cowper in a Funeral Sermon Preached in St Mary Woolnoth, Lombard Street, May 1800, *The Life of John Newton*, Richard Cecil, ed Marylynn Rouse, Christian Focus, 2000, pp. 362–364.
313 Miscellaneous Thoughts on entering the Ministry, John Newton, 1758, Lambeth Palace Library, MS 2937, ed Marylynn Rouse for *The Complete Works of John Newton*.
314 John Newton Diary, Princeton University, CO199, 1 February 1752.
315 *Olney Hymns*, 1779, p. 339, Book 3, Hymn 25, *Rejoice the soul of thy servant*, v 2.
316 *Olney Hymns*, 1779, p. 365, Book 3, Hymn 46, *Jesus my all*, vv 1, 6, 8.
317 Bristol Baptist College, John Ryland letters, G 97B OS Box C, Newton to John Ryland, 13 March 1782.
318 *Olney Hymns*, 1779, p. 254, Book 2, Hymn 61, *Power of prayer*, vv 1–2.
319 Newton fell in love with his wife-to-be when she was thirteen and he seventeen. They were married for forty years. After her death, he published his letters to her as *Letters to a Wife*.
320 John Newton Diary, Princeton University, CO199, Sunday 26 December 1790.
321 *Twenty-One Letters, written to a near relative at school*, John Newton (Religious Tract Society), 17 October [1781?].
322 Newton appears to have used this same text, Genesis 49:10–12, on Christmas Day 1780 at St Mary Woolnoth, London.
323 The Rev. James Webb, pastor of Fetter Lane Independent Church.
324 *One Hundred and Twenty Nine Letters from the Rev. John Newton... to the Rev. William Bull*, Thomas Palmer Bull, Hamilton, Adams & Co, 1847, pp. 160–61, Newton to William Bull, 16 November 1782, quoting Revelation 14:13.
325 This idea of the meaning of Shiloh does not command widespread support, though it is a nice one!
326 *Olney Hymns*, 1779, p. 151, Book 1, Hymn 122, *Peter released from prison*, Acts 12:5–8, vv 1a, 3b, 5.
327 *Olney Hymns*, 1779, p. 133, Book 1, Hymn 107, *Zacchaeus*, Luke 19:1–6, vv 1, 4–6.
328 *An Authentic Narrative*, John Newton, 1764, Letter 3.
329 Dr Williams's Library, MS 38.98.46–57, John Newton to David Jennings, 29 August 1752.
330 Bodleian Library, MS Eng Poet c.51, pp. 253–6.

Endnotes

331 *Olney Hymns*, 1779, p. 13, Book 1, Hymn 10, *My name is Jacob*, Genesis 32:27, vv 3–4.

332 *Olney Hymns*, 1779, p. 314, Book 3, Hymn 5, *Invitation*, vv 1, 5.

333 'Goel' is the Hebrew word for kinsman.

334 *Olney Hymns*, 1779, p. 74, Book 1, Hymn 59, *The Refuge, River, and Rock of the church*, Isaiah 32:2, vv 1, 4, preached from on Sunday evening 26 February 1775 (probably written for the service).

335 *Olney Hymns*, 1779, p. 262, Book 2, Hymn 67, *The hiding place*, February 10 1779, vv 1b, 2a. This hymn was written for the Fast Day on the same date. Newton preached from Zechariah 12:10 in the morning, Isaiah 63:15 in the afternoon and Deuteronomy 32:15 in the evening. His diary for that day concludes, 'May an answer to the prayers of thy people, and good effects of the preaching of thy servants on this day be visible throughout the land!'

336 *Olney Hymns*, 1779, p. 60, Book 1, Hymn 47, *The believer's safety*, Psalm 91, vv 1–3, 5.

337 No. 13 of the sermon series on the Transfiguration is based on Mark 9:9-10 and Matthew 17:9.

338 'This is all of your gifts', Horace, Book IV, Ode III.

339 John Newton Diary, Princeton University, CO199, 4 August 1789.

340 *Olney Hymns*, 1779, p. 60, Book 1, Hymn 47, *The believer's safety*, Psalm 91, vv 4, 6–8.

341 *Olney Hymns*, 1779, p. 287, Book 2, Hymn 88, *The flood*, vv 1–7.

342 *Olney Hymns*, 1779, p. 335, Book 3, Hymn 22, *Help in time of need*, vv 1–4.

343 *Olney Hymns*, 1779, p. 409, Book 3, Hymn 85, *Salvation*, vv 1, 4.

344 *Olney Hymns*, 1779, p. 228, Book 2, Hymn 39, *Man honoured above angels*, vv 4–5.

345 The Hebrew is 'Immanuel'; the Greek equivalent introduced is 'Emmanuel'. So either spelling is correct.

346 *Olney Hymns*, 1779, p. 25, Book 1, Hymn 19, *The true Aaron*, Leviticus 8:7–9, vv 1, 5–9.

347 John Newton Diary, Princeton University, CO199, 24 November 1774.

348 Newton added, 'Note "rivers" in the plural, intimating that variety, as well as abundance, that is in him—suited to all persons, states and seasons.'

349 *Olney Hymns*, 1779, p. 75, Book 1, Hymn 60, *Zion, or the city of God*, Isaiah 33:20–21, v 2, written for Easter Day 16 April 1775.

350 *Olney Hymns*, 1779, p. 74, Book 1, Hymn 59, *The Refuge, River, and Rock of the church*, Isaiah 32:2, vv 5–6, used on Sunday 26 February 1775.

351 *Olney Hymns*, 1779, p. 249, Book 2, Hymn 56, *It is good to be here*, vv 2, 5–6.

352 *Olney Hymns*, 1779, p. 226, Book 2, Hymn 37, *Praise for the incarnation*, vv 1–5.

353 *Olney Hymns*, 1779, p. 191, Book 2, Hymn 9 [Before Annual Sermons: *Prayer for a blessing*] *Another*, vv 1–2, for New Year's Evening 1774.

354 *Olney Hymns*, 1779, p. 209, Book 2, Hymn 24 [After Annual Sermons] *Asking the way to Zion*, Jeremiah 50:5, vv 1–2, written for New Year's Evening 1774.

355 *Olney Hymns*, 1779, p. 209, Book 2, Hymn 24 [After Annual Sermons] *Asking the way to Zion*, Jeremiah 50:5, vv 3, 5.

356 John Newton Diary, Princeton University, CO199, Saturday 18 December 1773.

357 *Olney Hymns*, 1779, p. 209, Book 2, Hymn 24 [After Annual Sermons] *Asking the way to Zion*, Jeremiah 50:5, v 4.

358 John Newton Diary, Princeton University, CO199, 21 March 1776.

359 *Olney Hymns*, 1779, p. 209, Book 2, Hymn 24 [After Annual Sermons] *Asking the way to Zion*, Jeremiah 50:5, v 6.

Newton's sermon texts are identified below with an asterisk *; the editor's substituted daily texts are marked with †.

Index of Scripture texts for sermons and daily readings

Index of Scripture texts for sermons and daily readings

Index of Scripture texts for sermons and daily readings

Index of Scripture texts for sermons and daily readings

3:1–17	31 May
1 Thessalonians	
2:1–16	26 Dec
2:17–3:13	16 Nov
5:12–28	23 Jun
5:25*	23 Jun
	24 Jun
	25 Jun
	26 Jun
	27 Jun
	28 Jun
2 Thessalonians	
2:13–17	4 Nov
1 Timothy	
1:1–11	26 Jan
1:8*	26 Jan
	27 Jan
	28 Jan
	29 Jan
1:12–17	2 Jan
1:16*	21 Mar
	22 Mar
	23 Mar
	24 Mar
2:5–6	30 Apr
4:9–16	29 Dec
2 Timothy	
1:1–14	30 Dec
2:15–3:9	28 Apr
3:1–4:5	14 Oct
4:1–8	25 Jun

Titus	
3:3–8	2 Aug
Philemon	
8–21	5 Nov
Hebrews	
1:1–2:4	10 Jul
2:3*	10 Jul
2:5–18	18 Dec
3:7–4:6	25 Jan
6:13–20	3 Aug
7:1–3†	2 Aug
7:1–28	1 Aug
8:1–13	22 Jul
9:11–28	10 Sep
10:11–18	10 Jun
10:19–39	14 Nov
11:1–7	26 Jul
11:8–16	20 May
11:23–29	31 Mar
12:1–3	21 Aug
12:5–13	4 Feb
12:18–24	19 Nov
13:9–16	28 May
13:20–21*	3 Sep
	4 Sep
	5 Sep
	6 Sep
	7 Sep
	8 Sep
	9 Sep
	10 Sep
	11 Sep
	12 Sep

James	
1:2–12	11 Oct
1:13–15	7 Mar
4:1–10	17 Feb
1 Peter	
1:3*	15 Apr
	16 Apr
1:3–12	11 May
1:13–25	12 Jul
2:4–10	8 Apr
5:8–11	20 Oct
2 Peter	
1:16–21	25 Dec
2:1–22	22 Aug
3:1–18	3 Oct
1 John	
1:5–2:2	9 Sep
2:3–17	27 Apr
2:28–3:10	26 Mar
3:1–14	24 Apr
2 John	
1–13	3 Feb
3 John	
1–14	22 Mar
Jude	
12–25	25 Jul
Revelation	
1:12–18	6 May

Index of Scripture texts for sermons and daily readings

In his Preface to *Olney Hymns* Newton wrote, 'This publication, which, with my humble prayer to the Lord for his blessing upon it, I offer to the service and acceptance of all who love the Lord Jesus Christ in sincerity, of every name and in every place, into whose hands it may come.' He divided *Olney Hymns* into three 'Books'.

Book 1: Upon selected passages of Scripture

Hymn 1	Adam, Genesis 3:9	17 Jan	[v 1]
Hymn 2	Cain and Abel, Genesis 4:3–8	5 Jul	[vv 2–3]
		8 Jul	[vv 4–8]
Hymn 4	Walking with God, Genesis 5:24	24 Jul	[vv 5–6]
		26 Jul	[vv 1–3, 7]
Hymn 5	Lot in Sodom, Genesis 13:10	4 Jun	[vv 1–4]
		5 Jun	[vv 5–8]
Hymn 7	The Lord will provide, Genesis 22:14	22 May	[vv 4, 7]
Hymn 8	They shall be mine, saith the Lord,		
	Malachi 3:16–18	15 Nov	[vv 1–3, 6]
Hymn 10	My name is Jacob, Genesis 32:27	4 Dec	[vv 3–4]
Hymn 12	Joseph made known to his Brethren,		
	Genesis 45:3–4	30 Apr	[vv 4a–5]
Hymn 19	The true Aaron, Leviticus 8:7–9	19 Dec	[vv 1, 5–9]
Hymn 21	Gibeon, Joshua 10:6	3 Aug	[vv 5-8]
Hymn 24	Sampson's lion, Judges 14:8	13 Jun	[vv 1–6]
Hymn 25	Hannah; or the throne of grace,		
	1 Samuel 1:18	29 Oct	[vv 1–2]
Hymn 27	The milch kine drawing the ark:		
	Faith's surrender of all, 1 Samuel 6:12	20 May	[vv 5–8]
Hymn 29	David's fall, 2 Samuel 11:27	4 Apr	[vv 1–2, 4]
Hymn 30	Is this thy kindness to thy friend?		
	2 Samuel 16:17	2 Oct	[vv 1-3]
Hymn 31	Ask what I shall give thee, 1 Kings 3:5	8 Nov	[vv 1–4]
Hymn 32	Ask what I shall give thee [Another]		
	2 Samuel 3:5	15 July	[vv 5-6]
Hymn 33	[Ask what I shall give thee], Another,		
	1 Kings 3:5	9 Feb	[vv 1–4]

Index of Olney Hymns

Book 2: Occasional hymns, suited to particular seasons or suggested by particular events or objects

An Authentic Narrative, John Newton, 1764

Letter 2		14 Oct
Letter 3		2 Dec
Letter 8		12 Feb
		5 May
Letter 9		31 May
Letter 13		28 Apr

Letters and Conversational Remarks, ed John Campbell, 1811

18 July 1795	16 Jun

Letters to a Clergyman, ed John Newton Coffin, 1845

28 September 1792	26 Aug
29 September 1792	2 Jul
27 June 1793	6 Apr
19 February 1799	17 May

One Hundred and Twenty Nine Letters from the Rev John Newton ... to the Rev William Bull, Thomas Palmer Bull, Hamilton, Adams & Co, 1847

27 October 1778	9 Jan
13 October 1781	10 Apr
16 November 1782	28 Nov

The Searcher of Hearts, John Newton, ed Marylynn Rouse, Christian Focus Publications, 1997

Romans 8:26	18 Apr
Romans 8:28	4 May
	18 Jul
Romans 8:30	22 Aug
Romans 8:32	15 Jul

Twenty-one Letters written to a Near Relative at School, or, Letters to a Niece, Religious Tract Society & Newton's Works

22 October 1779	20 Mar
3 August 1780	4 Feb

Bodleian Library

MS Eng Poet c.51, pages 253–6	hymn [undated]	3 Dec
MS Wilberforce c.49, f1	letters to William Wilberforce (MP)	
	22 December 1785	27 Feb
MS Wilberforce c.49, f12	15 November 1786	11 Sep
MS Wilberforce c.49, f14	1 November 1787	28 May
		1 Nov
MS Wilberforce c.49, f26	2 April 1789	8 Jun
MS Wilberforce, c.49, f29	1 July 1789	17 Sep
		26 Oct
MS Wilberforce c.49, f33	24 December 1790	28 Sep
MS Wilberforce c.49, f43	4 August [1793?]	7 Jul
		17 Aug
MS Wilberforce c.49, f50	19 June 1794	19 Jun
MS Wilberforce c.49, f52	2 October 1794	30 Sep
		7 Nov
MS Wilberforce c.49, f67	22 December 1795	29 Mar
MS Wilberforce c.49, f69	30 March 1796	29 Jun
MS Wilberforce c.49, f75	30 March 1797	19 Apr
MS Wilberforce c.49, f105	30 September 1800	14 Mar
		11 Oct
MS Wilberforce c.49, f112	21 December 1802	28 Aug
MS Wilberforce c.49, f83	letter to Barbara Wilberforce	
	28 November 1798	1 Oct
MS Wilberforce c.49, f119	letters to William Wilberforce (uncle)	
	19 October 1767	7 Apr
MS Wilberforce c.49, f121	4 July 1771	6 Jul
MS Wilberforce c.49, f125	letter to Charles Grant	
	18 April 1797	1 Aug

Bristol Baptist College

John Ryland letters, G 97B OS Box C: letters to John Ryland jnr

	14 February 1774	13 Feb
	28 January 1781	11 Nov
	5 June 1781	13 Jan

Index of manuscripts

The Works of the Rev. John Newton
letter to William Cowper

Index of Scripture meditations

Curate-in-charge of St Peter & St Paul, Olney (1764–1780); rector of St Mary Woolnoth, London (1780–1807). In Olney the morning sermons were generally for believers and the afternoon sermons for larger congregations. The evening service was informal, when Newton would often preach from a hymn he had written. The dates relate to when Newton preached from the texts, but not necessarily from his sermon notes.

Genesis

1:1	Sunday Evening 8 January 1769	5 Jan
9:14	Tuesday 20 Jan 1767; Sunday Afternoon 30 May 1779	
	(incorrectly written as 29 May in diary)	25 Aug
13:12–13	Sunday 2 June 1771	5 Jun
14:18–19	'Sunday 1 February 1767 [on verse 18, Melchizedek,	
	as type of Christ]	1 Aug
17:1	Thursday Evening 11 July 1776	12 Jul
49:10–12	Christmas Morning Monday 25 December 1769	
	[and Monday 25 December 1780]	28 Nov

Exodus

20:7	Sunday Afternoon 25 August 1776	30 May

Deuteronomy

33:29	Sunday Afternoon 28 December 1777	22 Jun

Numbers

24:17	Christmas Evening Thursday 25 December 1777	31 Jul

Judges

5:18	For the Bible Society at Aldgate Sunday 22 September 1782	22 Sep
		23 Sep

2 Samuel

23:5	Sunday Mornings 23, 30 April and 7 May 1775	23 Apr
		30 Apr
		7 May

Index of sermons with known dates

50:5   New Year's Evening Saturday 1 January 1774,
for the Young People   31 Dec

Lamentations
3:24   Sunday Evening 13 February 1774,
Funeral Sermon for Betty Abraham   13 Feb

Hosea
2:8   Harvest Sunday 14 September 1766   14 Sep

Micah
4:9   Thursday Evening 6 April 1774   6 Apr
     7 Apr

Matthew
2:2   Christmas Morning Thursday 25 December 1777   25 Dec
5:5   Sunday Afternoon 30 August 1767   30 Aug

Luke
19:10   Christmas Evening 25 December 1769   5 Dec

John
12:32–33   Sunday Afternoon 13 July 1777 [verse 32]   13 Jul
     [[add to above]]   14 Jul

Acts
16:31   Thursday Evening 20 July 1775   23 Jul

1 Corinthians
15:31   New Year's Morning Monday 1 January 1770   27 Sep

Galatians
6:7   Easter Sunday Evening 4 April 1779   4 Apr

Book 1

Hymn 4	*Walking with God*, Genesis 5:24	23 July 1775	24 Jul
			26 Jul
Hymn 41	*Faith's review and expectation*,		
	1 Chronicles 17:16–17	assumed 1 January 1773	1 Jan
			3 Jan
			4 Jan
Hymn 59	*The Refuge, River, and Rock of the church*,		
	Isaiah 32:2	26 February 1775	6 Dec
			22 Dec
Hymn 60	*Zion, or the city of God*,		
	Isaiah 33:20-21 (incorrectly printed		
	as 27–28 in some editions)	16 April 1775 [Easter]	1 Feb
			2 Feb
			1 May
			21 Dec
Hymn 69	*The Lord is my portion*,		
	Lamentations 3:24 [prompted by		
	the death of Betty Abraham]	20 February 1774	15 Feb
			16 Feb

Book 2

Hymn 1	[New-year's Hymns] *Time how swift*	1 January 1774	12 Jan
Hymn 7	[Before Annual Sermons] *Prayer*		
	for a blessing	1 January 1770?	10 Mar
Hymn 9	[Before Annual Sermons: *Prayer*		
	for a blessing] *Another*	1 January 1774	26 Dec
Hymn 15	[Before Annual Sermons] *Preaching*		
	to the dry bones	1 January 1775	28 Jun
Hymn 18	[Before Annual Sermons] *A prayer*		
	for power on the means of grace	1 January 1778	23 Jun
Hymn 20	[After Annual Sermons] *David's*		
	charge to Solomon, 1 Chronicles 28:9	1 January 1770	21 Jan

Hymn 21	[After Annual Sermons] *The Lord's call to his children*, 2 Corinthians 6:17–18	1 January 1771	29 Jul
Hymn 23	*Waiting at Wisdom's gates*, Proverbs 8:34-35	1 January 1773	7 Mar
Hymn 24	[After Annual Sermons] *Asking the way to Zion*, Jeremiah 50:5	1 January 1774	27 Dec
			28 Dec
			29 Dec
			31 Dec
Hymn 64	*On the commencement of hostilities in America*	11 June 1775	3 Oct
			9 Nov
Hymn 65	[Fast-Day Hymns] *Confession and prayer*	13 December 1776	6 Nov
Hymn 66	*Moses and Amalek*, Exodus 17:9	27 February 1778	22 Sep
			23 Sep
			24 Sep
Hymn 67	[Fast-Day Hymns] *The hiding place*	10 February 1779	7 Dec
Hymn 68	*On the earthquake*	8 September 1775	5 Apr
Hymn 85	*On the eclipse of the moon*	30 July 1776	30 Jul
Hymn 94	*Sheep*, written for Sunday 6 September 1778	6 September 1778	6 Sep
			7 Sep
			8 Sep

Book 3

Hymn 21	*The storm hushed*	September 1763	28 Feb
Hymn 30	*Why should I complain?*	September 1763	17 Oct